New Wineskins
for Global Mission

A Compendium
New Wineskins for
Global Mission Conference
Ridgecrest, North Carolina,
April 1994

Editor

Sharon Stockdale

Associate Editor

Helen M. Camlin

William Carey Library

Pasadena, California

Episcopal Church Missionary Community
P. O. Box 278
Ambridge, Pennsylvania 15003-0278
(412) 266-2810

Published by
William Carey Library
P. O. Box 40129
Pasadena, California 91114
(818) 798-0819

Library of Congress Cataloging-in-Publication Data

New wineskins for global mission / editor, Sharon Stockdale ; associate
    editor , Helen Camlin.
     p.   cm,.
   Proceedings of a conference sponsored by the Episcopal Church
Missionary Community, held April 27–May 1, 1994.
   Includes bibliographical references.
   ISBN 0-87808-269-7 (alk. paper)
   1. Episcopal Church--Missions. 2. Missions.   I. Stockdale,
Sharon, 1951- . II. Camlin, Helen M., 1938- .
BX5930.2.N48   1996
266' .3--dc20   96-19660
                                           CIP

Printed in the United States of America

DEDICATION

To Walter and Louise Hannum who had the vision and the faith to establish the Episcopal Church Missionary Community in 1974 and the persistence to raise mission vision in parishes, train hundreds of missionaries, equip Episcopalians to reach the unreached and encourage prayer for Episcopal missionaries ever since.

Contents

8 Bear More Fruit: Enabling Others

Acknowledgments

First of all, I would like to thank Jean Collins, ECMC's Office Manager, and Helen Camlin, the Associate Editor, who have both been Godsends and without whom this book would never have seen the light of day! Jean's gracious hospitality coupled with her efficiency (a really wonderful combination) made participants at New Wineskins feel very well cared for and enabled the conference to run so smoothly in the first place. She used those two qualities to equal effect in coaxing revisions of speeches and workshops out of the contributors to this book!

Helen devoted her tremendous editing skills to the mammoth task of making spoken presentations communicate from the printed page. Her enthusiasm months into the project ("I'm learning so much about the world!") was a great encouragement. Thanks also to Louisa Turner, Gina Reischman and Wendy O'Rourke for their help with editing, and to Cyndi Burns, Jane Mees, Jeri Ruby and Barb Wingert for their hours transcribing tapes.

I particularly want to thank all the contributors for their excellent articles and their heart to see Christ's kingdom spread. What a fantastic job Walter Hannum did bringing together such an outstanding line-up of speakers. Louise Hannum mobilized people to pray for the speakers and for the conference regularly for a year in advance. More than half the participants at New Wineskins raised their hands to say they had been impacted by the Hannums' mission vision and teaching over the years.

Some integral parts of the conference can't be reproduced in a book. The Rt. Rev. Bill Frey, Dean of Trinity Episcopal School for Ministry, was a great Master of Ceremonies, filling in on short notice when Bob Denig, Bishop of Western Massachusetts and President of ECMC's Board of Directors, was stricken with bone cancer. Many have told us that the worship led every morning and evening by the Rev. Greg Brewer and his team of gifted musicians was a highlight of the conference. The

Rev. Valarie Whitcomb's prayers after the main presentations enabled conference participants to respond corporately and became a very helpful role model for many of how to pray for missions. The early morning Communion services led by the Rev. George Pierce were inspired.

Bob Ainsworth's workshop isn't in this book, but his summary statement of John 21:4-11 "Ministry under the Lord's inspiration is easy, effective, and efficient" has been a mainstay to me as Director of ECMC.

Introduction

Nearly six hundred Episcopalians came from around the U.S.A. to the New Wineskins for Global Missions conference in 1994, as well as eight bishops and nationals and missionaries from twenty countries. A seminary canceled classes for five days so the entire student body, faculty and staff could attend. God did far above all we could ask, think, or imagine. One of the most unforgettable moments of the conference occurred during the closing service of Holy Communion, when Bishop Alexander Stewart, the Celebrant, asked, "Are there any who have not yet received the Bread of Life and the Cup of Salvation?" From around the room came the answers:

—One billion Chinese have never been invited to the Lord's Table.

—One billion Muslims have never been invited to the Lord's Table.

—715 million Hindus have never been invited to the Lord's Table.

—610 million Buddhists have never been invited to the Lord's Table.

—150 million Tribals have never been invited to the Lord's Table.

—17 million Sikhs have never been invited to the Lord's Table.

—13.5 million Jews have never been invited to the Lord's Table.

CELEBRANT: Who will go share the good news that the banquet is prepared for them?

PEOPLE: *We will go, by our prayers, our offerings, our lives, we will go!*

Episcopalians!? Yes, indeed! And New Wineskins wasn't just an emotional high with no lasting fruit. A year after the conference, participants reported that they are praying for unreached people groups, giving to missions, and their churches are becoming sending bases for missions. Episcopalians are catching the vision for missions, and churches and individuals are finding a variety of ways to implement that vision.

We have heard from participants that New Wineskins opened their eyes to missions in the Bible. A rector wrote us that New Wineskins changed the way he preaches. Vestries have made missions a line item in their budget for the first time. Another church is in the process of adopting an unreached people group and hired a full-time mission coordinator. Mission committees with well-thought-out strategies and priorities are being formed, and congregations are getting involved in hands-on ministry. Episcopalians are getting trained for effective service and are going on short-term missions with a view to long-term calls to be missionaries and tentmakers. A seminary professor wrote that he is trying to include more explicit reference to missions in his courses. People are befriending international students. Sunday school classes are praying for the 10/40 Window (North Africa to Indonesia).

Because of the tremendous response, ECMC has decided to put on New Wineskins for Global Mission '97, (April 2 to 6, 1997, again at Ridgecrest, North Carolina). New Wineskins '97 will continue to focus on the world's unreached people groups, partnering with churches overseas, and what Episcopalians can do at home and abroad, with special emphases this time on youth and urban ministries. Speakers from around the world, such as Norman Beale (unreached peoples), Dean Borgman (youth ministries), Lisa Chinn (international students), David and Rosemary Harley (training for mission), Colenzo Hubbard (inner-city ministries), Sam Kamaleson (World Vision), Bishop Benjamin Kwashi (Nigeria), Joseph Mai (Vietnamese in the U.S. and overseas), Juan Marentes (Honduras), and Marc Nikkel (refugees in Sudan) will again inspire and equip Episcopalians to meet the challenges of sharing the gospel in a changing world. New Wineskins '97 will enable participants to network with mission-minded parishes, sending agencies, and experienced missionaries. Parish teams will have the opportunity to worship, pray, reflect, and plan.

It is our prayer that this book of the plenary speeches (chapters 1– 4 and 10) and workshops (chapters 5–9) from the first New Wineskins for Global Missions conference will be used by the Lord of the Harvest as a tremendous resource for churches and individuals seeking to fulfill the Great Commission to go make disciples of all nations.

May God bless you and make you a great blessing!

Sharon Stockdale, Director,
Episcopal Church Missionary Community
January 2, 1996

April 2–6, 1997

1

New Wine Can't Be Contained: Foundations for Mission

JESUS, GOOD NEWS FOR ALL

The Gospel Is For Everyone

The Rev. Dr. John Rodgers

Let us begin with a prayer:

O God of all the nations of the earth: Remember the multitudes who have been created in your image but have not known the redeeming work of our Savior Jesus Christ; and grant that, by our prayers and labors, the labors and prayers of your holy church, they may be brought to know and worship you as you have been revealed in your Son; who lives and reigns with you and the Holy Spirit, one God, for ever and ever. Amen.

Book of Common Prayer, p. 257.

The gospel is for everyone! That certainly is crucial. To paraphrase Archbishop William Temple, "If the Son didn't die and rise for everyone, he didn't die and rise for anyone." You may say, "Isn't that obvious?" But if it were, we would be living it out—living out its truth and its mandate. Even more painfully, there are many in our culture (some even in the church) who deny both the universality and the urgency of the gospel. So our task at this point is to get God's perspective, for until our hearts and God's are one in this matter, we will continue to do a half-hearted, failing and falling effort.

I have taken as our text John 3:16, which appears in the midst of Jesus' dialogue with Nicodemus. The topic, as Jesus guides the conversation, is new birth. The key point of this dialogue is that everyone is beyond self-help—everyone. Becoming a Christian is quite simply impossible to all people in their fallen state. Therefore God's rescue is not a matter of advice for our self-improvement. We are beyond all that. The flesh is opposed to the Spirit; the natural man cannot receive the things of the Spirit for they are foolishness to him. But that which is impossible to us becomes real in us when and where the Spirit of God blows upon us, raising us from spiritual death to life through a new birth from above. Just as we cannot program the wind, we cannot program the Spirit of God. But the incredible news is that the Spirit of God has been poured out and he is on a mission in this world. God is committed to global, evangelistic renewal throughout the world. People are being regenerated and raised up to living, spiritual life—rescued, redeemed—and we are the ones that the Spirit uses to be his acolytes in this gracious work. The gospel *IS* for everyone because God *IS* for everyone.

I wonder how many of us, in our attempts to commend the gospel to others, have taken seriously this reality that only God can raise the dead. I think back to my early ministry, dashing out from seminary with my new collar, ready to change the world, thinking God certainly was blessed in getting me. All was dependent upon my cleverness and my hard work. There was little humility, little patience, little prayer and, also, little effect. Of course, I was pleased to see that those who were already believers could sometimes take comfort in some of the things I said. Even in such a poor spiritual state, God is gracious to use us to encourage one another. But when something good happens, we often take credit for it ourselves. I'm reminded of the story of the woodpecker on the telephone pole. Just as he took his first peck, lightning struck the pole and split it from top to bottom. The woodpecker spent the rest of his life boasting about the power of his beak. But slowly, by grace, one grows wiser. Humble prayer is our rightful posture—the power to give new birth belongs to God alone.

The condition of mankind is utterly hopeless except for the work of the Holy Spirit, and the Spirit's work rests upon the person and work of

Christ. We need to be set free as much as we need to be forgiven. Remember the old hymn, "Be of sin, a double cure," both from our bondage and from our guilty rebellion.

Some of us learned John 3:16 in the King James Version. It goes as follows: "For God so loved the world that He gave His only begotten Son, that whosoever believeth in Him should not perish, but have everlasting life." The RSV says, "For God so loved the world that He gave His only Son, that whoever believes in Him should not perish, but have eternal life." I hope we will use this text as a window to look through—to look at God, to look at ourselves, and to look at people in general—the world and humankind.

John 3:16 begins: "For God" (and already I begin to quake). Everything is decided at this point. Everything about the world, our lives, our mission. For if God be God, it is he then who calls the plays in our huddle. God is not one factor alongside other factors. He is the One—he is the Lord of All. To say "God" is to place everything else in subordination to him. The true greatness of God is beyond our comprehension. Did he not tell us through his prophet Isaiah that there is nothing in all creation with which we can liken him or to which we can compare him; that his thoughts are not our thoughts; that his ways are not our ways; that all the nations of the world together are but as a drop in a bucket in his sight?

Now think of that. I sometimes (under the helpful prodding of my wife) water the flowers in the yard. I fill a bucket and take it around and pour it out on the different flowers. At the very end, there is one very tiny drop in the bucket—how small it is—it's almost as nothing compared to the full bucket. The bucket itself is almost nothing compared to him who fills it and pours it out. And he is but nothing compared to the greatness of God. In fact, the whole of creation is but a drop in the bucket, says the prophet. Or as dust on the scale that doesn't even cause the weights to move. God forgive us when we take his name on our lips and have so little sense of his greatness, his goodness and his sovereignty. Through our familiarity with the word, we tend to devalue the greatness of God and fail to take off our shoes for we are on holy ground. My brothers and sisters, take off your shoes. Our text begins, "For God."

Now if God is this God who has revealed himself in the creation and in Israel and supremely in Christ, crucified and risen, the gracious and majestic God, then when he speaks, we must listen. Remember how in the old TV ads, "When E.F. Hutton speaks, everyone listens," everybody became silent so they could hear? May it be so for us. When God speaks, let his people listen.

So our text continues, "For God so loved the world." Now here our eyes are directed in two directions, to a relationship—one look toward the world and one look toward God. So first, the world: this world is the world which God loves. It is this fallen world which he loves. Amazing. God's love is unconditional. Salvation may be conditional in the sense that one must respond. God does not save the world simply in love, but rather love moves on into grace and takes a specific path so that people might respond. The foundation of this grace is this incredible love which God has for the world.

In our experience, things partly derive their preciousness from being desired and appreciated and treasured by others. Here is a world that is treasured and desired by God. If God treasures all the people, if our Father treasures and loves the world and the inhabitants therein, then so must we. For we are his children in Christ, we are imitators of our heavenly Father and of our Lord. His loves are our loves; his concerns, our concerns. Jesus both shows in his life and teaches in his word that our love is to be as perfect, that is, as embrasive as our heavenly Father's love, who makes his sun to shine on the just and the unjust (Mt 5:45). Not to love in this way is to depart from the heart of God. It is sin. It is to continually fall short of the glory of God. Now to be sure, as finite creatures, at any given moment our energies are limited and focused, but in principle our love is to include all and to be directed by God in his focused way as he guides and directs us, for it is the world which God loves. The very catholicity of his people, the catholicity of the church rises from this. Does this not begin to touch you in the heart and to challenge you as it does me? How often we limit our affection, our love, our willingness to be concerned for others. Have you written off someone, some group, some people group, some class, some race, placed them out of the bonds of your love? Then let us hear these words, "God so loved the world."

Bishop Alfred Stanway used to say, "You're going to have to forgive them sooner or later—why not sooner?" The world. What an amazing and surprising people we are when, in any real sense, we get hold of this, or the Lord gets hold of us, and we begin to reflect in this fallen world this wideness in God's mercy, this love of the Father for the world. For in the midst of the walls and the fences and the barriers and the hatreds of the fallen world, God's people recognize no boundaries, no exceptions, for there are none to our Father's love. "God so loved the world." But if it's a world God loves, it's also God who loves the world. It's not just that he loves the world but that he so loves the world, that is, he loves it in this fashion—to this degree and in this particular concrete way.

To apprehend the path and the intensity of God's love, we need to look at our text from the other end and ask, "What does God see in this world? When he looks upon us and sees us apart from Christ, what does he see?"

I weep as I think about this and certainly this is one of the places in my preparation where the Lord spoke to me most powerfully. I suspect each of us will need to repent deeply here. I certainly do. I mean by "repent" to think differently; to change our way of thinking, and hence, our way of behaving, to see things with God's eyes and not as the world sees, and, most particularly, not as our culture sees.

Apart from Christ, God sees us as perishing and void of eternal life. God sees people as moving toward a terrible and final judgment, with no ability to make restitution or to change their hearts. He sees them as perishing—not merely perishing as lacking food or as lacking safety or as engaged in warfare or as physically dying, though that would be horrible enough (indeed, as horrible as we see it is on the television), but as perishing eternally—as lacking eternal life; as heading toward eternal loss; as heading toward banishment from fellowship with God and from fellowship with each other as well. Here is a sight that, quite literally, breaks our Father's heart. Our Lord Jesus looked at Jerusalem and cried out, "How often would I have gathered you to myself as a hen gathers her chicks under her wings, but you would not." As horrible as the signs of judgment can be on sin in this life, it is to the final accounting and separation that our Father looks and beholds. He does not want to see us perish, lacking eternal life, moving toward the second death, to that condition where the Savior himself says there is "weeping and wailing and gnashing of teeth." It goes beyond our capacity to fully picture it, or to entertain it—as a matter of fact, we repress it. Jesus said, "It would have been better if he had never been born." What a thing to say. It is our awful guilt he sees. God is moved to take the path that his love will take— the path of grace. Let me put a question to each of us bluntly. If we really believed that those around us and throughout the world were perishing and moving toward eternal death, and if we believed that there were an alternative given by God and that God would use us to rescue the perishing—would we not act? As one person once put it to a Christian, "If I believed what you Christians claim you believe, I would crawl over cut glass, in love, to warn and to rescue those who are perishing."

When have you last climbed over cut glass to share the gospel with anyone? God says they are perishing and lacking eternal life. God have mercy on us all. We have cried "Peace, peace" when there is no peace, and we have said of the fallen and of the unconverted, "I'm okay and you're okay." I am reminded of that story where the one fellow says, "If I'm okay and you're okay, why is he up there on the cross?" When we should say, "Because he's up on the cross, you can be okay and I can be okay" in relationship to God through him!

I hope that you will never be able to hear this verse again without this word "perishing" suddenly blinking at you and asking you to look no longer after the flesh—to see people as man sees on the outside—but to see with the eyes of your heavenly Father.

The gospel is for everyone because everyone needs the gospel. For those who are well and those who are sick; rich and poor; near and far; male and female; educated and ignorant; our race, whatever it may be, and those of any other race; religious and secular; short and tall; thin and fat—for all have sinned and continually fall short of the glory of God, and unless they are given birth from above, they can neither see nor enter the Kingdom of God. Perishing. Man looks upon the outside—God looks upon the heart.

Will you repent with me for refusing to take seriously what God sees and tells us what he sees; tells us consistently through the entire New Testament? The third chapter of John's Gospel ends with these words: "He who believes in the Son has eternal life; but he who does not obey the Son shall not see life, but the wrath of God rests upon him."

The gospel is for all because God loves all and because all are perishing and lack eternal life and are headed for eternal death. Now I think we can understand the path that God's love takes. God so loved that he acted appropriately. He took the path of grace. He gave his only Son. God gave his best. In his loving identification with us he humbles himself, he teaches us, he models for us, he takes our place on the cross and bears our sins in his own body on the tree. On him, the Father placed the iniquity of us all—"and not for our sins only, but for the sins of the whole world." Love in grace plumbs the depths, but it also climbs the heights. In love, the Father raises the Son, victorious; exalts him to his right hand; and the Father and the Son, in love, pour out the Spirit—the Spirit of love—to open our hearts to Christ, to give us the new birth, to conform us to Christ, to bestow that love from which nothing shall be able to separate us. We are in his love—not that we first loved him, but that he first loved us and gave his Son to be the propitiation for our sins.

There is salvation in no one else for there is no other name given under heaven whereby men must be saved. So God's love, his Son and his Spirit meet us in the gospel through the body of Christ, through believers who commend the gospel in their life and in their witness, and tell the story. It is whosoever believeth that has eternal life, therefore Paul's words are addressed to us: "but how are they to call on him in whom they have not believed; and how are they to believe in him of whom they have never heard?"—heard in both the sense of hearing with the mind and heard in the sense of having received it in the heart through the witness of someone who knows him and gives testimony to him, that the Spirit might use both mind and testimony to touch the heart. How are they to hear without a witness, a proclaimer; how can they proclaim if they are never sent? The Lord himself says to us, "As the Father has sent me, so send I you."

The gospel is for all and we are sent to all. Must we not weep for our negligence and ask the Spirit to move us deeply and free us for this great service.

My brothers and sisters, let me conclude with several very simple and brief applications. Should there be anyone here who has never personally taken Jesus' gospel to heart, accepted Christ's love in their own heart, accepted him as the one who bore your sins personally on the tree (as the Apostle Paul says, "The Son of God loves me and gave himself for me"; and Luther says, "The secret's in the pronoun 'for me'")—if there is anyone here who has not underlined that personally, consciously; has not claimed all was signed and sealed at baptism; not cashed the check on Christ's account; then as we have a time of prayer and ministry at the ending of our time, I beg you to do so tonight. Tell the one praying with you that you would like to pray to receive Christ as your personal Lord and Savior—to open your heart for the Spirit is, even now, touching and drawing you to Christ.

I think most of us are going to have to ask the Lord for forgiveness; forgiveness because we have looked upon the outside and failed to look upon people as the Father looks upon them. Lord, give us the eyes, pray, give us the eyes to see people as perishing. Let our heart break with your heart. Let us see truly and honestly and faithfully as you see. Pray for the eyes of Christ.

Lastly, as we come to a time of prayer, I would pray that you would pray for a new freedom in the Spirit to bear witness to Christ, in your life and with your lips, no longer to be ashamed of the gospel of Jesus Christ—free and bold and yet sensitive (I don't think the Lord would have us drive people away, but rather, lead them to himself). Pray for the freedom to go where the Lord would have you go. Would he have you go across cultural lines to far places where the gospel is not yet heard or to where a church might be assisted by your gifts; are we free to speak in our families; are we free to speak in our parishes? Pray for the renewal of your heart and of your passion for the gospel.

For the truth of the matter is, God so loved the world that he, literally, gave his only Son, that whosoever believeth in him might not perish, but actually receive and have eternal life. In God's heart the gospel is for everyone—may it be so in our hearts as well.

THE HOLY SPIRIT AND MISSION

The Rev. Canon Kevin E. Martin

The Holy Spirit as the Author of Mission

My thesis is that the Holy Spirit is the Author, the Motivator and the Power for mission and for world evangelization. I would like to begin in Acts, the tenth chapter, a passage of Scripture that is so familiar that I will just make reference to it. Not only was this a pivotal time in the life of the early church, but most of us need to acknowledge that, had it not been for the tenth chapter of Acts, we would not be Christians today. Christianity would largely be, if it existed at all, a sect of Judaism.

The setting: until this incident the church was made up of people who were of the household of Israel. A few others had made their way in, but only a few. Samaritans had been welcomed, but they had acknowledged the God of Israel. There was that incident with the Ethiopian eunuch that I am sure was an embarrassment to many church people of the day. He was baptized and welcomed in by Philip. But for the most part, things had remained in the control of the early church. Just a few sprinklings, a few enthusiastic moments in which they felt a loss of control, but now something disconcerting began to happen.

Cornelius has a vision. In it he is told to send for Peter. Peter, in the meantime, is taking a nap and dreams of a sheet filled with all the living creatures of the earth. A voice from heaven says, "Do not call unclean what I have made clean." Then there comes a knock on the front door. And despite the offense for an orthodox Jew to even be in the household of a Gentile, Peter got right up and went to the household of Cornelius. There Peter begins to lay out, in a simple and direct way, the story of Jesus of Nazareth, "whom God anointed by the power of the Holy Spirit to be the Messiah of the Jewish people."

I don't know if Peter knew where he was going with that sermon, but something interesting happened. The power of the Holy Spirit fell upon the Gentiles, and, just as on the day of Pentecost, they received the

Holy Spirit. "What is happening here? How could this happen? Peter, what is to prohibit us from baptizing them, welcoming them into the household of believers?" Throughout this story the hand of the Holy Spirit is arranging the details to bring the church to that moment of WOW– insight! How did these people, Gentiles, get into this early Christian band?

What we need to recognize is that it wasn't the idea of the early church to welcome the Gentiles; it was the idea of the Holy Spirit. In fact, the Spirit had led the early Christians, kicking and screaming, to a place where they did not want to go. He brought them into a company of people they did not want to accept.

The people of the first century were not any different from you and me, their hang-ups were similar to ours, they had all the resistances we have. It was enough to just believe in the resurrection and to try to find their place in Judaism. Suddenly they are thrust into a controversy with a wider community because they let these people in. Well, they didn't let them in; God let them in. Luke is saying to us clearly, the author of mission is the Holy Spirit. I want to emphasize this as a person who has a long association with renewal. Renewal, the power of the Holy Spirit, leads to mission. If it does not lead to mission, then it is not renewal!

The Holy Spirit as the Motivator for Mission

A young priest of the Diocese of Texas has been doing a great job for Episcopal Renewal Ministries (ERM). I had lunch with him and talked about the church he has been serving. I noticed what seemed a mild depression, so I asked, "Why are you down? You're doing good things." His reply was, "Well, when I came here, there were forty people. I have been here a couple of years, and there are only forty-three people now. I had the idea that it would be different. I thought that if I preached the clear uncluttered gospel, somehow something would happen here."

"Really?" I said, "Where did you get that idea?" "What do you mean?" he responded.

I told him that we have an illusion that the church is just supposed to hold the hands of its members, encourage and make their existence Episcopal. It's an idea called "maintenance." It is riding a long trend which started about 1840-1880, the last great growth period in the Episcopal Church. We are supposed to be involved in evangelism, not in the keeping of some mausoleums, but there is a culture of mausoleums in the Episcopal Church; sustain the rose windows and the beautiful architecture that is so characteristic of the good taste of Episcopalians. Finally, I told him that if he wanted the church to grow, he must spend at least twenty to twenty-five percent of his time with people who are not members of his church.

Do you think he could find anybody in the state of Texas who is not a member of a church? How would he find them—if he wanted to? We agreed that he would get together four or five people from his church to answer this question: "How would we find people who are not members of this church?"

I said, "Now you are thinking missions! Now you are thinking of the institution of the church not as something to maintain, but as a force to mobilize for mission." That is the challenge of mission. Many of us in the church today need to resolve that we will leave maintenance behind.

It is disturbing for any of us to leave the close-knit fellowship of Christianity for a life with those who are not Christians. I know many churches who are not going to do any ministry in missions because people don't have any time. They are in church on Sunday morning, prayer meeting on Wednesday night, a house fellowship on Friday, Bible study Saturday morning, and on it goes. They spend all their time with Christians. Now there is nothing wrong with fellowship; certainly it should happen. But there are times when we need to leave the nest, leave the comfort of the Christian body.

How many groups of people do we walk around because "they'll never be part of the church"? We believe in the love of God, but to step across those boundaries is uncomfortable and disconcerting. Philip did it, and we, like Philip, must be willing to pay the price of mission. The price of mission is to let go of security and loosen the tight circle of Christian fellowship that we often create.

I need to add something else to the "let go of security." As an Episcopal clergyman, I am ashamed of the ongoing discussion, especially among our new clergy, of how much "package" one is going to get after seminary. If we continue with a maintenance mentality in the church, there aren't going to be any packages. We are going to have to learn to go out and find ten people who are not tithing members of a church, who do not attend a local congregation, who have not read a Prayer Book and disciple and train them. Maybe then we will know the meaning of the words of Paul when he says, "The laborer is worthy of his hire."

When we are in touch with the Holy Spirit, our motivation changes. We no longer want to maintain an institution. We no longer want to remain smug and secure among only our Christian friends. The Holy Spirit is the motivator for mission.

The Holy Spirit as the Power for Mission

Finally, the Holy Spirit is the power for mission. The Apostle Paul is an example of this power for mission. Not the stereotypical Paul; not the Paul we church people so often cast in our own image. No, there is another Paul.

I would like to challenge you to think about a way to re-envision the Paul on the road to Damascus. Paul is blinded by the light, of use to no one, not even himself. In comes Ananias, a great hero of Scripture, who says to Paul, "God has commanded me to come here to lay my hands on you that you might receive your sight and be filled with the Holy Spirit." From that moment, Paul is rapidly on the move for the Holy Spirit. When Barnabas and Mark say that maybe they should go back, it is Paul who says no, we have to press on. It is Paul who has the dream in which he sees the man from Troas saying come over here. It is Paul who takes the mission of the church into Mesopotamia and Greece. It is Paul who responds to the leadership of the Spirit, whether he is accepted, as he was among the Thessalonians, or rejected, as he was among the Ephesians.

Paul is persistent in his purpose. When others turned aside, even good people like Barnabas and Mark, what kept Paul going? We like to say it was the persistence of his vision, but when he was in Athens I'm not certain that he really knew what his purpose was. He just knew that he was supposed to be there, saying something. His purpose seemed to be something that unfolded over a period of time. It started first in the synagogue, and then moved to the God-fearers, then he actually established a church that was made up of only God-fearers. He seemed to learn from the Holy Spirit. He seemed to be an example of persistence in the Holy Spirit. The Holy Spirit's power was expressed by this persistence.

I hold Paul up as a person of the Spirit. One of the most striking marks of the Holy Spirit is not the mountain-top experience, but this tenacity not to be deflected from reaching the unreached. We must see the Holy Spirit in Paul's life, not in the explosive energy of the volcano moment, but in the steady persistence of the surging river of the Holy Spirit's consistency and purpose to reach the lost. That is why he is there in Acts. Not because Paul was the main character. It was because the Holy Spirit is the main character of Acts, and Paul followed unrelentingly the Author of mission, the motivation that this Author gave, and the power that flowed from this Author for one who single-mindedly and obediently followed.

Do we realize how important the Holy Spirit is to the church as the

Author of ministry and mission for the life of the church? Or are we still stuck in an old model where we believe mission activity is something optional for the life of the church? Recently, I read with shame and humiliation in *The Episcopalian* the announcement that our national office plans to close its mission office. As if mission is an elective for the church.

Many of us love our churches, but we're not crossing any boundaries; we're stuck in the maintenance mode. We are justifying this by saying that if we can't take care of the people we have, we won't be able to reach out to other people—as though it was an either/or formula. Those in the apostolic church had the love of Christ in them; they took the love of Christ to the world, and that is why they had the love of Christ among themselves. Fellowship, without mission, stagnates.

How does this square with our lives? Our churches? Our communities? We should stop in soberness and reflection and think about this Holy Spirit. Dare to say, "Come Holy Spirit, shed on us the fire of your love, give us the power to care for those who are not yet part of the church. Give us courage to step across some boundary somewhere for the sake of Christ." Be willing to be people who will live out on the edge of risk and rejection and hatred. Yes, the place where people may come to Christ.

THE DISTINCTIVENESS OF A MISSIONARY

The Rev. Walter Hannum

A reading from a great missionary support-raising letter, written in Greece by a Hebrew missionary on his way to Spain to those living in Rome who had committed their lives to Jesus Christ:

> For I will not venture to speak of anything except what Christ has wrought through me to win obedience from the Gentiles, by word and deed, by the power of signs and wonders, by the power of the Holy Spirit, so that from Jerusalem and as far round as Illyricum I have fully preached the gospel of Christ, thus making it my ambition to preach the gospel, not where Christ has already been named, lest I build on another man's foundation, but as it is written,
> "They shall see who have never been told of him, and they
> shall understand who have never heard of him."
> This is the reason why I have so often been hindered from coming to you. But now, since I no longer have any room for work in their re-

gions, and since I have longed for many years to come to you, I hope
to see you in passing as I go to Spain, and to be sped on my journey
there by you, once I have enjoyed your company (Rom 15:18-24).

There are two points I want to make. The first point is: The New
Testament was written by missionaries. Every word from Matthew
through Revelation was written by missionaries for missionaries. It is a
missionary handbook on how to present the gospel to the Jews, the
Greeks, and the barbarians and how to deal with the philosophical ideas
of the age. It is written to missionaries who are planting churches, telling
them how to nurture new congregations. Today, we have lost the great
insight that the Bible is a missionary book. In my own experience, I have
sat through days of lectures on the Letter of Paul to the Romans and never heard that the author was a missionary!

If you want to know how to write a missionary prayer/support letter,
study the Book of Romans. It is the perfect example. Paul did not tell
about how cold the weather was or how sweet the oranges were, but he
did write about the deplorable human condition and that the only way
that condition can be changed is through the supernatural loving power
of Jesus Christ.

The second point I want to make is: Paul was a missionary and not a
pastor. Peter was a pastor, an ambassador of Christ, to the Jews, his own
people while Paul was an ambassador to Gentiles, a people not his own;
thus making him a missionary. Peter did have a cross-cultural life changing experience when he went from Joppa to Caesarea and ministered for
a night to Cornelius the Roman centurion and his household. We do not
know if an active church was developed as a result of Peter's visit. Paul
not only ministered to Gentiles, but he planted churches and developed
leadership that could minister, evangelize, and administer the church in
his absence.

In his letter to the Ephesians, Paul explains that the ascended Christ
gives "gifts so that some should be apostles, some prophets, some evangelists, some pastors and teachers to equip the saints for the work of the
ministry, for building up the body of Christ" (Ephesians 4:11-12).

An apostle, a missionary, is a person with the unique ministry of going and living with a people who have not yet heard or received the gospel, to proclaim the good news and with believers to plant and nurture a
church. Before an effective missionary leaves, the people of the congregation can minister one to another, study the Scriptures, pray, break
bread and witness to their non-believing friends, relatives and neighbors.
They can discuss the important questions: "What is it God wants to do

for us in this place and time?" "What kind of people does God want us to be?" "What is it God wants us to do?"

A prophet is one who grasps the meaning of the gospel and shares how it applies to issues in their lives and society.

An evangelist persuades non-Christians in his/her own linguistic/cultural group to accept Jesus Christ as Lord and Savior, be baptized and be active in the life of the church.

The pastor/teacher usually has a long-term holistic ministry in one place, e.g. a rector, curate or vicar of a parish. Our seminaries basically train people to be pastors.

Paul was a missionary, which meant that he was constantly on the move. The Scripture passage above informs us that Paul had covered all the eastern end of the Mediterranean Sea and had gone all the way around to what is now Albania. The church had already been planted in Rome without his help. He now wants to visit the Christians in Rome to be ministered to and to minister. He knows the need to be encouraged and strengthened by the church community. He hoped the church in Rome would help underwrite his ministry and perhaps that some of them would be inspired to join him on the missionary trip to Spain. Paul thought that when a church was planted in Spain the gospel would have reached the ends of the earth.

Seminaries are needed to prepare pastors to minister where the church has been established. Even greater is the need for places to train missionaries to carry the gospel to where it is not. Are you aware that there are 12,000 identified unreached people groups in the world today? Dr. Ralph Winter of the United States Center for World Mission defines an unreached people group as: "A people group among which there is no indigenous community of believing Christians with adequate members and resources to evangelize this people group without requiring outside (cross-cultural) assistance." There are over a billion people in the world who have never met a Christian. A call needs to be made through the whole Christian church for at least 12,000 apostolic teams who will cross the cultural, linguistic, geographic and prejudice barriers to proclaim the gospel and plant the church.

I have been told that at Trinity Episcopal School for Ministry there is a rumor going around that "Walter and Louise love you and have a wonderful plan for your life!" Let me emphasize that I am not calling you to be a missionary, the Lord God will call whom he pleases. But everyone should proclaim the message that missionaries are needed, and needed for long-term service.

We need to raise up a generation of career missionaries who will plant the church in one place, move on to the next and then to the next unreached people group.

I ask you to read and study the Bible as a missionary handbook and to pray that there will be a continuous stream of people coming to faith from your congregation to join those 12,000 apostolic teams that are so desperately needed to plant the church among every people group throughout the whole world.

BREAKING DOWN THE WALLS

BIBLE STUDY: EPHESIANS 1:15 - 2:2; 2:11-18; 3:6

The Rev. Dr. Sam Wilson

Robert Frost has, in an inimitable secular poem, caught the essence of gospel mission. I use excerpts to set the stage for our exploration of the second chapter of Ephesians:

MENDING WALL
by Robert Frost*

Something there is that doesn't love a wall,
That sends the frozen-ground-swell under it
And spills the upper boulders in the sun,
And makes gaps even two can pass abreast.

... I let my neighbor know beyond the hill;
And on a day we meet to walk the line
And set the wall between us once again,
We keep the wall between us as we go.
...One on a side. It comes to little more:
There where it is we do not need the wall:
He is all pine and I am apple orchard.
My apple trees will never get across
And eat the cones under his pines, I tell him.
He only says, "Good fences make good neighbors."
Spring is the mischief in me, and I wonder
If I could put a notion in his head:
"*Why* do they make good neighbors?

---

*Robert Frost, *American Poetry,* edited by Karl Schapiro. Thomas Y. Crowell Co., 1960

...Before I built a wall I'd ask to know
What I was walling in or walling out,
And to whom I was like to give offense.
Something there is that doesn't love a wall,
That wants it down...."

Walls.
We run into them.
We hit them.
We hate them.
And yet we preserve them.

Secular history is written in exclusion and separation. As to sacred history, a flaming sword was set outside Eden to ward off our sinful first parents. Prideful humankind was fragmented and separated by linguistic confusion after Babel. Even worship in the tent and temple were forced to dramatize exclusion. A curtain in the tent and a wall in the temple left the symbols of God's presence accessible only once a year by one man. That same wall may have kept the Greeks from going to Jesus directly, when they came to Philip and said: "Sir, we would see Jesus."

I suggest to you that the essential character of the gospel of Jesus Christ is to destroy walls. Ephesians is a hymn to God's sovereignty in history and suprahistory. As such, it begins with the soaring enumeration of spiritual blessings in heavenly places in Christ Jesus. The recounting of these blessings makes Paul erupt into a thankful prayer. First, he prays for us to know Christ. Then he prays for us to know the hope to which we are called, the riches of his inheritance in the saints, and the exceeding greatness of his power.

I want to focus on the third part: EASTER POWER! To describe it Paul bankrupts vocabulary in a single sentence: "incomparable power, like the working of His mighty strength which He exerted in Christ when he raised him from the dead." Force, might, strength, energized.

By the resurrection, God has declared his Son Lord. The mystery of heading up and reconciling all in Christ is unveiled in the power that broke the bonds of death and the mighty clutch of the tomb to declare his holiness. He has seated him at his own right hand, and made him head over all; head of the created universe, and head of the church, his body. There is no power in heaven or on earth that remotely compares.

And that same power works in us. This might, power, energy also worked in resurrecting us from the dead; we who walked in the chains of a worldly mind, entrapped by its tastes, amusements, angers and goals.

We were dominated by the systems of men and the unseen spiritual powers that guided our lives. Their daily freeway reports influenced the routes our behaviors traced, and set, over time, the standards and the values that molded our pursuits. From the consumerism of our TV ads and junk mail, to the personal career ascendancy of business life, these goals justified our actions and who we are and became. They channeled our misbehaviors.

The scary part is who our heroes were. Look at who finds adulation and position. White collar and computer crime are admired, and the guy who can "make a buck" is apt to be extolled for the acumen, astuteness, and sinfully creative spirit that inspires him.

As to lifestyle, the Bohemian predominates in literature and art. Hemingway, Truman Capote, or people who suffuse our "culture" with machismo, sexual prowess, drunkenness, addiction, experimentation, abuse and rebellion. And we love it. We, too, fantasized lives like that, by the nature of non-conformity and rebellion we inherited from our first father.

Our innate sin and this world's evil system, shot through with rebellion, made us by "nature" children of wrath; our instinct and intuition joined with obedience to the commander of spiritual powers, and we became subject to his rationale for life and his evil plan for the ages.

BUT GOD... rich in mercy, brought us to life.

We were once ostracized, with no mark of God's ownership upon us. We were once separated from Christ, excluded from citizenship in Israel. We were once peoples who were no peoples, without hope, without God in the world.

BUT NOW! He is our peace, who has made us all one! He has destroyed the barrier, leveled the wall, torn the veil. What a marvel of grace.

But suddenly, Paul recalls our former sorry, excluded state, and rubs it in: "Remember, at that time you were separate from Christ, excluded from citizenship, foreigners to covenant and promise, without hope, without God."

Why should I remember, Paul? Don't put my nose back in that muck! It is because our selfishness tricks us. Paul knows we turn truth inward, we think only of our individual destiny, his choice of us, the wonderful plan he has for "our" life. Will you understand if I suggest that this is to trivialize this Scripture? Do you see that saving you or saving me, transforming our picayune habits is the mere beginning of what his power wants to do?

His purpose was and is to unite and reconcile all peoples and things, to enfold all nations, to reveal to the present authorities and the coming rulers the mystery of forgiving grace. The key phrase in the text is "He Himself is our peace, who has made the two one and has destroyed the barrier, the dividing wall of hostility....His purpose to create in himself one new man out of the two, thus making peace."

But I think that Paul knows how readily we forget. Apart from remembering our own sorry former case, we will forget those who live on in hopelessness. We will not take them the message of forgiveness unless we remember what it was like to be in dire straits like that. He says, "Remember," so that we will go, and we will break down fences.

Do you have a sense of the sweep and grandeur of this redemptive, reconciling mystery? Do we understand what the sovereign God is doing? Are we in line with his purposes, or dragging him into our personal agendas? What is life about in the church? Is this the drive of what we do: TO BREAK DOWN WALLS? Do the walls of our prejudice remain?—Built of the bricks of inadvertent snubs, subtle nuances of attitude and behavior that repulse or don't welcome, cues articulated in the silent language of gesture and dismissal, but that clearly say to "outsiders," "You don't belong, come no closer."

And what of our mission beyond ourselves?

The mystery described in this text has an unheard of scope. When this reconciling love is worked out through the church into transformed human relations, all outsiders learn of God's welcome for them. And, wonder of wonders, even spiritual rulers, both in this world and the coming age, learn that God really means it, all are welcomed. The church becomes the vehicle of declaring the message by word and witness to the desperate unreached who, to this day, have no promise, no passport, no visa, no hope.

In theory and theology, the hedges and divisions are gone in Christ. Yet we partition the church and neglect the unreached peoples. While they remain at a distance, the power and outworking of the mystery of Christ are restrained, for this is a mystery revealed and to be revealed. Christ's reconciling love constrains us to leap hurdles, and reach "them." We, if we continue the experience of the cross, will be liberated and sent.

The sovereign plan of God is the only source I know which gives total integrity and equality to the peoples, tribes, and nations. Other nationalisms and internationalisms culminate in loss of identity, or in incredible animosity and barbarity. Jesus Christ, in himself, makes us one. Why remember what we were? To reach others who like us languish still in hopelessness and exclusion.

And now you can begin to see why I think Frost has captured it so well.

From Wineskins to the World

Will we, for the sake of God and his Kingdom, look at our selves, our congregation, and the total church of Christ, in terms of the walls that may be broken? At issue is the eternal destiny of those who have no church among them. We can help make history. As an individual, a family, and as a congregation, we can share in God's age-long purposes. "They" need no longer be outsiders. That, I suggest, is the meaning of a missions conference.

What walls can we break? What unity can we build, what distance can we cross to communicate the power of the resurrected Christ?

"Something there is that does not love a wall..."

Resurrection power, unleashed in the church, destroys separating barriers and reconciles. Remember who you were, a nothing foreigner. But God. Then you will remember those still at a hopeless distance, and do something about it.

Everything about the gospel seeks to bridge gulfs, reach across chasms, plant expansive churches in unreached people groups. Eliminating barriers and reaching every human division could not be more central to the gospel of our Lord and Savior, Jesus Christ.

Are you and your parish a part? Will you be?

Our choice can be represented by the sadness of Frost's final lines, and we can be like his neighbor, who

> ...moves in darkness as it seems to me,
> Not of woods only and the shade of trees.
> He will not go behind his father's saying,
> ... "Good fences make good neighbors."

Or, we can be like Christ, leaping every barrier, sent to the unreached, rending and tearing curtains of separation; straining to leap hurdles, razing walls and bridging distances. This is the true nature of the church.

THE END OF HISTORY

BIBLE STUDY: REVELATION CHAPTERS 4 and 5

The Rev. Dr. Sam Wilson

The Scriptures are rich with a diversity of literary forms. I am indebted to John Howard Yoder for calling my attention to the fact that the fourth and fifth chapters of the book of Revelation are scripted for dramatic reading.

It is dramatic in its language. Notice a first key to deciphering the significance of the text: the dramatic use and play on triplets. There are at least three sets of three to talk about the God who exists in triunity. Relative to the action of history he is the God who was, who is and who is the coming one. There are three uses of the word "holy," and three uses of the word "worthy." Lost on the English reader is the lyric similarity of these two words in the original language, i.e.: hagios, hagios, hagios, and axios, axios, axios.

There is high drama in the scene and the events that are transpiring. Imagine, being down in the dumps in exile on an island, and suddenly being invited up into heaven itself. There the first thing you behold is the majesty of the Ancient of Days, seated on the highest throne, accent lighted in sparkling jewelry. A rainbow dome of emerald glow highlights him on the throne. One by one, John recognizes other elements. He becomes aware of twenty-four elders on their own thrones, announced by flashes of lightning and peals of thunder. Blazing lamps—seven of them—intrude on his awareness. The cadence of threefold worship dominates the heavenly world of sound. Four richly symbolic living creatures become visible, and their worship develops the threefold beat of the Trinity—Holy, Holy, Holy; was, is, is coming. This is the cue line for the three mentions of God as worthy: the worthy Creator, the worthy Redeemer, who extends his reconciliation to every people, tribe, tongue, and nation (able to take the scroll and open it), the worthy slain Lamb, worthy of power, wealth, wisdom, strength, honor, and glory and praise.

But *there is the highest emotional drama for John.* I present a puzzle; the apostle John sees that the Holy One holds in his hand a scroll, sealed from without and within. Suddenly, and strangely, the drama turns tragic; John weeps and weeps. The image puzzles us. A mature apostle on a crying jag over a scroll and a bit of sealing wax? What is going on?

The simple fact is that you and I scratch our heads over this scroll, but people of New Testament times immediately understood that the scroll stands for history and biography, and its sealing stands for meaning that is inaccessible. John weeps because he sees a scroll that would let him understand what life is about and why things happen, and that knowledge is denied him.

I have a special grouping of books on a shelf at home. In one way or another, they all plumb this question of life's meaning. None of these books gives me a compelling interpretation of history. But I don't weep. Yet John weeps bitterly. What does life and history mean?

What are these seals? The chapters which follow let us know, and the opening of the seals dispels the clouds which obscure our understanding.

Conquest and oppression, war and famine, death and plague, marauding wild beasts, martyrdom, earthquakes and meteors, and later, great tribulation, as yet incomplete, and after the seventh seal, silence, before the seven trumpets, bringing hail, brush fire, tidal waves and polluted water, blackouts and locust plagues, scorpions, demon worship and immorality. When the seventh trumpet sounds the kingdoms of this world become the Kingdom of our God and of his Christ forever. In the meanwhile, all these things keep us from understanding life's meaning. They seem so unfair.

As Christians we are confident that we ought to have a lock on the understanding of history; unfortunately, this gets joined to what has been called our triumphalism. We are supposed to be living God's victory in the world; we survive, and occasionally others even join the church. Do you understand what history is about? No, because it is sealed, kept from us by the same sorts of things enumerated in chapters six through eleven. Can you tell me please, why innocent children drown in a van in a river or are slain in drive-by shootings or must suffer lengthily from AIDS contracted at birth? How is it that good honest people, some of them our brothers and sisters in Christ, lack bread? Or what about those who have never had a swallow of water that is disease-free? What is the meaning of the growth of homelessness and slums? And why aren't clear rebels against God punished? Oh, I begin to understand all right why John weeps.

Why does Caesar appear to triumph? John is at the end of a long life. He has watched while all of his fellow apostles have gone to violent deaths, and he himself is exiled to Patmos. Why? You see, if we think of history from a selfish point of view, we can hear Bill Bright say that God may have a wonderful plan for our lives, but apparently the premium may not be on our happiness. Have you ever wept about that? And what is the meaning of a church rent by divisions, where people who are less respectful of the Word of God advance politically. Heretics get a hearing and are applauded, and faithful ministers are sneered at and caricatured. Yes, now we can understand why we should weep.

But there rings forth a voice, heard out of nowhere, "Weep not." You can't decipher history, but there is one worthy to break the seals and reveal life's meaning. "Don't weep," says one of the elders. The Lion of Judah has prevailed to break the seals and open the scrolls. And John, at that moment, turns his tear-dimmed eyes, expecting to see a lion, but sees, instead, a slain lamb. *The most meaningful dramatic event* comes as the Lamb takes the scroll, and John hears a new song, an ode to the Lamb. It wasn't there before. It's sung only when the meaning of history is revealed, the scroll is taken from the hands of the Creator by the Lamb, and he has authority to open it. And now *we hear the new song,* and lo and behold!

It's a new song, but it's the old, old story: the blood of Christ redeems! The reach of God's love encompasses every human division. John suddenly hears the elders singing and recognizes that the multitude that surrounds the throne comes from *every people, tribe, tongue, and nation.* What history is about is redemption and reconciliation!

How did John know? Did he see olive eyes, colored skin? I think Episcopalians ought to see readily from Revelation 5 that he recognized something new in worship. It is worship that tells the full-orbed meaning of God's love. All the nations are included because the redeeming Lamb has opened his arms in welcome.

I don't know whether John had a transformation in which he could understand all those languages. When we raise our voices to praise the Lamb, we do it in English phraseology, in expressions that other languages can't match. But our expression will be incomplete until the worship in their languages joins ours to tell the redemptive story of all. Every one contributing its unique genius of expression, until the praise of the triune God is complete and worthily sung. The meaning of history waits until the empty places are filled because we have reached the unreached. And worship will have full eternal quality only because of successful missions.

So why has history not yet closed, why hasn't Christ come? Why is it meaningful to keep on suffering? Why is it still worth being a martyr? Because history is in suspense until we reach the unreached. And the meaning of history is that God's redemption includes them—all nations, languages, people, and tribes. And our job is to reach them.

Caesar, sin and sorrow do not reign, but God and the redeeming Lamb do. The close of history waits for the fulfillment of the reign of the One who loves and takes away the sins of the world.

We have a book in the Old Testament that also challenges us with the meaninglessness of life from our merely human point of view. And the preacher says that all the things that are done under the sun, all of them are meaningless, as chasing after the wind; what is twisted cannot be straightened, what is lacking cannot be counted. He says: "I tried pleasure, I saw oppression. I saw labor and achievement, but what does a worker gain from his toil? In place of judgment, wickedness was there; in place of justice, wickedness was there. A righteous man perishes in his righteousness; a wicked man lives long in his wickedness." Who knows what is good for man during the few meaningless days he passes through like a shadow? No one can comprehend what goes on under the sun. And then there is an almost taunting scripture, "All the days of this meaningless life that God has given you under the sun, all your meaningless days." Does that sum up your life?

Well, if you see the world-encompassing worship of Revelation 4 and 5, that sense of meaninglessness can be dramatically changed to purpose and hope. The puzzles are gone, the Lamb is triumphant, and the nations are complete. This gives significance to all of history.

But we join that worship only as we strain every effort to reach every tribe and tongue, every class and clan, until all people are swept into the Kingdom. The Lamb takes the scroll and opens it for all to see. The church can contribute to the meaning of history once we understand that life is, indeed, meaningless unless we get on-board with God's purpose for waiting. The point is worship, robust only when all peoples and languages participate. Mission is the infrastructure of worship with eternal quality.

Let us worship then, dramatizing together why it is worth waiting, why it is worth suffering. But as you do, will you *make your worship a pledge to join in and be a part of what God is doing in history?* Will you offer yourself—and God might take you up on it—to live redemptively for the unreached?

Now, with deepened understanding, let us worship! And listen for his call for your part in mission.

2

New Wine for Those Who Never Tasted: Unreached People Groups

WHY INDIA NEEDS CHRIST

The Rev. Dr. Andrew W. Swamidoss

Why does India need Christ? The question has two major parts: Who is Christ and what is the situation in India which needs Christ?

In Mark 5:1-10 we read the story of the healing of the man possessed by Legion. No one had the strength to subdue him. Night and day, among the tombs and on the mountains, he was always crying out. Jesus said, "Come out of the man, you unclean spirit." The unclean spirits came out of the man and left him. In Matthew 12:22-32 we read that the stronger man, Jesus, bound the strong man, Satan. Jesus drives out demons. Exorcism is an integral aspect of Christology. The pages of the synoptic gospels are full of them.

India has a large tribal population, almost fifty percent, and they live in primitive conditions. Animism, worship of spirits, and a constant fear of spirits and black magic has a strong hold on many millions of Indians. If someone has a stomachache, the village "baghat" (doctor) would say it is because of a spirit and would not hesitate to put a hot iron rod on the patient's stomach. This "healing pain" will be more intense than the stomach pain. If someone dies, the family thinks that the spirit of the dead person is roaming around. They believe they are under the control of that spirit. Why does India need Christ? India needs Christ because people are afraid of demons and spirits. Christ alone can deliver them.

Let me point out two incidents that have taken place as examples: The field director of Friends Missionary Prayer Band told of a young missionary wife who felt very much disturbed by spirits when her husband wasn't home. He told her to quote Colossians 2:15 while praying and claim the victory since Jesus had triumphed over the devil on the cross. The missionary wife did that and from that time on she did not have any fear or difficulties with the spirits.

The field director shared this as a witness in a prayer meeting where an evangelist was also present. Sometime later the evangelist went to do village evangelism along with another friend. One family asked him to come to their home and pray for their sick son. The evangelist and the friend went to the home. The evangelist was led into the room of the sick son and the door was locked behind him! The sick man was circling the room wildly and the evangelist did not know what to do. He put his hand on the Bible and prayed, "Lord, I have heard the recent testimony of the field director. You are all powerful. You have disarmed the principalities and powers through the cross. Please heal this man." The man fell down and the demon left him. The healing was instant.

In Ephesians 1:21 we read, "Christ is above all rule and authority and power and dominion over every name that is named, not only in this age but also in that which is to come." Christ is the Lord of all, the One unto whom all authority has been given. He is supreme and unique.

Compare this with the rampant idol worship and the multiplicity of gods in India. There are different gods for different geographical regions—the gods in South India are different from the gods in North India. There are different gods for different castes—the gods of the Brahmins are different from the gods of the lower castes. There are different gods for different purposes—for education people pray to one god, for wealth to a different god, and for safety in travel to yet another god. The list is unending. India needs Christ because these idols are not gods and Jesus is the Lord of all.

People long for inner peace and deliverance from guilt. They take pilgrimages to holy mountains, rivers, seas, temples and birthplaces of various gods. Some people take this as an obligation and want to please the god by participating in as many pilgrimages as possible. I asked a

Hindu convert in Delhi how he came to know Christ. He said that he took many pilgrimages but could not get the peace for which he longed. One day a street preacher came to his street and preached about Christ. The Hindu invited the street preacher to his home and came to know more of Christ. He accepted Jesus Christ as his personal savior because he felt the inner peace he was seeking. A little later he was baptized. Christ alone can give inner peace. In Romans 5:1 and Colossians 3:15 and in several other places we see that the peace of God can rule in our hearts.

Superstitions bind many Indians. The bondage of astrology—reading of the stars and how they control the individuals, the bondage of palmistry—reading of the future through the various lines on the palms, the bondage of predicting fortunes through birds, picking up cards, etc. are keeping millions in fetters. In Colossians 2:20 Paul writes, "If with Christ you died to the elemental spirits of the universe, why do you live as if you still belonged to the world?" In India people believe that the elemental spirits of the universe rule the world and that these can be discerned by the use of the above means. Christ alone can meet such needs.

In India there are many philosophers: "Gnanamarga" is attaining salvation through knowledge—"Gnana" is knowledge and "marga" is the way. Thus this is the way through knowledge. There are people who go in for long meditation and try to know God through knowledge. Then there is "bhakhtimarga." This is attaining salvation through devotion. "Bhakhti" is devotion. This is the way through devotion. "Karmamarga" is attaining salvation through works. "Karma" is works. Thus this is the way through works. Good works will lead to salvation and bad works will lead to destruction, maybe rebirth in the next life into a lower caste or even into the animal kingdom. There are several other philosophies, variations of these and different ones too. There are universities in India which offer graduate programs in religion or philosophy.

All such attempts of philosophy are human efforts to know God. There is an intense search to know God through one's own ability. First Corinthians 1:20-23 says,

> Where is the wise man? Where is the scribe? Where is the debater of this age? Has not God made foolish the wisdom of the world? For, since, in the wisdom of God, the world did not know God through wisdom, it pleased God through the folly of what we preach to save those who believe. For Jews demand signs and Greeks seek wisdom, but we preach Christ crucified, a stumbling block to Jews and folly to Gentiles (RSV).

The Bible categorically says that man cannot attain salvation through his own efforts, be it knowledge or devotion or good works. Salvation is through Christ and Christ alone. It has been given as a gift through the grace of God (Rom 3:21-31). God took the initiative so that man can be saved. Human efforts cannot save. These philosophers need to see the light, that is why Christ is needed in India.

Hinduism does not have a concept of eschatology. Hindus do not have a hope for the future. They believe in reincarnation. The body and soul are separate. Upon the death of a person the body decomposes but the soul takes a new birth in the form of another human being or even in the form of an animal or bird. If one has exhibited good works in life he will be born into a better caste, then one can meditate, attain salvation, and merge with the Brahma, the supreme God. Thus it is a cycle of birth. The world does not come to an end. It goes on and on and on.

What does the Bible say about the life after death? In John 11:25, 26 Jesus says to Martha, "I am the resurrection and the life; he who believes in me, though he die, yet shall he live, and whoever lives and believes in me shall never die." This is realized eschatology. The blessings of the future are already present. The believer will have eternal life. The great hope of eternal life—living on and on with the Lord Jesus Christ in the Kingdom of God yet to come—is a magnificent concept in the Bible. There will be a new world. The unbelievers will be judged and will undergo eternal condemnation. Hinduism teaches immortality of the soul but the Christian faith teaches bodily resurrection. This is a sharp contrast. It is very difficult for a Christian to stand at the deathbed of a Hindu and watch the struggles since he suffers from a fear of death, having no hope of the life after death.

In Hinduism there is no concept of church. Individually each one is a Hindu and collectively they belong to separate castes and there is nothing that unites them spiritually. Worship is always individualistic. Large numbers will assemble in pilgrimage centers, but only to take a dip in the holy waters at the appointed sacred time or to take an individual "darshan" (view) of the idol who is kept in the holy of holies.

The New Testament teaches that Christ is the head and we are the members of one body (1 Cor 12:12-31). The church is the Body of Christ. In Christ there is neither Jew nor Gentile; all are one in Christ (Gal 3:28). We may belong to different races, may speak different languages, may belong to different countries, but we all belong to one another and together are the Body of Christ. This sense of belonging to one another is missing in Hinduism since it puts men into caste brackets and thereby separates them at their very birth.

There are more than four thousand people groups in India. These multitudes of tribal people live in remote areas and are exploited by the caste Hindus, government officials, politicians and others. Their living conditions are very poor. There is a great response to the gospel among these marginalized people. Once in southern Bihar I baptized a whole village, 192 people at one time. Matthew 9:36-38 reads, "When Jesus saw the crowds, He had compassion for them, because they were harassed and helpless, like sheep without a shepherd." Then he said to his disciples, "The harvest is plentiful, but the laborers are few. Pray, therefore, the Lord of the harvest to send out laborers into his harvest."

Millions of such people are exploited. Let me point out one. A young girl walked with a heavy bundle of firewood cut in the forest, one whole day's labor. Then she took the bundle to sell, walking down more than five miles one way to the village in the plain to sell the wood. It was worth more than thirty rupees. At one corner a man intercepted her and said that she should sell it to him and quoted five rupees as the price. When she refused to part with the firewood and began to walk away, the man started beating her. The missionary lady who stood nearby intervened and spoke for the girl and picked a quarrel with the man. Then he let the girl go free. She went to the next street and was able to sell it for twelve rupees, much less than its real worth. With such hard earned money when such people go to buy a pill for a headache, they are charged double the normal price. This is nothing but cold-blooded robbery and exploitation. Jesus rightly described the condition of such people— harassed and helpless, like sheep without a shepherd. It is a joy to see a good response among these people, but it is very painful to see that there are practically no workers to carry the gospel to such poor, needy, innocent people.

There is a large Muslim population in India, 120 million people. This is the second largest Muslim population in the whole world. The stumbling block for them is the divinity of Christ. They are able to accept Jesus as a prophet but not as the Son of God. In John 1:1-18 in the prologue to the gospel, the evangelist brings out very clearly the divinity of Jesus Christ. "The Word was with God and the Word was God. The Word became flesh." John brings out this concept in other parts of his gospel too. Much work needs to be done in the area of Muslim evangelism. As much as the Hindus need Christ, these Muslims also need Christ.

More than half of the 900 million people in India live below the poverty line. There are many children who are born in the street, live in the street, and die in the street. This leads to begging, stealing, violence, sex offences, drugs and all kinds of problems. Who shall meet the vast needs of these people who need to know Christ's love? Matthew 25:31-45 very graphically describes Jesus' concern over such needy people. Jesus says, "Truly, I say to you, as you did it to one of the least of these my brethren, you did it to me." The needs of the poor can never be belittled.

There need not be an unnecessary dichotomy between the ministry of church planting and the ministry of development. They are two sides of the same coin and go hand in hand. Church planting without caring for the needy neglects the physical realities and caring for the poor alone without doing any church planting neglects the spiritual realities. In the very next chapter, just five verses later, Matthew records an event in 26:6-13 where Jesus praises a woman for anointing his feet with a costly ointment. The disciples were indignant and murmured saying that the ointment could have been sold for a large sum and given to the poor. Jesus says that the woman has done it to prepare him for the burial. He adds that this act will be proclaimed in the whole world wherever the gospel is preached. It is in this context that Jesus says, "The poor shall always be with you."

The gospel of Jesus Christ is always a holistic gospel. He brings this out very clearly in the Nazareth manifesto, Luke 4:18-21. Any attempt to dichotomize the two—church planting and caring for the poor—commonly known as evangelism and social action—is not doing justice to the biblical text. The biblical mandate is to do both. The picture in India is so grim that the ministry of proclaiming the gospel—church planting and caring for the poor—must be done on a war footing with the utmost urgency.

Let me summarize: Why does India need Christ? India needs Christ because Christ alone can meet the vast need in the country. The strong hold of animism, the fear of spirits and black magic, the pantheon of having several thousand gods unable to grant inner peace, the varied superstitions, the manifold philosophies offering no solution to human needs, the hope for a bright future and resurrected eternal life with the Lord, the concept of the church, relief from the naked exploitation of the innocent multitudes, the vast Muslim population, the poor, suffering and the needy—all these can be taken care of only by our Lord Jesus Christ and him alone. Therefore India needs Christ.

Let me close with an illustration. About twenty miles from my hometown there lived a lady who was a powerful witness for the Lord Jesus Christ. I was young and as I was growing up I knew of many people who had gone there for physical healing who were touched by the Lord and were healed. It looked like the events in the Acts of the Apostles were being repeated once again. Many people were baptized. Once I asked a friend of mine to tell me her background. I was moved when I heard the witness. This lady was a strong Hindu lady. She had a next-door neighbor, a Christian lady who spent a lot of time in prayer and singing. This Hindu neighbor used to deliberately disturb her very much particularly when she was praying. One day the Hindu woman's children were sick with fever. She tried all her Hindu *pujas* (prayers), but nothing worked. The fever was increasing and there was no help. She went to her Christian neighbor and asked her to come to her house and to pray for her children so that they could be healed. The Christian lady accepted the request and went in. She asked the neighbor to remove all the Hindu ashes and fetishes from the bodies of the children. The other one hesitated for a while, but owing to necessity gave in and removed them all. Then the Christian lady prayed for the healing of the children. They were healed immediately. This changed the faith of the Hindu lady. She was baptized and became a powerful witness in the area. Soon the Lord began to use her mightily in the nearby areas, and she became a powerful witness for the Lord like St. Paul was. Many were touched by her and were baptized.

Power encounters are happening in India every day in the mission fields. The Lord wants more laborers for the vast amount of work yet to be carried out there in that large country with 900 million people. The response is overwhelming. Partnership in the great task of reaching the millions in India is the need of the hour. Are you willing? It is costly, but you will be a blessing to many. The result of such partnership will be "a great multitude that no one can count, from every nation, tribe, people and language, standing before the throne and in front of the Lamb, crying out in a loud voice, 'Salvation belongs to our God, who sits on the throne, and to the Lamb'" (Rev 7:9, 10). May the Lord grant us grace for this.

REACHING THE LEAST EVANGELIZED

The Rev. Tad deBordenave

More than ninety percent of the world's least evangelized people groups live in an area we call "World A" that extends from western Africa to most of China, and from Kazakhstan to most of Indonesia. It is an area where you cannot be a traditional missionary. It is very easy to be of good will in World A and yet not make an impact. With a little bit of understanding, however, we can be a lot more strategic and comprehensive. It is not like countries where you can get a missionary visa, walk in to start work and be met by the bishop who will tell you what to do. I want to outline a few things that are true of World A and then list some assets of the body of Christ today, to demonstrate how these can work together for the Non-Residential Missionary (NRM) strategy.

The first thing is *ethnocentrism*. In order to understand World A, it is important to understand people groups. Think about events in the former Soviet Union and the areas of Georgia, Armenia and Azerbaijan: the central issue is not politics and who is elected, but the enmity of one people group against another. Likewise, Yugoslavia cannot be understood without knowing about the Serbs and the Bosnians. And the situation in Kashmir is not simply India versus Pakistan, but the people groups of the Northern Punjab and Hindu Kush who are at war with each other. So if we are going to understand the undercurrents behind the scenes of the political and economic structure of a country, we have to understand people groups and how ethnocentrism is a dominant operative force today throughout World A, as well as in other areas.

Secondly, *information* is available in a new way today. When UN troops were preparing to invade Mogadishu, a political cartoon's punch line was not the arriving troops but the invasion of the news corps with floodlights ready to photograph the landing of the troops! CNN has told us about Somalia and Cambodia, the Kurds and Chechens. It is everywhere. I have CompuServe on my computer and I haven't begun to tap the information available to me. This is the Age of Information. I first went to Nepal in 1991 for four weeks. Beforehand, in Richmond, Virginia, I was able to gather precise information about the villages, people groups, climate and even the birds in an area I had never been to before.

Third, there are *restrictions* in World A. When my great-great-great-uncle Channing Moore Williams went into Yokohama harbor, nobody said to him, "You can't come." They might have said, "We don't want you," but the U.S. Navy gunboat that landed ahead of him cleared any restrictions about entering Japan. Passports and visas are an invention of the last hundred years. As Andrew Swamidoss says, "You can be a missionary to India, but only for six months." That's generous, really, when you think of other countries. I read the State Department information about visitors to Riyadh, Saudi Arabia. They want to know what time you are arriving, what you're going to do for all thirty-six hours of your stay, and what time you're leaving. And they don't want to hear anything about you being a Christian missionary interested in evangelizing: you won't get off the plane. The same is true of many other places. As some countries open up, others close. The restrictions on missionaries going into various places is something that must be taken into account as we consider work in World A.

Accompanying the restrictions is hostility. I read in the paper recently about a prison break in the southern part of Algeria in the mountains. Over two hundred Islamic fundamentalist political criminals were freed who have nothing to lose because they were under a sentence of death in the prison. They are now free in Algeria and their intention is to shoot foreigners. It's as simple as that. The hostilities didn't begin with the prison break, but certainly that upped the ante.

Ethnic cleansing is something that is going on deliberately in Tajikistan. Although we don't read about it, it is happening in places other than the former Yugoslavia. The hostility is intense and costly. For one reason or another, a government may be polite to visiting Westerners until they get on the plane and leave. But then sometimes dire repercussions fall upon the people who were visited. Sadly, many Westerners are not sensitive about this. For example, a Christian visiting China could go to one of the official churches, because the government already knows about it. But they shouldn't visit an underground house church because visitors are watched and followed, and government security forces will come in later with repercussions for the church. One reason for the hostility and restrictions is the fear of democracy from the West. But there is also fear of the church. China did a study of the causes of recent events in Eastern Europe, and they know that it all started with a church movement in East Germany which resulted in the wall coming down. The Chinese government is determined not to let Christian influence pervade China because they don't want their own wall to come down.

So these are the characteristics that we must understand as we think about how best to work in World A.

Now let me list two assets the Body of Christ, the church, has to use to reach World A. The first is cooperation. That means cooperation with the last person on the face of the Christian earth that you ever thought you would be collaborating with, because of the vast differences in your theology or style. The work is just too big and the urgency too great for us to get bothered by what really must be considered in the grand scheme of things as crossing "t's" and dotting "i's."

One of the images of this is the kaleidoscope, in which pieces of every stone are pulled together and make the overall image of what we see. What that means in terms of cooperation in the church in World A is that even though I may not doctrinally embrace some of the missionary societies I have heard about, we can sit down and find out how we can work together. We cannot let a lack of cooperation stop us.

The day is past for what Dr. David Barrett calls the stand-alone missionary agency which thinks it is going to set the world on fire without any outside help, thank you very much; you just stand back and watch us. The exception has been the missionary society that says to other societies, how can you help us? That needs to be the dominant theme in any missionary work today. Many agencies to whom I have written on behalf of the Qashqa'i are surprised to find that I am writing as an Episcopalian with an Episcopal missionary society, but they are pleased and eager to share, and we are working together.

Another asset that we must use is technology. We can say that William Carey did all right without a laptop computer, and so can we. But the word for that is "obscurantism," being opposed to the spread of knowledge. Technology is our servant. I hadn't turned on a computer until a year ago; now I am astounded at what I can do in my office with a telephone, fax machine, computer and printer. It's incredible what is available to me in a research library right across the street, and it's incredible what I can be in touch with, what I can generate and what I can learn.

In our newsletter "Out of Sight," I talk about a comparison of the Roman Roads and the Silk Road available to the early church to go east or west, and the information highway we talk about today. Paul was thinking strategically when he took the Roman Roads. Thomas was thinking strategically when he took the Silk Road. We must think strategically in terms of technology and what is available to us.

All information is not equally weighted: some facts have more value than others. Research and analysis should be done with a mind for what opportunities and possibilities may open up, or how this can redirect our strategy, or what this may mean for us six years from now. Research of our past shows us the future. In missions strategy in World A, we have to know what the future is, and we have to be there when it arrives in order to make a difference. Without research and analysis, we can have a lot of good will but probably not a whole lot to show for it. With it, in the midst of a very complex World A, with the people groups, information, restrictions and hostility, we can plan ahead.

The question is, "How can the church best mesh the realities of World A and our ability to tap the unparalleled resources in the Christian church today?" Often the more precise question is, "Where can this be done?"

If you can live inside the targeted country, communicating and pooling resources with the Body of Christ around the world, then you are ahead of the game. But many of these places today will not give visas for missionaries. A full-time missionary strategist desiring to plant churches will try to multiply the number of workers on the ground, using tentmakers of some sort, who are placed and recruited using all of the information available. If that can be done without opposition inside the country, so much the better. Many times, though, it is just not an option. Parts of Central Asia are a good example, because a missionary would not be given a visa to get off the plane. Three years ago, Greg Muffleman started a ministry in a country there, and I am going to let him tell what he has been doing outside of the country as a non-residential missionary (NRM).

GREG MUFFLEMAN: I am married and have two little girls, and when our family decided to become non-residential missionaries to this people group, we were not really sure of what we were getting ourselves into.

In high school, I was a foreign exchange student for a summer in Turkey, and that was my introduction into the Muslim and Turkic world. I lived with a Turkish family and had a blast. I came back a changed person because I had seen the world at the age of sixteen. In college, both my wife and I went on separate short-term mission trips, which further prepared us, opening our eyes to the unreached world. So when we were married, we knew that God was going to call us into some type of full-time Christian missions work in the unreached world. We thought of a number of different things, including becoming residential missionaries in Turkey. Then our rector told us about the non-residential missionary strategy, and shortly thereafter we visited Dr. Barrett, the "father" of the NRM concept. After listening to him for a couple of hours we were pretty much hooked. We considered being NRMs focusing on a particular city. We did a little bit more research and started seeing that there were unreached people groups of Turkic origin in desperate need of outreach.

Three different things appealed to us when we considered becoming an NRM family. First, the non-residential missions concept focuses one couple or family on one unreached people group. Looking at the vast needs of World A is overwhelming, but we knew we could make a difference focusing on one group. Second, the NRM approach seemed like a reasonable strategy to reach an unreached people group. A non-residential missionary looks at the whole people group, along with the world of resources available, and tries to put the two together to devise creative ways to get Christians in. Third and most important to us, it was an alternative to the surveillance we would have been under working residentially. We can do a host of things as NRMs focusing on this group that the missionaries—hereafter I will refer to them as workers—who are living full time in this country are unable to do.

There are three main focuses or functions of a non-residential missionary. First is to do research; to become an expert, however possible, on your unreached people group and the resources that could be used to reach them. We spent much time learning about this people group and studying the Christian world for who might be in a position to reach them. The second NRM function is to strategize. The Southern Baptists graciously trained us so that we could teach Episcopalians to become NRMs, and we brainstormed for two full days. Our task was to come up with one hundred ways to get the gospel to the people using traditional and non-traditional missionary approaches specific to their culture and society. The third NRM function is to implement strategies that are tailored to the person's particular gifts and abilities, and to get other people to implement other strategies. For example, there is an incredible human need in this country for medical outreach, for which I have no background. My job as an NRM is to gather information, to find and network with other people and organizations such as the Christian Medical and Dental Society who might have that expertise or interest, and to delegate those projects in which I cannot specialize.

The capital of the country is a small Soviet city; its buildings, streets, cars, trucks, pavement and sidewalks resemble Moscow. The people are very different; they are darker, more Middle Eastern, and their clothes are very colorful. Their language is close to Turkish. They are warm and friendly; in most cases they really want to get to know you. They are nominally Muslim, as many in the USA are nominal Christians. In some ways that is helpful because they might want to talk about what you think and believe. In other ways, you have to be careful. There is no public preaching, but one-to-one friendship evangelism is very effective.

Most of the workers' apartments are bugged and most phones are tapped, which means that when we talk on the telephone we have to use creative language. We talk about churches as fellowships, seminaries as shepherd schools, workers instead of missionaries, and we never use last names or specify affiliated organizations.

Out of several million people who live in the country, we estimate that in 1994 there were twenty indigenous Christians (ed. note: over 100 in 1995). What is being done to reach these people? There were no missionaries or workers there three years ago when we first started. Now there are about two dozen workers living in the country; some are short-term for two years, and others are long-term. These include Americans, British, Canadians and one German, representing eight different mission organizations. Some of them teach English at the university and a few teach at institutes which are for upper-level education. One group of people installs water filters in orphanages and hospitals, as the availability of good drinking water in the capital is extremely limited. Finally, two people are there to foster cultural exchange, and are trying to form a joint venture with the Ministries of Construction or Culture. We have been involved in placing some of them, in helping them get over there and find housing.

In addition to the long-term workers, there are also short-term teams going in and out. A couple of churches sent a few small teams in during the fall. We helped them find housing and they went primarily to encourage the workers, to do friendship evangelism, to walk the streets and to pray for the city. Right now I'm excited about two short-term teams, one just finished and one just starting. Four Englishmen from London went for two weeks of personal evangelism. They all had experience in the Turkish world and were able to speak Turkish. They purposely kept themselves separated from the permanent full-time Christian workers so as not to compromise their security. Then another team of eleven, affiliated with the Caleb Project, just left for three months to do research, with the goal of developing ministry tools like prayer journals that we will be able to give to people in churches to raise awareness and intercession for this ministry.

We have two main roles right now. Primarily we are facilitators of a group of international organizations who desire to reach this people group. Cooperation with other missionaries and organizations takes concerted effort, prayer and real commitment, and those involved in ministry to this people group have agreed to come together. We found two or three logistical projects, such as raising prayer support, where we can work cooperatively. Unity in reaching the people is a primary focus of all of our work. If we go in there fighting and arguing with each other, we are not going to get very far. Since I live outside of the country, I have been asked to do the work of bringing this group together for consultations held twice a year in different locations in Europe. We gather to bring in other organizations, to talk about our work and to move ahead in what we are doing.

I just spent a week in Istanbul in conference with organizations committed to Central Asia. We had a good meeting talking about security issues, the status of the church, and obstacles we face in our ministries. We also talked about the future. How exciting it was for the eight of us to discuss all the different things that we knew were coming in the next six months: this group and that group are coming, this project should be finished soon and this one needs to begin; and how to prepare for our next consultation. We are hoping to interest another five to ten organizations in ministry to this people group. And to think that three years ago there were no Christian workers there! So we rejoice in what is happening.

The second important thing for us to be personally involved in is raising prayer support and channeling prayer requests from workers in the field to people here in the US and around the world who have expressed an interest in interceding on behalf of this ministry. One worker in the country has volunteered to gather prayer requests from the others every two weeks. Another worker encodes and sends them to me via e-mail, and then I forward those requests to a network of churches, organizations and individuals who have promised to pray. It is really important to keep those prayer requests updated every couple of weeks and not let too much time go by.

Where is the work headed? The most important need is for workers with a commitment to planting churches. We can look at various projects and creative ideas, but if we lose the focus that the end goal is to establish the first indigenous church in this people group, then we are not doing the best possible job. So we need workers who have skills in teaching English or to do a host of other things, who can be there for the long haul to plant churches.

A short-term team from another part of the former Soviet Union wanted to rent the university auditorium for some public meetings but the Minister of Religion said no. They prayed and went back the next day, and he said yes! So there was one week of public meetings last summer, and about twenty-five to thirty people came.

Some of the workers have suggested forming an international church. The government would be more open to something like that because it would be started by, and for, expatriates.

However, we believe the indigenous church will start in homes. Small, one-on-one groups of believers will gather and form house churches. We pray for the day when there will be a registered church of indigenous believers. There is a Russian Orthodox church, a Russian Baptist church and a Russian Pentecostal church that are registered and we have made contact with some of them. Very few people are involved. There was a KGB person heading up one of those churches, so obviously it was not a very safe place to be open about what we wanted to do. So we pray for a softening of hearts, but we believe that the indigenous church will probably begin with house churches.

There are a hundred things we could do to get other workers into the country, and slowly but surely we will implement them as time allows and as the Lord puts us in touch with other people who share this burden. One man dreams of bringing in large amounts of medical supplies, books and all types of humanitarian aid. In order to do that we will need to cooperate and raise some funds. It started a couple of years ago when one person had an idea, and it could be one or two years away, but this is how these things begin.

One of the university teachers is a single woman. She is in her late 40s and her hair is graying, and that has helped her a lot. For the first few months she didn't actively seek out too many opportunities to share her faith. People got to know and love her, and she built friendships and relationships with fellow teachers and students. She now has more opportunities to share the gospel than she can handle.

The men do not treat women the way American men try to treat women in our country, and that sometimes makes it difficult. Women do hold more of a subservient role, but that's something that can be worked with, and the Western women who are there have dealt with it.

We have colleagues in another organization who are also NRMs to the same people group and because we started out in cooperation from the very beginning it has really paid off. It has not always been easy, but we have a good working relationship and the partnership has been great. We have been able to figure out what they can do, what I can do, and how we can best work together.

We want to work together, we need other people, and we desire unity. We are the first NRMs in the Episcopal Church, and at various meetings I have been one of the only Anglicans present. It has been wonderful to blow away some stereotypes, both for myself as well as others.

OPEN DOORS TO CLOSED COUNTRIES

Ms. Sharon Stockdale

I would like to quote a sentence from *Operation World:* "Foreign experts and businessmen: China aims to recruit about 30,000 experts annually." Did you get your mind around that number? Thirty thousand experts annually "to teach English, Japanese and German, as well as other subjects, and also to build up China's technology and industry. Pray that many may be radiant Christians able to impart their faith while on the job." Thirty thousand—can you imagine?

Every Christian organization that sends Christian teachers to China has more openings than people. Some of the broad categories in which there are job openings are: agriculture, applied sciences, architecture, business, design, computer science, engineering, English language, journalism, law, science, technology and translation. And that's a short list. There are many more openings. We had a request for a perfume specialist once, and we found someone!

This isn't a new way to serve God in the world. There are many people in the Bible who worked for their living while attending to God's purposes. For instance, Abraham had a cattle business. In Egypt, Joseph served a general, a jailer, and Pharaoh himself. As for Amos, he was accused with the words, "Go, prophet," and he answered, "I'm not a prophet—I didn't go to prophet seminary. I'm a shepherd; I tend sycamore trees." Daniel was a high government official in Babylon. Of course, Paul worked to support himself making tents. That's where the name "tentmakers" comes from.

You may be thinking, "I know somebody who could be a tentmaker." I would like to recommend the book *Working Your Way to the Nations: A Guide to Effective Tentmaking.* It is very helpful for training any prospective cross-cultural workers in your church, whether they go in a traditional role or as a tentmaker.

I tried to go overseas for years, but I ran into one closed door after another. Finally, I was praying about whether the Lord wanted me overseas at all. Maybe I had been barking up the wrong tree for years, wasting years of my life. I had worked with international students, earned a master's degree in linguistics, and gotten some theology and Bible training and a Certificate in Teaching English as a Second Language. I remember praying, "Lord, I don't know what you want me to do! It would be so nice if somebody would call and say, 'Hello, Sharon! This is for you!'" That wasn't a request, just an expression of my frustration. Well, the next day I got a telephone call and this is how the conversation went:

"Hello, Sharon?"

"Yes."

"You don't know who we are, but we know who you are. How would you like to go to Beijing and teach English on a team for two years?"

As far as I know, I went with the first known group of Christians to go to China since the 1950s. The Chinese leaders in 1981 were extremely nervous about us. During the four years I was in China I had four hundred students who were businessmen and university teachers. Churches were growing in the countryside in China, but we were the first Christians all but one or two of our students had ever met. Everybody was nervous about us at first. Our mail was opened. With rare exceptions, I was not in a room alone with one other Chinese person the entire first year. Sometimes people were questioned by the police after talking with us. It was severe.

People didn't know anything about Christianity, and on our first day at school, the administration told us, "You cannot invite your students to church. Do not give them any literature. You cannot talk about religion in class. However, you can talk about the holidays." We were very limited in sharing our faith. It was also before the free market system, so the food wasn't very good and we were malnourished and often sick. There were very few foreigners in China, so there were always curious people staring at us everywhere! It was like airport radar—if anyone wanted to reconstruct anywhere we had been, there were hundreds of people who could report on the exact route "the foreigners" had taken. We might as well have had flashing lights on our heads!

I remember walking one night with one of my teammates because we couldn't talk inside the hotel. We were asking, "Why did God bring us here? What can we accomplish?" People had been so wounded in the Cultural Revolution. It was breaking our hearts. There was just a handful of us. We prayed, and I remember saying, "Well, God, you brought us here for some reason and we may be limited, but you are not limited. You can do something great." We prayed daily that even though there was nothing we could say, the Lord would shine through us and give us a special rapport with our students. He did, and he gave us a deep love for our students that was reciprocated. They started to learn English like nobody's business! The Lord gave us great success with our teaching.

They all had been warned that we were Christians. We didn't have to tell them. They could just watch us for months, and they did! Thanksgiving was the first time I mentioned God. I said, "Thanksgiving is a day that Americans thank God." Now, when Chinese people get really nervous, they make a sucking noise through clenched teeth. They did that. I thought, "Lord, you know my students love me, and they are worried that I'm going to be on the next plane out!" So I said, "The families get together and eat turkey. Here's a picture of a turkey." I can't remember whether it was that year or the next year, one of my students said, "Well, why didn't they thank the Indians?" I said, "Well, I think they did thank the Indians, but God sent the rain."

When Christmas time came I wondered, "Oh God, what can I say?" I thought I would start with the safest, most mundane thing first. I drew a picture of the Mediterranean on the board and talked about where Jesus was born. I said that we had tried to date our calendar from the day of his birth, and that's what AD and BC was about.

One of my students raised his hand and asked,"You mean Jesus was a real person?" I said, "Oh yes." The whole class was shocked. They had been taught he was a fairy tale. You can "safely" hear a lot about Jesus Christ if you don't even know he ever existed. The class reaction was "another lie the government taught us."

I also talked about Santa Claus because I had to bring in the cultural information. I taught them Silent Night, ("Jesus, Lord at Thy birth") and some other wonderful Christmas carols. There is a lot of content in some Christmas carols that I didn't remember really hearing that way before!

One of my students said, "America is such a technologically developed country, I can't understand why so many Americans believe in God." I said, "What kind of God do you think we believe in? The God I believe in is the God who created the laws of nature. Actually, science helps me believe in God." I said, "If I took my watch apart and put it in a box, and shook it, how long until my watch would tell the right time?" Someone in the class said, "That would never happen!" I said, "A watch has an order, pattern, and design—it looks like somebody made it. My brain is a lot more complex than a watch. The whole universe is even more complex. It looks like somebody made it. Science helps me see the order, pattern, and design, so science helps me believe in God." They were stunned at my "incredible wisdom." I didn't think it was that profound, but they had never heard anything like that! They had never heard a rational, intelligent explanation of the Christian faith.

A few days before Easter, I still hadn't prepared anything to say. I had a "free conversation" class, meaning the students could set the topic. I went in and asked them, "What do you want to talk about today?" A student said, "Tell us about Easter." The one thing about being told not to talk about something is that it makes people really curious!

I said, "What do you want to know?" The student said, "It's a religious holiday, isn't it?" I said, "Yes. It's the day that Jesus rose from the dead. He came back again, and he was really alive—not like a ghost!" The looks on their faces—I cannot tell you what it's like to talk to somebody about Jesus' resurrection who has never heard the idea! They were staring at me as if I was crazy. How could I believe something like that? I told them it was kind of a long explanation, was that okay?

The students loved and respected us. One of the students, a party member, said, "Oh teacher, there's freedom of religion in China. You can say anything you want." I thought, "Well, I guess I will!" So I asked them, "Why do I believe in God in the first place? How do I even know he's there? I can't see him." I said, "The Bible says in the beginning that God and people were friends. They walked in a garden and talked together as friends. (I was praying like mad: 'Oh God, Oh God! I'm really over my head! What am I going to do?')" Then I was thinking that we "sinned" against God, but they wouldn't know the terms "sin," or "rebel." So I continued, "We had a revolution against God." (Everybody in China understands the word "revolution!") (Then I was thinking of the concept that the wages of sin is death, and prayed, "Oh God, how am I going to explain that?") I said, "When you have a revolution, you kill your enemies." People around the room started nodding their heads. I realized that they knew a lot more about that than I did. I said, "All people have said we don't want God to be our God—we want to be our own God. We want to do what we want to do. But God had a problem because he loves us. He didn't want to kill us. That's why he sent Jesus Christ."

I had a wonderful time in the People's Republic of China talking about how Jesus loved the poor people, the threat he was to the religious leaders and the miracles he did. I talked about his resurrection from the dead, the kind of person he was, and the way he loved people. I thought I had better talk some more about the cultural side of Easter so I said, "Now there's another way we celebrate Easter, and it has nothing to do with Christianity. There's the Easter rabbit that brings eggs. I don't know why it isn't an Easter chicken, but it's a rabbit." I talked about that, making it clear that they were quite different. Finally I asked if anyone had questions. One student raised his hand and said, "Teacher, why does the President of the United States swear on a Bible?" ("Oh God, why does the President of the United States swear on the Bible?") I said, "The Bible is a record of what God has done and said in history, so swearing on the Bible is kind of like swearing by God." I was trying to think what the parallel would be. I said, "You know, it's better to swear by God than to swear by the people, because someone might do something in secret that the people wouldn't know about." One student raised his hand and said, "Does God know what we do in secret?" I said, "Oh yes." Another student said, "Does he know our thoughts?" I said, "Oh yes." The whole class sucked air in through their teeth!

Then one of my students said, "Would you still say Easter was good news if you lost your job, would you say that God didn't love you anymore?" I said, "That's the really good news. We haven't done what we're supposed to. We haven't loved people, been kind, or loved God. But Jesus died in our place so we can come to God without being afraid." The whole class breathed a sigh of relief!

When the class hour was about over, I went out to get a glass of water. We had an "English only" rule that was strictly enforced. The students were preparing to be interpreters for foreign businessmen, and they spoke English one-hundred percent of the time. The classroom door was locked when I came back. I had to knock on the door to get back in. I was surprised to find them all speaking in Chinese! One student explained, "Teacher, we never heard anything like this before. How could we talk about this in English?" They were making sure they got the story right, and they were so excited that they just couldn't stand it. They didn't want to get into trouble, so they locked the door and spoke Chinese!

The next day I was teaching another class that also happened to be a free conversation class. I asked, "What would you like to talk about?" A student said, "Tell us about the Easter chicken!" The word was getting around! The next day they asked my teammate Karen, "Why do you believe in the God?" She answered, "Well, I grew up in a Christian family, and my father is a believer." The students remembered that when she introduced herself on the first day she had said her dad worked for NASA. That was the pinnacle of human achievement to the Chinese. A student blurted out, "If your dad works for NASA, then he is smarter than God!" She said, "My father knows who gave him the brains." Another student said, "I knew you were going to say that!"

I taught university faculty at schools that are the Chinese equivalent of Harvard and MIT. People really did not know about Jesus, and what grieved me was that they had no way to find out. Many of my students told me I was the first Christian they had ever met.

Now the situation has changed some. Since Tian'anmen Chinese intellectuals are asking really serious questions. I never got into political discussions with my students; I was not there to push a political system. But they have burning questions: Is there any foundation for truth that doesn't change according to who is in power? How would you have a democracy? What would prevent you from just shooting the people who disagree with you? What gives a human being worth? They are not asking so much "How can I be saved?" but "How can China be saved?"

The gospel really speaks to those issues. They are different from the issues that Americans have, but they are burning ones for Chinese people. They need people who can tell them the good news: There is hope for their country! They need people with servant hearts. It's important that we go as a blessing to China.

Although the leaders are very nervous about Christians, there has been a real turnaround. Most schools have had very positive experiences with Western Christian teachers. Now, most places would prefer Christian Westerners to non-Christian Westerners; they don't have as many problems with immorality, broken contracts, or complaining. Christians are more likely to truly care about their students and want to teach well.

There are thousands of openings around the world for Christians in all kinds of professions. In the Muslim world, "closed" to missionaries, or in places like Japan, where you can go as a missionary, secular jobs open contacts with different levels of society. Tentmakers require the same kind of prayer support that a missionary does. I was very blessed. The people at the Cathedral of St. Philip in Atlanta prayed for me, and I felt it.

That's why I knew what to say when I was asked why the President of the United States swears on the Bible and why I drew a map of the Mediterranean to show Jesus' birth place. It just happened to be the most important thing I could have done. I could not have known that on my own. But people were praying for me. The people back at home have a vital role in terms of prayer support and spreading vision.

One of my prayers for each person who reads this is that God will put on your heart maybe one person to whom you should talk about this. It may not be China; it may be another country. Is there a doctor, lawyer or teacher God might want to send overseas—someone who just needs some training in cross-cultural sensitivity and on how to explain the faith and who could go and make an impact? Pray and ask if there is someone specific that God wants you to tell about this opening of secular jobs in closed countries around the world.

REACHING MUSLIMS

The Rev. Don McCurry

In seminary, when professors for missions came and spoke, I would become all agitated. I didn't know why I was agitated about what these people from Pakistan and Sudan and Egypt and Ethiopia were saying. I wrestled with the question: Am I called to be a missionary?

I accepted a pastorate to a broken-down church in Colorado Springs. It had asked its three previous ministers to leave and had been on Home Mission help for thirty years, and I wanted to see if God could fix that church. He did. But after we were filling up the church with young people, and some of their families were coming to Christ, I said,

"Maybe it would help this church if we brought in missionaries, so the church could open their eyes to the world out there."

So I brought in missionaries on six successive Sundays. And while they were preaching, I was praying: "Lord, do you see these beautiful young people? I want you to call them to risk their lives for you at the ends of the earth." Wasn't that generous of their pastor? I heard the Lord: "You hypocrite! You're asking me to send those young people to risk their lives, and you're not willing to go first!"

I was interviewed back in Philadelphia for a missions career, but I didn't know that the people on that board had heard negative information about me. A moderator of the general assembly had come to our church in Colorado Springs. We had a blizzard every day he was there, so the elders didn't come to his evangelistic services. Then the lady who was going to provide hospitality for him got sick, so he heard me making last-minute arrangements, etc. His son was on the interviewing committee, so I was on the defensive through the entire interview.

When I got on the train to go see my parents, all I could hear with the clickety-clack of those wheels on the rails was, "McCurry, you don't have what it takes, you don't have what it takes." All the way to Washington! When I met my mom and dad, I gave a sick laugh and said, "You don't need to worry about me going anywhere. That'll never happen!" Ten-thirty the next morning, a telegram arrived: "You have been appointed to career mission service. Return to Philadelphia at once." I was in total shock!

I went back to Philadelphia and met with the board's secretary. I said, "Dr. Grice, when I left here last night all I could hear on the train was: 'McCurry, you don't have what it takes, you don't have what it takes.'" That godly old man leaped out of his chair, stuck his finger in my chest, and said, "McCurry, don't you ever forget it! The day you think you have what it takes, you're finished with God, because he resists the proud and gives grace to the humble." Then Dr. Grice asked, "Would you be willing to go to Pakistan?" And I said, "Of course!" I didn't know what I was doing! Pakistan is ninety-seven percent Muslim. It's the only country that was ever carved out of another country because of its religion. It's the most doctrinaire Muslim country in the world; and it would cease to exist if it refused to defend Islam. That's where I was sent.

I was absorbed into the high-velocity activities of an old mission that had more than enough positions to fill. The older generation of missionaries were retiring, and the younger missionaries were used as "hole-pluggers."

But at the end of four-and-a-half years there, lying flat on my back with hepatitis and realizing I had not seen a single Muslim come to Jesus, I asked Jesus, "Would you give me a second chance? Would you teach me how to work with Muslims?" I thank God for those lessons! The other missionaries hadn't learned the lessons, I'm afraid, so they couldn't teach me. He used Pakistani brothers and sisters.

I remember the first lesson. I was competent in Urdu now, doing some Bible studies in Ephesians, and I'd had five days of marvelous exposition with the staff of Taxcella Hospital. I got to Ephesians 6 on the sixth day, where it says, "We wrestle not against flesh and blood, but against principalities and powers." I made the mistake of saying to my Pakistani audience, "You know, the first day I set foot on Pakistani soil, I felt Satanic oppression in this country." I lost my entire audience.

When I was finished, the senior superintendent of nurses came up to me and said, "Mr. McCurry, you have no right to speak that way to us. We think you've come from the most Satanic culture on the face of the earth. We don't know anyone who has a higher per capita crime rate than New York City at high noon. We don't know any people so corrupt who have made an industry of exporting films of violence and pornography like America. We don't know any hypocritical people who preach equality and have failed to solve their race problem. We don't know of anyone with a higher standard of living than you people, and you still have twenty percent of your population living below the poverty level." She went on and on. I had nothing to say. She had fingered my blind spot. I could spot demonic influences in any other culture but mine.

On another occasion, during an argument between white-skinned ordained missionaries and brown-skinned pastors and elders, one of the missionaries lost his temper and walked out, followed by ten other missionaries. Two of us remained seated. The oldest pastor stood up and said to the retreating backs of those missionaries, "Yes, this is what we always thought about you! You are Americans first and Christians second." I was stunned.

I staggered out of that meeting, looked down at myself dressed as a Westerner and said, "Why am I dressed this way?" I walked into my house that was built by a missionary predecessor: "Why do I live in this kind of a house?" And I began an examination. I asked myself, "Am I allowed to change? Could I actually become like a Pakistani?" I decided to try. It polarized the mission. One missionary said, "Why have you lowered yourself to the standard of these people? We're trying to lift them up to our level. We are the most advanced civilization on the face of the earth."

But when I got into the streets, and stood with all the people dressed like me, I began to have doors open to me that were not open to other missionaries. Muslims started saying, "You love us. You learned our language. Now you dress like us. When you come to our house, you eat like us, and we don't feel like we are entertaining foreigners. When we come to your house, we feel like we're in one of our houses." Slowly, I began to learn how to work with Muslims and how to understand their worldview. I eventually had to read the *Koran* to get inside of their thinking. I had to understand where these people were coming from.

Eventually, towards the end of our residency (we were there eighteen years) I was invited to the seminary to teach. I introduced courses called "Christianity and Culture" and "Cross-Cultural Evangelism." I taught the students that missionaries had been in Pakistan ninety-nine years when I took that position, and no one had ever taught them how they could live among the people. We loved being patrons! We never wanted them to become equals!

Teaching that course on "Christianity and Culture," I had a nightmare one night. Two leaders of a 5,000-member Muslim village came to me in a dream. They said, "Mr. McCurry, you've been teaching us about Jesus Christ for at least two years. We finally believe. We've talked it over in our whole village. All 5,000 of us believe, and we now want to be baptized." The next question was the nightmare: "Would you come and teach us the Christian culture?" What is the Christian culture? British Anglicanism? American Presbyterianism? Swedish Pentecostalism? Indian Brethrenism?

There is no answer to that kind of question. It's the wrong question. The real question is, how does Jesus relate to culture? To use Niebuhr's paradigm, is he above it? Is he against it? Is he in it? Does he want to transform it? The answer is "all of the above." Jesus is in the business of transforming culture. Naturally, he's against things that are wrong. Of course, he approves things that are already right. And, he's transcendent above it all.

Those are the paradigms, then, that we begin to apply to Muslim work. Would God treat a Muslim the way he treated me when I came to Jesus? How much dislocation does there have to be culturally? You couldn't tell the difference between me and my pagan classmates at first glance. Would God allow a Muslim to be that way? The consensus of the missionary community at that time was no. I was one of those who had to conclude the answer would be yes. He would accept them culturally the way they are, with the exception of the reprehensible things that had to be judged. That is what led to a whole new career in missions.

Now, since that time, I have had the joy of actually praying for

Muslims, praying country by country, people group by people group—and not only seeing God give marvelous answers but also being part of the answers. I was in Heidebek, at the YWAM training base in Holland, and a team was forming for Uzbekistan—two hundred Europeans to go in as teachers. As we were worshiping, God gave me a vision of ominous black clouds over the map of Uzbekistan. The clouds scattered madly in every direction, and light began to pour down on Uzbekistan. The Lord said, "I dwell in the midst of the praise of my people." I shared that with these two hundred young people in training, and I said, "Whatever else you do, sing! Praise and worship the Lord in Uzbekistan!"

In January, they had to keep 300 people out of the meetings because they could only take 150 in the basement of the Baptist church in Uzbekistan. One hundred of them had been Christians for less than three years—already on fire for Jesus! Twenty of them were Uzbek converts and four of these were leaders. Twenty more were converts from Kazakhstan, Tataristan, Muslims from Georgia, Azerbaijan, and Tajikistan. Ten were pastors. They were all on fire for Uzbekistan. The government is trying to shut it all down, but it's too late. The fire is spreading.

We are seeing Muslims coming from people groups that we have never seen before. God is doing some of it sovereignly.

In Teheran, during the days when Khomeini forbid male doctors to treat female patients, the male doctors went on strike, saying, "Who will care for our wives, our mothers, our daughters, and our sisters?" Then one of Khomeini's lieutenants needed emergency surgery and the revolutionary guards with guns pointed gathered a team of surgeons. The patient died on the operating table. These Muslim doctors prayed something like this: "God, you know that we're as good as dead men. But we read in the Koran that Jesus can raise the dead, and if you will raise this man from this table again, we will follow you." The man came back to life. This is a well-attested story. Those doctors are now baptized members of the downtown church in Teheran. This story has spread like wildfire throughout the city of Teheran, and the churches are full of Muslim converts. People are having visions and dreams about Jesus, and they are asking for Bibles, but we can't get them in.

Another story is from a Koran reciter in Pakistan, from the town in which I lived. He had memorized the entire Koran in Arabic, even though his mother tongue was Punjabi. He knew that in the Koran, Jesus was greater than Muhammad. He went through the town asking, "Where can I find a Christian, or where can I find a Bible?" He bumped into a young man I was discipling. The man got him enrolled in a Bible correspondence course. The reciter found in John 8:12 that Jesus said, "I am the light of the world." He went out into the mustard fields about 4:30 in the morning. He began to pray earnestly, "Jesus, if you are the light of the world, appear to me so that I will never have a doubt about what you said." Jesus appeared in dazzling light to him! And he never doubted afterwards!

The reciter gave his witness in the mosque by chanting the Koran and explicating from the Bible, until the audience became restless. He did this for forty-five minutes, until a Mufti jumped up and said, "This man has a demon! We do not know how to control him!" The reciter was taken all the way up to the Minister of Religion in the government to try to explain what had happened. He bore his witness bravely, in the face of threats before cabinet ministers in the government of Pakistan.

Yes, there is trouble—sometimes there are executions and drive-by shootings. We have that here in the States, so what? In the middle of all of that, the gospel is spreading. In Islam, we're working with a people who have been told a lot about Jesus, but not the heart of the gospel. They have not been told that he really is the Son of God, that God became a man, that he was the sin-bearer, that he successfully died on the cross, was buried and rose again, and that he is the ascended Lord. That is the part they have been lied to about.

It's different working with Muslims. In fact, there are five levels in which we have to engage Islam, and I give you these five challenges. Some of you will fit in at different levels:

We need massive intercessory prayer for the Muslim world, country by country—all forty-seven of them—and the 408 major people groups.

We need those at the highest government level who will battle for religious freedom and human rights, and force the issues on Muslim countries that refuse to concede.

We need people who will enter the battle for truth against the lies, because we are being lied about by a false religion.

We need to respond to human need, because with the exception of the oil countries, the Muslim countries are the poorest in the world, and Jesus has told us to remember the poor.

We need people who will preach salvation. First Timothy 2:4: "God wants all men to be saved and to come to the knowledge of the truth." Second Peter 3:9: "God is not willing that any should perish, but that all should come to repentance." Colossians 1:27 and 28: "Christ in you, the hope of glory, whom we preach, warning every man, and teaching every man in all wisdom that we may present every man perfect in Christ Jesus." To know God is to agree with him in how he looks at every other human being, and that includes Muslims.

Matthew 24:14 says, "This Gospel of the Kingdom shall be preached in all the world as a witness to all nations and then the end will come." We are at a historic moment. The stage is set for a new heaven and a new earth. And you, my friends and fellow workers, hold the key.

MINISTRY TO THE INDOCHINESE

The Rev. Duc Nguyen and Mr. Reachsa Uch

REACHSA UCH: I saw the Khmer Rouge kill my mother, my sister and other people. It was so painful. I tried to open my mouth, to scream, to get their attention so they would come kill me. The first time I tried, I was paralyzed. I could not scream at all. I tried again, and it didn't work. Finally I saw there was a reason. Maybe I wanted to live so I could kill all these people. I made three promises. Wherever I lived, I would take revenge. If I could not, I would dedicate my life to be a Buddhist monk to pay more credit due my family. If I could not do this, I would not live in Cambodia any more.

When the Vietnamese came in 1978, I went to live with my uncle and I finished high school. Then I joined the police force because I wanted to take revenge.

Six months after that, my dream of taking revenge became a reality. I saw the commander who ordered my family arrested. I was a police commander, and that's when I decided I was going to kill him—just to take revenge.

I asked him, "Are you afraid?" He said, "Yes." "Do you know what happened to me when you ordered people to kill my family?" He didn't answer. I pointed the gun and tried to kill him. My finger didn't work. I tried to kill him again, and then my heart surrendered. I felt discouraged. I could not kill to take revenge for my family! I cried. One of my friends said, "Reachsa, let me finish the business for you." I said, "No, don't kill him."

I didn't know why that man killed my family. I freed him. Life is painful. I fell down and asked for forgiveness, saying, "Parents, brother and sister, I cannot do this. Forgive me."

In 1984, I heard that a Vietnamese expert wanted to send me to study in Vietnam for three years and then somewhere else for six years. I was unhappy with that, so I escaped to Thailand. I wanted to find peace. I heard about Jesus. Many times I went to church, but I did not receive

Jesus Christ as my personal Lord and Savior. In 1988, I applied to receive training in the United States. My background was involved with communism, so American immigration would not accept me. I prayed that if God would take me to Canada, I would believe in him. Six months after that I was accepted by the Canadian embassy to come to Canada.

When I went to Canada, I was assigned to stay in a reception center. There one of my friends came to talk to me about God's Word. He gave me a Bible, and read it to me. He prayed for me and stayed with me. Six months later, I received Jesus Christ.

Then I went to a Bible college. After I graduated, I began to realize that I had gone through a lot of pain and suffering in my life—it is very hard for me to tell you how much—and I decided to go to seminary and study biblical counseling. I came to realize that a lot of Cambodians had gone through pain and suffering, and I thought that counseling was the best choice so I could help my people. God could use me in many ways to reach out to Cambodian people.

DUC NGUYEN: The preceding was a living testimony of the power of God unto salvation. Reachsa told me that he wanted to come to Trinity Episcopal School for Ministry. I asked him why he didn't come and he said he didn't have the money. I said, "Lack of money is always the problem in life. Whether we are rich or poor, it's always a lack of money. So just come! Believe and God will provide." I feel that God does the financing for all our missionary activities.

Just five weeks ago I took a group of eighteen people back to Vietnam. This time, they had a healing experience when they met the people. A few months ago, I helped a group in Pittsburgh return to Vietnam. They drove from Hanoi to Danang, in the central part of Vietnam, they did a prayer walk for every province in that part of the country. Another group connected to a village. Every year they return to Vietnam bringing their tools and some money. They have built clinics through the church. They have given of themselves to the village. This is the way they tell the people that they love them. Many times, whole villages cry at the outpouring of love.

In Vietnam, at the present time, there is no freedom to preach the gospel. But there are many ways that we can share the gospel. Someday we will start a missionary society. This time the Americans would come back with love. We would go there to find the people who are missing—not missing in action, but missing the gospel of Jesus Christ.

ADOPTING A PEOPLE:
COMPLETING THE UNFINISHED TASK

The Rev. Ralph D. Winter

As we talk together about what God is doing in the world, we must be thankful that he has already made himself known to us. He spoke to Abraham four thousand years ago saying he wished to bless him and his lineage, and that through him he wished to bless all the peoples of the earth.

We must be thankful for that divine initiative which intervened in the sordid evil of a planet already tyrannized by Satanic power. But God has been faithful across four thousand years, pushing back that power and that darkness. His glory has penetrated many darkened peoples already.

We must be thankful for our own historical background, for the presence of his Word in our language, as we look forward to the completion of his global penetration, His expanding Kingdom reaching every people on the face of this earth. We need his blessing in this awesome endeavor which belongs to him.

In a word, the background of our subject goes way, way, way back. There is a lot we do not understand about what God is doing in the world. Despite all we don't understand, what we do understand begins to unfold in the very first pages of the Bible. Genesis 1 to 11 talks about three things: 1) the beauty of God's creation, 2) the entrance of evil, and 3) the hopeless result. And that result really was hopeless. That exceedingly pernicious "fall" affected nature as well as man.

At that precise point of hopelessness, in Genesis 12, our topic is introduced. Our topic is actually the theme of Genesis 12 through 50 and, indeed, through the rest of the entire Bible. *In fact, the theme of the entire Bible and all of history is that of God reclaiming all the peoples that were alienated and estranged across the world.* In the very first few words of Genesis 12 we see the plot of the next four thousand years.

Blessing or Adopting?

When God called Abraham, he said, "I want to adopt you." Now, wait a minute, you say, the word *adopt* is not in the text! Oh, yes it is! We must look more closely. The translators unfortunately preferred the word *blessed* to *adopted*. So they translated 12:3 "I will bless you and through you all the families of the earth will be blessed." But the meaning of the Hebrew word here translated *blessed* means something closer to the idea of *adoption*. For example, the same word comes up when Jacob was *blessed* rather than Esau. It wasn't that Jacob got a blessing like a box of chocolates! His "blessing" meant he was now bound into the family name, in fact, declared the firstborn, and thus now accorded privileges and obligations within a particular family more than ever before.

Thus, the word *blessing* is not a very good translation of what it says in Genesis 12:2 and 3. Rather, it might better be "I *will adopt you into my family*. You will be my son, with the privileges and responsibilities of the firstborn. And it is through you that I will include all the other nations of the earth."

In the New Testament we see phrases like "sons of God and joint-heirs with Christ." That is the same precise imagery. So you can see that the word *blessing* in Genesis 12 is just an unfortunate word thrown in by translators, in whose own culture there is no longer a ceremony for the conferring of primogeniture. The word *blessing* is really quite misleading. When a family goes to an adoption agency to adopt a child, they don't say "We want to bless a child." That may be part of it, of course, but it is not the main thing.

Thus, as far back as Abraham we see God setting out to push back the darkness by embracing, re-adopting, taking control over people after people after people. *This is the essential story of the Bible.* It is the story in the Bible. The Bible simply is the story of an expanding kingdom (an image similar to a *family* image). It is essentially what we ask for when we pray, "Thy kingdom come, thy will be done on earth as it is in heaven." Seeing things this way enables us to understand the Lord's prayer as a missionary prayer, to see the Bible as a missionary book, and recognize God as a missionary God. And, we see that the adopting of peoples, the reconciliation of whole groups is the very essence of the process.

Personal Evangelism, Planting Churches, Penetrating Peoples

Note, then, that this essential missionary process is not just winning individual souls to Christ. To see this more clearly you can think of a three-level universe where personal evangelism is merely the essential first level. Most everyone in evangelism knows that if you just win people to Christ and then say, "I'll be seeing you," and don't follow through to the next level of planting churches, you won't bind individuals into accountable fellowships, and you will be losing people as fast as you find them.

So, while you can't plant churches without personal evangelism, note the dread possibility that you *can* win souls without planting churches. That is, you can go the first level without going to the second. And, you can go to the second level of planting churches without thinking in terms of the third level of *penetrating peoples*. It is very basic to know that missionaries are uniquely in the business of *penetrating peoples*. They don't just *plant churches,* or just *win souls.* Remember that you can be busy planting churches without penetrating any new peoples just as you can win souls without planting churches.

However, we must be clear about what is meant by planting churches. By *churches* I don't mean buildings. By churches I mean fellowships that are like a family with interpersonal accountability. *That is part of the adoption process we are talking about in which the love and the authority of a Father God is revealed with power.*

Thus, in reality, missionaries are basically *adoption facilitators.* They go around the world facilitating the re-adoption of the nations, binding people into the "nurture and admonition" of the church and the global family of Christ. I say *re-adoption* because it isn't as if all these peoples on the earth were *always* estranged from God. After all, God created them in the first place. They were clearly in touch with God originally. Yes, the astounding thing is that wherever you go in the world, very often, though they have never heard the name of Jesus they have a concept of *a high God.*

Don Richardson has written about this in his book *Eternity in Their Hearts.* (He got that phrase out of *Ecclesiastes.*) He shows that in every culture there is still a point of contact in peoples' hearts. Of course, what awareness peoples still have within their group is the residual glimmer of something they once knew. It is not a spark to be fanned into flame in the old liberal sense so much as the potential for REcovery and REconnection to the living God. That is why we say *RE-adoption.*

The Bible itself talks in these terms and has from the beginning. All the way through the Bible this is the primary, organizing theme of the Bible: the consistent, outward expansion of this family, kingdom—whatever you want to call it—where God is in charge, the sphere of God's domain. Jesus said, "If I, by the finger of God cast out demons, the kingdom of God is here." Thus, the presence and the power, the signs and wonders of the living God are part and parcel of the missionary movement!

Now, as Kevin Martin has said earlier, "If that power is conceived of as a *blessing* rather than as a *provision for outreach,* we have really asked the wrong question." And that is one more reason why I don't like to use the word *blessing.* People get confused; they may want the blessing without a real relationship to God. But Kevin says, "Don't ask what it is; ask what it is for."

What is it for? *Adopting a people*—that's what it's for! This *adoption* process is the Holy Spirit's power reaching out across the world, pushing the darkness out of the lives and hearts of individuals by penetrating whole peoples and bringing them back into the global kingdom, the very family of the living God. God is in the adoption process and we are helping him.

Genesis 12 starts right out with this idea of *blessing* or *adoption*. All of this is actually the Great Commission. It is the same thing. There is no distinction whatsoever between this statement of the Commission in Genesis and Jesus' rephrasing of that same Commission in the New Testament.

But, note that in the wording of this Commission, whether in Genesis or Matthew, the concept of *peoples* is crucial. God deals with us not merely as individuals—although that is the great stress of pietism in the evangelical historical tradition. God deals with us as part of a *family*. He takes seriously our cultural tradition. He doesn't want us to forget our roots. He doesn't downplay the linguistic and cultural inheritance of anyone. He doesn't say that everyone has to speak English to get into heaven. He accepts us in our cultural clothing, where we are in our own group.

What is a People?

Let's look more closely at the question of "What is a people?" It is both exciting and confusing. For example, you could say in one sense that the Chinese are one people. But you can't say that *Chinese* is "a" language anymore than you can say that *European* is "a" language. Have you ever heard of anybody trying to learn Chinese? Sure, we have all heard that phrase. Do you realize that it's total nonsense? There is no Chinese language. There is a Chinese *family* of languages, just like there is a European *family* of languages. But Mandarin and Cantonese, both part of that Chinese family, are, as languages, about as different as German and Italian.

God takes each people separately and significantly and seriously. There are also peoples within peoples. The Cantonese sub-family in south China, for example, has twenty-five mutually unintelligible languages and peoples *within it*. If you set out simply to adopt the Cantonese, you have made a big mistake.

Mission vs. Evangelism

The unique function of a mission agency is to plant a church where there is not yet a church within a particular group. Oh, the group might be scattered or it might be in three places at once, but it is an *unreached* group if there is not yet within that group—in any part of it—a breakthrough, a breakthrough that makes sense within that group (and if that group is sufficiently homogeneous, or unified, so that one breakthrough will suffice). We need to be sure that every person within that group will be able to understand the gospel as a result of that original breakthrough. Every person may not have yet heard the gospel but it is a case of the need for further evangelistic work, not specifically mission work that needs to be done.

We understand the slogan of the AD2000 Movement in this sense. "A Church for Every People" means that "the gospel is now there FOR every person." Just as when the Bible is translated into the language and culture of a given group, then, no matter how scattered that group may be, the Bible is now there FOR every person, whether they have seen it or read it or not. It is not necessary to translate it again *for* a group geographically separated. It has been done!

In this sense a missiological breakthrough into any one part of a group is a breakthrough of "the gospel *for* every person in that group." It is a separate, additional, and simpler process to keep taking the gospel TO each person in other parts of the same group, and in each new generation which daily and hourly grows into the age of accountability. In this sense the mission breakthrough can be completed while evangelism never can.

At this point we can sum up that the kind of entity or *people* we are talking about is one in which, once there is a culturally relevant church, the gospel will then be available FOR every individual in that group. Such a group is a type technically defined in the following terms:

> It is the largest group within which the gospel can spread as a church planting movement without encountering barriers of understanding or acceptance.

Notice, this says *understanding* OR *acceptance*. You might say, well sure, at least *understanding*, but why *acceptance*? Well, what if the people in one corner of an apparent group can understand but they just don't like those other people who are doing the talking? In that case the missionary better arrange for other missionaries to come around the other side with a different denomination to try to reach those people. Never fear, when people finally get into the Bible they will all come to the same Billy Graham Crusade. But in the early stages they may hate each other, and kill each other, even though they *understand* each other. So, *acceptance* not just *understanding* is what we need to define the essential unity of a group that is a single people in missiological terms.

How Many Groups to Go?

Now you may wonder, If you are going to divide groups down to such levels, how many groups are there in the world that constitute this essential "missiological" unit? Answering this question would not tell us how to finish evangelism but it would tell us how to complete missions. The problem is that no book in print was designed to tell us precisely how many such groups there are because not many people out in the field have been thinking in these technical, missiological terms. We can at least make estimates.

Our estimate in 1990 was that there were between eleven and twelve thousand groups still remaining without a missiological breakthrough—not a large number of groups! At the same time we freely admit that these eleven to twelve thousand groups cluster together in a much smaller number of "clusters" or groups possessing their own subgroups. The AD2000 movement, as a first step, for example, is aiming at 1,685 groups that are larger than ten thousand in population, and less than five percent evangelical. Many of these are in fact clusters of smaller groups too badly alienated from each other to receive the gospel from their neighbors.

For example, Don McCurry has said that there are four hundred and eight major languages within Islam. Well, if you pressed him further he would tell you there are probably another fifteen hundred smaller languages—subgroups—which we have to take seriously, groups that are hard to describe and list.

It would be like setting out to list all American groups, including black Americans, brown Americans, Asian Americans, southern Americans, western Americans, and maybe even listing "Americans." Wait a minute. *These are overlapping categories.* Lists like that aren't ideal, but they are better than nothing.

Take the Chinese. First of all, not all the people in China are even Chinese, and not all Chinese are living in China. So far as I know, there is no word in the Bible that could be translated properly "country." Countries are the result of modern geopolitical divisions. The Bible knows nothing of countries, only empires and peoples. It talks in terms of ethnic, linguistic, cultural identity.

The "peoplehood" structure of human society is very complex, and we will not know exactly how it works until we finish the job. Most people still see the world in terms of individuals in geopolitical areas of the globe, but whatever you do, don't get group boundaries confused with country boundaries, which are not really to be found in the Bible at all.

A Missionary Looks at the Globe

Using people terminology (rather than country terms), let's take a missionary look at the globe. First we'll look for the number of Bible-believing, committed Christians. I'm not suggesting that these are the only people who are going to get to heaven. I'm a Presbyterian, and I am aware that there are a lot of wandering, confused Presbyterians. Only God knows where they stand. But, we can say with confidence that most of them are not interested in missions. That we know—you can't count on them to help finish the job.

The kind of Christians down through history who can be counted on are the ones who have *expanded in number*. They are the ones who are spiritually alive enough, who have enough faith and Spirit and power to go to the ends of the earth to share their faith. Below is the picture of their growth. In about 1430 AD such people were about one out of a hundred, etc.

1430, 1 out of a 100 (1% of world population)
1790, 2 out of a 100 (2% of world population)
1940, 3 out of a 100 (3% of world population)
1960, 4 out of a 100 (4% of world population)
1970, 5 out of a 100 (5% of world population)
1980, 6 out of a 100 (6% of world population)
1983, 7 out of a 100 (7% of world population)
1986, 8 out of a 100 (8% of world population)
1989, 9 out of a 100 (9% of world population)
1993, 10 out of a 100 (10% of world population)

Note the great acceleration in the last twenty-five years. We are coming to the end of something at express-train speed. At least one out of ten people in the world are now active Christians! And *active* Christians are only about one-third of all Christians—Christians in general now constitute one third of the population of the world.

Isn't that just amazing? Another way to depict this would be to say that one out of ten is a *useful* Christian. Remember, I'm not saying these are the only ones who get to heaven, or that these are the only *true* Christians.

The key point for us in a conference like this is to note that we can say *one out of ten ought to be recruitable*. They will, I hope, come to the next New Wineskins for Global Missions conference, because just think how many people are going to go out from this conference to recruit people for that next conference! It's going to be amazing. But there are still twice as many Christians who aren't going to come, who aren't interested, who are burdened down, confused, groping, stumbling, hurting. They just aren't *useful*, though they may be Christian.

Okay, we've now talked about the one-out-of-ten active (and recruitable) Christians. They number well over 500 million. In addition to these half a billion *active* Christians, there are a full billion additional *inactive* Christians. Let's go on to classify all the world's people in half-billion sized groups.

Group A: *one* half-billion *active* Christians
Group B: *two* half-billion *inactive* Christians
Group C: *three* half-billion *non-Christians with access* to
            the gospel in their own culture, and
Group D: *four* half-billion *non-Christians without access*
            for whom the gospel is not available apart from
            additional missionary breakthroughs.

It is necessary to point out that rounding things to half-billion sized units isn't quite accurate because that way these four groups only add up to five billion, while the world's population is now closer to six billion than five billion. These 500 million units of size are actually speeding toward 600 million each.

Alternatively, it might be easier to think of the entire world's population as being represented as ten men standing in a row. In that case we can speak of

Group A: *One* of the ten is an *active* Christian
Group B: *Two* of the ten are *inactive* Christians
Group C: *Three* of the ten are non-Christians *in the shad-
            ow of the church*
Group D: *Four* of the ten are non-Christians *who can only
            be evangelized if their group is first missionized*

Once again, in terms of rapid change, Group A is not only rapidly growing closer to 600 million, it is growing even more rapidly than the other groups! It is beginning to grow too large to be represented by only one man in ten! This will soon spoil our neat summary, but it rewards our soul to realize that the category of active Christians is growing more rapidly than any other group anywhere near that size—whether Islam, Buddhism, Hinduism, etc.

What All This Means

Let's be sure we have a clear understanding of the significance of this fourfold breakdown.

Group A constitutes the Christians who are ready to help evangelize the world. There are more than a half billion of them.

Group B is another billion Christians who are not likely to help because they are tied down with their own concerns.

Group C is a billion and a half who do not describe themselves as Christians. They live in the shadow of the church. They already can hear the gospel on the wavelength of their own culture. The Bible has been in their language for maybe a thousand years. There are vibrant churches within their society. Individuals among them may be just as lost as anybody else, but individuals within these societies *do have access.*

Then there is Group D, another two billion who *do not have access.* Now these are the ones gathered together within unreached peoples—the groups that we are to help God "adopt."

Your congregation doesn't need to adopt the peoples which contain Groups A, B, and C. Such groups are already "adopted." God has already broken through into the hearts and souls of a substantial number of people within their culture. Not all of the individuals living within these peoples are believers—some are in Group C—but all of them have access. All peoples but those in Group D are already adopted, or, in technical terms "Reached." Now, how many of these Group D peoples still need to be adopted? In 1990 we estimated eleven to twelve thousand.

Is This an Optimistic Picture?

From the viewpoint of individuals you can certainly look at the global situation as a rapidly declining burden on the rapidly increasing number of those *individuals* who are true, active, believing Christians, ready to finish the job. The job certainly is so much smaller now than it ever was before in history. You have seen the decline from one out of a hundred to *one out of ten.*

James Wong showed us that what I refer to here as one out of ten could also be said to be a ratio of nine to one (nine *other* people for every active Christian). And it can be said to be seven to one if you compare the number of active Christians only with those people who do not consider themselves to be Christians, that is, with Groups C and D.

Here we can go even further since it is only Group D, the last four men in our representative population line-up, who are sealed off behind walls of language and culture from any Christian witness. Thus, you can also say, equally truly, that those last four portray "four to one"—four people in unreached groups for every active Christian. Can you believe that? For each active Christian there are only four other people in the world who have yet to have access to the gospel, whose people group needs to be adopted, whose language needs to be penetrated. These are the individuals who are sealed off behind cultural and linguistic barriers that can be crossed only by true, pioneer missionary techniques.

We have been looking at *millions of individuals in four categories.* Let's see if we can relate these facts to the number of peoples to be penetrated. It is, after all, the number of *unreached* peoples (cultural groups) that is the true missionary measurement.

Nevertheless, even if you recognize that the missionary task (as compared to the unending evangelistic task) does not deal with *millions of individuals* but merely *thousands of doorways into people groups,* you still get a very optimistic picture because, say, eleven thousand groups yet to be penetrated is a very small number in terms of the enormous global total of active Christians. Theoretically, there must be about five million congregations of active Christians, and that means that there must be on the order of five hundred congregations for each group that is yet to be reached! The true measure of the size of a task is not the absolute size but the size relative to the resources available. In this case the size is very small.

Tools Tell Totals

Looking at the chart, we can stand back and see the global challenge in terms of the different tools of outreach. We can compare what is left to be done in terms of a certain communication tool, noting the size of the task suited to a particular tool. My list goes from the largest of the mass media to the face-to-face level. You will note that the goal numbers get larger as you go down to the church planting level.

1) Satellite TV. A man once said to me, "If you use satellite TV, you can reach the whole world at one time. You don't need any more missionaries! Forget it!" He wasn't really trying to downplay missions; he was just trying to up-play his new gadget. Now, this was fifteen or twen-

GOD'S SYMPHONY OF EFFORT

What can be done: "A Church for Every People by the Year 2000 and (in that sense) the Gospel for Every Person"

Communication Tools Employed		The TOTAL ORIGINAL TASK as defined by tool used	=	PROGRESS as of Jan 1995	+	What is left to do!
Sattelite TV	1	7 "World" languages	=	One "World" language now (English)	+	6 more languages to be on satellite
Major Missionary Radio	2	372 languages spoken by over 1 million people	=	170 major languages now broadcasted	+	202 languages yet to be broadcast
Film Ministry Campus Crusade's Jesus Film	3	1,154 languages spoken by over 50,000 people	=	315 sound tracks now	+	839 sound tracks to go
Scripture in Print Wycliffe and others	4	6,675 "Visual" languages	=	2,961 either have some scripture or don't "probably" need it	+	1,201 do need 2,513 possibly need
People Lists Lists of names (sometimes "clusters" of unreached peoples)	5	12,000 "Ethno-politico-linguistic" peoples	=	9,500 no unreached peoples remaining within	+	2,500 yet to be approached
Audio Casssettes Gospel Recordings and others	6	14,000 "Audio" languages	=	4,588 now on cassette	+	9,412 yet to be put on cassette
Church Planting within Unreached Peoples-- 15% of missionaries involved	7	roughly 24,000 needing Church movements	=	roughly 13,000 now possess church movements	+	roughly 11,000 needing a church movement

ty years ago. And this is how our conversation went:

I said to him, "Are you going to try to reach Muslims with your satellite?"

"Oh sure," he said, "we can broadcast the television signal in seven languages simultaneously."

I said, "Great, what language will you use to reach the Muslims?"

He said, "Um, well, Arabic, right?"

I said, "Most Muslims don't speak Arabic."

So he said, "What do they speak?"

I replied, "Well, about four hundred major languages, plus fifteen hundred additional smaller languages."

His face fell. The *reality* of human society is usually underestimated. I'm not saying a mass medium is not a useful tool, but the more the "mass" of the medium, the more *minor* the adjustments are possible for human diversity. Seven channels? You can use them up pretty easily.

2) Missionary Radio. Suppose, however, that you run a major missionary radio station. We can truly rejoice over the fact that the missionary radio enterprise in the world today constitutes the most extensive use of electromagnetic communication that has ever been achieved. There is no secular, communist, capitalist—whatever—use of radio that is anywhere near as powerful or as extensive as the global network of Christian radio.

But they are so big, their air time is expensive. You can't focus on a little tribal group someplace at a hundred dollars or so an hour. I mean, they've got radio equipment that is so big they can't readily deal with *thousands* of languages. They figure there are two hundred and eighty major languages in the world spoken by a million or more people. And they feel sure that everybody in the world can partially understand at least one of these two hundred and eighty languages.

Now isn't that relatively simple? Well, if you are using a big gun, it's obvious that you can't shoot at flies. *At every level the goals have to fit the tool.*

3) Film Ministry. Suppose you are using a film ministry, as does Campus Crusade. They initiated an amazing program for their *Jesus* film, and at the beginning were going after the same 280 major languages. But they have been making midcourse corrections. As they got out on the field, they felt 280 was not enough. And so, they shifted to a thousand different languages. More recently, they shifted again. They have now trimmed down and simplified their method of soundtrack development. They are not quite so perfectionistic as before. For smaller groups they can produce in two weeks what used to take six months. And costs are going down. Accordingly they now have a much larger goal.The *Jesus* film is a marvelous outreach. But, again, the tool determines the goal.

4) The Printed Page. Suppose you employ the printed page. It's so inexpensive that you can focus on six thousand languages. You can aim for the "mother tongue" rather than just a trade language for contact.

As in the case of all these tools, we've gone a certain distance but we still have further to go. And, as in the other cases, you measure what's left to be done in terms of the tool being used.

6) Audio Cassettes. But suppose we jump over row #5, since we have already talked about that, and go on further down. We'll go from Scripture in print to Scripture on tape. With cassette tape we are now using the ear gate. The ear gate is far more sophisticated than the eye gate.

This is why people who can't hear are far worse off than people who can't see. I don't know how old I was before I began to realize that. All over the world there are people who can't hear, or who can just barely hear. They can't learn to speak or to understand speech. In many societies they are beaten and kicked around like animals. They may even be kept in cages and thrown slop to eat. And they are used for work like a kind of intelligent animal. You cannot believe how they are treated! Two hundred and sixty million hearing-impaired people are probably more bitterly treated than any other category of human being. Why? Because the ear gate is the most important gate.

Visible writing is always an abridgment of the marvelous complexity of the sound of a human voice. This means that three or four different groups may be able to read the same New Testament even if they don't pronounce the words the same way! However, it also means that if each group pronounces it differently, they won't listen to the same radio broadcast. It means they won't listen to it on cassette unless it is pronounced their particular way. It means they won't all go to the same church even if their different groups employ the same printed New Testament.

In other words, dealing with people on *paper* is the most economical and efficient way to go in the sense that you can reach a lot more people with the one printed New Testament than you can with just a single set of cassettes. But cassettes have their own advantages. They can be used by people who cannot read, and thus are worth the extra trouble to deal with more subtle dialect differences.

Know also that in many "non-literate" societies, people are able to cope pretty well with an outside world that uses printed material—even if only a few within their group can read. The readers are often leaders who get up on Sunday and what they have read they try to explain in the local dialect. A little reading goes a long way.

Comparing Two Approaches

Let's take note of the two special organizations which are connected with tools #4 and #6, respectively. These two incredible organizations spread the Word on paper and on cassette.

Wycliffe Bible translators is the paper and ink organization. They are the world's largest long-term mission agency. They have something like six thousand missionaries coming from forty-two countries and working in seventy countries. They are the world's experts in their field.

But so far they've only dealt with a thousand languages because getting just the New Testament into print is a very complex, lengthy process. But it is worth it because of the permanence and economy of the medium. It also enables more people to read than if you were going directly into cassette.

The second organization specializes in cassettes—Gospel Recordings. They don't have six thousand workers; they may have only sixty but they've dealt with four thousand, five hundred languages instead of one thousand because it is far, far easier to work with cassettes than with printed paper. If you go right straight through to the *ear gate* with audio or video cassettes, you don't need to worry about writing problems. You can get there quicker and faster. But what you do is not quite as permanent and costs a lot more than paper and ink, so the printed page still has real advantages. So you would not want to choose between written and oral media.

Wycliffe's brilliant people took many, many years to figure out the best way to do what they are doing. You won't believe the statistics of their work. Wycliffe was a remarkable bunch of people from the start, and they started off rapidly. They didn't just add one person this year, and two people the next year. Even so, it took them thirty-five years to produce thirteen New Testaments. But in the next ten years they completed another one hundred New Testaments. In the following two years, they did another one hundred! See the acceleration? This does not reflect increased staffing, although that is part of it. It reflects increased competence.

If your church wants to send a missionary couple out to some tribal group that doesn't have a written language, tell them to go to Wycliffe's Summer Institute of Linguistics. They'll send you to the University of Texas at Arlington where they run the whole linguistics department. They know what they are doing, and they are perfectly willing for any church or mission to work with them. They always have been. I took their course years and years ago without any thought of ever being a Wycliffe worker myself. They have devised a marvelous program. I highly recommend it.

Gospel Recordings also know what they are doing. Again, they stand ready to help any mission working anywhere.

7) Church Planting. We come, finally, to church planting, where we began, because that is where all these tools must end up. In church planting efforts there are cultural barriers and prejudices even more subtle than those picked up by either the ear gate or the eye gate. As a result, when you set out to plant a church, you need to anticipate the necessity of dealing with even more groups than the people who spread the word in cassettes.

The key point here is that even if we deal effectively with the level of Scripture in print or even with audio cassettes, the cultural complexities of face-to-face fellowship involve other barriers that produce more Adopt-a-People targets than any one communication tool would predict. *What pioneer church planting missionaries are up to involves more sensitive handling of more different groups than any other approach whatsoever.*

Mobilization

You know, doing all this talking about what God is doing in the world, and how much more is to be done, or how little is to be done, leaves out another whole subject: *mobilization.*

As we observed earlier, a job is no bigger than the resources available. We have amazing resources but, like Christians, most of them are inactive rather than activated.

I truly believe that no one missionary can be as effective as one mission mobilizer. This is where we must be grateful for the wisdom of Walter and Louise Hannum. They could have gone back to the Yukon Valley to work. They chose to stay and mobilize. This conference would not have happened without them.

I decided not to continue on the field for the same reason. My work in this country undoubtedly outweighs what I did in Guatemala. What about you? Are you more valuable as a mobilizer than you would be as a field missionary?

The concept of a missionary is known widely. What is not known widely is the cruciality and urgency of MOBILIZATION. Right now in history what God is doing is held back more by the inactivity of the gargantuan human and financial resources of the vast global Christian family than it is by the obscurity of the missionary option.

You may not be able to go to the field. Being "stuck" in a local parish may mean God wants you to be a mission mobilizer. In fact, even if you could go to the "field," God may want you to be a mobilizer. Some of the most influential mobilizers in history were never missionaries.

If for any reason anyone absolutely cannot stay home, then the next best thing is to go to the field to be a mission mobilizer there.

It is tragic but true that many churches and individuals do not yet understand how important it is to support people who do not actually "go to the field." Flying over saltwater seems very important to them. The special hardship of the mobilizer is the matter of support. How many are willing to join Walter and Louise in their office and make the ECMC a success?

Take heart. In my denomination (Presbyterian Church, U.S.A.) in just the last year we have gained five full-time frontier mission mobilizers and they have churned up close to a million dollars a year for frontier missions. Right now we have work in forty-six such groups!

Remember the phrase "My utmost for his highest." It is easier to give our utmost than it is to seek out his highest. I always think that if you are willing to go you are qualified to stay home to mobilize. If you are not willing to go anywhere for God you are not likely to do much of anything for God. If you are not willing to stay to mobilize—since that is the greatest need right now—you may not even be qualified to go!

3

Partners for a Harvest: Working with the Church Overseas

THE CHANGING FACE OF WORLD MISSION

The Rt. Rev. Dr. David Gitari

Africa is a large and complicated continent and I am not an expert on issues of mission on the entire continent. Kenya, where I come from, is in East Africa and I can address the changing face of Third World Mission in that area with some authority.

The Anglican Church in Kenya is celebrating the 150th anniversary of the arrival of the first Church Missionary Society missionary to Mombasa. Dr. Johan Krapf, a German, was seconded to CMS, England, by the Evangelical Lutheran Church of Württemberg and sent as a pioneer missionary to East Africa. He arrived at Mombasa in January 1844, paid a brief visit to Zanzibar and returned to Mombasa in March of 1844. Shortly thereafter both his wife and child died.

Dr. Krapf was a gifted linguist and the first person to publish the Swahili Dictionary and Swahili Scriptures. He began his work among freed slaves and also went on geographical exploration tours upcountry. History books tell us that he was the first man to discover Mt. Kenya, though the Africans had discovered and seen the snow-capped mountain on the Equator centuries before that time. Although Dr. Krapf established some stations, the response to Christianity was slow and discouraging. However, it was from this small beginning that the gospel first reached East Africa and now a vigorous and dynamic church is celebrating 150 years of the coming of Christianity to East Africa.

In the story of any new church, the foreign missionary contribution tends to progress through three phases:

Missionaries are first pioneers;
then missionaries become pastors / teachers;
finally, missionaries become partners in mission.

Note the three P's—pioneers, pastors and partners.

Missionaries as Pioneers

The Third World church owes great gratitude to God that there were men and women from the Western world willing to leave the comfort of their respective countries to go share the gospel of Jesus to tribes and nations who had not heard the Good News. These pioneers risked their lives for the sake of the gospel. They responded willingly and enthusiastically to the Great Commission. The living, dynamic church in East Africa could not celebrate its 150th anniversary without paying tribute to these great pioneers.

Unfortunately, the great missionary pioneers also made some great mistakes. We revisit their mistakes so that we do not repeat them; we may be called upon to become the next pioneers. The day of the pioneer missionary is not yet over. There is still a need in some lands for the old type of pioneer missionary who will penetrate the jungle and mountains and venture into deserts to find tribes that are dying without having heard the gospel. Our plea is that such possible pioneers take note of some mistakes made by their predecessors.

The first mistake was in coming to Africa with a gospel wrapped in Western culture instead of presenting the pure gospel of Christ. This would have allowed the gospel to confront the community culture directly. Then the converted community would be able to express the new faith in its own cultural context. One of the responsibilities of the African church today is to remove the Western wrapper which may be hindering the gospel. For example, some pioneer missionaries condemned African music as pagan. They translated modern and ancient Anglican hymn books into the vernacular and Africans were taught to sing hymns that had no African context. So the Christmas carol which says, "Snow had fallen, snow on snow . . . in the bleak mid-winter long time ago" does not speak to the East African. In East Africa we have no experience of bleak mid-winter and falling snow!

Any modern pioneer missionary must learn to respect the culture of the people he goes to evangelize even if he does not fully understand it. Condemnation of cultural practices is only valid when such practices are contrary to the Holy Scriptures, especially the Ten Commandments. As the Lausanne Covenant declared, "The gospel judges every culture on its own criteria of truth. Because man is created in the image of God, some of his culture is full of beauty, but because he is fallen, some of his culture is demonic."

The second mistake made by some pioneers was to try to evangelize individuals by plucking them out of their communities. I will discuss this in detail later in this chapter when I discuss missionaries as pastors/teachers.

The third, and probably the worst, mistake some pioneers made was to desire to become permanent missionaries in the stations they founded. Having established the church, the pioneer was tempted to feel he was so indispensable that if he went away the church could not survive. This can only be true if he made the believers dependent on himself and not on the Holy Spirit. The story is told of some Anglican and American missionaries who had labored for about fifty years to plant a church in Southern Ethiopia. In that time they had only baptized about one-hundred people. The Italians invaded the country and conquered Ethiopia around 1936. Foreign missionaries were expelled and unable to return until after World War II. When they returned in 1946, they found 6000 baptized Christians. One of the missionaries embarked on a Ph.D. research program to find out why the church grew so fast in the absence of the missionaries!

Missionaries as Pastors

During the pioneering stage, when there are no Christians, the missionaries must be the ones to win souls to Christ. If there are two or three, they become the nucleus of the church, for Jesus said, "Where two or three are gathered together in my name, I will be there" (Mt 18:20). But, after a group has been won and a church started, the missionaries must expect the evangelistic activity and work of building up new believers to be carried on by that church. At this stage, the missionaries take upon themselves the care of all the church and the training of indigenous leadership. As John V. Taylor has observed,

> Almost always missionaries have allowed this second phase in their relationship to the "younger church" to drag on far too long. It is a pity that "paternalism" has become a bad word in missionary circles, for what it describes is a form of love. But it is a love which is too possessive and protective; it cannot bear to take the risks with the church which God takes. The church which grows up under such conditions is, in certain respects, a distortion of true Christian community.*

This stage is symbolized by MISSION COMPOUNDS. The missionaries built for themselves beautiful houses in a compound surrounded by a wall with a well-trimmed fence. Every morning the missionaries would leave their compound in a vehicle to visit outstations and then return to the Ivory Tower where no natives could enter unless they were servants. It is no wonder that when Father Vincent Donovan, the author of *Christianity Rediscovered* (SCM Press, 1978) went to Lolino Mission in 1966 to assist in evangelizing the Maasai of Tanzania, he found the work of the mission in 100 years was zero.

Having failed to win any adult Maasai to Christianity, the missionaries decided to build primary boarding schools and hospitals supported fully by the mission. The missionaries believed that by the time the Maasai children had completed their primary school education they would be Catholics, and by the time the patient left the hospital, he/she would be a Christian. However these children, who were plucked out of their communities, reverted back to the religion of their fathers when they left the school. Father Donovan believed that this approach to mission was wrong. This was not the way to evangelize these proud pastoralists of East Africa who believe all cows in the world belong to the Maasai. He asked permission of his bishop to try a new approach in mission.

With the bishop's permission, Father Donovan left the mission compound and went to live among the Maasai. Each morning for one whole year the entire community gathered around him to hear him tell the story of Jesus. They shared with him their own concept of God, salvation and

---

*John V. Taylor, *For All the World: The Christian Mission in the Modern Age* (Philadelphia: Westminster Press, 1966), p. 62.

forgiveness. He, in turn, told them about God who has come down to search for the Maasai, about Jesus Christ his Son, about forgiveness and salvation. After one year of instruction, he left them for one week so that they could decide for themselves whether to accept the gospel. When he returned, the chief, on behalf of the community, said the whole community had decided to accept Christ and were ready for baptism. Father Donovan said that he was going to baptize everyone except for the three people who did not regularly attend the instruction. The chief answered, "If you do not baptize everyone in the community, then you do not baptize anyone because those three had been sent by the community to look after the cows. Each evening they were told by others what they had learned about Christ." Father Donovan baptized the entire community and the community became a eucharistic community. His work having been completed, he moved on to other Maasai communities and worked for a maximum of five years. He established churches in four other communities. Of the communities he evangelized only one community rejected the gospel after one year of instruction. Though humbled by their rejection, Donovan learned to bear the gospel whether it was accepted or rejected.

Donovan's approach to mission may rightly be called the INCARNATIONAL approach. As the writer of the Book of Hebrews says, "In the past God spoke to our forefathers in various ways by the prophets at many times and in various ways, but in these last days he has spoken to us by his Son, whom he has appointed heir of all things, and through whom he made the universe" (Heb 1:1-2 NIV). The Son of God has come and camped in our midst so that he can reveal the Father to us; for us to see Jesus is to see God the Father himself. He chose the twelve disciples and formed a community, and for three years he taught them about the kingdom of God, so that in turn they could become his messengers of the Good News to the world. The incarnational approach calls upon the missionary to live and work among the people he is evangelizing so that they, together with him, can articulate the message of the gospel and at the end accept it or reject it.

The Western world has become too individualistic and there is a tendency by missionaries to prefer to pluck individuals from their communities and evangelize them with a hope that they can go back to their communities to tell the Good News. I believe it was Descartes, the French philosopher, who summarized the Western philosophy of the being of a man by saying, *"I think. Therefore I am."* In African philosophy, we would rather say with professor John Mbiti: *"We are. Therefore I am."* The being of a person can best be understood within the community to which he belongs.

Missionaries as Partners

Today, in most parts of the world, missionaries have moved into the third phase of their relationship and have become partners with their fellow Christians. Mission boards have handed over to the local church all land and property previously held in their name. The local church invites the missionaries and decides where they are to be located. The mission board is responsible for their housing, language study and even pastoral care. As John V. Taylor said,

> Old attitudes on both sides die hard, however, and there is plenty of room for misunderstanding and tension. The true partnership which all are seeking can only be born out of full surrender to the Lordship of Jesus which gives His glory and His mission to the world priority over everything else.*

In East Africa, the church grew rather slowly during the missionary pioneer period (1844-1900 AD). Then the church grew fairly rapidly (mathematical progression) during the first half of this century and until independence. That was the period when the missionaries assumed leadership of the church. But after leadership was handed over to the local church, the growth has been astronomical—the church has grown by geometrical progression. For instance, for about eighty years (1880-1960), the whole of Kenya was one diocese and had one bishop. By 1975 there were six dioceses, and by 1994 there were twenty. Within the last two years the dioceses have increased from ten to twenty.

When I became Bishop of the Diocese of Mt. Kenya East in 1975, there were nineteen parishes and about 150 congregations. By 1990 it became necessary to divide the diocese into two dioceses because the number of parishes had increased to ninety-three and there were 400 congregations. Every month we were beginning two new congregations. I knew the church was growing rapidly because of the number of candidates being presented to me for confirmation. Many times I confirmed 300 or 400 to 600 candidates in a single parish. One day I went to Sagana Parish and I was presented with 895 candidates to confirm. After con-

---

*Taylor, *For All the World*, p. 65.

firming 400, we had to take a break for a cup of tea!

One of our priests noted that Jesus did not only have twelve disciples, but also recruited an additional seventy disciples whom he sent two by two ahead of him to every city and place where he himself was going to come (Lk 10:1-20). So the priest chose seventy people in his parish and trained them to assist him in evangelism and pastoral work. They visited every home, every school and every marketplace. Many more believers were added to the church. In their pastoral visitation they found many Christian couples whose marriages had not been blessed in church. When they were asked why they did not have church weddings, they said that church weddings were too expensive—white dress for the bride, suit for the bridegroom, four-story cake, and of course, the cost of the wedding party. The pastor assured them that the church did not demand these things. The minimum requirement by the church is the presence of the bridegroom and bride, their witnesses and, where possible, parents. One day he conducted church weddings for 267 couples. The couples filled the church and all the witnesses were outside.

Among the nomadic people of Northern Kenya, we have tried the incarnational approach to mission. The pastors and evangelists live among the people, move with them when they go in search of water and grass. When I ordained the first Gabbra priest, the Rev. Andrew Adano, he requested that I buy him a camel and mule to use for evangelism. He wanted to live among his own people, look after goats and travel using a camel as they did. Whenever possible, he would tell them about Jesus. Starting with three converts, there are now many Christian believers among the Gabbra, and in July last year Andrew was consecrated an assistant bishop with special responsibility for overseeing the church among the pastoralists.

While realizing the fact that it is the work of the Holy Spirit which has made the church grow fast, and the commitment of our own people to preach the gospel of salvation, we nevertheless recognize the fact that not much could have been achieved without the contribution of our partners in mission. We owe a great deal to our partners in prayer, our partners in evangelism and in theological education, partners in development and partners in the struggle for justice, peace and reconciliation.

Partners in Prayer

We could not have achieved what we have without those partners who have devoted their time and energy to pray for us. St. Paul urged the

Colossian Christians to devote themselves to prayer, keeping alert in it with an attitude of thanksgiving. Then he urged them to pray for him and his team of supporters, "So that God may open up to us a door for the word, so that we may speak forth the mystery of Christ, for which I have been imprisoned, in order that it may be made clear the way I ought to speak" (Col 4:2-4). After the ascension on Mt. Olivet, the disciples returned to Jerusalem and with one mind they continually devoted themselves to prayer. After ten days there was the outpouring of the Holy Spirit on the day of Pentecost. Peter boldly proclaimed Jesus and three-thousand souls were added to the church. Formula: Ten days of intense prayer + Outpouring of the Holy Spirit + Courageous proclamation of the Gospel = Three thousand souls won to Christ.

Partners in Evangelism

The Christian Missionary Society, England, and British Christian Missionary Society Cross-Links sent pioneer missionaries to Kenya. Now our relationship is that of partnership in the gospel. Other partners have joined this partnership. Two CMS Australia couples are working among the unreached peoples of Northern Kenya. In about 1983, we entered into a tripartite agreement with the Diocese of Southern Virginia in the United States and the Diocese of Bukavu. The Diocese of Mt. Kenya East provided Archdeacon Linus Njuki to go to Zaire as a missionary. Funds for his expenses were provided by the Diocese of Southern Virginia, and the Diocese of Bukavu gave Linus an opportunity to serve as a missionary in Zaire for a period of two years. The Evangelical Lutheran Church of Württemberg invited Moses Jnue, one of our priests, to serve as a missionary in Germany for five years after which we consecrated and enthroned him as a bishop of Embu. St. John Stone Church in Canada has long supported the ministry of Andrew Adano in Northern Kenya. We are deeply involved in evangelism, but we have our partners whose contributions have been significant.

Partners in Theological Education

From the beginning of the diocese, we made the preparation of men and women for the ministry of the church a priority. St. Andrew's Institute for Mission and Evangelism was started in 1977. More than eighty percent of the clergy serving in the Dioceses of Kirinyaga and Embu have been trained there. From its simple beginnings, St. Andrew's has now become the largest and best equipped theological college in the Church of the Province of Kenya. It has also helped to train personnel for the church in Sudan, Zaire, Tanzania and Ethiopia. In December of 1993 we ordained fourteen women who were trained at St. Andrew's for the priesthood. Some of the women priests have proven to be among the best pastors in the Church of the Province of Kenya. Partners in Mission who have joined us in making St. Andrew's what it is include World Vision International who gave the first grant to purchase beds, utensils and other equipment for the eight students enrolled at St. Andrew's in 1977. They later gave a generous grant to construct the dining hall. The United Thank Offering gave a generous grant to construct dormitories. The EZE of Germany provided funds for the construction of staff housing and classrooms; the Tear Fund helped to provide for the improvement of the water supply and the British Royal Air Force sent a team of water engineers and plumbers; the Diocese of Chelmsford, England, provided funds to construct a library; the Evangelical Lutheran Church of Württemberg, Germany, granted student scholarships, and CMS and BCMS Cross-Links have sent theologians to teach at St. Andrew's.

Partners in Development

The Lausanne 1974 Congress on World Evangelism had a great impact on me. Prior to that, I did not quite know how to relate evangelism and social action. The study of scripture convinced me that a human being is a psychosomatic unit and we cannot separate the spirit from the body. Our evangelism must go together with acts of mercy and development. In 1979 we started the Department of Christian Community Services which became the development arm of the diocese. Since that time we have established health committees in every parish, trained more than 400 community health workers, operated sixteen mobile clinics for immunization of children and held training in areas of family planning and prenatal and postnatal care. We have established Rural Development Programs for better agriculture, provided training for farmers, operated veterinary clinics for livestock and assisted with the provision of water. In some parts of Northern Kenya, women have to walk thirty miles in search of water for the animals and their families. To provide a borehole in such places is a great blessing to the people. During times of drought and famine, we have provided food. We have a saying that a hungry stomach has no ears. The Development Program has been one of the most effective in the Church of the Province of Kenya. Funding support from agencies in both Europe and America has been invaluable.

Once again, we could not have succeeded if it were not for the support of our partners in development. Partnership in development began when the Episcopal Church of America sent one young missionary, Kerk Burbank, from Pennsylvania to our diocese. We appointed him as the first Director of Christian Community Services of Mt. Kenya East in 1979. He wrote the first Community Health Proposal which was funded by EZE of Germany. He served a two-year term and returned home to marry. He then returned to Kenya with his bride to serve an additional two years.

Partners in Search of Justice, Peace and Reconciliation

As long as the church is involved in such humanitarian activities as famine relief, healing the sick and providing care for refugees, the government is quite happy. But when the church questions the root cause of famine, sickness or refugees, the church is told that these are political questions and the church should not be involved in politics. But the church cannot just be content to do humanitarian work. The church must become involved in finding the root cause of these problems and in responding with a hope of transforming unjust societies to make them more humane.

We have challenged election rigging and worked for multiparty democracy. We have challenged corruption and the exploitation of the poor by the rich. Our involvement in challenging these evils has made us even risk our lives. The Kenya Parliament debated me for two and one-half hours because I issued a statement in 1987 saying that the ruling party had used a national delegates meeting as a rubber stamp to pass twelve resolutions in five minutes. In April of 1989 my house was invaded by a gang of forty-three people who had been sent to kill me. I was saved by climbing on to the roof of my house from where I could shout for help. The gang ran away. We say that it is good for a person to die for his country, but it is also good to live for the gospel. Jesus said that if they persecute you in one city, flee to the next. And I say, if they come through the door, run through the window, and if they come through the window, go to the roof top.

Africa is bleeding from Cape Town to Cairo and from Monrovia to Mogadishu. Much blood has been shed in Rwanda. We invite you to become our partners, especially in preaching the sanctity of human life. Man and woman are created in the image of God and therefore every human life is sacred and should be respected, not exploited or eliminated.

Rwanda is a country with one of the highest percentages of Christians. Yet they are shedding the blood of innocent people by the thousands. Cain is very much alive and he still says, "I am not my brother's keeper." If there is anything that you can do to work for justice, peace and reconciliation in your own country, and then become a partner in search of justice on the mission field, that will be a great blessing to the mission of the church.

CHURCH PLANTING IN LATIN AMERICA

The Rev. Canon Tom Prichard and the Rev. Alfredo Smith

A movement in mission is underway in the Episcopal Church. We are experiencing it with the South American Missionary Society (SAMS). In the past six years SAMS missionaries have tripled in numbers. We have gone from fifteen missionaries to forty-five missionaries: thirty missionaries in the field and fifteen missionary candidates preparing for the field.

Now for the bad news. Did you know that of the requests that are coming to us from overseas dioceses asking us for missionaries, seventy-five percent of these requests are going unmet? I have had Latin American bishops say to me over the phone, "I am on my knees begging for help." Missionaries are needed for church planting, as evangelists, Christian educators and theological educators. Missionaries are needed for a wide range of compassion ministries: school teachers, administrators for children's homes, medical personnel, people to help provide clean water systems.

Our overseas partners in mission are faced with an extraordinary challenge and they have very limited resources with which to meet that challenge. By the year 2000, fifty percent of the world's population will be concentrated in the cities. In Latin America by the year 2000, seventy-eight percent of the population will be in the cities: enormous, sprawling urban centers. It is estimated that by the year 2025, one-quarter of the world's population will be the urban poor, living in squatter settlements, surrounding the mega-cities of the world. Right now there are an estimated 100 million children growing up in the streets of the cities. The extraordinary challenge of reaching the cities of the world is the challenge facing the mission of the church.

Working as a missionary in Bogotá, Colombia, I saw some of this firsthand. Bogotá is estimated to have from seven to nine million people. It was exciting to see the way the Lord was at work changing lives. People were hungry for the gospel, and those who came to the Lord were excited and inspired. They were reaching out and expressing that faith in ministries of compassion.

We had a team of four South American Missionary Society missionaries, and our vision was not terribly profound. Our vision was to build up a church that would be self-sustaining. We held our first service in 1983 with nine folks present. We soon grew to fifteen, then twenty and then twenty-five.

On the other side of Bogotá, however, there was a church-planting effort by the Christian and Missionary Alliance. When I first met their missionaries, I learned that our progress and theirs was similar. Not long after that, when I met them again, I reported that we now had fifty and they reported seventy-five. When we reached seventy-five, they were at 150. I began to notice a trend! Pretty soon they had two hundred people on Sunday, then four hundred, then six hundred. They reached one thousand and they planted two daughter churches. By then they had my attention!

I found out that they had a strategy called the "Encounter With God" church-planting strategy, and, in fact, Bogotá was not even thought of as a very good example of it! "Encounter With God" had begun in Lima, Peru, in 1973, in a church with 180 members. Twenty years later, that 180-member church has grown into thirty churches with a combined Sunday attendance of 30,000.

I have seen not only the evangelism and discipleship that has gone forth from those churches, but I have seen their ministries of compassion as well. In a city estimated to have 200,000 children living in the streets, one of these churches feeds three hundred of them breakfast every morning. Another has, from its own funding, created an orphanage.

When the South American Missionary Society saw what was happening with this strategy and how it worked, we sent a team to the capital city of Hondouras, Tegucigalpa, to plant a church using the "Encounter With God" strategy.

Alfredo Smith was the senior pastor of the mother church in Lima, Peru, where the "Encounter With God" strategy was started. Prior to that, he served for fifteen years in Argentina as an evangelist and pastor of the Christian and Missionary Alliance Church. This is his report of the work of God in Lima, Peru.

SMITH: The Christian and Missionary Alliance Church has a history of almost forty years of ministry in Latin America. The population of Latin America is approximately 450 million people and growing rapidly. The largest cities of the world are in Latin America. Mexico City is on the verge of 20 million people, São Paulo is near 16 million, Rio de Janiero has 14 million and Buenos Aires has 12 million. There are cities along the Pacific coast from Santiago, Chile, to Caracas, Venezuela, with populations ranging from five to almost ten million people each. We have to look at the cities and be sensitive to the concern of God's heart for them.

The foundation of every spiritual enterprise the church may ever face is prayer. Have you ever pondered the fact that not to pray is a sin? When we think of sin, a long list of indiscretions comes to mind. Yet I am afraid that we never stop to realize that there is such a thing as the sin of prayerlessness. This sinfulness is tragic. The ministry of our Lord Jesus Christ was focused and centered on prayer. The book of Hebrews tells us that during the days of Jesus' life on earth and when he was ending his ministry, he offered prayers and petitions with loud cries and tears to the One who could save him from death. Scripture tells us that he was heard because of his reverent submission. Although he was a son, he learned obedience from what he suffered. He ministered from a life of prayer, prayer that issued from the very heart of the living Son of God. If we mean business, we have to start at this very point. It is Samuel who states very clearly in 1 Samuel 12:23, "As for me, far be it from me that I should sin against the Lord by failing to pray for you." This type of sin is burying many churches and finishing many ministries.

Have you ever pondered the words found in Ezekiel 22:30-31? "I looked for a man among them who would build up the wall and stand for me in the gap on behalf of the land so I would not have to destroy it, but I found none. So I will pour out my wrath on them." Ezekiel is revealing a principle, a spiritual law. Prayerlessness shuts the door to grace and opens the door to the operation of law. May God help us to understand what this means. If there is no prayer, there is no proper atmosphere created to allow the grace of God to move.

Do we realize this spiritual principle when we come to the theme of missions? When prayer is offered in the right way, then power comes from God. The strategy of the Holy Spirit will become clear before our eyes. The ministries of the Holy Spirit can flourish and the resources will come. God has abundant resources; he is a God of abundance—there is no limitation in him.

Let me share with you how things started in Lima, Peru. The setting

was an exploding city economically, culturally, demographically and politically. A yearly influx of 350,000 people came from all quarters of the
nation. The city is now over seven million people. Peru is one of the
poorest nations in Latin America; it is the poorest in South America.
(Latin America includes Central America and Mexico, which are in
North America, and South America, which is from Venezuela and Colombia downwards.)

Lima is the capital city of one of the poorest nations of Latin America. The church was stagnant. In this exploding city, within an eight-year
period, the congregation stayed at 117 members with a regular attendance of two hundred. They had been without pastoral leadership for
two years. A group of some fifteen to twenty-five people started to pray
together. "Lord, we need the ministries of the Holy Spirit moving in our
midst. We are asking, Lord, that you may give us a pastor. We are also
asking you, Lord, for an awakening—a mighty revival." This group
would gather two, three or four times a week, interceding in the presence
of God. They did this for two solid years.

The first evidence of answered prayer was the Holy Spirit of God
calling people from different areas of the continent to come to Lima to
form a team. A Canadian couple serving in Colombia felt a burden for
the city and came. I was called from Buenos Aires, with my wife, to
come pastor the church. Two other U.S. couples living in Lima joined
the team. Added to that were a few Peruvians and a team was formed, all
with people burdened for the city of Lima. It was a soverign movement
of the Holy Spirit; no one on the team was sent by any organization.

This team came together with a deep awareness of the presence of
God. Our strategy was as old as the Bible. We realized that if something
was to be accomplished in that city of Lima, we would have to begin
with a systematic evangelistic effort. That effort was the one outlined in
the Bible, in Matthew 28, of preaching, baptizing and teaching.

The challenge was in developing this strategy. The prayers had assembled the team and now the need was for the right type of facility in
the right location to attract people. This would be costly but God moved
a man in Texas with great resources to sponsor this. God gave us a facility on one of the main aveunes of the city of Lima.

The evangelistic effort was systematic and aggressive. The first fif-
teen-day crusade gave us a harvest of 175 people. Our major problem
was handling that many new people in a congregation of 117 members!
We had planned for moderate growth with some thirty counselors prepared to deal with the newcomers.

After the initial crusade, we felt led by God to organize what came to be known as the Bible Academy. We had systematic evangelism and now we had systematic teaching. Newcomers could be taught the principles of faith: repentance, conversion, new life, temptation, sharing their faith and personal evangelism. During the fifteen days of recess between evangelistic crusades, we were working with the new believers in the Bible Academy. This continued for the entire fifteen months. When new believers completed their first course, then they would pastor the next course and worked side by side with the team. In fifteen months we had 225 evangelistic meetings.

Prayer was sustained, the evangelistic thrust was maintained, the teaching was upheld and the whole thing just began to snowball. Our sanctuary had a seating capacity of one thousand and it was necessary to duplicate services. A lay seminar program was organized from those who were being saved and incorporated into the church. We asked God to show us those whom he was calling to participate in the various ministries of the church. This was a tremendous amount of work, but these people were key to the continuation of the whole strategy.

The next step which God revealed was to prepare a group of people within the church who could be "hived off" to form the nucleus and birth a church in another quarter of the city. We were now at two thousand members, having duplicate services and the facility was at maximum capacity. In the "hiving off" process, the mother church would sponsor a daughter church by supplying a full-time pastor, providing the financial support and helping them to continue the Encounter program.

The next need that became apparent was a ministry training center to prepare those God was calling for full-time ministry. There were believers trained at the Bible Academy and there were also believers who had been trained at the laymen's seminars to work alongside the team. Now the need was for those who felt the burden and God's clear call to serve in full-time ministry. So a seminary was created. Certainly there were many good seminaries in Lima, but we were preparing new wine and realized that new wineskins were required. Thus, The Bible Institute of the Alliance was started. Presently the enrollment is nearly three hundred students who study in a five-year Bible study and seminary program.

All Encounter With God work has now passed into the hands of nationals. There is not one single foreigner running the Encounter Program in Lima, Peru. It is self-supporting, self-governing and self-expanding. The church has caught the vision of serving its own nation and the Encounter program is now covering the whole nation of Peru. It is spilling over the borders and has become established in Quito, Ecquador. What began there with a group of some ninety people now numbers almost 1,100 people and is reaching the highest levels of Ecuadorian society. It is being very effective in reaching those levels never before reached by evangelicals.

Tom Prichard has seen evidence of what happened in Bogotá, Colombia, where over one thousand people have responded. God has opened the doors to Caracas, Venezuela, which is a very difficult city to evangelize. Encounter is also moving south into Chile and into Argentina.

As poor as the Peruvian nation is, the Peruvian people came to me when I was in Quito, Ecuador, with an idea. They told me, "Pastor, you were with us for twelve years, and you have been in Ecuador. Don't you think it would be good for you to team up with us in order to evangelize a continent?" I returned to Buenos Aires, my own city for years, and served as an itinerant speaker/evangelist and ministered at conferences for pastors all over the continent.

Then they came to me and said, "We will be supporting you full time and we are thinking of sending you to Miami, U.S.A." Poor people sending missionaries to the United States—isn't that something? They have been faithful and have supported us for these last years. The hand of God has been mighty upon these Peruvians. They are experiencing church growth and seeing the hand of God move in marvelous ways.

Where do we go from here? Our objective is to "Fill all with the Gospel of Christ." Those who are in the trenches need proper logistics, the backing and support to continue, remaining humble and sensitive to the promptings of the Spirit, in submission to the Word of God. We live in days in which subjectivism and spiritualism are displacing the Word of God and it is important that we not lose our bearings. It is the objectivity of the Word of God that keeps us alive and going. Submission to the Word of God and sensitivity to the prompting of the Spirit allow us to be ready to adapt to the changing scenes we have to face. The one trap to be avoided is uniformism. The goal is to spread the gospel; the method employs integrated planning and flexibility.

The whole Encounter strategy started with prayer, prayer and more prayer. It has been blessed by God and led by his Spirit. The Bible says, "Give and it shall be given unto you." Put another way, "Don't give and you will be choked." The Peruvian people have learned the lesson and they are putting it to work.

GOD IS AT WORK IN OUR DAY

The Rev. James Wong

The hour is late. Has it ever occurred to you that we may be that last generation? God is, in a sense, putting everything in our hands to finish the Great Commission. I feel as if the gospel of the Kingdom of God has gone one big circle.

Beginning in Jerusalem, in 1800 years the gospel had reached the whole of Europe, crossed over the Atlantic to North America, and then from Spain down to South America. In the second half of the last century, the gospel went from Europe and England, down to Africa and came across Asia and the Pacific Islands. In a sense, the gospel has been preached to the whole world!

Acts is one of the most fascinating accounts of mission strategy. As Paul was evangelizing Asia during his first missionary journey, he was greatly encouraged by the receptivity and response of the unreached people of Asia Minor. He wanted to go back for a second time around! Of course unknown to him, God had a different strategy. God has different timetables and programs for the nations of the world. Thank God that Paul was obedient and sensitive to the Holy Spirit! While he was at Troas, he wanted to go farther up north into Asia Minor to modern Turkey, but there was a restraint in his spirit. Still, he wanted very much to evangelize the whole of Asia. So, while he was asleep, God spoke to him. That night Paul saw the vision of a Caucasian man from Macedonia who said, "Come over here and help us."

You know, when I go to heaven, the first question I'm going to ask is, "Why did you go west? Asia is so much more important! There are so many more people in Asia." And God's reply may be something like this: "The people in the West are so stubborn and so slow!" or "They had to be given 1,800 years' start!"

So that's why the mission of the church has been western Europe—from Europe to North America to South America. It's only in the last one hundred years that a tremendous spiritual movement has started in Asia. That's a compliment and consolation that we were a little more obedient and a little faster in responding to the Great Commission. It took you and your forefathers 1,800 years to get converted and the last two hundred years to get you to hear the Great Commission! Here I am, reversing the order—a man from Asia calling you brothers and sisters to come over to this side and help us now. Are you having a dream now? I'm the man from Asia, beckoning you to come over here to help us! Praise God!

In 1986, at the Missions Agency Conference held in Brisbane, Australia, there were a few people from the Third World, a few from Asia, a few from Africa, and a few from Latin America. We were invited as guests, as observers of this missionary agency meeting of the Anglican Communion. While at the meeting, some of the Third World leaders, bishops from Africa and Asia and Latin America, got together and asked themselves the question, "Why is it the only time we meet as brothers in the family of God is when there is a conference called by the people from the North—from Europe or from North America, from the Western countries—and then we come as guests? In between we hardly meet one another." Out of that concern, a movement was gathered called "Anglican Encounter in the South." In January 1994, in Kenya, seventy of us came together representing twenty-three provinces of the Anglican communion from about thirty-three countries. For the first time, Anglican leaders (including bishops, priests and lay people, women, and youth) from South America, Africa and Asia met together to ask ourselves, "What is God saying to us as Anglicans in the non-Western cultures? What is God doing in our midst?" We were surprised to find that the center of gravity, as far as Anglican Christianity is concerned, has been tipped over to the south. More than sixty percent of the total Anglican family are found in the southern continents rather than in the north.

We need to encourage one another, to share our experiences and insights, and ask ourselves, "What is God saying to us? How can we be faithful to the Great Commission? How can we really get the gospel out to the nations in Africa, Asia, and in South America, as well as share the gospel with our brothers and sisters in the north?" Out of that encounter, there has been follow-up ministry that will go on, and I believe that by the next Lambeth Conference, there will be a very strong contribution from the Anglican constituencies from the south.

At the conference we realized that one of the greatest needs among the Anglican Communion, parishes, dioceses, and the provinces in the south, was to learn to be more self-reliant—to look to God to provide the resources, manpower, gifts, talents, visions, financial capability and creativity to fulfill the Great Commission. Mission was number one on our agenda at that conference. Then we asked ourselves, "How can we at the same time be faithful to our Anglican heritage, and be biblical and faithful to the Word of God?" We feel that this is consistent because, after all, Anglicanism came out of the Reformation and the principles of the Reformation are what the Scriptures teach. For us, we needed to ask ourselves, "How can we be Anglican in the south, true to the Bible, true to our Christian convictions, true to our historic creed of beliefs, and yet at the same time culturally relevant and dynamic in our context?" We looked at the church, the mission structure, the leadership structure, some of our programs, and we were determined to find ways and means to transform our churches in the south to become dynamic mission centers instead of maintenance centers.

In 1 Thesslonians, chapter one, Paul wrote these tremendous words of encouragement, and in a sense, it is my testimony to you beginning with verse 5:

> For our gospel did not come to you in word only, but also in power and in the Holy Spirit and in much assurance. You know what kind of men we were among you for your sake, and you became followers of us and of the Lord, having received the Word in much affliction, with the joy of the Holy Spirit. So you became examples to all in Macedonia and Achaia who believe, for from you the Word of the Lord has sounded forth, not only in Macedonia and Achaia, but also in every place. For your faith towards God has gone out so that we do not need to say anything, for they themselves declare concerning us what manner of entry we had towards you and how you have turned to the living God, away from idols, that you may serve the true and living God.

What a testimony Paul wrote to this group of baby Christians, literally several months old! He said, You received the gospel and were changed! You live by the gospel. Not only that but from you the gospel has gone forth with great power so that everywhere they testify of your faith!

Let me ask you this question: Has the gospel lost its power? No, it is the same gospel. Then why are we not more bold to proclaim it within and without? We have waited almost two thousand years, and as a result, two-thirds of the world's population are still not Christian. Almost twenty-five percent are totally unreached. How are we going to finish it in the next six to seven years before the year 2000 A.D.? I believe it is possible, and I'm going to show you statistically a strategy of how we can do it together.

First of all, the days ahead of us are ones of great excitement and challenge. Never before in history have there been more open doors for the preaching of the gospel, if we only have eyes to see, ears to hear, minds and hearts that are willing to obey God. People are hungry for the gospel. All over the world, there are more people who are receptive to the gospel rather than resistant to the gospel.

Secondly, I want to show that the growth and development of Christianity has been at a fantastic rate in comparison with all other religions.

Thirdly, in our generation, we have more resources and abilities to fulfill the Great Commission than in any other generation before us. Think of the information technology, speed of travel, modern equipment, and the vast resources of the Lord's people; education, ideas, creativity and skills to communicate the gospel.

Fourthly, there has been tremendous progress in understanding the great missiological task—the strategies, opportunities, various methods, and great worldwide attempts to evangelize the nations before the return of Jesus Christ.

These are some of the great opportunities before us. Our concern is to reach the unreached peoples of the world in our generation by doing what we've been doing: praying together, planning together, and proclaiming the gospel of Jesus Christ. We have learned that no one nation, no one denomination, and no one Christian group can do it alone. That's why God has brought us together so we can really work together. The world we live in is composed of almost six billion people. After almost two thousand years, we have barely reached two billion. There are still four billion people who are not Christians today. The way we have been going you can calculate that mathematically it would take four thousand more years to reach the other four billion. Four more millennia! I don't think Jesus Christ wants to wait that long!

So how are we going to reach the world, to fulfill the Great Commission that the gospel of the kingdom shall be preached as a witness to all the nations and then the end will come? Do we mean political nations? If so, there are 235. Are we going to reach one nation at a time politically? Many of the nations are not easy to go to. Or are we going to reach the individuals—almost 5.5 billion and still multiplying. By the end of this decade there will be six billion people; that will take another four thousand years. Or, are we, as we've been told again and again, to reach the twelve thousand unreached people groups? I think this is one of the most significant strategies for world evangelization that calls for the whole church to take the whole gospel to the whole world. The unreached peoples concept applies in all the continents of the world, the greatest number of unreached people are still found in Asia today. This is a most significant concept in missionary strategy.

Here is a good example of an unreached people: there is a group of thirty million people in central Java with less than two or three churches among them. That's a large people group that is within our geographical distance to communicate the gospel. It is a group of people where there is, at present, not a sufficient indigenous community of Christian believers who have adequate resources among themselves to reach them. So they need outside help.

The twelve thousand unreached people groups consist of people who are tribal, animistic, not religious, Hindu, Chinese religions, Buddhist, and all kinds of others. I believe that one of the greatest challenges in modern missions today will be the mission to Islam, in areas where eighteen percent or more of the world's population live. At the moment, only two percent of all the missionary resources are dedicated to evangelizing the Muslim world. It's a great challenge for us.

What about the needed resources? I want to suggest that God, in his wisdom and sovereignty, has raised up adequate resources, but he's calling the church to redistribute and refocus. For example, there are over four million full-time Christian workers of every sort. But the largest part are all in "World C." World A is the unreached people, World B is their neighbors, and World C is Christian. Almost all our Christian resources are in World C. About twenty thousand missionaries are in World B, and less than one percent are dedicated to the twelve thousand unreached people groups. As long as this continues, we will wait another four millennia before the whole world can hear the gospel. We have to change and go to obey the Great Commission!

Now, look at our financial resources. God has enough financial resources for his work to be done, but it is not well distributed. For example, it is estimated that the total personal income of Christians worldwide is close to nine trillion dollars. Now, one billion is one thousand million. One trillion is one million million. That's a lot of money. There are nine trillion dollars among the Christians. But what is used for foreign missions? Not even one percent! Christians are not even giving one percent of their resources for world mission!

The challenge for men and women in the pews, the Christian churches, is that we need to pray, not to ask God to send more missionaries, but to convict us to release our resources. Why do we accumulate? We can't use it in heaven! We must release the finances so that resources are adequate to meet the need.

Now let's look at the positive side, and see what God is doing in the world today. It has been estimated that every week over a thousand new churches are being opened up all over the world! The U.S.A. has more than 1,500 Christian radio stations. Why not give some of these away? Why do you need so many radio stations in one country? Send them to Russia! Send them to Asia! In Southeast Asia, we need some of the gospel!

Africa is the site of one of the most thrilling moves of God—twenty thousand new believers are coming into the Kingdom of God every day. It's the same in South America. It's happening more slowly in Asia, but even in Asia, for example, South Korea is a bright spot. God is taking the nation of Korea, and in the south he's bringing revival to Indonesia, so it is like Asia is in a nutcracker. The Holy Spirit is going to apply the pressure to break the hard nut of the religious beliefs of the people in Asia. God is doing it!

And there are many exciting stories all over the world. God is at work! Our responsibility won't wait. God is at work. God is calling people to come to him. It's not the will of God that any should perish, but that all would come to the saving knowledge of him. Look at the growth rate of Christianity compared with all the other religions. Sometimes, we think of the great Asian religions of Buddhism, Hinduism as great obstacles to evangelism. Statistically, it is not true. All over the world Christianity is growing at a faster speed than all of the other religions, two or three times faster. The Muslims, Hindus, nominal Christians and Buddhists are much slower. There are far more people who are being converted and brought into the Kingdom every day by born-again, Bible-believing Christians who know Jesus Christ than by any other ideology or religion. We saw the collapse of communism in Russia and many parts of Eastern Europe. So there are more people coming to faith in Jesus in Eastern Europe, Central Asia, and even in Russia today! All these are God's marvelous works.

4

Harvest Field on Our Doorstep: Mission in the U.S.

NEW WINESKINS - ¡GRACIAS A DIOS!*

The Rev. José D. Carlo

The title of this conference is New Wineskins for Global Mission and I would like to take a few minutes with you to examine the makeup of these new wineskins. While my comments arise from my experience in Hispanic mission and ministry, they are equally applicable to other combinations of languages and cultures.

1. The new wineskins must be of many tongues. One of the great challenges to the English-speaking members of the Anglican communion is to lift up, honor and rejoice in the fact that the majority of Anglicans are non-English speaking. Today, as many Christians speak Spanish as speak English. It will require a changing of our minds and of our hearts to accept the fact that even in the smallest of our congregations there

---

*This presentation was done with a very Latin flavor with the participation of and input from the whole plenary group in a bilingual dialog which included the singing of two hymns in English and Spanish.

needs to be more multilingual opportunities for expressing and living out the love of Christ.

We need wineskins that reach out and say, "Christ loves you and died for you," not only in English but also in Spanish, "Cristo te ama y murió por ti," or in Chinese or in Swahili, etc.

2. *The new wineskins must be of many cultures.* Respecting and valuing each other's culture is important and Christian. Music, dance, traditions, foods, holidays, sports, etc, are all part of the fabric which defines our cultural identity.

For instance, if I were to ask you for the date of the independence day celebrations you would probably all answer, July 4th. But, depending upon the makeup of our congregations, we might also pray and give thanks on September 15 (Mexico) or September 16 (Central America) or August 5 (India), etc. How about Mother's Day? Second Sunday of May (USA), fourth Sunday in Lent (Canada), December 8 (Panama), August 15 (Costa Rica), etc.

Our task is to be sensitive to these different dates in the cultures represented in our congregations and to lift them up in prayer and thanksgiving. The different cultures should be a part of, and reflected in, the tapestry of the new wineskins.

3. *The new wineskins must emphasize more of the cross in our celebration of Easter.* We live in a situation where we can, so easily, glory in Easter. We talk about it, rejoice in it and even look for Easter eggs on Easter. But how good are we at giving thanks to God in times of adversity, pain and sorrow?

Half the world must carry a heavy cross if they would celebrate Easter. In one of the workshops it was mentioned that the Russian Orthodox Church went underground for over seventy years and that during those years over fifty million Orthodox Christians died just because they were Orthodox Christians. Silently that part of the universal church suffered, persevered and gave thanks for their resurrection in Jesus Christ. Their Easter celebrations had to wait seventy years.

About fifteen years ago, China rescinded its prohibition of the practice of Christianity in that country. Expectations were that maybe ten thousand Christians remained in China. Joyfully we learned that millions had remained faithful in the face of great persecution. Their Easter celebrations waited thirty years.

When was the last time you were spit upon, or insulted, or imprisoned or lost your belongings, just for being a Christian? Did you give thanks and realize how blessed you were? (Matthew 5:11). Easter faith requires a well-carried cross. We must learn, in the name of Christ, to increase our sharing in the cross of others and to better carry our own cross. The new wineskins will bring us greater participation in the cross and the Easter of the whole church.

4. The new wineskins must be on fire with the Holy Spirit. They must reflect a continuous celebration of the Pentecost experience in many tongues, peoples, nations and cultures; a deeper sense of the meaning, in our lives, of the cross and of the resurrected Christ. Hopefully, these new wineskins are already being forged within and among us.

¡Gracias a Dios!

INTERNATIONAL STUDENT MINISTRY

Mr. Leiton Chinn and the Rev. Paul Frey

CHINN: Last night, the Lord impressed me with the familiar passage of the Great Commission, Matthew 28. When I think of the Great Commission, I remember all those action verbs:

Go! Make disciples of all nations! Baptize! Teach! Sure, that's the Great Commission. But the Great Commission also has a great promise. He showed it to me last night. What's the promise? It is summed up in the word, "Emmanuel." And lo! I am with you—Emmanuel. With you in the great unfinished task!

Let the floodlights flash "Emmanuel" in your ministry, in your mission. In the unfinished task of world evangelization, we are going to labor in vain if Emmanuel is not walking with us. And, remember, your labor is not in vain with the Lord Emmanuel.

Come with me now on my sojourn in missions. Why? That I might remember how he has been Emmanuel.

I was baptized as an infant in an Episcopal church in Honolulu. When I was four, my parents got divorced. I stopped going to the Episcopal church.

Suddenly, all my other friends had both parents, and I didn't. And I used to wonder, "How come I am different?" but I don't think I suffered from any kind of dysfunctional syndrome. You know why? God has a special heart for the foreigner, for the widow, and for the orphan, and I was a quasi-orphan. So I would go to my neighbors, who were Japanese. I am an American-born Chinese. These Japanese neighbors became sort of my adopted family. I remember at an early age, I felt that the world was my home because I could go to that house any time, go in, and they would receive me.

After I became a Christian in high school, I was at a Baptist conference center in Honolulu. A Southern Baptist summer missionary sang a
missions song called, "Follow Me." The phrase that God used to pierce
my heart goes like this: "Oh, Jesus, if I die upon a foreign field someday,
it would be no more than love demands, no less could I repay."

I sobbed in the pew. I had a vision. In my mind's eye, all I could see
was whiteness and a little pile of dust. The Spirit of God said, "This is
what you are." I knew it. I gave that pile of dust back to him. I call that
the "Lordship decision." I said, "Take this pile of dust, mold me and
make me and if I stray from you, bring me back. Oh, Lord, thank you for
your faithfulness."

The potter will take us in our marredness, our crackedness. Let's not
struggle too much. He will remake us to be a vessel fit for the Master's
use.

God had a funny way of preparing me for ministry among internationals. God is just tremendous. I am an American citizen, but thanks
be to God, the Foreign Mission Board of the Southern Baptist Convention gave two scholarships to the state of Hawaii. Hawaii, before state-
hood, was considered a foreign mission. Thanks be to God, because like
many international students, I couldn't afford to go off my island to some
big country, or, in this case, the mainland. I wouldn't have made it to college away from Hawaii. By God's grace, I was given one of those foreign student scholarships. I went to California Baptist College, and I experienced what it was like to be a foreign student.

Even though I am an American, I belong to a sub-culture. I discovered that Hawaiian culture is different from mainland culture. Also, at
Thanksgiving, when most of my fellow Americans went home, I, like
many international students, had no home to go to. I could not afford to
fly back to Hawaii. So I went to a Thanksgiving conference for international students.

Later, when I was in the Army, God sent me to Korea, even though
the rest of my class went to Vietnam. In Korea, I truly experienced what
it is like to be a foreigner. Thanks be to God again. I was lonely as a
Christian in Korea, and God brought a Korean Christian, an older man,
to become like a Paul to me. He discipled me through his manner of life,
and I attended the Korean church. All I am saying is that God met me as
a foreigner in a foreign land through a national. I am glad to say this, because so often we in the West think we are the ones that are going to
minister to the rest of the world.

I was a very needy American. God built me up. I came back to the
States, and I needed more training. The Navigators trained me to share

my faith. Even though our target was military people at Fort McPherson, Georgia, I met some internationals and shared the gospel with them. One of them I just saw two years ago back in Seoul, Korea. He has been a faithful pastor and evangelist all these years. Another one was a Christian Taiwanese. He was a great scientist. He just resigned and has enrolled at Trinity Evangelical Divinity School.

At this point in my life, 1973, twenty years ago, I was very much convinced that I would be most effective as a "tentmaker missionary" outside the United States. I thought that a layperson might have more credibility than a "paid professional." Secondly, I believed I should be in an area of the world that had not had as many opportunities to hear the gospel as we have in the United States.

To make a long story short, in the last seventeen years I have been a professional missionary back home, not a layperson in Asia. How did that happen? I had to come back to sell the house that my brother and I inherited when our father died. Instead of returning to Korea, where things were very fruitful, I felt the Lord saying, no, stay home and go to seminary.

I went to seminary on the East Coast. In the second year, I had the urge to go back overseas. I said, "God, you showed me that you wanted me to stay in the States but now I have this overwhelming desire to go back overseas." Guess what? God brought it together—the impossibility of two directions, stay here and go there.

Peter had a vision three times. I only needed two visions, not three. I bumped into a person working with international students and he told me what he was doing. The next day I got a letter from a mission agency. One line popped out: "A life given to ministry to international students would be tremendously rewarding." God, are you trying to tell me something? Stay home, and minister to the world I am bringing to you. Foreign missions at home!

During the seminary's summer break, I worked as a volunteer with international students at a church in Atlanta. By the end of the summer, I had a great burden to share with the North American church the tremendous mission opportunity of reaching the world in their neighborhood.

I took some international students out to a conference in Colorado Springs. The night before the conference ended, International Students, Incorporated (ISI), a ministry specializing in reaching international students, had a banquet. They said they were going to send a traveling team all across North America to share the vision with churches. When I heard that, I went back to the prayer room. I thought I was going to have a long night in prayer. As I began to sit down, the word of the Lord came into my mind: "Behold, I have set before you an open door which no man can shut." I said, "Thank you, Lord!"

The next day I went in and talked to the president and he invited me to join the special traveling team. So I traveled across North America sharing the vision, then went back to seminary. I knew God was leading me into missions, and I wanted to go to a school that had the best menu of courses in missions. For me, it was Fuller School of World Mission, at that time. I wrote a paper on "Ministry to Iranians" in 1978. There were seventy thousand Iranian students in the United States. The next largest group was thirty-five thousand from Taiwan. Then, boom! We heard shots as Americans were taken hostage in Tehran. And I said, "Lord, let your church show your love and forgiveness to these seventy thousand Iranian students over here!" I still don't know how we did.

The last paragraph of that paper I wrote in seminary in the winter of 1979 was the following:

> In thirty years, the foreign field of international students in the USA has grown from less than thirty thousand to nearly 300,000. While the increase of the international student foreign field has grown substantially, the increase in laborers in international student ministries has grown moderately. During this next decade, may God grant a great awakening in response to the validity, vision, and mission of reaching international students in the United States.

I want to give you an update. There are now over 500,000 international students. God has answered the prayer for a great awakening. In 1981, a couple years after that was written, the Association of Christian Ministries to International Students was formed. And God is causing churches, parachurch ministries, denominations, and individuals to catch the vision of reaching the foreigners in our midst.

It is lovely to see how God works with us. And who are we? We are dust. I don't forget that I am a marred clay vessel. God doesn't let me forget that he is the potter. But, praise the Lord, we will all sing "Have Thine Own Way" together some day.

FREY: In seminary a few years ago, a classmate asked, "What major things do we, as North Americans, miss when we read the New Testament?"

The instructor didn't miss a beat. He said, "Hospitality!" Hospitality is a major New Testament doctrine, and North Americans are blind to it.

It is also an Old Testament doctrine. Leviticus 19:33 says,

> When a stranger sojourns with you in your land, you shall do him no wrong. The stranger who sojourns with you shall be to you as the native among you, and you shall love him as yourself; for you were strangers in the land of Egypt: I am the Lord your God.

Don't harm the stranger in your midst. America is probably about to go through another wave of xenophobia. That's a Greek word which means fear of foreigners. We've done it before. We feared the native Americans, and we need to repent. We exterminated people right and left, out of fear. We have on many occasions been blessed by people coming to this land, and we have tried to throw them back out—Hispanics, Japanese, Chinese. This is not the first time that people have come to our country in great waves. Even some of us who are Irish were not well received. The Bible, however, says treat them like your own people. And what does that mean? Love them like yourself! Then the Bible gives the reason why: Do not ever forget that you were strangers in a strange land, that I saved you. You were strangers.

I don't know if you have ever been a stranger. I was fortunate enough to be a part of a family that was thrown out of a Latin American country and had nowhere to go. I am so thankful to the people who showed hospitality and took us in.

There are 500,000 international students, and there are probably three million immigrants in the USA. Nearly a million immigrants a year come legally to this country from many parts of the world. Some of them are going to want to go to our homes. Hospitality.

Of those 500,000 students who come for a short time, three years, five years, six years, or more, eighty percent of them never see the inside of one of our homes. Eighty percent of them do not meet an American anywhere except perhaps standing in line for a driver's license, or in a classroom where the teacher lectures like I am doing here. God is bringing the world to our doorstep, and He wants us to respond. Now, we are going to make a lot of mistakes. Stepping over cultural barriers, you do stupid things. You say things that you discover later you should not have said. But there is no gain in any enterprise without taking a risk! Let's make some new mistakes! Step out! Find creative ways to reach internationals in our midst.

I met a woman recently who wants to do international student ministry. She works with a campus ministry among your average North Americans. She said the leaders gather together and the campus minister has someone who will give a testimony. That individual will get up and say, "I came in and met Jesus Christ and I gave my life to him!" The person working with internationals will say, "Well, we had a really good potluck, and I had some interesting conversations. It just doesn't sound like a whole lot. We sort of feel bad."

But Jesus started and ended his ministry at potlucks. I want to encourage and challenge you in your hospitality. I want to challenge you, before this year is out, to have invited someone from another land to have dinner in your home. That's all. You don't know where that will lead. You never know.

My friend's family has a woman from China living with them. My wife called me since I have been here to tell me that a Brazilian couple is in-between apartments and is moving their furniture into our garage. You don't know where that will lead. But God will bless you mightily.

GOOD NEWS FOR THE URBAN POOR

The Rev. Antoine (Tony) Campbell

I am going to talk a bit about mission in America, about reaching out to people in our neighborhoods, in our communities. I want to begin by talking about a premier missionary in America, Martin Luther King, Jr. I remember Martin said that there had been many threats on his life, but he was not worried, because he had been to the mountain top, and he had seen the promised land. He wanted the people to know that, as people, they were going to get to the promised land. He might not get there with them, but the people would get there. So he said, "I have no worry, I am not fearing any man, because mine eyes have seen the glory of the coming of the Lord." The next day, he died.

King could make that promise to us as a nation, not based on history, but based on the strength of events that happened two thousand years ago. In the cool of the morning, the women disciples were the only ones who came to the tomb. They came looking for the end of a ministry, but instead they found the beginning. They discovered a new call and a new purpose. They moved from being disciples to being the first evangelists and apostles. They found their reason for living, and our reason for living: to share the Good News that Christ is risen, Jesus is alive, to tell a world that is starving for love and mercy that God loves, cares, redeems, restores and gives us—not just to everlasting life—but wholeness of life in this world. This message frees us to be new people, peculiar people, people who live in contrast to the world.

Bishop Allison used to tell a story about a young alcoholic in a rehabilitation center who felt as if he could not be forgiven. Nobody could reach him and he was about to be expelled. Before someone could be sent away from the center, they were required to have an interview with the director. When the director sat down with the young man, the young man began to break down and confess. What the young man didn't know was that the director had also been a recovering alcoholic who had pulled his life together. The young man told the director, "I have destroyed my family, I have lost my job, and I think I have just drunk too much liquor in my life for God to forgive me." The director looked at the young man and said, "Son, I have lost three families, and I have lost more jobs that I can count. I have spilled more liquor on my shoes than you can drink in your whole life, and still God has saved me!"

Whenever we share the love of Christ, we become evangelists. I remember, as a young boy growing up, visiting my grandmother and my aunt. Sometimes I would sit in the kitchen as they were cooking, and they would sing an old hymn. They would sing, "I'm coming up on the rough side of the mountain, but I'm holding onto God's strong hand. I'm coming up on the rough side of the mountain, but God is leading me home. I'm coming up." They would keep singing that song in the kitchen, and sometimes they would go over to a corner and begin to pray. It was my grandmother and my aunt who taught me how to pray.

It is important that we share this love, because it is the command of Christ in the Great Commission. It is also important because, in our world, so many people still come to the tomb of Jesus Christ, like Martha and Mary and Johanna, looking for death instead of life. So many who stare at the cross and at the tomb see, not life, but only despair. Look at the statistics. Between the 1970s and the 1980s, the Presbyterians, the Methodists, the Lutherans, the Church of Christ, and the Episcopalians, all lost about three million members. Between 1960 and 1980, together we lost ten thousand congregations. That is coming up on the rough side of the mountain!

Our children in America are dying. In America, there are fourteen million children living in poverty. Fifty-five percent of those children live in female-headed households. One in four of our homeless in America are children. Over 100,000 children will go to bed tonight without a home. Twelve percent of all children have no health coverage. Thirty percent of all first graders do not graduate from college. Fifty-one percent of all African-American males do not graduate from high school and

cost our society over $250 billion each year in lost salaries and taxes. To-
day there are more African-American males in prison than there are in
our colleges.

I remember visiting in a prison for teenagers where I saw a young,
pretty girl with blonde hair and blue eyes. I couldn't understand why she
was in this prison. As the group went by, I went in to talk with her. She
rolled up her sleeve, and I saw how she had lacerated her arm. She told
me that she tried to kill herself because she had been sexually and physically abused by both parents. She didn't think life was worth living. She
said, "Reverend, my parents don't want me. My teachers don't want me.
The prison guards in here don't want me." Then she said something that
chilled my soul. She looked at me and said, "Reverend, even your God
doesn't want me." My brothers and sisters in Christ, that is coming up on
the rough side of the mountain!

As the people of God, we are called to reach out to people with
hurts and needs. In a football game, people pay to see what a team is going to do when they hike the ball. They know that teams have to huddle
together. They want to see what the team is going to do when it's actually time to play on the field. The world knows that the church has to huddle, that we have to gather together in worship and conference. What the
world wants to know is, what we are going to do Monday through Saturday, when we are faced with sin and sickness, death and injustice? Will
we have the courage to be evangelists?

All too often, when we in the church have been called to face the
pain in the world, we have been reluctant to trust God and proclaim a
message of life and hope. The church is afraid of mission and evangelism
because we have lost our faith in the God who can redeem and restore.

I have a friend who regularly rode on a train. At every stop he
would cover his eyes. He did this for three or four stops on the subway in
New York, so I asked him why. He said, "When I was growing up, my
mother told me that whenever I saw a woman come on a train or bus, I
was supposed to get up and give her my seat. So if I close my eyes when
women get on, I don't see them and I don't have to get up." Well, too often, our church has been like that!

We had an unchurched neighbor who was going through a painful
divorce. Instead of inviting him to the church, we just covered our eyes.
We saw the homeless people down the street and instead of reaching out
to them, we just covered our eyes. When we saw the child who needed to
grow up in a Christian place, we just covered our eyes. When we saw the
foreign student next door to us, we just covered our eyes. Helen Keller
was asked if there was anything more terrible in life than being blind and
not able to see. Her response was that having sight and being unable to

see was worse. We must see again as Christian people. We must believe again in the God who is able to bring Jesus back to life. I don't know about you, my brothers and sisters, but I believe that if Jesus can rise from the dead, then he can handle any hurt or difficulty we might face in this life.

In my little church in Pawleys Island, South Carolina, when we were hit by the devastation of Hurricane Hugo and we didn't know where to turn, God got involved in our lives. The first thing we did was to gather twelve people and we worshipped. Within two days we were serving 2000 meals a day. We were feeding an entire town! Six years later, we had rebuilt over 3000 homes in that community. We had brought the hope of Christ.

As a young man, I hated South Carolina. My parents are from South Carolina. As a six-year-old, I went to drink from a water fountain, and as I bent down, a man grabbed me by the back of the neck and shook me. He said, "Hey, Nigger, you go drink in the back." He pushed me and I saw my father with tears in his eyes, a grown man who couldn't to anything to protect his son. But, my brothers and sisters in Christ, from Selma to Memphis to Montgomery, black and white people marched together and died together because they had the faith and the courage to believe in a dream. Today we can live together, worship together, and drink water from the same fountain.

If God can change the South, then God can restore the hope that our nation needs. It is with this faith that we must face our future.

An old farmer had two mules, Willing and Able. Willing was willing, but he wasn't able. Able was able, but he wasn't willing. In our churches, we have too many who are willing, but they aren't able. We have people who are able, but they are not willing. The task of the church is to take those people who are willing and give them skills so that they will be able. We must convict the hearts of those people who are able so they will be willing to be evangelists. We must become reckless for Christ.

I had a good friend who was dying of cancer. When Henry went to the University of South Carolina, he was told that he was too small to start as a fullback, or even play football for the University of South Carolina. Henry just kept plugging away. By his senior year, he was a starting fullback on the football team. The day he died, his wife called for me to come at 5 o'clock in the morning. She sat on one side of the bed, and I sat on the other. I was holding Henry's hand. I could tell he was in pain, and he was breathing his last. He looked at me and said, "Tony, I don't want people to worry about me. Because, Tony, there are people who said that I couldn't make the football team at the University of South

Carolina, and I surely couldn't start. But, Tony, there is no quit in me. I want to tell you something else. There is no quit in my God, so I am not afraid."

My brothers and sisters in Christ, I am not afraid today for our church, nor am I afraid for the world because, like Henry, I know that there is no quit in Christ, and therefore there is no quit in his Body. Like Henry and Martin, I am not afraid, because we as people have been to the mountain top, and we have seen the promised land. We have been to the tomb of Christ, and we have witnessed his glory and resurrection. So, I am not afraid, because our eyes on this day have seen the glory of the coming of the Lord, and we will share in that glory.

5

Build the Arbor: Develop Mission-Minded Parishes

LIGHTING A FIRE FOR MISSIONS IN YOUR PARISH

Mr. Tom Telford

I spend three nights a week visiting churches all over America, helping them with their mission programs. We have come to a point where mission is on a decline in America in many, many churches. I am convinced that the church has many responsibilities, but only one mission: the evangelization and discipling of the nations.

It starts in Genesis 12:1-3, with the Abrahamic covenant.

> The Lord said to Abram, "Leave your country, your people, and your father's household and go to the land I will show you. I will make you into a great nation and I will bless you; I will make your name great, and you will be a blessing. I will bless those who bless you, and whoever curses you I will curse; and all peoples on earth will be blessed through you" (NIV).

Then there is Genesis 22:15-18:

> The angel of the Lord called to Abraham from heaven a second time and said, "I swear by myself, declares the Lord, that because you have done this and have not withheld your son, your only son, I will surely bless you and make your descendants as numerous as the stars in the sky and as the sand on the seashore. Your descendants will take possession of the cities of their enemies, and through your offspring, all nations on the earth will be blessed, because you have obeyed me."

I am amazed that even though I grew up in a home where we studied God's Word, I never grasped the mission concept in the Old Testament! Psalm 67 says this:

> May God be gracious to us and bless us
> and make his face to shine upon us;
> that your ways may be known on the earth,
> your salvation among all nations.
> May the peoples praise you, O God;
> may all the peoples praise you.
> May the nations be glad and sing for joy,
> for you rule the peoples justly
> and guide the nations of the earth.
> May the peoples praise you, O God;
> may all the peoples praise you.
> Then the land will yield its harvest,
> and God, our God, will bless us.
> God will bless us
> and all the ends of the earth will fear him (NIV).

There are still somewhere in the neighborhood of a billion-and-a-half to two billion people who have never heard the gospel once!

There are four problems you are going to face in going to your churches and doing mission effectively. The first one is the common perception that mission is peripheral to Christianity. Lots of people just think of mission as a program in the church when it is the central theme of the church.

The second problem is the ineffectiveness of mission enthusiasts—you and I—in relating mission to contemporary audiences. I just heard a report from the leading denominational mission and faith mission agencies that said that eighty-five percent of the money given to world evangelization is given by people ages fifty-five and older. We must become more effective in communicating mission to younger people!

The third problem is in the nature of pastoral ministry that tends to focus on local needs. Some of us are near-sighted when it comes to looking at the world.

The last problem is one of the influence of the North American culture on the evangelical church. The North American culture wants everything coming in, and mission is God giving out of himself. Even in our leadership, we want to keep the best things for us, and God wants the best given away. The model of that is found in Acts 13, at the church in Antioch, where they gave their leadership, Paul and Barnabas, to go on mission. Think about it.

I teach at a couple of Bible colleges and seminaries. At one of the schools in the South, at Columbia, I asked my students to write a paper on "Your Church and Mission and What You Think of It." One young man wrote this:

> It is clear that our church is in the midst of a period based on a philosophy of isolation. The parallel to the situation the United States found itself in back in 1941 is striking. We've gone through a very profitable and growing period in our church, followed by a couple of leaner years as well. The church, at the beginning, grew because it reached out to people, especially families, and it emphasized a strong discipleship program, prayer and fasting, and sacrificial Christian living. This is the church I grew to love and appreciate very much. As time went by we grew faster than our facilities could handle. We began looking inward, wondering how to build a building and pay a staff that would suit our ever growing needs. I believe we began to look more at how to serve each other in the church rather than in reaching out from the church. There were isolated pockets of outreach but nothing was ever emphasized with the congregation as a whole. We found ourselves with a church full of good, godly people who were increasingly preoccupied with what was going on in their own lives and circumstances. Not only that, in the process of enjoying each other's fellowship, we gradually forgot about a world out there that

was lost and being attacked and being taken over by the enemy.

I think that's typical in many churches.

There are five prerequisites for mission that we must realize in our churches. The first is that we have one purpose. Our church needs a unified vision for discipling the nations. If we intend to reach the world, we should select and design our church programs and activities to equip us for this purpose. Most people have a very poor understanding of why the church exists. Do your people understand that? Do they have down pat that the church is here, not for their benefit, but for the benefit of reaching the world? That's scriptural and we need people who have a vision for seeing the world reached for Jesus Christ. Does your church have a good purpose statement, a good mission statement? It's very interesting to me today that fast food chains and businesses are now printing their mission statements. Have you seen some of those on the wall? Do people have a clear understanding of why your church exists?

The second thing we must realize is that the key to a mission church is prayer. How much time does your church spend praying? E.M. Bounds, one of the great writers on prayer, made this statement: "A local church can develop fantastic programs, channel hundreds of thousands of dollars into world missions, yet if it is not first a praying church, its efforts and dollars are in vain." He goes on to say, "The reason is simple: God will not share His glory with anyone. He alone deserves it and the prayerless efforts on the part of a local church indicate an independent spirit—one that does not acknowledge that God, alone, is in charge."*

A number of years ago I was teaching at a conference, and in the course of the day I found myself sneaking into the library to lay down and just get off my feet and have a little rest. I went into the library, and there was a woman in there on her knees praying. She would mention someone's name and then ask God to call them into mission and into his ministry. She repeated that prayer over and over again—it went on for twenty or twenty-five minutes. She happened to be the mission chairperson in a large church in New England. When she got done I said to her, "Betty, what have you been doing in here for the last thirty minutes?" She said, "Tom, when I became the mission chairperson of our church, I was challenged to pray for every child in the Sunday School between the

---

*E. M. Bounds, *The Complete Works of E.M. Bounds on Prayer* (Grand Rapids, MI: Baker Book House, 1990).

ages of seven and seventeen." She said, "I've done that for twenty-five years." I said to Betty, "What has happened as a result of your prayers for twenty-five years?" She said, "We've seen 227 young people from our church become full-time career missionaries."

I wonder how many parishes across America have some dear women who are doing that? One of the reasons that I am in the ministry today is because I came from a church where people prayed for me, even when I wasn't going the right way. We need people who are going to pray that God chooses people from our congregation and thrusts them out into mission all over the world. We need to model that. We are not going to go anywhere without prayer. There is a war going on out there and prayer is where we are going to win the battles. Jim Elliot, that great missionary martyred by the Auca Indians said this, "The saint that advances on his knees never retreats."

Thirdly, we need a strategy. We need to give priority to unevangelized areas, to church planting and leadership development. We are at the point where the missiologists tell us that we can reach the world by the year 2000. We are not going to do that unless we develop a strategy for reaching the people groups of the world. I think one of the keys to having a successful mission program in a church is to personalize it. I like the statement that says, "Tell me and I will forget, teach me and I will learn, involve me and I will understand."

There is a church mission conference going on in New England right now. They have adopted a hidden people group in a remote part of Africa. They now have fifty-eight percent of the people in that church praying for the Tuareg people. They have identified three additional people who want to go there. They have found a man who is preparing in a college, and they are taking on some of his support. Their whole church is starting to pray for those people.

We need to personalize mission. In many denominations today, mission giving is going down because people will not give to a fund anymore. Churches do not become excited until they see sons and daughters from their own church go marching off into mission. Is your church a sending church? I think short-term mission is one of the ways that we are going to get lots of people turned on to career mission. Send them out for vision trips, vacations with a purpose, whatever, but let them get to see the world as God sees the world. By the way, I would recommend that we also send our pastors out. We need to send every pastor of every church in America overseas for two to three weeks.

I think we are going to have to change our lifestyle. Someone said a few years ago that in the sixties and seventies we gave out of a great affluence to world mission, and in the nineties we are going to have to give out of great sacrifice. Are we willing to sacrifice to reach the Muslim world, the Hindu world, and to reach out to China? It is going to cost us something financially.

Scott Wesley Brown sings this song:

> Things upon a mantle, things on every shelf, things that others gave me, things I gave myself; things I've stored in boxes that don't mean much anymore, old magazines and memories behind the attic door. Things on hooks and hangers, things on ropes and rings, things I guard that bind me to the pettiness of things. Am I like the rich young ruler, ruled by all I own? If Jesus came and asked me, could I leave them all alone? Oh, Lord, I look to heaven beyond the veil of time, to gain eternal insights that nothing's really mine. And only ask for daily bread and all that contentment brings, to find freedom as you're serving in the midst of all these things. For discarded in the junk yards, rusting in the rain, lie things that took the finest years of lifetimes to obtain. And whistling through these tombstones the hollow breezes sing, a song of dreams surrendered to the tyranny of things.*

About three weeks ago I was in a church where a young woman had been called to the mission field. She had been properly trained. Because the church was lacking in funds, she was about to postpone her trip. The youth pastor stood up in front of 600 people and said, "You know, if we really love Mary and we know she is qualified to go, I have a proposal to make to all of you—a way to get her to the field immediately." (She needed $30,000.) He said, "If everyone in this congregation would stop giving $32 a month to cable television, which is rotten anyway, and send that money to her mission agency, she could probably go." Then he said this, "How many people are willing to do that?" Approximately forty percent of the congregation came up with $14,000 above the $22,000 offering they had taken in church for the regular budget! There is a biblical principle: you cannot outgive God when you assist him in reaching the

---

*Scott Wesley Brown, "The Tyranny of Things."

world. If the people in your church are in the doldrums and not doing mission, get them doing mission—they will come out of the doldrums!

Lifestyle is an issue. I think of the young woman who coordinates a Perspectives class in New England. She was driving me to the train station one night. She had been overseas as a short term missionary, and she apparently had an experience that was not too good. I said, "Patty, what happened?" She said, "Well, I just found out that I just could not serve in another culture—just couldn't do it. But," she said as we rode to the station, with tears streaming down her face, "my roommate went overseas, and she definitely has cross-cultural missionary ability given to her by God." She said, "Her problem is that she has about eight or nine thousand dollars' worth of college loans. So you know what I decided to do after praying about it? I went down and took out a loan from the bank and I'm going to pay off my roommate's loan, so she can go to the mission field." Patty is the kind of person that we need involved in mission!

I often think that mission funding is why God has given many of us good salaries. Maybe your job is being the person that funds someone else to go. These are the things that are the marks of a mission-minded church and these are the marks of world Christians.

Lastly, I think we need to spread the vision. Your denomination will not move ahead in mission unless you begin getting your church turned on, but it doesn't stop there. Are you willing to take on four or five other congregations and help them become turned on to mission? That's mobilization. Your church alone is not going to reach the world for Jesus Christ. That's what the Association of Church Mission Committees is about—advancing churches in mission commitment. We encourage churches to mobilize other churches. We would like to see six thousand churches mobilized and moving out in mission by the year 2000. We believe that can happen.

If you are going to have a mission committee, identify and recruit committee members. Who are the mission-interested people in your church? I would suggest that you recruit those people; don't ask for volunteers. In the New Testament, the Lord never had in his circle of relationships a volunteer—he recruited people. Recruit people with a deep concern for the church, a close relationship with Jesus Christ, an interest in evangelism, and a burden for their neighbors. Most importantly, find people who want to pray.

When recruiting, it is important to offer specific assignments to prospective committee members. When you oversee the annual mission conference, provide a written job description for the mission committee.

During a typical term of service, members of the mission committee should be expected to maintain a personal walk with the Lord, including the practice of spiritual disciplines of prayer and Bible study, attend the meetings, and be involved in the committee's mission education efforts. The average Christian is illiterate when it comes to world mission, so they need to be trained and educated if they are going to make important committee decisions.

You know that God has brought the mission field to us today. For instance, I live in a very rural community outside Philadelphia. In Henning's Market where my wife and I shop, we often see Muslims. In the Philadelphia area we now have fifteen mosques within a ten-mile radius of City Hall. Could you lead a Muslim to Jesus Christ? We have that opportunity right here in this country, so education is very, very important.

Attend one training event. Host a Mission Awareness Seminar at your parish, pray over it and see who comes. Maybe that is where you start your missions committee. I assisted one little church in putting together a mission conference, and then I watched that church grow every year. Their mission budget is now $40,000, with 120 people. They have adopted a hidden people group, they have hosted the Perspectives course, they have sent at least fifteen to eighteen of their young people on short term mission trips, and their pastor has gone on two overseas trips. They hold a mission conference every year for all the churches in their area. We need people who are willing to fight some battles to get the mission program in their church going and then to help another five churches do the same.

Here are some of the other job requirements for the mission committee: correspond quarterly with each one of the church missionaries and attend educational seminars. A good training program for your mission committee is a Perspectives course—it is offered all over the country. *Mission Frontiers* magazine lists locations for Perspectives courses. Committee members should also serve on a subcommittee. In all, involvement on a mission committee requires approximately ten hours per month.

Here is what makes up a good mission committee meeting: fifteen minutes of worship because mission is God's business, and at least a half hour of education. Study a book together, or *World Pulse,* or just discuss the issues in mission. Finally, divide into subcommittees; and then go home.

Have one night a month where you just gather and pray for the world. A number of committees list all the countries mentioned on the

6:00 news and pray for each one. This is a creative tool for educating the church.

There needs to be a mission emphasis in churches fifty-two weeks a year. One way to do this is to start a weekly three-minute long "spot" on mission at your Sunday morning service to inform people about what is going on in the world. Call it a "Moment for Mission" or "Focus on the World."

One of the best ways to reach young couples is through their children via the "trickle-up" effect. Get their kids turned on to mission. I got my interest in mission when I was about seven years old. Every night before bed, my mother used to read stories to me about William Carey, Hudson Taylor, and Adoniram Judson. Mission is exciting! We have to get that excitement back into our churches and mission committees.

A person named Gordon Aeschliman wrote something that summarizes how we should view the world and ourselves as "world Christians."

> We are world Christians; we put God's love for all people first. No race is superior to another; no government is more loved than another. No country is dearer than another. We don't put our nation's economy before God's economy. He tells us to seek first His kingdom; He will then meet our needs. We are driven to action daily with the knowledge that two billion people do not know our Savior. Our passion in life, our unquenchable desire, is to take God's love to them. No task is too small for us; all that limits us is our unwillingness to believe God can enable us to do it. We are sold out to Jesus Christ, our Savior and Lord. Nothing less. It costs everything to be His disciple. Don't give us blessings, give us grace to be unquestionably obedient to Your very last command and desire. Don't give us status—give us a place to serve. Don't give us a mansion to live in—give us a spring board to take God's love to the whole world. Don't give us things for our use—use us. Don't give us good jobs— put us to work. Don't give us comfort—command us. Don't give us pleasure—give us perspective. Don't give us entertainment—enable us. Our great joy in life is in pleasing our Lord and there is no other joy comparable.*

---

*Gordon Aeschliman, *Trends: The Changes Affecting Christians Everywhere* (Downers Grove, IL: InterVarsity Press, 1990).

I am more and more convinced that our ultimate significance is found in God. Are you part of God's global cause? We face a humanity too precious to neglect. We know the remedy of the ills of the world which is too wonderful to withhold. We have a Christ who is too glorious to hide.

NUTS AND BOLTS OF DEVELOPING A FRUITFUL MISSION COMMITTEE

Mr. Tom Telford

A missions committee can have fun learning about the world. That's the idea of the following quiz. You can create entertaining quizzes relating to missions, adding learning points that will educate the committee.

Question #1: The population of what country will exceed that of China in the next century?

Answer: India. Demographers predict that by the year 2000, India's population will exceed that of China because the Chinese are practicing birth control, while Indians are not. We don't hear much about India.

Question #2: Name five members of the Commonwealth of Independent States.

Answer: Russia, Ukraine, Georgia, Belarus, and all those with "stan" on the end of them; Kazakstan, Turkmenistan, and all of those. When the communist government was overthrown, all these countries started. This question is important because we used to smuggle Bibles into these countries. Now you could drive a tractor-trailer load, and it would not be enough. A study of the history of missions reveals that whenever there has been an overthrow of government, a window opens for only a couple of years, then it often closes back up or reverts. So we need to take advantage of that!

Question #3: Which continent is the least populated?

Answer: Antarctica. That's not a good investment for missions, unless you are interested in reaching penguins!

Question #4: Name the top three cities of the world based on population expected by the year 2000.

Answer: By the year 2000, the biggest city in the world will be Mexico City, with 32-34 million people. Next will be Tokyo, and the third one will be São Paulo.

The point of this question is that urbanization is the big change in missions. Before long over fifty percent of the world is going to live in an urban setting, not in jungles. I went to Mexico City on a missions trip, and all the ministry was done open-air with microphones, with evangelism on the streets. The people were trained by an organization called "Open Air Campaigners." That's the wave of the future, with most missionaries living in high-rise apartments. The people at most of our mission agencies in this country say that for many years, most of our missionaries have come from rural areas. It is difficult for rural people to adapt to seventeen-story buildings.

Question #5: Name six countries with "z" in their name.

Answer: Tanzania, Zambia, Zaire, Zimbabwe, Switzerland, Brazil, Swaziland. One of the weaknesses of most of us is that we know very little about geography. God says he loves the whole world, so you and I should know something about the world. He loves the people in downtown Hong Kong as much as us. That's difficult for us as Americans, isn't it? God loves the world equally. That means you and I have to love the whole world equally. We can't be prejudiced and love Jesus Christ.

Question #6: Name the top four Muslim countries in the world, based on population.

Answer: Bangladesh, India, Indonesia and Pakistan. Most people say "Turkey," because we hear Turkey often on the news, but the masses are in the other four countries.

That's my quiz. Make up some mission quizzes, and see how you can get interest up and missions conversations going.

The Three Dimensions of a Local Church

Our churches need three dimensions. The first one is upward: worship. The second one is inward: edification. The third one is outward: mission. The problem is that most churches just do upward and inward, never outward. For some it is all worship, but true worship should force us outward. If all you do is worship God, you are going to become an obese Christian. There's a balance with worship, edification and mission. My contention is that the toughest one for us to do in America today is mission, the outward part.

Purpose statements are important. One church I know has this as their vision statement: "Communicate the gospel message to every person if God gives an open door, beginning in our Jerusalem." Churches that are doing missions very well are churches that have people being won to Christ right in their own church. I was in one church that had a candle in the front of the sanctuary. The pastor said, "Every time someone in our church leads someone to Jesus Christ, we light the candle the next Sunday." This church is willing to communicate the gospel message where they are, in their own Jerusalem. They are beginning there and extending out worldwide through missions outreach. The Great Commission should be at the core of every church's activities with worship and nurture. Does it lead to fulfilling the Great Commission? The idea of a soup kitchen is not just to feed street people, but give them the gospel while you are feeding them. That fits. The purpose of vacation Bible school is to reach children in the neighborhood who have never been exposed to Jesus Christ. That fits. Look at every church ministry in that light.

Peter Drucker, a Christian businessman, who writes a lot of business books says this: "The mission of the organization has to be clear enough and big enough to provide a common vision. The goals that embody it have to be clear, public and constantly reaffirmed."

Every so often the leader of a rapidly growing megachurch says, "I am not going to preach this morning. I'm just going to tell you what our goals for this church are and where we are headed and what we are doing, so everybody knows." He is constantly reaffirming their purpose. We wouldn't have the hard job of selling missions if we had done that more.

Calling and Mentoring the Missions Committee

Selecting and training the members of the missions committee is crucial since your church's mission outreach will never move beyond where your leaders are at any given point in time. That is why the selection process should not include an open call for volunteers. Jesus never asked for volunteers. When you ask for volunteers, sometimes you get more than you bargain for. You often get people that are going to take you the wrong way. I'm convinced the devil has people in every church that are going to take you away from where you want to go. How did Jesus recruit and select people? He prayed, sought out those men, and conversed with them.

One way Jesus trained was through mentoring, going alongside someone. When I left the first church I was in, the missions program fell apart. With the second church, someone told me to find someone and pour my heart into them, duplicate myself. I selected a young man, took him to conferences, trained him, and now he's doing a much better job than I ever did at that church.

We need to develop people who will become better than us. One man who wrote a book on mentoring says that most of us want to mentor people who will never become better than we are. I thought about the first time I went back to my church to a missions conference. I saw the guy that I mentored on the platform, doing what I did. I was jealous; that's sinful human nature coming out.

There's a great story about General Marshall. When Roosevelt realized there was going to be another war and all his generals were leaving, he knew he needed someone to discover and mentor all the young men who would lead in the next war. Marshall wanted to lead the army, but Roosevelt wanted him to search the military schools and army bases for the young leaders. So Marshall discovered and trained them, and he recorded the name of each one in his little black book. When World War II was over, an Associated Press correspondent said to Marshall, "There's a story that these soldiers tell about your black book. Can you tell me the names that are in that book? I won't print it, I just want to know if it's true." Marshall shared his black book, and the names included General Eisenhower and Omar Bradley. Who really was responsible for winning the war? I honestly think it was the man who mentored those people. Most of us who are concerned with missions are getting a little old. Are we willing to train someone else with our hearts?

Qualifications for Membership

There are qualities, or even character traits that committee members need. 1) A Healthy Spiritual Life: The missions committee is not a place to win people for Christ. If they are going to make decisions concerning church finances in your church and who is going to the mission field, they need to be mature Christians. Mature Christians have a love for the world, an interest in missions and a desire to learn more. When I tell mission committee members they should read at least three missions books a year, I'm amazed at how many of them say they can't. Well, then, they shouldn't be on a missions committee! Missions is changing so rapidly; committee members are going to have to learn. They also need to be people open to change, because missions is changing very rapidly. When my father was ninety-two, he said that the sign of a mature Christian is the willingness to accept change.

2) A Deep Concern for the Lost: In 1 Peter it says, "He is not willing that any should perish." In Acts, it says that people are not going to

get into heaven unless they have made a confession of Jesus Christ. One reason why missions isn't popular is that we have preached love and grace exclusively in our churches. We don't preach a God of justice and the existence of hell. We need people with a deep concern for the lost.

David Bryant heads up the Concert of Prayer Movement in this country. If you go to his house and eat supper there, one of the things they do before they eat dessert every night, is they play little games about countries of the world, little quizzes. He has about four or five children, he has adopted a couple of children from other countries, and they play a game where they give you a card with a country on it, and you have to guess the capitol of that country or you don't get dessert. And then they pray for them. He's got kids aged five, seven, eight and nine; they pick up some country and they name the capitols of these countries and then they pray for them. Those kids will never be prejudiced. We need to model something, and I think as Christians, we need to model a concern for the lost of the world because our God is a missionary God.

3) A Sense of Humor: A sense of humor is important, because we all make mistakes—even on missions committees.

4) A Willingness to Go: One missions committee I chaired decided we would add some younger members. I went to a girl in our church who was very creative and said, "Joyce, how about coming on the missions committee and becoming an intern? You are a lot of fun, and you've been to Bible college." She said, "Tom, that is the last committee I would ever want to be on. Number one, I don't have any desire or concern for missions at all. Number two, I can't stand you." So I said, "Joyce, you might not like me, but I want to tell you that, as a Christian, how can you say you don't like missions? What did they teach in that Bible school you went to?" She argued until I just gave up. But before I left, I said, "Joyce, you're on my prayer list."

About three weeks later, Joyce followed me into the church office and said, "Tom, I am willing to become an intern. Send me the books." She apologized and came to the missions committee. Within one year, she said, "Tom, God is calling me to the mission field." That was nine years ago. She has taught at Faith Academy in the Philippines for seven years.

I have watched four people on that missions committee quit jobs and go off on missions. Are you willing to go if God calls you? If we get interested in missions, it's dangerous.

Training Strategies

We are woefully ignorant of missions in our culture, so we need training to be effective committee members. Here are ways to get members "up to speed."

1) *Perspectives Course:* This is a sixteen-week course that meets one night a week. It provides a life-changing overview of missions. It is offered around the country through the U.S. Center for World Missions.

2) *Conferences and Seminars:* Go to a number of different seminars, and buy some of the tapes from others that you can't attend. The Association of Church Mission Committees (ACMA) has a conference with thirty-one workshops basically geared for missions committee people. The Urbana Missions Convention held every three years in December will convey the excitement of missions.

3) *Reading Lists:* Make up a good reading list of books. Develop a good reading list. I would get a copy of the William Carey Catalog and find the list of missions books. Don Richardson's books *Peace Child* and *Lords of the Earth* are good. Thomas Hale has written three tremendous story-type books about Nepal and India. Greg Livingstone has written a great book *Planting Churches in Muslim Cities,* and Bill Sahl has written a book on how to win a Muslim to Christ. These books are educational and exciting!

4) *Missions Training Program* for the entire church. Do creative, attention-getting things about other cultures, history and mission activities. Bring different people in. Find out what other churches are doing. Get the whole church on board and interested.

5) *Vision Trips*: I think short term mission trips are very important. Look for sales and send people on "vision trips." We live behind such walls that we need to go and see how other people are living. It has a powerful effect on Americans.

6) *Retreats:* Many missions committees go away once a year, pray and lay out plans for the next year in missions. They get far more done. Missions committees normally meet at night, when they are all tired, trying to do business at 7:30 at night. If you are not good at planning and organizing, find a church member who does that for a living. For the last five years, a member who works as a consultant has come to our meetings to organize and prioritize our ideas.

Lessons in Leadership

Expect the best from people. Develop a climate in which to grow.

Have a written job description for everybody on the missions committee. Make sure meetings are fun and learning times. It's important to have an educational time. Be willing to take the blows and criticism that come with leadership. I think God was preparing me for what I am doing by being a baseball umpire and a bus driver. People are not always nice in church.

You also have to say no to many good things. You cannot do it all. The sign of a good missions church is that they don't say yes to everybody and everything. That's why we need a missions policy and strategy. It's not easy saying no to people, but we have to sometimes. Here are some other lessons I have learned about exciting positive leadership in a missions committee:

1) *Be Willing to Change Directions with God's Leading:* I got my church all excited about adopting the people group in Tanzania. Then Sue Jacobson came to my office and prayed with me because she felt called to mission work in China. After that first time I met with her, I put her in the pulpit on a Sunday morning to do the three-minute missions spot that I do. She did it on China. Now, my pastor is very protective of the time. If I go over three minutes, I hear about it. At three minutes, I heard my pastor lean over and say to her, "Keep going; say all you want." So I knew it was the Holy Spirit! We liked her so much that Sunday that the missions committee gave her the money for mission work in China. She came back and started recruiting people from our church for China. All of a sudden, Tanzania started getting more and more distant. That's been nine years ago. We now have six of our church people in China teaching English as a second language. When Sue went over there the second time, she stayed for two years. She taught American culture at Beijing University. She asked if she could teach religion since that's part of American culture. So she was able to teach the book of John as a religion course in Beijing University, and she was paid by the communist government! On the final exam, the last question was, "Will you accept Jesus Christ?" Four students accepted Christ. One wanted to come to the U.S. to go to school. I called my friend Tony Campolo and asked if he could get this young man a scholarship. He said, "You get him over here, and I'll give him a free scholarship." We got him here, and he stood in our pulpit and told how he had accepted Christ taking that exam from the girl in our church!

Now, in my church on Sunday mornings there are at least thirty-five to forty Chinese people always in the balcony. They have headsets through which the pastor's message is interpreted by volunteers in our church.

I wanted the church to go to Tanzania, but God wanted them to go to China. We can't always structure things the way we want.

2) *Build Relationships:* Relationships take time. A member of one missions committee I was leading was a parole officer for juveniles. He was really trying to be a witness on the job, but he was struggling. Often I would take off work and go to court with him. There is a relationship that has lasted for life. If you are a leader, you have to take time for relationships. A committee should become like a community, where you share each other's problems. You straighten those out, and then you do God's business of wrestling with the world.

3) *Give Credit Where Credit is Due:* Become a Barnabas, a "son of encouragement." That's a gift and the job of a leader.

4) *Share What You Have:* The most important thing that ACMC does is the Membership Manual. It lists every church that is a member of ACMC and their strengths. These churches are willing to share all that they are doing with any other church that phones them. The whole idea is mobilizing churches in missions.

Find a couple of churches in your neighborhood and just start praying for them. Then go and find out who the missions person is in their church and say, "Let's talk and share resources. This is what our church is doing in missions. What are you doing?" All of a sudden, you will see relationships being built. Maybe one of those churches could use some help. The only way we are going to see the world reached is by coming together.

MISSION IS THE GOLDEN CABLE THAT HOLDS THE BIBLE TOGETHER

The Rev. Walter Hannum

I spent twenty years in the villages of Alaska. One of the things I did there was train village men for ordained ministry. They were leaders in the community, but they had never been to school or had just a fourth grade education. Several of them knew no English, and I didn't know much about their language. Our textbooks were the Book of Common Prayer, the Bible, and a couple of hymnals. I learned that the New Testament is a missionary handbook. That was a great revelation to me. But I discovered when I studied at the Fuller School of World Mission that people for hundreds of years had known that; it's just been kept a secret. John Wesley said that reading the New Testament without being a missionary is like reading a book on swimming and never jumping into the pond. You don't know the full meaning of these things until you start to use them. The other thing I learned there was that the entire Bible is the story of God calling all the peoples of the earth back to himself. Mission is not a thread running through the Bible; it is the cable that holds the Bible together.

When you look at the Bible, let these words jump out at you: "nations," "all peoples," "all the families of the earth," and "Gentile." "Nations" is the word "ethne," which literally means every ethnic, linguistic, social, cultural group of people. Whenever you see the words "nations" or "Gentile," it's the same word, meaning those who aren't in the fold yet. You were either a Jew or a Gentile, or a barbarian. A "barbarian" meant a people without a written language. If you had a written language, then you were a Gentile. You were still garbage, but you were higher class [garbage]. The barbarian was just one step above being an animal in their eyes.

After Zacchaeus repented, Jesus said, "Today salvation has come to this house, because this man, too, is a son of Abraham. For the Son of Man came to seek and to save what was lost" (Luke 19:8-10). Another reason Jesus gave for his coming to earth is to preach the good news of the kingdom of God (Luke 4:43). God the Son is a missionary Savior crossing the cultural barrier of heaven and earth. The Holy Spirit is given to believers so we can be effective witnesses of Jesus in our Jerusalems, Judeas, Samarias, and to the ends of the earth (Acts 1:8). To my knowledge, this is the only reason given in the Bible for us to receive the Holy Spirit. The fruits and the gifts of the Spirit are to be used by us in making disciples of Jesus in all nations. God is a missionary God.

Why is God going to bless Abraham? So that Abraham would be a blessing. In no place in the Bible does God talk about blessing people because they have won brownie points. Every single person that God calls in the Bible, he calls to service. Nobody was called to privilege. The disciples had the privilege of being with Jesus, but the purpose was to empower them to go out and minister to a hurting, a dying world. He also had nice little things to say, such as, "I am going to bless you so you can endure crucifixion." My natural response to that is, Lord, if that's the way you treat your friends, no wonder you have so few. But it is a blessing that a person can be willing to make a sacrifice and be fulfilled in a life of service for Jesus and for the people. God blesses Abraham so Abraham himself will be a blessing. "The things that I give you, Abraham, you are to use these to improve the quality of life of other people. It is through you that in some way I will be able to reach them and pour my life into them as I have you, because you will go and tell them of me or witness to me. The skills that I give you, you can use to have other people's lives be fulfilled."

When I was in Alaska, I had to travel around to many villages and celebrate Communion. I learned very quickly that I could train an adult with a fourth-grade education to celebrate Communion, perform marriages, and have burial services. The purpose of preparing them was not for their benefit; it was, rather, so their villages could have pastors who could serve the sacraments, preach at Sunday services, and visit and counsel people. Also, we had a hospital in Fort Yukon, which served an area half the size of the state of Pennsylvania. The farther away you got from Fort Yukon, the smaller the villages. It was so hard to get to the hospital that they used to say in those places that if you were well enough to make the trip, you didn't need to go. So we began to train people to be health aides. They did some mighty things as the years went on. They were not blessed so that they could have better health. They were trained so they could be a blessing and all the villages could have better health. That's what a blessing is.

God told Abraham that this blessing was to continue until it reached every family on earth. In Alaska I was with Athabaskan Indians first, then I went to the Eskimos. There I discovered that they didn't like to be called "Eskimos." They wanted to be called "Inupeks." Eskimo means "raw meat eaters." "Inupek" means "the real people." I wasn't an anthropologist, but I began to ask questions, and I found out that they first used that word to differentiate between themselves and animals. They saw they were different from all the other animals, not only as a bear is different from a moose, but there was something different about people. The uniqueness was that people knew right from wrong. This is a phenomenal thing for pagan people to recognize. They would say, "We don't always act like Inupeks; at times we act like animals." That is exactly what St. Peter talks about in 2 Peter 2:12, how, without the grace of God, we are like irrational animals. The Inupek didn't get along at all with the Athabaskan Indians. They had one word for them and that was "Alikek," and one always had to say it with oomph. The word meant the "enemy" or the "bad guys." So everybody was either "Inupek," which meant they were to be treated morally, or enemies who could be rightfully killed, robbed, raped or destroyed.

There is only one way to become an Eskimo and that is through an Eskimo mother. It's very interesting to live among a group of people who feel superior to you, especially when you think you are coming to bring great things to them from the outside. I thought this was unique to Eskimos. I discovered at the Fuller School of World Mission that every tribal people in the world, including the tribes that you and I came from in Europe or wherever, have the same belief, that they are the ones who are truly human. The rest are in gradations according to how they compare to that particular culture. But that was not the picture the tribes of Jacob had. I don't know when the book of Genesis was written, but early in the literature of the Jews, they saw that all the people of the world were human. Adam was not a Jew, he represented mankind. Abraham was not a Jew; he became one. He was a pagan, a heathen, a Gentile that God redeemed for the benefit of all the peoples of the earth. It was a tremendous insight which had phenomenal implications.

Why is it that we are blessed? It is so we can be used to bless others. What blessings do we have that we can share? How can we make a real difference? Who needs to be blessed by us? Maybe we can also ask, in what ways can other peoples bless us? Sometimes mission becomes a two-way street of being fulfilled by others.

At the dedication of the temple, a high point of Israel's national and religious history, Solomon gives a tremendous prayer, quite a litany of things: that the people be forgiven, have good crops, and on and on and in the middle of this he prays, "Likewise when the foreigner, who is not of Thy people Israel, comes from a far country for the sake of Thy great name, and Thy mighty hand and Thy outstretched arm, when he comes and prays toward this house, hear Thou from heaven Thy dwelling place, and do according to all for which the foreigner calls to Thee; in order..." Why does he want the prayer answered? "For all the peoples"—all the ethnic groups—"that the peoples of the earth may know Thy name and fear [or reverence] Thee as do Thy people Israel, that they may know that this house which I have built is called by Thy name" (2 Chr 6:32-33). This is a phenomenal missionary concept!

The missionary strategy that the Jews had, and have today, is that Jerusalem was on the trade routes. It was a very strategic place for people traveling in that part of the world. Their idea was that the temple would be a place where the worship of God and the singing of Psalms would attract people. People would be drawn to this place. At the temple they had a large area set aside for the Court of the Gentiles where the Gentiles could hear and see what was happening. The idea behind this was missionary outreach, that any Gentile could come close and see if he or she wanted to become a Jew. One significant fact about the Jews is that anybody could become one! You could be a slave or free, man or woman, rich or poor, young or old. The convert had to do several things, however. If the convert was a man, he had to be circumcised. Also, they were to be baptized, which was symbolic of washing away all of the old cultural background. It was said that all the people who came in that way were orphans because they renounced their own family in order to be part of the family of Abraham. The convert had to learn a very different lifestyle.

Anyone could become a Jew. Of course, the tragic thing was that at the time of Jesus, they had turned the Court of the Gentiles into a place where they sold animals. That's what often happens to missions; the church starts putting on bazaars to raise money rather than reaching out to the nations. When the budget is tight, the first thing that usually goes is college work; and the second thing is mission.

Out of 150 Psalms, fifty of them contain missionary statements about going to other people. "May God be gracious to us and bless us and make His face to shine upon us that Thy way may be known upon earth, Thy saving power among all nations. Let the peoples praise Thee, O God, let all the peoples praise Thee" (Ps 67:1-3). The vision that the psalmist had, inspired by God, was that the day would come when every people on the earth would sing God's praise.

I want us to look at one reference from Isaiah which refers to when the Israelites were in captivity in Babylon. "It is too light a thing that you should be my servant to raise up the tribes of Jacob and to restore the preserved of Israel. I will give you as a light to the nations that my salvation may reach to the ends of the earth" (Is 49:6). To me that is the most pungent missionary statement in the Old Testament. God said it is too small a thing to be dreaming about political independence and the reestablishment of worship in the temple. It is going to happen, but that's not why you were called. I will give you as a light to the nations that my salvation may reach the ends of the earth. Can you imagine if at the next big presidential convention, the candidate said, "I really think it is too small a thing to worry about the economic security of the United States or our political independence. I think it is more important that we see that the Kingdom of God is extended throughout the world, that there be peace, justice, and human rights proclaimed in the name of Jesus Christ." Did a cheer go up? I believe Isaiah got bombarded by tomatoes! People don't like to hear that blessings are for other people, especially at their expense. Can you imagine the Presiding Bishop at the next General Convention saying, "God is not pouring out his Spirit to renew our church, but so that we can go out as his ambassadors to renew the world. You are empowered for a purpose. Not so you can have better parishes, but so the parishes can be better launching pads for mission. The missionary movement throughout the world is far more important than the survival or renewal of the Episcopal Church."

Daniel had a dream in which

> there before me was one like a son of man, coming with the clouds of heaven. He approached the Ancient of Days and was led into his presence. He was given authority, glory and sovereign power; all peoples, nations and men of every language worshiped him. His dominion is an everlasting dominion that will not pass away, and his kingdom is one that will never be destroyed (Dan 7:13-14 NIV).

Daniel was told that God wants to be worshiped by all these pagans. Daniel may have thought he would have a dream about lightning coming from heaven and destroying the Babylonian soldiers. God said, "No, I want those people to worship me, Daniel. I want them to know who I am. I want the Israelites to be a tremendous missionary force!"

Another one of the great missionary books in the Bible is Jonah. People remember the whale, but the purpose of Jonah's trip was to take the message to Nineveh. He tried every way he could to escape. God's message to Jonah was to go to the people who were his enemies. The book of Jonah gives us a picture of Israel's refusing to be a missionary to the nations!

The Gospel of Matthew was written by a Jew for Messianic believers. There are three things Matthew wanted to do. First he wanted to give an overview of the redemptive work of Jesus. The second thing was to make it very clear that this Jesus is the long-awaited Messiah, the fulfillment of what the prophets said. The third thing was that he is not only the Messiah for the Jews, but he is the Savior of the world. A lot of people want their own Messiah; Jesus is the world's Messiah. So at the very beginning of the story, the Gentile kings come to worship a human being, which is unheard of for the Jews. Who is it who says that Jesus is the Son of God in that story? Gentiles. Throughout that book it is the Gentiles who recognize who Jesus is. Where did Jesus have the disciples assemble when he gave them the Great Commission? In Galilee of the Gentiles, the trade routes. The whole book is a missionary book.

The great word to Abraham was "GO," and when Jesus was giving the Great Commission he started out with "GO therefore and make disciples of all nations, baptizing them in the name of the Father and of the Son and of the Holy Spirit" (Mt 28:19 RSV). In the Greek, there is only one imperative in that whole sentence: *Make disciples.* The purpose is to make disciples! The question isn't how many miles you go, how many people you baptize, how lengthy or interesting the teaching is, or how many observances you hold on Christmas or Sunday. The question is, "Does this produce disciples of Jesus Christ?"

What are some of the statements in the Bible about a disciple? How will Jesus know you are his disciple? He will recognize you if you bear much fruit, if you will keep his word, if you will pick up your cross and follow him. I think that picking up the cross means that we do things to bring redemption, health, or healing to other people at our own expense. Disciples are people who are willing to do those things. It's too light a thing for us to consider how do we have people become Christians. How do we make disciples? A disciple is someone who makes another decision. Discipleship is service, and it can be dangerous. It's a laying down of one's life. It's not a light thing.

A major milestone that is recorded in the New Testament is that Gentiles didn't have to become Jews to become Christians. It was all right to eat ham. You can remain 100 percent Chinese and still be a disciple of Jesus. You can wear Chinese clothes, speak Chinese. In Islam, people have to read the Koran in Arabic to make it count for religious experience. Translations do not count. But Christians can read the Bible in all languages. It's really a baptizing of whole peoples, whole societies.

Jesus said, "The Father sent me." Where? He sent him into the world. Where does he send us? Into the world as well. Sometimes we think we are sent into the church. You have heard many times, I am sure, about the guy who went into the ministry to be a fisher of men and ended up being the keeper of an aquarium!

There is a great question in Romans: "For everyone who calls upon the name of the Lord will be saved, but how are they to call upon him of whom they have not believed? And how are they to believe in him of whom they have never heard? And how are they to hear without a preacher? And how can they preach unless they are sent?" The idea here is that preaching is for decision-making. When somebody puts a gun to your head and says your pocketbook or your life, you make an important decision. It isn't just filing away information. It's like the proposal: Will you marry me? It requires a decision, followed by action. Not to answer means the answer is "no."

Then comes the victory in Revelation 5:9-10. "They sang a new song saying, 'Worthy are you to take the scroll and to open its seals, for you were slain and by your blood ransomed people from every tribe, tongue, people and nation'"—every tribe in Zaire, Alaska, and Los Angeles. There is a great cry of victory at the end of the story of world mission.

Missions is a major theme throughout the Bible, but not many Episcopalians know it. Missions needs to be preached from our pulpits, and studied by our vestries, missions committees, small groups, adult forums, and Sunday schools.

A number of churches have found it productive to use the "African Bible Study" with the mission passages listed below. In a small group, one person reads the passage aloud. Each person gives one word or phrase that catches their attention. Another person reads the passage aloud. Each person tells where it touches their lives today. The passage is read aloud again. Then each person shares how they believe God wants them to respond. Finally, each person prays for the person on their right.

Genesis 12:1-3
2 Chronicles 6:32-33
Psalm 67
Isaiah 49:5-7
Daniel 7:13-14a
Matthew 28:18-20
Mark 16:15-16
John 20:21
Acts 1:8
Romans 10:13-17
Revelation 5:9-10

INVOLVING YOUTH IN MISSION

The Rev. Whis Hays and Mr. George Anglin

WHIS: I believe young people are inextricably linked to the global mission of the church. They are a primary target of mission. Young people are "goers." Young people are senders. And, if we are wise enough to see the strategic advantages, youth ministry itself becomes a model that teaches young people to see all ministry through missionary eyes.

First, young people need to be recognized as a primary target group for mission. In the booklet "The Changing Shape of World Missions," Bryant Myers asks, "Are children and youth a blind spot in Christian mission today?" Let's ask the question, what does the typical unreached person in the world look like? Where are they? Some would say World A. Others would say the "10/40 Window." But few seem to notice that the typical unreached person in the Third World is young. The average age in Mexico City, the largest city on the planet, is fourteen. The same pattern holds true across the board in the major metropolitan areas of the Third World. If we think that mission means adults going to adults, we will miss a tremendously responsive target group.

Eighty-four percent of all Americans who will ever make a personal decision to follow Jesus Christ as their Lord and Savior make that decision by age twenty. When you talk about a "Decade of Evangelism," you are talking about evangelizing youth and children; otherwise, you may be focusing only on sixteen percent of the responsive population.

We are clueless about the global demographics of the world partly because our country is not youthful. We have one of the lowest percentages in the world of people under fifteen. If you look at World A, the countries such as India, between thirty-seven and forty-one percent of the population are under fifteen. What does this have to say about evangelism? If that evangelistic response statistic from the United States, eighty-four percent by age twenty, holds true across the globe, what does that say about our missionary strategy? We have a big, big blind spot. What we are doing is not wrong by commission; it is wrong by omission.

What do we know about the people who haven't heard the gospel? The typical person we need to reach with the Great Commission lives in a city in the Third World, is poor, and is *young*. What this tells me is that people who understand urban ministries, cross-cultural missions, and youth ministry need to be talking to each other and working together. If we fail to recognize young people as a target group, we will overlook major opportunities for spreading the gospel.

Second, young people are also important agents of mission. There is a Western cultural assumption limiting the vision of the missionary community. We have a concept in our minds, played out daily, that teenagers are irresponsible and unpredictable. They cannot really be trusted to get anything done.

Western industrial society invented adolescence. The word "teenager" did not appear in an English dictionary until the mid-1940s. The word "adolescent" was coined in 1904. American teens have been relegated to a waiting pattern where they languish until they can do something that is going to be worthwhile in the world. As a result, we are raising a generation of young people who describe themselves as having strong feelings of worthlessness, loneliness, and uselessness.

The assumption that youths are somehow incompetent and irresponsible really is an assumption of *our* society. Once you cross over into the Two-Thirds World, in World A or World B, you do not necessarily find the same pattern. In Mexico City, Pastor Alfonso Navarro leads a growing, dynamic Roman Catholic Church. The church growth, renewal and planting movement in that church has spread from Mexico City throughout Mexico and even into the United States in the Roman Catholic Church. I went to one of their Christian Education nights. They were offering six classes and two of the teachers in those adult education classes were teenagers.

Bob Linthicum of World Vision, MARC, their urban ministry expert, has lived in twelve cities in Latin America, Asia and Africa. Bob's impression was that people in the Two-Thirds World don't have the luxury of telling people that they have to get their graduate degrees before they can become productive members of society. One mark of this, he said, was that in those twelve cities, seventy percent of the police are teenagers.

The assumption of incompetence and irresponsibility that has gradually emerged in our own society doesn't apply globally. Furthermore, I think Scripture rebukes us on this point. The word "teenager" does not occur in the Bible because it was invented in the twentieth century. But start looking for Biblical teenagers—let's try listing a few. David was probably old enough to be in junior high when he hit Goliath. Samuel may even have been a little younger than that when God called him. When Mary said yes to God about having Jesus, she was probably thirteen or fourteen. Timothy is another one. John was almost certainly a teenager when he was following Jesus around. We could go on for a while.

My favorite biblical teenager happens to be Josiah. He is the only person specifically described in the Bible as having loved the Lord with all his heart, soul and mind, obeying what Jesus called the "Great Commandment" in Deuteronomy. When Josiah started reforming his whole country as the king, he was eighteen or nineteen years old. Or consider Jeremiah. He was called into a prophetic ministry as the spiritual leader of the people of Israel. When God called him, do you know what his objection was? "I'm too young for this." When Jeremiah made that objection, Josiah the King was nineteen or twenty! The point is that in the time of Josiah and Jeremiah, God was doing something extraordinary through young people. I think that it is happening again. What God is doing through young people in this decade is truly extraordinary compared to what I saw him doing in the first ten years that I was in youth ministry. The Spirit is doing something through them! I think this raises a question, along with that list of examples from the Bible: what about rethinking the place of young people as primary recipients and as agents of mission?

Students, particularly college students, have a huge role in the history of missions. Ironically, one of the places where the Episcopal Church is the weakest is in our ministry with college students. We are bad enough with high school and junior high, but at college it gets downright pitiful. We can take some comfort in the fact that we are not the only ones. Southern Baptists did a study a couple of years ago where they discovered that if you track people who are active in their churches at the point of graduation from high school, eighteen months later only four percent of those people are still active in churches. The Christian Education model, the program model that the Southern Baptists use with their kids (and looks so successful as long as they are under their parents' roofs), doesn't necessarily produce continuity into college.

Why is it that young people are the ones who respond to the gospel and the ones who respond to the call to missions? Why is it that youth and mission are so intimately connected with each other? In the first place, especially in Western industrialized societies, there is a vocational window of opportunity in adolescence and in young adulthood. "What am I going to do with my life?" That's one of the big questions that kids have to answer. Ask clergy when they first felt God was calling them into the ministry. The vast majority will answer sometime during their teenage years. I would be willing to bet the same is true for missionaries. When kids go on a short-term mission, the question begins to get answered: "What am I good for?" If they discover God working through them on a short-term missions trip, a very large percentage of those people begin to hear God calling them to the mission field. I have been told that eighty percent of all people who are long-term missionaries start by going on short-term missions. Why not start them when they are teenagers, when they are asking the question, "What am I going to do with my life?"

The second reason youth and mission are connected is that kids have a willingness to take heroic risks. This is why recruiters go to high schools when they are trying to recruit people into the army. They don't go to graduate schools. Kids have a sense of invulnerability. They are more willing to take the risk. Kids are more willing to be heroic than older people are. Most adults won't go on short-term missions in most congregations, even mission-aware congregations. Kids are far more likely to go.

Last but not least, I think there is a strategic advantage in sending American kids to kids overseas. This is not because of some superiority of American culture, but because of the global media culture. Kids in Russia, Tierra Del Fuego, and Indonesia know about Levi's. What is the most popular TV program on the planet? "Baywatch." American youth culture has been exported through the media. Not that it's all American, because certainly the Brits and the Aussies influence it, too. The great arbiters, however, are Hollywood and Madison Avenue. That global-mediated English-speaking youth culture has broadcast the allure of American youth all over the planet. Do you think most long-term missionaries are particularly in tune with that culture? No! One of the great advantages of sending American kids short-term overseas: kids over there see these Americans, and they want to know all about them. Those kids are more curious about our kids than our kids are about them. You have to be careful in your preparation so that the American kids don't think that they are God's gift in an egotistical sense. But their age and nationality do provide an opening for our kids to say, "The stuff you see on TV, some of that is real, but there is something that American TV isn't telling you about—Jesus! He is the most important thing in our lives!" You can use that to tremendous advantage in short-term situations.

GEORGE: I had the opportunity of working as a youth group leader in a small church in Manassas, Virginia, in my second summer of the Josiah Project, a Rock The World: Youth Mission Alliance leadership program for college students. I knew that God was calling my Josiah Project team to go to Honduras on a short-term mission trip, and, at the same time, I knew that God was calling me to stay with my youth group and continue to minister as a youth group leader. Eventually, I discerned that God was calling us to go together to Honduras with the Josiah Project.

We were a congregation of about sixty members; fifty percent of our parish was under the age of eighteen. There were many different things going on with our church financially. We were trying to get our own facility at that time. Because of our financial bind, the vestry had to cut off my salary for a period of time. I was in one vestry meeting, listening to all these older people who knew so much more than I did. At the end of the meeting, I had the opportunity to be able to say, "By the way, I would like to know if we could go to Honduras?" They took me seriously; they prayed about it, and the following Sunday they said, "Yes, we believe God is calling you to do this. You have to realize you are going to have to raise all of your support outside the church. We also feel maybe one other person is called to go with you; one other person in the youth group as a Timothy, someone who might get on fire for missions." There were seven other people in the congregation who wanted to go, some of them adults. I tried everything I could to scare them out of going on this mission trip just to be sure that they were hearing God's call.

I don't know if you have ever worked with kids when they think they hear God's call—it's like, "Yeah, that's what he said, so I'm gonna do it!" "Well, you have to raise on thousand dollars." "Yeah, God wants me to do this." "Well, you could die if you are down there; there are minefields." "Yeah, it's okay. I know God wants me there." It went on and on like that. I couldn't persuade any of them to back off this trip. They knew they were called.

On May 15, the bishop commissioned us. We had a total of seventy-five dollars in the bank when we stood up and were prayed for. We had to raise $8000 in forty-five days. I remember the stress of it. This was a giant leap of faith for our congregation. About a month after that, I got a phone call telling me we had all the money.

Let me say now, when parents hear you are talking about their kids on a trip to Honduras, suddenly every parent in that congregation is talking to you and wants to know all the details about the trip. I remember talking to one girl in the congregation and she felt so strongly, she knew this was what God wanted her to do. She knew that everything would be taken care of in God's way. Her attitude was an example to me that sometimes it takes three things to get started on a mission trip. One is a call, which we definitely had. One is faith, which is also what we had. And the other thing, and this is something that young people have better than adults, is ignorance. That's what we had. We had a lot of kids that only knew that God had called them to go on this mission trip.

The parents, on the other hand—I remember her parents exactly. "She just doesn't understand. This is one thousand dollars. She has this to take care of, she has that to take care of; she has to get a passport, shots, all these other things. It can't be done. I tried to talk her out of it; she won't listen to me. I don't care anymore." That is honestly what happened. I will tell you though; the next year her parents did not think twice about sending their daughter on another mission trip, and their son went along as well.

We finally left on the mission trip. Being there was a tremendous opportunity for young people who (in our country) can't drive a car, who get little respect, and who have parents constantly telling them what to do. Can you even imagine the impact of arriving in a village with all the villagers lined up in the yard of the president's home, cheering and singing songs of welcome to this group of young people who had come to help them? This was the first time they had ever seen a large group of Americans in their village, and, gosh, we were nothing in America. But to these people, we were going to build a water system and change their lives. And we did.

They changed our lives, too. The kids came back knowing that they had made a difference in the world for Jesus. Kids, who are considered useless by our own standards at home, who are lonely, felt such love from the people in La Solicias, Honduras. It was just tremendous. When you get back home, the first thing you feel as a leader is success! No one died! God was right; we were supposed to go on this trip!

Later on, one by one, teens started coming up to me and saying, "George, I know why God called me to go on that trip. I'm going to be a missionary later on in my life!" Colin, one of the youths on that trip, is now trying to find out how to be a long-term missionary in Honduras himself. Another girl, Megan, went back last year. A couple of kids went back last year, and they are looking into ways of becoming missionaries, too. This is a perfect time in their lives to say to them, "Hey, God has something that he can do with your life. You don't have to go into the rat race. You could be making a difference in someone's life over in another country."

When we got back, we were able to stand up in front of the congregation and tell stories about little kids who loved us so much that they gave us their marbles, which was their wealth for some of them, to say thank you for coming down there. The difference that made in the congregation was really something. Even though we didn't have the resources or the time to put it all together, God's call, God's timing, and God's preparation were there. That trip worked because of God. That congregation, now in their own building, numbers over one hundred people. It is a tremendous testimony of what Jesus did through kids on one little short-term mission trip, which was the first mission trip for anyone from that congregation.

One last story. One of the mothers in the congregation said, "I always felt called to be a missionary, but I never really had the opportunity to do something like that." This summer she is going to Africa for the first time as a short-term missionary, partly because of the testimony of her daughter. So youth going on short-term mission trips really changes the lives of the kids that go, changes the people over there where we serve, and changes the people in the congregation that sends.

WHIS: I want to emphasize that it does make a huge difference when a group of kids sent overseas reports back to the congregation in a public forum. It won't have the impact on your congregation if you demand that they be professional speakers when they get up front. It is okay for kids to just share what God did in them and through them in a quite unprofessional way. We are all used to that in Christmas pageants. We can get used to it with reports about short-terms as well. If you don't report to the congregation, you will be depriving your congregation of the impact such trips have.

I want to make very clear that a whole congregation, if not already committed to missions, can easily make the leap to direct involvement this way. You can bring missionary after missionary after missionary through your congregation and still not move your congregation any more than a small increment towards where they will get with just one short-term mission trip by the youth group. It's their kids that are over there! It changes the congregation. All Saints' (Dale City, Virginia) had never had an overseas mission trip in its nine years of existence prior to the mission trip our youth group took to Mexico, never sent anyone cross-culturally. Since then, dozens of people have gone out from that congregation on short-terms. In fact, that congregation became home to SOMA, Sharing Of Ministries Abroad. It has become a missions congregation, and the ice was broken by that group of kids that went to Mexico. It is the fast way to educate your congregation as a whole about missions. The benefits in terms of the congregational life were aptly summed up by the quote Tom Prichard cited about what he would do if he were the rector of a church that burned to the ground. The answer: "The next Sunday I would take an offering for mission." There is something about giving that waters the giver. I just can't recommend this highly enough.

We have talked about youth as the target group and youth as the goers. Now, let's look at youth as senders. We know that the missionary enterprise requires both people who go and people who send. Young people aren't normally thought of as senders. In fact, I never thought about that very much until this last year when our youth group took on the project of sending two of their own members on a longer short-term mission with YWAM. The impact it had on our kids of sending off people, getting the letters back, having their friends come back and hearing the stories about what they had experienced was phenomenal.

If you want to see tremendous support for the goers in terms of prayer support or letters being sent (there is no group better at writing letters than teenage girls), kids are a great group to have as senders. They do have some financial resources they can put into it, and sometimes they do that sacrifically. They have tremendous ability to pray; being "ignorant enough to go" also applies to being too ignorant to "know" that God won't answer some of your prayers. There is nothing I would rather have than a group of turned-on teenagers praying for me, because they are too ignorant to "know" what God won't do!

And last but not least, the whole business of the personal support that goes out that way is just fantastic. It has a beneficial effect both on the people who have been sent out and the kids themselves as senders.

Finally, the missionary mentality is crucial to youth ministry stateside. One of the things that Rock The World stands for is relational youth ministry and incarnational youth ministry. The relationship that the leaders have with the kids is the starting point. We want to take that whole relational strategy a step further because, frankly, it is what we see God doing. There is a sociologist and anthropologist named Alvin Toffler who has talked about a phenomenon called "Future Shock." Future shock is culture shock that is created among people as they grow older because the culture that they grew up in vanishes on them. It's partly induced by the need for novelty and entertainment in advertising, but is also partly induced by technological change, by migration and contact with other people around the world as information and transportation systems shrink the globe. What that means is that, as a forty-three-year-old, the thing that I remember as normal adolescence no longer exists. It is not even an option.

The logic of future shock has driven us to understand that youth ministry is, by its very nature, missionary—even inside our own country. One of the things that we are obsolescing in our vocabulary is the term "youth minister." It dies hard, but what we are really trying to produce is "youth missionaries," people who are capable of bringing the gospel into the youth culture, to walk the gospel into that place relationally. That's the pioneering phase. You go through a pastoral phase, just as you do in an overseas context. Finally, you get to the point where some kids emerge with the spiritual gifts and the respect of their peers as spiritual leaders. Then you train and bless those people and bring them up to the level of leadership. What you are really trying to do is start Christianity as an indigenous people movement within the youth culture. It never becomes quite independent of the adult culture, but you want to equip kids because kids will listen to other kids about Jesus faster than they will listen to adults.

I no longer speak to youth groups without taking kids with me who already know me. It opens doors a whole lot faster. It collapses nine months into nine minutes. We have to approach the whole youth ministry task as missionaries, I think, if we are over twenty-five-years-old.

The significance of this for our youth ministries is really profound; but it also has significance in terms of missions. Kids learn by modeling. If what you are doing in your relationship with them is deliberately modeling missionary behavior, you are already training them to be missionaries themselves. That's part of the central vision of Rock The World. We see the whole business of youth ministry as a missionary enterprise, and see the global task of world mission as inextricably linked to youth ministry. Please join us in calling and equipping kids to lead the world to Christ.

MAKE SHORT-TERM MISSIONS HAPPEN IN YOUR PARISH

The Rev. Marty O'Rourke

MARTY O'ROURKE: Evangelist Billy Sunday once called the Episcopal Church a "sleeping giant" because of its unrealized potential. There is a correlation between denominations that emphasize missions and those that grow. The Episcopal Church has not stressed cross-cultural missions, and we have a great untapped potential in our congregations.

Sometimes parishes raise the question, is it cost-effective to send people? In the long run, it is. Studies show that once you go on a short-term mission, your giving to missions doubles.

One fruit-bearing sign is that short-term missions encourage long-term missionaries. Eighty percent of long-term missionaries went on a short-term mission; as many as ninety percent of all missionaries are either children of missionaries or have been on short-term missions. Short-term missions are really a great way for people to "test the waters" and decide to become full-time missionaries.

Paul said, "Pray for us, that God may open a door for our message" (Col 4:3). Right now, we have a great door that God has opened for us, and it is imperative that we step through it. I recently read in an article that something new has happened just in our generation to blast the Great Commission wide open. Today anyone can go virtually anywhere in the world in just a matter of hours for a comparatively low cost. The advent of jet transportation along with telephone and radio communication has shrunk the globe. When William Carey travelled to India in the 1700s, it cost him the equivalent of $400,000 in today's money—one way. The affordability and accessibility of travel, combined with technological advances in communications, are opening the door as never before.

Today it is possible to visit a foreign field for a short time of weeks or months. This opportunity did not exist even fifty years ago. We can now go to a foreign land for a month and have an impact for the gospel: to help the local church with physical and spiritual needs, to bring people to Christ, and then to return to our regularly-scheduled lives. I just learned about a man who for four years had been working to bring people to Christ in Spain, a difficult country. A short-term mission group visited, and in a couple of weeks tripled what the man had been able to do.

My parish has sent a number of teams to Jamaica. While there, we were invited to speak at a public high school simply because we were foreigners. In those schools, unlike our own, we could speak freely about Jesus. We gave the children an opportunity to accept Jesus, and a teacher got up to say, "I hope you all heard what they said, and I hope each of you will ask Jesus into your heart."

Our ministry there started with two people going on vacation to Jamaica. They got a burden for the Jamaican people and began to pray, even after returning home. Through a remarkable series of circumstances, they made connections with an Anglican priest from Jamaica and invited him to attend a renewal conference sponsored by our churches in Ohio. It turned out that he was about to quit the ministry because of burn-out. At our conference he experienced a wonderful time of spiritual renewal, invited us to visit his parish, and became our principal contact for ministry there.

Bishop Alfred Stanway of Australia, who helped found Trinity Episcopal School for Ministry in Ambridge, Pennsylvania, liked to give this advice: Pray, start small, pick the right people, and don't let money be a determining factor. I think there's a lot of wisdom in that. Prayer is the foundation. Then, the people who comprise your first team are very important. Obviously, you want people who are leaders.

Sometimes in churches, if we have people that we don't quite know what to do with, we think that maybe we should encourage them to go into missions. However, we have been challenged to send our best people; those who have already proved themselves in local ministry and can be flexible in varying circumstances.

Don't let money be an obstacle. We have a young man who is going to Africa this summer. He needs to raise $3,000. Our parish budget is very tight, but the money is coming in. I know this experience is going to change this young man's life, and he is using the trip to explore a possible call into full-time missions.

I will never forget the word spoken over our first team during the church's send-off prayers as we prepared to depart. We were told that the team was like the lead in a pencil, which would have the actual contact with the paper, but the church was the pencil itself, and by its prayers and intercessions it was supporting and bearing down upon the point as it made its witness. Of course, the Lord is the hand that guides and moves the pencil.

Make sure that missions are part of the regular life of your body, and that it's not done off on the side. Pray for your missionaries regularly during services and put frequent updates or even newsletters in your bulletins. We commission our teams during the Sunday morning service when they go out, and when they return we have them briefly share their experiences.

You have to be sensitive about what and how long people should share during a Sunday morning service. We found that a good outlet for the team members who are bubbling over with enthusiasm is to hold a "Jamaica Reunion" soon after each trip. We invite anyone in the congregation who wants to hear more to attend a potluck dinner where we cook Jamaican food, show our slides and photographs, and compare notes.

We recommend a book entitled *Stepping Out: A Guide to Short-Term Missions,* edited by Tim Gibson, from YWAM Publishing, P.O. Box 55787, Seattle, WA 98155, and also available through the U.S. Center for World Missions. This is a wonderful book full of practical advice about short-term missions. It's a compilation of writings from some of the top short-term mission experts in a number of denominations, not just from Youth With A Mission. Whether you are just beginning to consider short-term missions, are actually in the planning stages, or have already been on one, this is a book that will interest you. One chapter, called "Ways to Ruin a Short-Term," suggests: "When you report home, castigate your congregation and friends for their lack of commitment, prayer and giving to missions. This is one of the few times you will have their deferential respect, so make the most of it!"

We learned this the hard way. Somebody returning from one of our outreaches basically went back to their home church and told people they weren't as spiritual as we were because we were making these trips, and why didn't more people go, and they had better get on board. Now, did that build a sense of community? No, it caused separation, and impeded the cause of mission.

There will be resistance, and you may be asked, "What about these poor people right in our city who need help?" This question is a trap. God is not an either/or God; he's a both/and God! Yes, those local people do need ministry. But we found that people who went to Jamaica and did ministry there often suddenly realize, "Hey, I can do this very same thing right where I live, too!"

Brother Andrew, who smuggled Bibles into closed countries, said, "The Bible says to GO. It doesn't say anything about coming back again." I have found that when people step out of their comfort zone, they have to trust the Lord. When they come back, they want to continue that deeper dependence upon God.

A young man from Church of the Apostles in Fairfax was a member of one of our teams. Later, he chronicled this experience: "The first night we had some transportation problems (which isn't unusual), so we didn't get into Jamaica until late at night. I was dropped off in Colgate, and briefly met my host before she went back to bed. I began to relax in my room. Suddenly I heard dogs barking outside, a car engine shut off, and a door slam. I heard shouting in Patois (Jamaican dialect), then someone banged on my window. My first thought was that someone had seen this white American drive up, and they were coming to kill or rob me. I realized that I was totally alone: I had no idea where I was, I didn't know the people I was staying with, I had no idea where anyone else from the team was, and I was helpless. I was absolutely, totally dependent on God. My intellect and my American Express card could not get me out of this one. I began praying, and God gave me peace. I heard my host open the door, and it turned out to be just some relatives visiting late at night."

We all have our everyday routines. When you are out on one of these trips, however, nothing is routine. You are trusting God to supply transportation and provisions for that day.

As an American on my first trip there, I was frustrated and angry because of the time schedule. One Sunday we did services in three different churches and were driving to our final service. We were already an hour late, and the church was another half-hour away. I thought we might as well not even go, because there would be nobody there. The rector was driving us, and along the way spotted a woman he knew. He stopped the car and talked to her as if he had all the time in the world. Meanwhile, I was going crazy! It was a hard lesson, but we learned that if something isn't happening on schedule, God has something else planned, and we had better be watching for it. When we finally arrived at the last church, we found those folks had just continued to praise the Lord for an hour and a half until we got there!

It's important to make disciples. My simple definition of a disciple is anyone who can make other disciples. Early on, I determined not to do it for them, but to do it with them. It was a partnership. God showed me this clearly on my first trip. After I preached at the morning service, the senior warden of the church, who was a very well-respected man, apologized that he was unable to attend the evening service because of a persistent cough. I simply asked, "Would you mind if I prayed for you?" God healed him. It was his first miracle, and he was changed. At the evening service, I asked him to pray with me for others, just as I had done for him. He prayed with great faith! At the next evening's service, a young lady stood up, pointed to the senior warden, and said, "God healed me when he prayed for me." God was giving me a sign of our purpose: to share the ministry so that it continues without us.

We must never have the patronizing attitude that we are just trying to help "the poor natives." We go to another country and see that they don't have the material items that we have, so we tend to think we are better. Here is a sad example. Some churches in Florida sent people to Jamaica to do some building. When one of the Florida churches needed to build something for itself, the Jamaicans offered to come and help in return. The Americans replied, "No, no, we don't need your help; you go help yourselves." Right away, the Jamaicans recognized the relationship was a one-way street, and they ended it.

One of the poorest Jamaican churches we worked with took an offering when my home parish had a building campaign, and they presented us with a check for $50. It was humbling to accept such a sacrificial gift. It was like the loaves and the fishes, and God wanted to take it, break it and multiply it for us. Of all the gifts we received, that was the most precious. Typically what they give back to us is intangible: it's not something we can clearly see or touch, but we can feel it because it's deep and real. We must always tell them what they have taught us and given to us, and thank them for it. The ministry must be a two-way street.

First Peter 3:15 says, "Always be prepared to give an answer to everyone who asks you to give a reason for the hope you have in you" (NIV). On these trips, you must always be ready because you never know what is going to happen next. An ordained priest was on one of our trips and saw others on the team leading people to Christ. Discouraged, he wrote in his prayer diary, "I guess I am just not an evangelist." He then went to catch a bus, and as he was waiting for it to arrive, a Jamaican approached him and asked, "What must I do to be saved?" What was the Lord saying to this priest? We must always be prepared for God to use us in any way that he chooses, and we have to be flexible.

WENDY O'ROURKE: One of the crucial things we learned was the value of operating under indigenous authority. We submitted all of our work to the Anglican rector who was our contact in Jamaica. We did what he asked us to do, and if we had any questions we went to him. He helped Marty decide which people on our teams should serve in his various congregations. We wanted to avoid being seen as "the great American Santa Claus," so when people would ask us for shoes for their children, we filtered all such requests through the rector. He would then distribute the things we had brought, ensuring that those who truly needed them received them, rather than the people with the best persuasive skills.

As a musician, I was delighted to see how easily music bridges those cross-cultural barriers. I used my guitar to teach some of our favorite praise choruses, but the people were especially delighted when I played some of theirs, which can really rock the church! If you take a short-term missions team, try to enlist a guitarist or keyboard player on the team; you will find you've brought along a ready-made bridge to the community.

One couple, the Hendersons, from our church served on two Jamaica teams. Bing is a doctor and Karen is a nurse. In 1991 this family sold virtually everything to serve aboard YWAM's medical mercy ship, the *Anastasis*.

KAREN HENDERSON: Bing and I became full-time missionaries as a result of exposure to short-term missions in Marty's church. You just never know who is going to be interested in mission trips. We have three school-age children, so we would be unlikely candidates. But, even more than adults, kids need to be exposed to missions. People touched by missions at a young age will always have that seed in their hearts.

We have a son who is eleven years old. We read *God's Smuggler* by Brother Andrew together, and he was so excited about it that we got *God's Smuggler to China*. One of the people in that book heard God's call to be a missionary when he was seven years old. That put a real excitement in my son's life, that he could hear now what God has for his future.

Before we left home to go into full-time missions, a lot of people asked how we could take our kids away from a good, American life. The Lord gave me Genesis 22:18: "And through your offspring, all nations on earth will be blessed, because you have obeyed me" (NIV). I'm excited that God didn't wait until our kids were all grown.

MARTY O'ROURKE: In Luke 10, Jesus sent the seventy-two on a short-term mission, and they came back as changed people. I encourage you to take young people. I once asked our youth group why they believe in God. Two of them mentioned their experiences in Jamaica. Years ago Karen Henderson asked me a question that still haunts me: "How can I teach my kids not to take what they have for granted?" Part of the answer lies in appreciating how people in other cultures live. I took my eight-year-old daughter on a short-term mission which included a visit to a Jamaican orphanage. Katie noticed that in the dormitory every bed was perfectly made and some—but not all—displayed the owner's single toy on the pillow. Her heart went out to the children, especially those with the empty beds, and she will never forget this. Some of the kids nicknamed her "Bleach," because she was the first white child that some of them had seen. I think that's going to help her understand racism.

Children do benefit from missions. It was discovered that out of every ten thousand families in which the father was a skilled craftsman, one child would be listed in Who's Who. From five thousand lawyers' families, one child would be listed. Of twelve hundred Episcopalian priests' offspring, there would be a single entry. But for every seven Christian missionary families, one child would grow up to be included in Who's Who! Why? These are children who have been out in the world and have seen that there is more to life than having two cars in the garage. They see that whether they become doctors, economists, scientists or teachers, God can use them to change the world.

WHAT HAS WORKED FOR US

Panel of Mission Committees

The four churches represented on this panel are very different from each other—large and small, urban and rural—but all of them have accomplished something significant in missions. Two of the parishes represented also have strong programs to international students or immigrants.

GARY JOHNSON: I have been a full-time member of the staff of Truro Episcopal Church in Fairfax, Virginia, for nine years as lay Staff Director of Outreach and Mission. Truro is a large suburban church of three thousand members with an average Sunday attendance of 1700 to 1800 people. Mission at Truro has evolved into a fairly large ministry that literally reaches around the world. We have diocesan relationships with four foreign Anglican bishops, three of whom are in Africa. A number of short-term mission teams have been sent to different parts of the world and I have been a member of seven of those teams. Fifteen active missionary units consisting of either one person or a couple are supported in a variety of situations including Wycliffe Bible Translators, Youth With a Mission, and other similar groups. One individual is connected to the Episcopal Church's Volunteers for Mission program. Our parish has a strong local outreach as well, feeding the poor and serving the homeless. We have established a facility called the Lamb Center in the Fairfax area, which is a daytime drop-in center where people come in off the street, get a shower, their clothes cleaned, receive mail, leave their belongings for a night or two, make telephone calls, participate in a Bible study, etc. Last year we saw over five thousand people. Our parish also supports four seminarians from Truro as well as one seminarian from another church. We are deeply involved in ministry to international students and our proximity to metropolitan Washington, D.C., and many colleges and universities provides great opportunities in this ministry. In short, the parish is involved in a multiplicity of programs.

The parish felt it was important to establish a vision statement; in fact, it has crystallized our direction as a church and defined our reason for existence. While the statement has undergone several modifications, currently it is basically: "Be a Christ-centered community which is actively concerned with making an eternal difference in other people's lives." Sub-elements of that statement include: "equipping the saints, serving the community, helping to renew the Episcopal Church, and reaching the unreached." From that we developed a statement pertaining to outreach or mission activity, which is defined as anything done by the parish off the parish property.

John Howe, the former rector, now the Bishop of the Diocese of Central Florida, challenged our vestry back in 1976 to make a substantial commitment to mission by asking them to "pray about giving away as much to others as you spend on yourselves." After a time of fasting and prayer, the vestry unanimously agreed. At that point, about eleven percent of the budget was directed to outreach, and most of that was going to the diocese. A seven-year plan to achieve fifty percent in outreach was developed, increasing by five percent per year. The goal was achieved within a five year period! Concurrently, the parish was involved in a major building expansion program, during which time the outreach budget did not suffer. The increased facilities, including 350 more seats, expanded educational facilities, and a paved parking lot, were completed without incurring debt! I cannot overemphasize how totally this was bathed in prayer and accomplished only because it was of God.

Presently our parish is preparing to plant a mission church in western Fairfax, about eight or nine miles from Truro. As many as 120 families have attended there, dedicating themselves to pray and work for its success. A site and a vicar are presently being sought. The area includes a new multi-cultural lower income housing complex of mostly unchurched people which provides a fertile mission field.

The mission committee at Truro parish feels that it is important to have a vision, a clear-cut sense of what outreach or mission is, so that priorities can be developed. We see evangelism, discipleship, church growth, Bible translation and support for overseas nationals as some of our priorities. A clear sense of structure helps to facilitate where investments of people and money are made. This also undergirds us in being good stewards and aids in making difficult choices regarding which ministries receive support.

My responsibility is for oversight of the mission structure, consisting of four committees each chaired by a vestry member. Each committee has a funding responsibility and a defined level of authority. If that level is exceeded, then it proceeds to another level of review, and finally to the full vestry.

Some determining criteria involve answers to such questions as: Is it gospel-centered? Is it consistent with the vision of the church and priorities for the year? The committee believes that we are about the business of mission because God has called us to that and because of Jesus Christ and what he did for each person. Noble or humanitarian reasons do not necessarily fit this criteria.

Applications for funding are submitted on forms designed for specific categories which outline the budgetary requirements. The committee reviews the applications along with written reports received throughout the year, newsletters, prayer letters, and the goals that were established with the applicant's mission agency and whether or not they were achieved within the past year. We ask such questions as: Are their budget projections realistic? Have they been good stewards of the funds entrusted to them? Do they have a broad base of support so that they are not totally dependent on one or two individuals or churches? Does the ministry have an effective means of keeping supporters regularly informed? The level of parishioner involvement is particularly important at the local level. As an example, there are twelve parishioners actively involved in a jail ministry directly across the street from our church.

I would encourage those who are mission-minded to look at where your church is now and begin there. Don't let large churches with multiple staff and a large budget be intimidating, but rather look at what God is already blessing, start there and ask God for the growth and the wisdom to find the next step that is important in mission development.

JOHN McBRIDE: I am a member of Little Trinity Anglican Church in Toronto, a thriving, vibrant downtown Anglican church in Canada's largest city. The parish has a membership of five hundred with an average Sunday attendance of 350. There are three Sunday services: 9:00 a.m., 10:30 a.m. and 7:00 p.m.

Little Trinity Parish has nineteen home fellowship groups that meet weekly, a paid staff of five, three honorary assistants, a part-time organist, ten layreaders, and hundreds of volunteers. The budget is $430,000 Canadian, which goes up about five percent every year.

We have been sending out and supporting members who have been called to be missionaries for over a century. Most of them go out with an interdenominational society such as Wycliffe Bible Translators, World Vision or Africa Evangelical Fellowship. An overseas mission committee of eight to twelve persons oversees all aspects of the mission and reports directly to the rector. I am currently a member of the missions committee. A policy document explains the responsibilities of the committee towards the missionaries, the rector and the parish. The primary task of the committee is to provide support for the missionaries, and their secondary task is to keep the congregation informed so that everyone can pray specifically and respond to needs. The committee meets ten times a year to review letters from missionaries and take appropriate action, plan parish-wide mission events, process missionary material received, and pray for each missionary.

Each committee member writes a letter to a missionary once a month. The church office sends out financial support quarterly. Within our worship service, we pray for missionaries and their families every Sunday on a rotation basis and we list them in the Sunday bulletin. Plans are coordinated with the rector when missionaries return from short term assignments or furlough so our entire congregation can hear of the work firsthand, learn of the needs, and respond with special gifts such as eyeglasses, books, or medical supplies. Excerpts from missionary letters and addresses are printed in our monthly parish newsletter.

The committee screens new candidates, provides advice and assistance, debriefs missionaries when they return home, and responds to emergencies as they arise. As an example, a young couple went out to the Philippines and it was a disastrous experience. They came home disillusioned. There was a long period of recovery that involved the mission committee and intervention by the rector. In another instance, supplies were sent by ship to the coast of Africa, but delivery to the inland site required an aircraft at a cost of twelve thousand dollars. The men's group of our parish was able to raise fifty percent of that amount in two days.

The committee attempts to supply the needs of missionaries who come home on furlough by arranging for such things as a car or a house for a few months. While the missionaries are home, the committee has one or more informal meals with them to get well acquainted and learn first hand of their experiences, some of which they could not write about or would not be appropriate for the whole parish.

The overseas portion of the church budget is about ten percent ($40,000-$42,000 Canadian), which the committee is responsible to defend at the annual general meeting. In addition to that, the members of our parish sponsor lunches and other activities which raise another twenty thousand dollars. Additionally, the outreach budget includes the diocesan assessment, which is about $75,000, much of which goes to run homes in downtown Toronto for various needs. Presently, the total outreach portion of our $430,000 budget is about $135,000—not yet at fifty percent.

Support for a missionary is based on the individual's need and the ability of the committee to budget that support. As a general rule, the committee strives to provide twenty-five percent of the need, relying on the missionaries to obtain the other seventy-five percent from the mission organization and through their families and friends. Attempts are made to increase the budget annually to cover cost-of-living increases.

Other related areas of involvement include parish members serving on mission boards, such as World Vision, AEF, Interserve, SAMS, SOMA and Mission to Muslims. Support is provided to theological students at Wycliffe College, an evangelical college in downtown Toronto, and one or two students are engaged yearly in assignments with our rector. Support is also given to InterVarsity Christian Fellowship. About $4,500 is donated to send people to camp as staff and campers, and encouragement is provided to have as many students as possible attend the Urbana world mission conventions held every three years. Homefront mission support is encouraged through Stephen Ministries, Neighbor Link, World Vision, downtown relief agencies, and neighboring parish programs.

The youth of our parish are very involved in short term mission, often staging lunches to raise support. Since 1990, they have served in such places as Angola, Costa Rica, France, Egypt, St. Vincent, Venezuela, and Zambia. Several have used their annual Spring break to go to Mendenhall, Mississippi. For the past five years, they have done a benefit event for Africa, raising two thousand dollars or more each time by doing skits, singing, and playing musical instruments for the whole parish. Medical doctors who are members of our parish go away for one or two weeks to serve in eye clinics, often accompanied by other parish members who serve as administrators.

It is our intention to encourage more people, especially the youth, to become involved in mission, to increase the support of the present missionaries, to continue to pray for very specific places and very specific needs, and to increase the general giving for mission overall.

GEORGE FLEMING: I serve as the rector of St. Paul's Church, Bailey's Crossroads, Virginia, six miles from Washington, D.C. When I came to St. Paul's in 1968, it was a suburban community. Now it is urban, with a very high diversity of nationalities and cultures. The local high school has forty languages represented, almost like a Tower of Babel! There has been a very big change within our congregation. We are still wrestling with issues of an aging Anglo congregation and its surrounding international neighbors. We also have an Hispanic congregation with us, under the supervision and support of the Diocese of Virginia; St. Paul's provides space and utilities. This came about after fifteen years of trying to make contact with the large Hispanic community. About one-fourth of the congregation are West Africans (Liberian, Ghanian and Nigerian) who participate in the vestry, acolytes, choir, etc., which represents a merging of cultures. St. Paul's has been involved with shelter ministry since 1984 when a man was found dead a couple of hundred yards away from our church one very cold Christmas Eve. This began in the church basement continuing for three winters. It has evolved into a permanent building nearby supported by churches and the county. Our parish is also involved in summer backyard evangelism, neighborhood Vacation Bible School with outreach programs to the local housing projects.

We have had good Daily Vacation Bible Schools in our area, but it seemed like the children that we wanted to attend, the children of different ethnic groups, never came. It was basically our own children and those from another parish. This past year our Christian Education group found a book called "Backyard Evangelism." This suggests that you go to wherever there are children collecting, say, near your backyard, invite them in, set up some simple games, and end it up with a short Bible study. We have come in behind some apartment houses where there are many latchkey kids whose parents are working two shifts a day. These kids are wandering all about.

We did it at two locations. The first time, we put out a big tarpaulin on the ground and started playing some games. We brought a couple of kids along from our church just to prime it, and then all these kids started coming by. They would circle around, and then come in closer and closer. Before we knew it, they were there with us, because children love to play games. We ended with a short Bible passage, and then had popsicles, which we brought in a cooler. This took about an hour and a half each day. The first day a couple of kids came, the next day they brought others. It kept snowballing. Their mothers would come along, too. Some mothers wanted to find out who it was that was over there. Our church is only two blocks away. If you can't get them to the building, then you go out to the street.

Our congregation also supports a Campus Crusade worker at Duke University and Annandale Christian Community for Action in which St. Paul's participates through its outreach with emergency food deliveries to families in crisis, furniture deliveries, and a daycare center.

The possibilities which exist for smaller churches who often feel a lack of resources are as limited as the imagination. St. Paul's has an average attendance of 110 on Sundays, a budget of $115,660, with ten percent, or $11,540, for mission.

Even a church of no more than two hundred members can have a very unique way of listening to a missionary call. As an example, Fran from our parish had a vision and a call. It was through Fran that our church was drawn into mission. As members of the congregation heard about Fran's vision to go to the Middle East, they formed a group who prayed for her. Initially I was not supportive of Fran's focus on the Middle East. So I began a mutual discernment with her of the call of the Lord as she went first to Indonesia to test out her vocation and then studying at Fuller Theological Seminary and the U.S. Center for World Mission, and finally going to the Middle East with the blessing of our congregation.

Each time Fran returns to St. Paul's, there is a quickening of the Holy Spirit. She preaches once a year. She knows the people, and they love her a great deal. For a small church, this sense of relationship is what encourages mission. Fran is considered a tentmaker, in that she began using her skills as a teacher and librarian to support herself, but relationally she is what makes mission real in a small parish.

JIM SIMONS: I am the rector of a rural church located in Ligonier, Pennsylvania, called St. Michael's in the Valley. Our Sunday attendance averages about 150 people. Although we are located about sixty miles east of Pittsburgh, the community of Ligonier is a place of extremes. Of the Fortune 500 wealthiest people, four of their addresses are within five miles of our parish. In contrast, the parish sits in the foothills of the Allegheny Mountains, real Appalachia. When I came to the parish in 1988, attendance was about seventy people and giving was $80,000 a year.

Right or wrong, our parish became involved in mission as a strategy for church growth. We made a commitment to continually raise the amount of money given away every year. Currently we are at fifteen percent and are working toward the goal of fifty percent which is a significant amount of money for a congregation of 150 members. The giving is divided into "local" and "non-local." Locally, our parish is involved in three particularly exciting areas of mission. One area involves a relationship with Blue Cross/Blue Shield through which health insurance is provided for the children of the working poor. Presently there are 180 children on the program, and approximately 400 have participated in the program in the past three years. A reevaluation of the program is underway to determine whether it might be better to self-insure and create some sort of medical consortium using physicians in the area and attempting to obtain some grant money.

The second component of this program is educational. A major issue in the program is that many of the people insured will get in a program and never use it. It's an educational dilemma because many of the people consider medical care only in emergencies. These people are not familiar with preventive care and only seek medical help when a child has progressed from a sore throat to convulsions, or when a toothache has become an abscess.

The third component is a weekly program called "Priority Two." It is a Christ-centered unemployment counseling service that includes a seven-week course which teaches individuals how to identify their gifts, network, write resumes, answer want-ads, and find jobs that fit. It is also a support group.

Locally, a food bank operates out of our church, run in conjunction with the ministerium, which feeds 150 families. Internationally, our parish supports five full-time missionaries and we are adding a sixth. We support a seminarian in St. Petersburg, Russia. We have entered into a relationship with an orphanage in Guatemala and have taken two ten-day trips down there to work, with teams made up of both adults and children. Presently a trip to Uganda is being planned for the summer of 1995.

The missionaries with whom we, as a parish, interact are required to report back to the congregation monthly and to show financial accountability. We support a missionary doctor in Bombay, India, who is not affiliated with an oversight organization such as South American Missionary Society, so the requirements placed on him are somewhat stricter. Missionaries are also required to come back and visit our parish on a regular basis to maintain the connection and involvement between parish and missionary. We place strong emphasis on the relational aspect of mission within our parish.

The importance of maintaining purity in outreach giving cannot be overemphasized. At St. Michael's we *give away* fifteen percent. A staff person administers all of the outreach, especially the local efforts. Neither her salary, the diocesan assessment nor any overhead is included in the fifteen percent. It is important that the congregation understand that it is truly given away—to missionaries and to outreach. The result of this attitude has been an exponential increase of twelve percent in giving in the first year when our increase goal was 2.5 percent. When people see the church doing the mission of God, it is exciting for them.

Another area of outreach for us at St. Michael's involves establishing a covenant with a church over the mountain which has never been able to support a full-time rector. St. Michael's is going to hire a priest, and I will have pastoral oversight which will enable this parish to become a full-time, self-sustaining parish. The parish of St. Michael's has committed $12,000 to this agreement with the diocese.

As a parish, St. Michael's is experiencing God's blessing bountifully as we seek to be a blessing to others. What we thought was a strategy for church growth has become the vehicle for wondrous spiritual growth within our parish and we are, indeed, blessed to be a blessing.

6

Tend the Vines:
Prepare for Effective Mission

DISCERNING A MISSIONARY CALL

Mrs. Louise Hannum and the Rev. Geoffrey Little

LOUISE: This workshop is designed to help individuals and churches discern their call to world mission. We can look to the Bible passages that speak about an individual's and the church's call to mission. In Mark 1:16-20, we read of Jesus' call to Simon, Andrew, James and John. And what are they called to do? Jesus calls them in order to prepare them to be fishers of men.

In Mark 3:14, we are given an account of Jesus' appointing these four and eight others to carry out ministries in his name. Before they are sent out, Jesus wants them to be with him and learn from him.

Again, in Acts 9:4-6, we learn about Saul's call. It was dramatic and certainly caught Saul's attention. He was called to obedience, "Get up and go into the city and you will be told what you must do."

Saul's story continues in Acts 9:11-17, after he arrives in Damascus. Ananias, a member of the Christian community, obeying the Holy Spirit, went to Saul, a known enemy of the Christians. Ananias laid his hands on Saul's head to pray that his sight be restored and that he would be filled with the Holy Spirit. Ananias also spoke about the difficult ministry to which Saul was being called.

As church members, we do help discern persons who are being called for ministry service. A major concern as we help in this discernment is that people who are called be healed and filled with the Holy Spirit.

The account of the church in Antioch helps us to see further responsibilities of the church in its call to world mission. Acts 11:20-26 describes the church in Jerusalem sending Barnabas to visit the new, growing church in Antioch. Finding more work than he could do in teaching these new Christians, he called for Saul. He trained Saul to work alongside him in a teaching ministry.

In Acts 13:1-3, we find the church in Antioch fasting and praying and allowing the Holy Spirit to direct them to send out Saul and Barnabas, their leaders, to be missionaries throughout the rest of the Mediterranean world. I am convinced that these new Christians had friends and relatives in that part of the world and they were eager to have them hear the Good News of Jesus Christ. The church in Antioch wanted to hear from their missionaries on their return. "They gathered the church together and reported all that God had done through them and how He had opened the door of faith to the Gentiles. And they stayed there a long time with the disciples" (Acts 14:27-28).

These passages can be summed up in the following: (1) a call requires discipline and obedience; (2) we need to pray, pray, pray, and we need to send people out; (3) the church needs to call and affirm an individual's call.

The question for the church is: will you be a missionary church that calls out missionaries to be your representatives, or, are you going to make those who are called spend a great deal of energy interesting persons in missions?

If you feel called to missions, by all means try to find persons in your church who will join you in your call. Should they turn a deaf ear, look for a church that will. The individual responding to the call to missions needs a sending church that cares about them and the persons to whom they are going. The prayers of a sending church are essential.

GEOFF: Let me begin by reinforcing the idea that it is crucial to view the missionary call of the Christian individual only in the context of the missionary call of the whole church. In the last five years, I have gone through two different but parallel experiences. First, I observed for three years how other people in the church treated me as a missionary;

and now, for the past two years, I have observed how they have responded to me as a newly ordained priest. On the part of many lay people I have received a whole lot of undeserved kowtowing as if I were something they are not, a special holy man. On the other hand, those of us who have professional positions in the church encourage this behavior by pridefully enjoying the attention. These attitudes of exaggerated deference coming from the lay person to the missionary and/or priest, in my opinion, is doing a tremendous disservice to the gospel. It creates a false class system of Christians that God never intended, a perceived division between those who serve in the church and those who do not.

What Louise has shown us from the Scriptures is what I like to call the "missionhood of all believers." We must understand that all of us are called into missionary service in some form. The question of whether or not Jesus is calling you into missions is really irrelevant. That question was answered positively when Jesus died on the cross, rose again, and issued the Great Commission. The proper question is, do you have a special vocation to go overseas or to work in a cross-cultural context as part of the larger missionary calling of the Church?

Where Missionary Calls Come From

A common misconception about missionaries is that they are special Christians who receive a supernatural calling, like a voice from heaven or a vision of an angel (otherwise, why would they ever do such a crazy thing?!). Our tendency to think this way is often nothing but a defense mechanism to wiggle out of doing sacrificial things God wants us to do. In fact, missionaries are special only in the sense that all Christians are special in the eyes of God. In 1 Peter 2:9 we read: "But you are a chosen people, a royal priesthood, a holy nation, a people belonging to God, that you may declare the praises of Him who called you out of darkness into His wonderful light." In most cases the missionary call to go overseas is discerned in much the same way other Christians perceive what their vocations should be.

In my experience, I have heard only a few missionary candidates speak of their call in terms of dreams or voices. Most have said that it was Bible study, or prayer, or the suggestion of others, or circumstances, or a combination of such factors that first led them to pursue missionary service. It is simply not true that a calling from God to ministry must be somehow proportionate in drama to the difficulty of the ministry. For every missionary called into service like Paul with a dream and a voice (see Acts 9), there are many others called more like Barnabas who first learned what he should do simply through prayer and the fellowship with the church (see Acts 13).

Practical Steps for Confirming a Missionary Call

When a person initially senses a call to missionary service, or any call for that matter, two mistakes are to be avoided at all costs: doing nothing at all and doing everything at once. On the one hand, making no changes in your life at all is tantamount to ignoring God. On the other hand, rushing out to buy a one-way ticket overseas may land you in a place where God (and everyone else) does not want you to be. The key to responding to a missionary call is to look for confirmation. God loves to reveal things to us, to make things more clear, and he has unlimited resources under his control to do it.

I want to suggest a three-step process for confirming a missionary call. The three steps—inquiry, involvement and investigation—are presented in the order in which I believe most people should, and naturally, will proceed. The suggested activities under each step, however, are not in any significant order.

Step 1: Inquiry

The first, and perhaps most obvious, thing to do with the idea that you may be called to missionary service is to take up the matter in detail with God himself. The faith assumption to make as a Christian is that God is willing and eager to confirm his will for you, especially as you inquire of him directly in prayer and in reading the Bible. This does not mean the answer will come easily and without struggle, but you should not assume that these basic spiritual disciplines cannot be of any help in such a matter.

Prayer. To commit the possibility of a missionary calling to prayer is the first step toward responding. Experienced Christians know this because to pray is essentially to submit to God as Governor of your personal life. We do not pray to God the way we go to an attorney seeking advice. In the latter case, we go to hear our options so that we can decide for ourselves what to do. In prayer we go to God with a willingness to follow his leading, even before we know exactly what direction to take. If we were not willing to obey, we would not pray.

To pray about the possibility of missionary service is not a step to be taken lightly, but it is absolutely essential if you are looking for confirmation of a missionary calling from God. Dare to pray. And be specific. Add the issue of missionary service to your daily routine of prayer. Pray with others whose confidentiality you can trust. Jesus said, "Ask and it will be given to you; seek and you will find; knock and the door will be opened to you. For everyone who asks receives; he who seeks finds; and to him who knocks, the door will be opened" (Mt 7:7-8). God will give you direction about missionary service when you pray.

Bible Study. Psalm 119:105 says, "Your word is a lamp to my feet and a light for my path." The basic idea here is that the Scriptures, inspired by God, give guidance to the people of God. My experience has been that, coupled with prayer, a discipline of reading the Scriptures with an openness to apply what is learned is a sure way to confirm a missionary call. This is not only because God is eager to reveal his will to us, but also because the Bible is all about missionary service—God reaching out to the nations of the world, using his people as his instruments to do the job. So on the matter of calling missionaries, the Bible is especially well-suited!

Be sure to maintain your daily habit of reading the Scriptures as you wait for God to confirm his direction for you concerning a missionary call. There is no need to engage in any special Bible studies or to refer to selected verses on missionary service, which, in fact, may lead you to think you should go overseas when you might not be called. It is better simply to trust God to direct you within your everyday routine of devotional study. The bishop who ordained me to the priesthood once told a group of us who were newly ordained not to fret about doing great things for God: "Just show up, and he will do the rest." Just show up in prayer and Bible study to inquire of God about missionary service, and God will do the rest.

Step 2: Involvement

The advent of high technology in this century has radically changed the way overseas ministry is done. It has also greatly influenced the way people decide to do overseas ministry in the first place. Advanced technology has served to bring millions of people from other countries to our own towns and cities in the United States, and the same technology has created significant possibilities for doing short-term mission work overseas. Cross-cultural ministry in the United States and short-term service overseas can help provide confirmation of a long-term call to overseas ministry.

Local ministry. Today more than ever before we are blessed to find people from Asia, Africa, and Latin America in the mainstream of the

United States. They are in our churches, neighborhoods, and places of work. For anyone sensing a missionary call from God, it is easy now to get a sense of what it would be like to work with people of other cultures before making a long-term commitment overseas.

This local involvement with internationals may or may not be organized. A church in your area or the local Chamber of Commerce may have a program you can plug into. If not, try simply inviting internationals from your church or neighborhood to a meal. Either way, a key question to ask yourself is this: When you come across people with different habits and thought patterns than your own, are you interested and drawn in or are you fearful and repelled? It may be a little bit of both, but the experience might help you clarify God's direction concerning missionary service.

Short-term experience overseas. It is no longer necessary for prospective missionaries to make a multi-year commitment to go overseas without having any experience of the place and people they are going to serve. There are hundreds of organizations in the United States, and some associated with the Episcopal Church (check the Resources at the end of the book), which can arrange a mission experience overseas lasting anywhere from one week to six months. Some long-term agencies will even help missionary candidates arrange a short-term trip to the very place they are considering for long-term service.

The benefits of a short-term experience are legion. Not only will you see what it is like to live overseas, you will gain experience in applying to a mission agency, in communicating with your church about mission work, and even, perhaps, in raising funds to make the trip possible. Some have said that short-term trips give a distorted picture of what long-term service might be like. My experience, however, is that this is to be preferred over having no picture at all. So, if the opportunity is available for you to go short-term, do not pass it up.

Step 3: Investigation

In Acts 13, we learn that sending the first cross-cultural missionaries was an affair between the Holy Spirit and an entire congregation. It is significant that Saul and Barnabas did not receive their call individually, or even as a team, but in the fellowship of the gathered church. I take this to be a worthy model for discerning a missionary call today. A person considering missionary service should, even at the initial stages, bring the idea before the local church and any church-based missionary organizations as a way of further investigating the will of God.

Your local church. Bringing your local church into the decision-making process is helpful for two reasons: first, your church has people filled with the same Holy Spirit who is seeking to lead you into service; second, the people of your local church know you. This combination is available to you in very few other relationships you have, so take advantage of it. To consult your local church, it is generally not a good idea to make an announcement on Sunday and see what happens. You may get too much feedback that way, and much of it will not be helpful. It is far better to start by privately sharing with your rector your sense of call. Bringing your pastor into the process is vital for church involvement in your missionary service. He/she will likely have an idea of what steps to take from there. If not, you might request that your pastor appoint a committee made up of mature Christians whom you know and trust as a "support committee" for prayer and counsel. Over time such a group can be helpful to you for discerning a missionary call and suppoorting you afterward.

Mission agencies. Many potential missionaries make a mistake in thinking you should not contact a mission agency until you know you are called and are sure where you want to go. This cuts the very people who have the most experience and expertise in international ministry out of the discernment process. Most mission agencies are not anxious to take just anyone as a missionary. If you are not called, they stand to lose just as much as you do by taking you on without proper screening. So contact mission agencies early on in the process, and they will generally be of great help. In the Episcopal Church we have a number of mission sending and support agencies which would love to speak with you if you sense a call to international ministry (see Resources section at back of book). Most will seek to engage you in a process of inquiry and application. This may even involve a meeting or conference with agency representatives. Trust the process, whatever it may be, to confirm or change your course.

A Message to Married Couples

Much of the above applies to both individuals and married couples. But what should be the approach of a couple when the partners do not see eye to eye on the subject of missionary service? In fact, I have met very few couples who are equally convinced they should be missionaries, especially at the earliest stages of considering a call. It is quite normal to see one spouse pushing the issue forward while the other is at least cool or even hostile to the idea. But it is not normal or right for a married couple to embark on missionary service when one partner feels they are not called. This is the issue I want to address here.

If you are a couple considering missionary service and do not agree on the matter, here is a simple covenant which you can make for yourselves. The terms are both faithful and practical: If you are the one against it, agree to explore the issue fully with your partner; and if you are the one for it, agree to drop the issue if, having explored it, your partner does not want to move forward. It is vital that such an agreement be made when the issue of missionary service first comes up, before either spouse begins to feel their point of view is not being respected.

Beyond that, let me say again that you should trust the judgment of the mission agency on such a matter. Remember, it is not in the interest of the mission agency to send out people who are not called. The issue of agreement between spouses is (or should be) one of the first things an agency looks for when considering a married couple for service.

A Call to Act

In Psalm 32, God challenges his people to follow him with these words: "I will instruct you and teach you in the way you should go; I will counsel you and watch over you. Do not be like the horse or the mule, which have no understanding but must be controlled by bit and bridle or they will not come to you."

These words challenge Christians to respond willingly and appropriately to the leading of the Lord Jesus Christ. Those who do enjoy the promise that God will guide and protect his people.

If you sense a call to missionary service, act on it willingly and appropriately. I have mentioned a few simple steps you, as a couple or individual, might take to confirm a missionary call; but the key step is to decide to take action. What you do to confirm your missionary call may not require much effort—inquiring of God in prayer and Bible study, involving yourself with people of other cultures, and investigating your call in the fellowship of other Christians—but you can be assured God will honor your efforts. Remember, he is eager to make his will known to you.

Discussion

An interesting way to apply the previous principles is to have a "test case." T.J. and his wife, Audrey, have a sense that they are being called to missionary service. They shared with the workshop group this "inkling" and received input as a plan of action was discussed.

T.J.: I am a youth pastor at a church outside Philadelphia. I have been there for five years; been married for three years, and my wife and I have an inkling of a missionary call. We are praying about what this means. We are in the very initial stages of inquiring. We have some folks telling us to go, go, go, and some folks saying no, no, no. We are both unified and eager, but don't have any idea where we want to go. We know we need to check out some of our motives. My wife isn't sure what she would do; we don't have any clue about who to ask what she would do, or what I would do. I am interested in youth; she is a news director at a radio station.

GEOFF: First of all, let's explore some questions of clarification. Do you have children? How important is her job? Have you thought at all about the type of work you might do? Have you investigated overseas opportunities for using the positions you presently have?

T.J.: We do not have children, and my wife is willing to give up her job and go if that is what God is calling us to do. Both my wife and I have degrees in broadcast journalism and we have wondered if the Lord would ever put that into play. My background is with youth and we have wondered how our gifts and talents would apply to that area. We have just begun to investigate opportunities which might use the positions we currently have.

GEOFF: Based on the information we have, what would you (the group) suggest as a plan of action for T.J. and Audrey in sensing a missionary call?

GROUP: Since you have mentioned radio, is there any hope for that? Is there an organization with information on positions available throughout the world? What are some of the opportunities available through agencies represented at this conference?

GEOFF: Most agencies, like SAMS and EWM have an opportunity list available and you would be surprised at the variety on that list. Radio and journalism skills are wanted. There are exhibition booths at the conference which will have opportunity lists available. InterChristo is a computer service that lists opportunities for mission.

LOUISE: Information is available through Global Opportunities for those considering tentmaking. They can connect you with support groups in other countries, they have a network of Christian tentmakers from all denominations.

GROUP: First seek out your pastor and those closest friends, the ones you pray with all the time. Let form follow function as your personal gifts begin to emerge. I wouldn't even look at this list until you have really committed yourself to prayer about it.

GEOFF: I believe God's wisdom is in that. The suggestion about starting with prayer, consulting your local priest and with that priest, having a plan of action, bringing that plan to the local church, has the ring of the Lord to me. Consulting InterChristo and looking at lists is for that time when you are much further advanced.

T.J.: I have done that in an introductory way and my priest sent me to this conference.

GROUP: Do you have a regular home group with whom you meet every week? The concern here is that you have a small group that is committed to pray with you, so that together you might hear the Lord as they pray for the Lord's will in your life. This group should be committed to the point that they know you well enough to tell you whether you are on the right track, to keep you accountable.

T.J.: The closest thing I have to a small group are the volunteers that work with the youth at our church.

GEOFF: It is a good idea to inform the vestry early on because later on if you are called to missionary service, you are going to have to go to that vestry, if for nothing else, for money. In my experience, the earlier they are brought in, the more sure and more quantitative will be the support you receive. The earlier you gather support, be it prayer, encouragement, or money, the more sure it is going to be with you for the rest of your ministry.

When you consider whether you want to share this "inkling" with people with whom you are involved in ministry, consider confidentiality and use caution. Certainly, you are working with youth and the Holy Spirit works through younger folks just as much as the rest of us.

LOUISE: If your church has a strong missions committee, I would suggest that you see them.

GROUP: One thing about having a group of people who are praying for you is that they are already in tune with you and will not need to be convinced. Also, if you hear some negatives, accept that sometimes it is spiritual warfare going on. Not everybody is glad to see that battle won.

GEOFF: That is why it is important to choose carefully those with whom you confide and keep that number small at the beginning. There is a war going on and Satan is perfectly willing to use people in the church to convince you to go the wrong way. Be selective.

CARING FOR MISSIONARIES: BEFORE, DURING, AND AFTER

Mrs. Gwen Burbank

I have had a variety of different levels of experiences, both as a missionary and as a missionary supporter. I did not know what a missionary was until I married one. My husband and I went to Kenya, East Africa, and worked for Bishop David Gitari. At the time I was a corporate trainer dealing with computer systems in the medical and hospital area, so I was like a fish out of water. I did not know how to translate my skills.

There are stages of adjustment for overseas living. The vertical axis in Figure 1 represents levels of comfort or levels of satisfaction and effectiveness. The horizontal axis represents different times, such as before you go overseas, during your overseas time, and the "after" overseas stage. This research was done with five groups such as the Ford Foundation, the Peace Corps, and several missionary groups. I have seen some adaptation of this type of graph which incorporated across the board overseas living experiences. First, the missionaries are called, and they want to go overseas. All of a sudden, stress may occur because the family is beginning to think about the implications. How am I going to do this? Am I going to sell my car? What am I going to do with the kids? What type of job is my wife going to have? How are we going to learn the language? How are we going to raise the money? All these practical details come into play. Unresolved issues in the couple's life will begin to surface. Take it as a good sign that these things are happening; it's

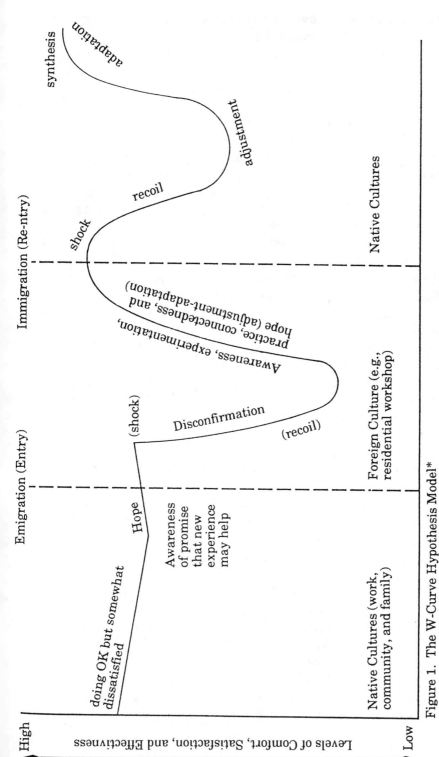

Figure 1. The W-Curve Hypothesis Model*

*From "A Strategy for Managing 'Cultural' Transitions: Re-entry from Training" by Art Freedman, p. 26 in *Cross-Cultural Reentry: A Book of Readings*, ed. by Clyde N. Austin, Ph.D, Abilene Christian University, 1986.

normal. Assist your missionaries by getting them the help they need. It is crucial that personal issues be resolved before the missionaries leave, because nine times out of ten, the resources are not available overseas to deal with them. And they will have many more stresses overseas than in their own culture with their own support system.

Every family member will go through this process in a different time frame and role. If you have studied family systems, you will know that one person may take on the role of mourner, feeling everything in the family. Another may release the tension through laughter and jokes. A third person might be the doer, always busy, never taking time to feel. That's normal. The people who are involved with the missionaries may pick up on this while the missionaries may be so engrossed in the process that they are not even aware of their tendencies.

Once you get overseas, initially there is euphoria. Then all of a sudden, a hundred decisions bombard you, and you are not able to operate on the same efficiency level as you did in the United States. This can be particularly hard on Americans because we expect to keep running, not allowing time for adjustment. It is very important to allow yourself time. In all the literature that I read, the things that you can really do to survive are first, have a sense of humor and lower your expectations of yourself; slow down, give yourself some time. It is important to allow missionaries the liberty of being learners, to say they are there to learn, not to get anything done for a year, or for short term, a month. After that they will feel more able to move into the role they planned.

In this next stage, if the missionary or cross-cultural worker does not adjust and come to a positive attitude, they can simply crash. I have seen this happen often, and now I understand that it was those without a support group at home who crashed. The correlation was very interesting to me. Those who had someone in the U.S. who prayed for them, or they could write to, or who listened to them, were able to get through it and move toward a positive adjustment. Throughout the rest of this stage, there is increasing efficiency and increasing levels of comfort until you go home.

Then re-entry occurs. You come back into your original social system and you expect to be able to operate as before, and it doesn't happen. When you go overseas, there is a tendency to forget about the bad things in your own culture. You tend to glamorize all the good things. This is my personal list: I thought that things would work better and that the people were more efficient in America. That was because in Africa, the whole dimension of time was different. Things took longer, but it didn't necessarily mean that people were less efficient. In some ways, they may have been more efficient. I remembered America as being always very clean. I thought that my friends would be the same, and I could just resume my relationships where I left off. I was very proud and I am now humbled by this—I thought that maybe because of my cross-cultural experience, people would be interested in what I did. I thought that maybe my experience was valuable, and I could use it when I got home. That's the kind of thinking that goes on.

I got home and found these things weren't true. People are dynamic, and if you have not been in good communication, you are not going to be able to pick up where you left off. Your whole system of values has changed. You will feel an overall sense of disorientation, like you don't fit anymore, and truthfully, you don't. You are no longer truly American because you have had this overseas experience, but neither are you truly (in my case) African, because I'm not African. Generally, the only place missionaries really feel comfortable is in the airplane between one country and another. You have to help the missionary be able to deal with that. During re-entry, the missionaries are often tired and irritable. They have just expended themselves overseas, and, now, back home, everybody has all these expectations which they can't possibly fulfill. Because of all this, they may withdraw, and it can lead to depression.

You can help your missionary with preparing for re-entry even before the missionary goes. Realize that the stress is not abnormal; they have to live it out. Counseling helps a lot of missionaries. There are agencies throughout the United States who do re-entry training, even for children. It might be helpful for them to take some time to just rest while coming home. Maybe if they are going through another country, they might take a week or two and just decompress a little bit before arriving home. The most important thing is really to allow your missionary to be honest about what they are feeling. A lot of times the sending church wants to hear the wonderful, victorious stories when missionaries come home. They want to hear how their dollars won the world for Christ, and that doesn't always happen. Sometimes God is planting seeds and not reaping a harvest, so sometimes missionaries feel very guilty.

We were very blessed by our church. When we came home, we were really in a lot of pain. One woman in our church said, "We need to do something for our missionaries." She started the missions committee. She invited us to do a forum and said, "We just want to hear from your heart." Our friends, who had supported us, just sat there and listened to the time when we were exhausted and had no money to go on vacation, and some of the hard things that happen to missionaries as well as the wonderful things. That did more for our healing than anything because then those who felt called in the congregation were able to minister to us through inner healing prayer or through having us over and just letting us be us. That is a key role for a missions committee.

Another way to help missionaries is to make sure that they go through adequate good-byes. It is a mourning period and sometimes they get so wrapped up in the details that they don't even say good-bye. It doesn't hit them at first, but it may hit six months later when all of a sudden, things just don't feel right because they haven't adequately gone through the mourning period and said those good-byes.

Some teenagers have to go back to their host country one more time because they tend to glorify the experience, to think only of the wonderful things. It costs a lot of money, but it may help to send them back to regain a sense of reality.

Now I would like to cover the rationale for the mission committees. For every missionary we need at least ten very committed people for support. I believe that any person going overseas should not leave home without a group of people who are equally as committed and excited about that mission. This is the ministry of senders. If anyone knew about the missionary experience, it was Paul. In Romans 10:13 he says, "How can they hear unless it is preached? How can they preach, unless they are sent?" The ministry of sending is biblical, and it is wonderful to study Paul's communication with the people who sent him. I look at it as a tripod, with God as one leg, the missionary as one leg and the senders as one leg, all important and working together to do the job. If you shorten one leg, the tripod is off balance, losing its effectiveness.

Members of the mission committee play various roles. They are the liaison with the vestry and clergy. They are the group in the church that may identify the cross-cultural worker. A number of mission agencies have stressed asking mission committees to take their jobs of screening very seriously. In other words, it would be better for the person who "feels the call to go overseas" to hear "no" from you than to get halfway through the process and hear from the mission agency that they are not really suitable for overseas work.

A very important job for the mission committee is encouraging short term missions. A short term mission is a critical tool for discernment if someone feels called to a long term mission. It's the mission committee's job to set up lines of accountability to assure that the missionary is really fulfilling a role that is strategic in God's plan for mission and not over there just shuffling paper. It is a very hard question, but you have to ask it. Ways of maintaining accountability are by letter writing, requiring a yearly report, periodic phone calls, and best of all, a visit on the field. Never feel guilty about spending money from the mission committee to send somebody over. That could mean more to a missionary than anything.

Another key role of the mission committee is seeing to the spiritual life of the missionary. People often think that doing all this great work for the Lord is going to nurture one's relationship with Jesus. Well, it doesn't; it is draining! Make sure that the missionary is spending time in the Word and in prayer. Good sermon tapes are appreciated. Oftentimes overseas, the sermons are so dry. The missionary is dealing with a totally different culture and can't even understand the sermon, even if it's in English.

Lastly, assure that the missionary's training needs are met. There are many different training institutions throughout the United States.

Part of the fun of being on a missions committee is brainstorming. When people think creatively, I have seen wild things done for support of missionaries that are really going to bless them. For instance, in the area of communication, write to them and have others sign up to write once a month, put up a bulletin board with their name and address on it, send one secular and one religious magazine, have a project of sending cards, have somebody donate $50 to $100 a month and just call, make a mat with the missionary's name with arrows to the country and laminate them as placemats to take home so families can pray for that missionary. One church has a missions family album. They include pictures with their names, addresses, prayer requests, birthdays, anniversaries, and other information that might be helpful.

There are a number of financial considerations for the missionary committee. It's very important for the missionary to know that they have their start-up money. You have to ask them some hard questions, such as are they really so far in debt that they are running away from something? Have they paid all their back taxes? Missionaries, if they are living overseas, do not have to pay U.S. taxes on earnings of less than $75,000. I have yet to meet a missionary who has made more than that. But they do have to pay overseas taxes and often that is more than they would have to pay here. Overseas taxes could bankrupt a missionary because, even though they are making little by our standards, they may be making top wages by local standards. Help them to make sure they have figured that out. And who is going to cover the insurance? Is it the church or do they have their own? What happens if the missionary dies overseas? Make that plan before they go. Are they going to be buried there? Who has their will? If a relative dies or becomes seriously ill, set up the policy ahead of time. It is easier for them to know in advance if the church does not have money to bring them home for a funeral.

Today it probably costs about $35,000 for a single missionary and between $45,000 to $60,000 a year for a family. That would include, of course, the full retirement and health package. That's a good bit of money. It's important to make sure that it is really necessary for a missionary to go overseas. Because for that same amount of money, you could support at least ten or fifteen local indigenous priests. In Kenya, there were individuals in the church called "evangelists" who had gone through seminary. That same amount of money could support probably around thirty Kenyan evangelists.

Another important question is, are those missionaries working themselves out of a job, or are they creating dependency? If I go overseas and do this job, but nobody else can ever do it, then I may be doing more harm than good. These are questions the missions committee should be responsible enough to ask. Another question involves comparable salary and housing. Is your missionary making ten times more than the bishop? We were paid the same amount of money as someone local was paid, and we lived in the same type of housing. That opened up doors in the community.

Another potential resource is retired people. These people have lived life, raised and educated their children, and now have time, and in many instances, retirement packages. Short term mission might be a good option, if it is set up right. Bringing people from foreign countries over here, and training them so they go home and do the job far better than we could is another option.

Do one little thing at a time. Your committee needs to decide upon measureable, attainable goals and steps to reach them. Don't get overwhelmed. And, remember, prayer undergirds it all.

AVOIDING DISASTERS: PREPARING FOR MISSION

The Rev. Dr. Sam Wilson

One of my favorite cartoons is one of Dennis the Menace sitting in his high chair, leaning forward as his mother comes through the kitchen door with a great, big glass of milk. Dennis tilts his head, looks at her, and says, "Who told you milk was good for me, the milkman?"

I present myself to you as a missions educator—for the moment as the milkman—to say frankly and directly that I could not be a stronger advocate of missions training. Such preparation is not only good, it is essential. It is essential in order to avoid repeated disasters. It is essential to avoid the tragedy of missed opportunities to plant the community of faith among people groups who have no fellowship of Christians where Christ's reconciling message is lived out in ways that are understandable.

There is an organization in the United States that exists to provide pre-crisis training to mission agencies. They came into existence initially to prepare agencies before they face hostage situations, i.e., they prefer disaster prevention. They will, however, send consultants after the fact, even where training has not been given. I am sure you can understand their preference for the former circumstance.

There are currently, in Latin America alone, five persons who are hostage. The ongoing hostage situations have this agency so strapped that they must deal only with the direct disasters where agencies are already in distress. There are mission agencies which spend too large a share of their energies and resources dealing with problem situations, with near and real disasters that could have been avoided or attenuated. Like the hostage agency, I would much prefer not to deal with the disasters, but with disaster prevention. That is why I am a strong advocate of missionary training.

The Anglican Communion has a noble history of mission sending, the roots of which go back to the SPCK and the CMS. This is a denominational history that has few rivals. Probably no mission society in the world has entered more unreached peoples in its history than the CMS. Included in that history are some of the most compelling contributors to missiological thought. The mere short list of names like Henry Venn and Roland Allen would be impressive enough. They faced, thought about, and dealt with situations in the nineteenth century for which no experience and no thought out training existed. Their writings and actions as supervisors of missions moved to correct that deficit. A rich body of both literature and experience exists to supplement and expand their training. Yet our current situation is that once again little, if any, preparation for the most challenging, daunting task in history is being required. I refer to taking the sacred Word and the divinely ordained community of faith and planting it in unreached people groups. That is missions.

Shortly after we convened the Stanway Institute Board for the first time, the head of an Anglican agency told me: "I can't use an ordained

Episcopal priest as a missionary." What did he mean, and what does that tell us about missionary training?

For instance, how much of what is meant by being Episcopalian is essential or contributory, and how much is secondary or even an impediment to being a missionary? Even with all that noble history, we are now looking at a church which, for decades, has suffered eroding membership and has progressively and deliberately stepped down its missions commitment. The predictable corollary has been a decline in available orientation, education, and selection processes. Neither the structures of sending nor the means of preparation have been available. And we have fallen into thinking that preparation for "normal" ministry is automatically valid for cross-cultural situations.

Adding to the mix and perplexity of our current situation is that career missionary service has been redefined and curtailed. Too many Episcopalians have either inaccurate data or erring missiology. By and large, they believe that the day of church planting mission is over, and that we live in a time when mission should be defined only as partnership with existing national churches.

At the same time, the breath of the Holy Spirit is prompting a rediscovery of a continuing call to missions and a recognition of the church's missionary nature. Where renewal has come, and matured, there is a push toward mission. This has occasioned, for example, exploratory attempts on the local parish level to find outlets for the energy of the Spirit. The existing denominational avenues are closing. In these circumstances, the consequence of the natural pressure of the Spirit of God toward those who have not heard leads to "irregular" sending. Local parishes have to entrepreneurially discover new ways of sending. The most natural avenue is short term missions from the local parish. In these circumstances, it is the most predictable thing in the world that preparation will lag behind or be non-existent. Over the long haul, this is a prescription for disaster. The parishes are underprepared to provide screening, accountability and training, or are so small that their resources are taxed by the effort. Much of this type of mission sending is occurring that is never reported. And equally unreported are the disasters that occur when preparation is deficient or non-existent.

The Southern Baptists, who have four million members, and around five thousand career missionaries, discovered they also have at least 180,000 laypersons overseas. What a challenge that would be—to work with 180,000 people who are already in an overseas situation!

So an appreciable amount of sending that is not sending goes on. A lot of people go overseas with virtually no preparation. The Baptists, by the way, were able to establish that a large percentage had some formal training in personal evangelism, although, of course, it was training in the monocultural situation, and very much method bound.

We need to do some thinking about what is the minimum preparation. I wish I could say that we could always prepare someone for what we call "culture shock" and have ways to handle that culture shock. Perhaps the worst case of culture shock of which I have personal knowledge involved a businessman who landed in Peru with his wife. Neither he nor his company had given her any preparation whatsoever. The day after their arrival, he took her to the kitchen to introduce her to the Peruvian maid who was to serve her every whim. Although he thought he was giving her the ultimate in luxury, she was so spooked by the notion of a stranger in her house so different in appearance, whose language she could not speak, that she said, "That's it!" She went up to her bedroom, began to bawl, and insisted on going back to the States immediately. A week later that's just what they did. They had to give back all the guaranteed funds and repay the travel and incidental costs themselves according to company policy.

Can such occurrences be diagnosed and avoided ahead of time? Not always, necessarily, but some instances can be eliminated and others lessened with preparation.

Unfortunately, some mission agencies do not even have a boot camp. In a week of orientation much time is exhausted telling people about the agency and its policies, how to run the accounting, how to make appropriate reports, what the agency stands for, and what it is as a mission. Extra time, if there is any, is used to prepare people to go.

By nature, I am an educator. As such, my preference is to educate people so they are prepared to react to the different contexts that they will find. One way of looking at culture shock is to ask about the things that are viewed differently. The sense of time, as well as the use of space, vary drastically. Learning not to expect things to happen on the United States time schedule means gaining an understanding of the question of when is late late. Often three days is fast in the Third World. That would completely fly in the face of everything that we North Americans expect in our hurry-up culture.

So how is a missionary prepared for a change in the sense of time? Perhaps you are familiar with the story of the agency board member who was supposed to examine a missions candidate because the full board was unavailable. So he waited a week, and then he called the candidate up one day and he said: "At 3:00 in the morning, I would like you to be on my porch." The candidate arrived on the porch promptly at 3:00 a.m.

He sat there, and he sat there, and he sat there. At 5:00 a.m. the door finally opened and the mission board member invited him inside. He sat him down on his couch, looked him square in the eyes, straight-faced and said, "How much is two plus two?" The candidate, raging internally, controlled his emotions and said, "Four." And thus it went on. The candidate was waiting for the real interview on his qualifications to begin, when the board representative said: "Fine, that will be all. I'll be sending my recommendation to the board. You should know it will be positive."

The letter he wrote to the board gave the following detail:

> I tested the candidate's expectations as to the use of time by surprising him and asking him to come at an absurd hour. I then tried his patience by leaving him sitting there for two hours. I tested his humility by asking him questions that a third grader could easily have answered, and he passed all my tests with flying colors. I have a patient, humble, adaptable person that I am fully able to recommend to the board as a missions candidate.

We do not need more missionaries if the cost is sending the wrong people. When we start talking missions training, we can ask: How does that person submit to taking up her cross, his cross and following Christ? How is a spirituality for mission developed? There are a whole set of spiritual disciplines, spiritual training and education required to prepare the individual to be a woman of God or a man of God. The difference will be the cross, because the cross opens the way for the life and fullness of the Holy Spirit to flood that person, to gift them and to use them.

Traditionally, we have turned to a seminary residential setting in order to provide a community of faith that can be the disciplining factor. These years are really supposed to be three years of spiritual formation.

What elements would we immediately suggest as making up the educating of a person to be a person of God? We certainly think of the need for flexibility and adaptability, the possession of a servant heart, the ability to experience change positively, and a tolerance for ambiguity.

The Apostle Paul said, "I have become all things to all men so that by all possible means I might save some" (1Cor 9:22).

As an educator, I look for what I take to be the hallmark of the fullness of the Spirit in anybody's life. For me, it is the spirit of the learner, a readiness to learn. With a group or with a prospect for a short term mission trip, I would say emphatically, "Do you understand that you are going as a learner? The purpose for your going is to learn, not necessarily to give." We North Americans have this arrogance that we have got the gospel right, the message right, we have got it all down; all we have to do is go teach them to do it our way. That notion is contrary to the working of the Spirit of God.

I used to take student groups for a two- or three-week overseas study trip and they would know they were going to learn. I would structure the trip so there would be a mix of both academic and experiential learning. Also included would be an absolute requirement of a pre-field orientation commitment and a post-field processing or debriefing commitment so they could process and learn from the experience once they had returned.

Another major area of preparation is developing a disposition and readiness to work together in the Body. How should we train missions candidates so that a true team spirit is learned? Where in the church do you find a congregation that has a structure or a mechanism that produces real bonding and fellowship, that models the kind of support we are talking about? We need to give attention to the spiritual characteristics of the person and to the spiritual development and mutual interdependence of the Body, because we don't want lone rangers going out there. Lone rangers are almost universally recognized as detrimental.

How do we make people think, not of how good we are and how much we have or how well off "they" will be if they come to be like us, but the exact opposite? The exact opposite is the essential mindset of the missionary and the church. How must I change in order that others may hear?

All of our Western stuff, powerful, majestic, familiar and moving as the liturgy may be to us, may need to be examined in terms of how must we change to be missionaries. That's the start. Please understand, I am not calling for change for change's sake. Change is not comfortable, but it is the character of the New Testament church. If I am to prepare missionaries, I must prepare missionaries to do the bridging, the reaching, the changing.

No matter what preparation model we look at, that model should include an experience and a process piece that forces people to put the experience together with the content. This helps guarantee that out of that thoughtfulness comes an improved attitude, an improved understanding of structure, an improved understanding of potential cross-cultural goals. Content matched with experience worked through process. Preparation must include cross-cultural experience that is evaluated.

What should that content include? Characteristically, missions preparation programs include three content areas. Number one, of course, would be basic biblical and theological studies. Along with them, follow the social and behavioral sciences. They are an absolute necessity. Then, there are the specifically missiological studies: mission history, mission theology, and strategy and models of mission. With those three areas a person gains perspective and has a good start on becoming the person capable of doing the job.

At the parish or church level, what would that mean? It could mean hosting the Perspectives course, which immediately brings together the three components of historical, biblical and missiological materials. Or, it could mean making use of the marvelous influence of missionary biographies. If we look at the generation we are trying to persuade to go into missions, they are most receptive to the MTV type of presentation. Using talented youth to dramatize portions of missionary biographies as skits would be a double blessing—both to the ones who read the biography and choose the chapter and to the ones who see the presentation.

There is a good reason why the Southern Baptists have 5,000 missionaries. They advertise publicly and practice within their church the slogan: "Baptists are a mission-minded church." There are 1,700 Christian and Missionary Alliance churches and over 1,000 missionaries. Within the CMA Church a missions conference of at least three to four days is expected of each congregation every year. Sunday school classes are dedicated to a specific mission field where they study the country and the people. As the youth grow, they are absorbing mission. They know God wants people to go. The Mormons plan the financing of a missionary term from the birth of each manchild. There is no question of whether, only how.

The church has to begin by believing that it exists for mission. The Episcopal Church supposedly has 2.5 million members and has less than one hundred missionaries. The South American Missionary Society alone has almost fifty; the Church Army has a couple. In 1994 twenty-two Volunteers for Mission and Appointed Missionaries are in the field who have just been advised that their current term is their last.

The local parish can be made into a missionary parish. The training, the motivation starts in the parish. It begins, I believe, by asking one critical question: "What does it mean to be a Great Commission parish?" This does not mean that local needs are neglected or that the liturgy is discarded. It does mean that, as the accidents of history and time and place and country change, we must be open to change in order to be faithful to the Word of God. Permission to do this is even granted in the preface to the Book of Common Prayer and validated by Article XXXIV of the Thirty-nine Articles. There are prayers for mission in that book that are supposed to be prayed every day. Every parish must have missions as a primary focus for existing.

The question then comes up, "How can this be done in a parish?" As a response to that question, let me present a little bit about a background for modeling. Are you at all familiar with the generational divides that are currently being used to analyze the U.S. sociologically? Seniors are considered the builder generation. They are followed by the boomer generation, and they, in turn, by the busters. Then follow their children whom we haven't named yet, but simply call Generation X. We don't know what they are going to be like. The reason I raise this is because what is distressing everybody in all churches and agencies is that the builder generation, now in their fifties and sixties, are the major donors, the major support for missions. But something happens as you move to the boomer generation. The boomer generation shows little denominational loyalty. They share that with the busters, by the way. But they still can be enlisted for things in which they believe.

What has this got to do with mission? If we are talking about educating boomers and busters to do mission, you have got to know that the only thing that will motivate both of them is a cause in which they can believe. They will not be motivated by denominational loyalty. They will not just fall in line; they have to be convinced that the task is worth doing, that it is worth supporting. There is also another obstacle. Every generation that ever lived probably hated the bureaucracy that they had to live with, but some of us learned to live with it. These guys won't. They will pick only those organizations that suit them. Now, is God going to write Ichabod across the whole boomer generation, the whole buster generation, and there are not going to be any missions? We are pretty close to that with the boomers. We see largely later vocations now. The task for us is to evolve a parish program that puts children, teenagers, and the buster generation in tune with the cross-cultural needs of the world, the mission challenges of the world, that allows them to get invested in that world in a way that they can use their gifts and know that they can modify the program. That requires inspired, tough leadership.

Every three years a Mission Handbook is published detailing all approximately 900 mission agencies in the U.S. and Canada, their ministries and their denominational connections. You would think a boomer or a buster could find something in that book that is worth doing. Instead, they are so antagonistic to organizations that they don't even want to look at the book. Describing an organization will not involve them, will not educate them to commit their lives to mission. They will not be motivated unless they are presented with a clear, persuasive statement that this is what the world is all about; this is worth doing.

They need to see in the Word and modeled in life, men and women of God, sensitive to others' needs, who recognize when a need exists and respond. That's a first step toward becoming a missionary. Dramatize for them the need that is the peculiar mission need of the world and be a role model for them. You can't simply tell them, "go."

The model of the minister training the minister, in ministry together is a truth that we have got to recapture. We have got field-based education, decentralized education, distance education, and interactive education, the high tech stuff: Internet with a satellite hookup so we can talk with the TV camera to students in Tanzania, but they need to know *why*. The student needs to see a missionary doing without potable water, meat once a week and still being a joyous Christian concerned about reaching others. When he sees that model, it will make him a missionary or a minister. Build ways in your church to model reaching out. Recognize and be sensitive to those around you who are different and glorify bridge-building. These after all are the essential missionary gifts.

INTERCESSORY PRAYER:
PLUG INTO THE POWER

The Rev. Valarie Whitcomb

God has the task of world evangelization and world mission on his heart as never before. Now, that may seem to be a presumptuous statement to make about God because it is obvious that God has these concerns on his heart and has had them on his heart forever. However, I think God has turned up the burner on the stove, and there is a fire burning in God's heart today for world evangelization and world mission which appears to be greater than ever before. It appears that God is right on the edge of doing a great thing in the church and through the church, in reaching the world. What we need is God's heart. If we really had God's heart, then we would pray, because we would have the same passion that he has for the people; we would have the same passion for the lost, for the nations. I know that God is going around the world today touching churches with this passion. God is touching churches across denominational lines. God is lighting a fire and motivating churches to become churches that pray, especially that pray for world mission and evangelization.

We had a prophetic word come forth at All Saints about a year ago.

God was saying something like this: "My heart cry for the nations has reached its full measure. I can no longer contain the fire of my love. I require now also the hearts of my people." His heart, I think, is bursting with love for the nations and the lost, and he wants us to catch that fire in our hearts.

About seven months ago the rector of our church, John Guernsey, and I felt that the Lord was calling our church to be "a house of prayer for all nations." At all vestry meetings, we gather around the altar. We mostly pray throughout a large portion of our vestry meetings. We don't make any decisions unless we pray and listen to the Lord, and we don't make any decisions until everyone is in agreement. If we are not in agreement, we figure God isn't ready to give us the answer yet. We spent a fair amount of time praying through this prayer concept to see exactly what the Lord *did* want to show us. What we began to understand was that he wanted this call to be a house of prayer for all nations, to be the foundation in our church on which everything else was built. Once that call was laid as a foundation, it would influence all the other programs. For example, we now have our children praying for the nations. We are beginning to have more courses in our adult education program related to prayer and how to pray. We had some before, but we are increasing them now. I think God wants to call churches to "major" in prayer.

Now, I am going to make a true confession as a clergy person, and it is that most clergy (as well as highly motivated, godly lay leaders) can come up with a thousand and one bright ideas in any one 24-hour period. These ideas can keep the church really busy. One of the things we are having to come to terms with is that we are not to do or decide anything about any future program or activity without submitting it to the Lord. We are to ask him how it fits with his concept of a house of prayer for all nations. For me personally, this means I really have to submit my bright ideas to the Lord. It is very easy to create a lot of stuff, even a lot of stuff around prayer, and not have it be God's stuff.

About seven months ago, as we began to try to pull this together and understand what God was trying to teach us, we began to see many important truths. We are discovering that God is moving the same way in many churches, mobilizing people and teaching the same principles: "God's Prayer Principles for World Mission."

1. God has all the time in the world.

It is only us Westerners who do not have all the time in the world. God made time, and he is the One who has the purposes, programs, ideas, etc. He has enough time for whatever he wants to do. We need to submit ourselves to his guidance and *his timing*. God is working his purposes out. The scripture for this principle is Habakkuk 2:14, "For the earth will be filled with the knowledge of the glory of the Lord, as the waters cover the sea." We can rest and know that God is going to do what he is going to do. Our job is to cooperate, listen, hear, obey and be faithful.

2. God is looking for consecrated hearts and lives.

We have been hearing about the cost of world missions. Not only does world mission cost us everything, but prayer and intercession for the nations costs us everything. If we are really going to be serious about prayer, there are a lot of other things we are going to have to give up. We have to find more time to pray, one way or another. We either have to get up earlier, stay up later, or carve out some other time and this is not easy. I know that, because I battle it daily, but it is absolutely essential. It requires giving up activities that were fun, or entertaining. I have had to give up a lot of needlework I used to do. The scripture I want to use is Romans 12:1. *"In view of God's mercy, offer your bodies as living sacrifices, holy and pleasing to God"* (NIV).

3. God uses imperfect vessels.

All of us are somewhere on the road to holiness, complete sanctification, total healing, and to knowing what in the world we are going to do when we grow up. It is a process. There is a tendency, in our culture more than anywhere else, to want to get there and have it all together. God is much more concerned with the process than with the end result. Obviously he wants and likes the end results, but it is the process that is important. When we begin to intercede for the nations, world vision, and world evangelization, we are going to find that God is much more interested in what he is working into us than he is on the outcome of any individual prayer. He is interested in the process in us, but the result will be mighty prayer for the nations. This scriptural principle is revealed in 2 Corinthians 4:7, *"But we have this treasure in jars of clay, to show that this all-surpassing power is from God and not from us"* (NIV).

4. Humility must be one of the cornerstones on which we build a house of prayer.

We cannot even pray without God. Jesus says in John 15:5, *"I am the vine, you are the branches. If you remain in me, and I in you, you will bear much fruit. Apart from me, you can do nothing"* (NIV). God has quickened that Scripture to our hearts almost every time we pray. "Lord, apart from you, we can do nothing. Apart from you, we can't pray, know what we are supposed to do next, teach Sunday School...whatever it is, apart from you, we can't do it." It is absolutely critical that we understand that our capacities, whether they are spiritual gifts, natural talents, our physical energies, must be yielded so that he can flow through us. If we are not humbled before the Lord, the result will be a lot of good projects and maybe an exciting church, but God's not going to get the glory. Instead, men and women will get the glory, and that is not what he wants. Psalm 127:1 says, *"Unless the Lord build the house, its builders labor in vain"* (NIV).

5. God begins his work in us by changing our worldview.

One of the popular terms today is "paradigm shift." It means a change that has to do with the very foundations of what we believe. Once we begin to make those changes in our lives and in the life of the church, it is like an earthquake. Maybe that is what God means when he says he is going to shake things! We need to change the way we see and understand the world. We must learn that we live in the Kingdom of God and that the kingdom of darkness is against us. We must come to the understanding that our struggle in prayer is not against flesh and blood but against the rulers, the authorities, the powers of this dark world, and against the spiritual forces of evil in the heavenly realms (Eph 6:12). We must get that paradigm shift worked into the base of our being.

I want to show you several worldviews. "Probably there is some kind of heaven somewhere, probably there is even a God, but all of reality is down here on earth. Everything is lived in the concrete, the here and now." That is the one that we function in, unless we stop and think about it.

The second view is what I will call a "Western *Christian* worldview." This is the one that most of us are all learning to operate in as we learn to live in the Kingdom of God. In this one we believe that there is a heaven. We also live down here on earth in the reality of everyday life.

We believe that there is a certain interaction here between heaven and earth; that there are angels that seem to come down from time to time, and the power of the Holy Spirit can affect our world. Generally we believe this, but we don't act like it much of the time. It takes a great effort to stop and think of the reality of the Kingdom of God and that there is this continuous interaction between the supernatural world and the natural world.

The last view is a "Third World view" or another name for it is the "biblical worldview." This is the one in which we should be operating all of the time. In this one, too, there is a belief that there is heaven and there is earth, the physical realm and the supernatural realm. The difference in this worldview is, that instead of having a solid line that keeps us from going back and forth from the supernatural to a natural realm, there is what science calls a "semipermeable membrane." There is always interaction, a continuous flow between the supernatural and the natural world. In fact, right now I'll make an outrageous statement: there are more than likely some demons here. There are also some angels here, and if we pray we have access to the power of the Holy Spirit in this room. That's the perspective that we need if we're going to be intercessors. We must have that understanding because we intercede in two ways:* One way of intercession is to draw someone to God, for healing or whatever the situation is. The other way of intercession is to stand in the gap so that the person or situation is divided from the evil one. Both ways of intercession require living in the biblical worldview.

Our problem with these worldviews is that, if we don't stop to think about it, we operate in the non-Christian worldview. If we do stop to think about it, we might operate in the Christian worldview. But the biblical worldview is where we need to be all the time. Our heart's desire needs to be a more continuous living in the Kingdom of God. We are seated in the heavenly places and have authority in the name of Jesus to do mighty works, to destroy the works of the evil one, and to build the Kingdom of God. This is only done through prayer. However, we have to engage more and more in the biblical worldview if this is going to be accomplished.

6. God is going to begin this work by cleaning our hearts.

I have a personal experience of this, and I have been a Spirit-filled

---

*I got these from some tapes on intercessory prayer called the "Lightening of God" by Dutch Sheets. Order by phoning 719-548-8226.

Christian for twenty years. Before this call to prayer for the nations began, I thought God had done some stuff with me. I had been through inner healing. I had seen God work in a progressive sanctification in me. When God began to get hold of us at All Saints Church about being a house of prayer for all nations, we began to discover layers and places in our hearts that God had not touched. It has been very painful, but absolutely essential. What God is doing today is not a superficial work, because he needs our heart to contain his love. He has to do something to enlarge our hearts. If he does not do that, he will not be able to use us to intercede.

There are several ways that God does this heart cleaning. First, we need a great cleansing from our Western lifestyles and selfish desires. That is one thing that God has been doing in our hearts at All Saints!

The second thing that God needs to do in cleansing hearts is a great cleansing of the past sins. If there is unconfessed sin, there are places where the enemy can attack. Praying for the nations is not like praying for your Great-aunt Susie who has the flu; it is much more serious. I find that this confessing and cleansing is not particularly effective in my personal prayer closet. I find this to be true of our lay leaders also. If you have got something to confess, go to a brother or sister. We can say it to God, but we'll never know we are free until we say it out loud, bring it out into the light, and have someone assure us of forgiveness.

The third thing God does when he starts to clean our heart is a great healing of our past from the effects of the sins committed against us. This means we are going to have to forgive things that we do not want to forgive. Obviously this is painful, but it is essential if we are going to intercede.

We can present our hearts to God so he can prepare them to be intercessory hearts. It involves an act of our will to say, "Lord, I hear your heart cry for the nations. Here I am, use my heart." We need to have pure hearts to hear how he wants us to pray. Some of you who are already intercessors know that God wants to give his intercessors his secrets about individuals, families, churches and nations, so that we can pray those things into being or in whatever way he leads. But he has to have pure hearts and people who can keep his confidences. Hearts that are unhealed and harbor sins like anger, bitterness, unforgiveness, and resentment cannot be used fully for God's purposes, partly because they are unclean, and partly because uncleanness leaves places for the enemy to debilitate us and our ability to engage in the prayer battle. Do not become discouraged. My own discovery is that this is a process. God will use us at whatever stage we are now. He is a gracious God of mercy and forgiveness. He wants us closer to him. As we get closer he begins to burn off some of what has been hindering us. The cleaner our hearts, the closer we can come to God's heart (see Ps 24:3, 4, and 7).

7. He wants to begin by working with his leaders, both clergy and laity.

These people in our parishes are the vision carriers. Many of you may be in churches where you have a real desire to see this kind of thing happen, but you don't know what to do because your rector is not on board and neither are your lay leaders. The role of the intercessor is to get God's heart and to begin to pray for it to be manifest in your church, for God to begin to change the hearts of those whom he is calling to be vision carriers. It is our task to love them and intercession enables us to love. The more we love them, the gentler we will be with them, and the more wisdom we will have about approaching them.

As leaders at All Saints, we have experienced that this season, which has been going on for about a year, is a season of great revelation and unearthing. There has been a lot of stuff that God has brought up in our personal lives and about the way we operate as a church. There has been a lot of repentance, a lot of weeping, a lot of teaching about the vision. We have experienced a great tearing down of false beliefs and assumptions and we have also experienced a great restoration in our lives. Even as he breaks down the old, he is building up the new. As we learn experientially, he takes us also to a place where we must understand it theologically and biblically, so that it can be taught.

8. God will provide hands-on learning situations in order to give us the encouragement we need.

I am going to give you one clear example: One night I was watching a news special on Ethiopia. The people were starving, and there was a lot of war. Now, I have seen hundreds of pictures of starving children on television. As I looked at those pictures, however, I began to weep. I knew it was God because I had seen so many pictures that I had long since lost sensitivity to them. I was broken-hearted over these children in Ethiopia. The rector and I were teaching our first class on intercessory prayer and had been seeking ways to apply the principles of intercessory prayer practically so the people could begin to experience it. My weeping experience led us to set up a project which we called, "Target: Ethiopia." We did a lot of research on Ethiopia. We had people make summaries of newspaper articles. We had others copy maps of Ethiopia into manageable portions. Then we worked out a prayer list together. Every Friday we had a prayer vigil from late afternoon to nine or ten o'clock at night. People committed themselves to pray for an hour. We provided material and prayer requests. The class lasted six weeks, and we did fifteen prayer vigils. Every week we would get the latest information off the news wires. We summarized fresh prayer requests each week so people could see if there was any change in the situation, if any progress was being made. Eventually, we got to the end of the class, and the crisis in Ethiopia seemed to slow. As we prayed throughout the class, we came to identify the closed port of Mogadishu as the key target for our prayers. There were many relief agencies with their ships out in the harbors loaded with food to bring into the country but they could not bring it into the port since it had been closed because of fighting.

Now I want to read to you from a portion of a book on intercessory prayer, written by a professor at General Theological Seminary, John Koenig. He used "Target: Ethiopia" as an example in his book.

> All during Lent in 1990 a large group of church members gathered to learn about the needs of Ethiopians on both sides of the conflict and to pray for them. Most of these Christians prayed—every Friday for five hours—that people would be fed. I learned of this concentrated effort in April. Some two months later I chanced upon an article in the *New York Times* entitled "Millions Are Fed As War Rages—With Luck and Ingenuity Ethiopian Aid Gets Through." The story concerned an unusual series of breakdowns in the government bureaucracy that had enabled international church agencies to deliver huge amounts of food to remote rural areas. Luck and ingenuity? Yes, and very likely something more. Of course one can never prove sequences of cause and effect when it comes to prayer, but here the coincidences are arresting.*

That was our first venture into praying for a nation. It was small, it was manageable, but it produced awesome results. Now, I'm not saying it was just us praying. Obviously, God was mobilizing people all over the world, because he loves Ethiopia. He gathered up all the prayers of his people everywhere so that he could release his answer and the people could be fed. God will provide hands-on learning situations and will give us the encouragement we need!

---

*John Koenig, *Rediscovering New Testament Prayer* (San Francisco: Harper, 1992), p. 88.

9. God will not teach us to intercede in a vacuum.

He wants to give each church deep and warm relationships with real-life missionaries and nations. I want to give you an example—a tiny country called Brunei. It is illegal there to be anything other than Muslim. Therefore, the church in Brunei is a struggling church. There are maybe two thousand Christians in Brunei. Last summer, when the March for Jesus was going on, the March for Jesus Organization in the U.S. supplied each community a nation in the "10/40 Window"* to pray for. We got a phone call from March for Jesus saying we were assigned the country of Brunei. So we began to do research as we did for Ethiopia. We had a prayer assembly at the close of the March for Jesus. There were about five thousand people who participated in the March, we all prayed for Brunei, for various things, one of which was that the Sultan would become a Christian and that unity would begin to occur between the churches in Brunei. There were other things, but those were two of the main things.

Later in the year our rector and I were invited to go to Korea to pray as a part of a gathering of people who prayed during the focus in October on the 10/40 Window. There was a woman there from Brunei. This woman was so excited when she learned that five thousand people in Woodbridge, Virginia, had prayed for her country! In the meantime, our rector had been invited to go to a conference in Malaysia. He thought, "While I am in Malaysia, it's not that far from Brunei, why don't I stop by?" Our friend said she believed God wanted our rector there during their spiritual warfare conference. Those happened to be the exact days that fit in with his schedule. He went to Brunei, met the Christians, and began to feel burdened that somehow God was going to enable him to meet the Sultan of Brunei. He thought, "This is crazy, we all know you don't come to the United States and meet Bill Clinton." When he got to Brunei, the people who met him at the airport said, "How long are you going to stay?" He said, "Till Tuesday (or whatever it was)," and they said, "Oh, you can't go home then. You have to stay another day." "Why?" "On that day we are going to go and pray for the Sultan." The Sultan was holding a special festival open house and every Brunei citizen had been invited to come and meet the Sultan through a long receiving line. The Brunei Christians believed that if they went through the line and shook his hand, they would be "laying hands" on him. They were go-

*The "10/40 Window" is that band of countries from Africa to China between 10 and 40 degrees latitude.

ing to pray silently for him as they did so. Well, our rector went through the line and prayed for the Sultan. All Saints now has contact with the country and with real live people. We continue to fast and intercede for Brunei.

10. In these days, God is raising up an army of prayer warriors, a network of intercessors and a new breed of missionaries, short and long term.

One of the things we have learned is that every person who is an intercessor needs intercessors; every person who is a pastor or lay leader needs intercessors; and every person who is a missionary needs intercessors. I have nine personal intercessors. I keep them informed of my prayer needs. God is trying to teach us that intercession works together with missions. When we went on a trip to Uruguay, this is the kind of intercession we had going. It was a two-week trip to do two conferences for clergy and lay leaders on inner healing and intercession. We were going to do some teaching on spiritual warfare and deliverance as well, so I knew we needed a lot of intercession. I had nine personal intercessors praying for me and the team. At All Saints we also have what we call "Intercessors for Uruguay." These are nine people who feel called to pray for Uruguay. I put the Intercessors for Uruguay on red alert during that mission trip. A priest who went with us had maybe nine personal intercessors, so we had a total of about twenty-seven intercessors praying for our mission trip. As the intercessors at home began to pray and listen to the Lord, the Lord guided, and he began to give them scriptures. The next day they would fax the scriptures to us. The scriptures were encouragement, but often they were also specific words of instruction that we needed to apply to the situation we were facing the next day. The mission trip was extraordinarily blessed by God. The first day we did a teaching on the baptism of the Holy Spirit to thirty people. All were baptized in the Holy Spirit, powerfully, with signs and wonders following. It was perhaps one of the easiest times of ministry I have ever had. I flowed with the Spirit; it was not difficult; and our team experienced the same thing. The interesting thing was that there was almost no spiritual warfare at all for us while we were in Uruguay. However, at home, our intercessors were bearing the brunt of the warfare. Some of them became physically ill. There was great travail going on, and many tears as they, together and independently, interceded and prayed through for us. The result was that they began to love Uruguay. Many did not have the same connection that we do at All Saints Church, but they, too, began to have God's heart for Uruguay as they interceded and did spiritual warfare.

I really believe that is the kind of missions God wants in the future. We cannot do this stuff alone. It is impossible. We must have intercessory prayer support, and we must have people out on the field doing the ministry. You cannot separate it. It has to be together.

PRAYING FOR THE CITY

Capt. Steve Brightwell

I would like to tell you a story of what God is doing in my life and in the lives of some other people with whom I pray. I cannot do this as an expert; I feel like I have just entered the first grade of prayer. The Lord had impressed on me earlier, when I was a missionary in Honduras, that he wanted me to become a man of prayer. He has gone to great lengths to get me there, and it is beginning to happen.

As the new National Director for the Church Army, I was in a very isolated position. I had been a missionary in Honduras, but moving into the inner city was a bigger cross-cultural jump for me. The Billy Graham Crusade was on its way to Pittsburgh. I got a call from a man who was trying to rally people together who had a cadre of men they could mobilize and get the Crusade going. I said, "John, I don't have a cadre of anything. I am isolated." He said, "Well, would you like to get in on a group that prays on Thursday mornings for an hour and a half?"

Now I want to tell you how God made John ask me to come. Months before, I had gone to St. Louis to meet with a consultant. His secretary showed me a newspaper article about a new store that had opened up on Liberty Avenue near us in Pittsburgh called "Condom Nation." The article broke my heart, and I have a hard heart. When my heart breaks, it's the move of God. The Lord impressed on me that I was to go and lay on the sidewalk in front of Condom Nation and pray. I thought, "That would be kind of neat, I might do that." And God said, "You have to do this." I'm walking into town, gritting my teeth. It's noon rush, in downtown, on the busiest street. As I walked around the corner onto Liberty Avenue, there was Condom Nation. There are sleazy sin spots in the area of our headquarters. They are the regular, dingy, dark, shame-covered places where people scurry quickly to their cars or from their cars to the front door. But this one was different; it looked like a mall shop. It was bright, clean, the windows were clear and you could see right in. There was no shame. People were going in and out of a bus stop right next to it. I annointed the store with oil, and people started looking. I threw my black bag/briefcase on the ground, and I fell on my face. I have never had a sweeter time of prayer in my life. The Lord just broke my heart.

The first principle he taught me in intercession was that we are not separate from the sin; it is in us. We are not separate from the sinners; they are us. I think I knew that intellectually, but he put it in my heart that day. Praise God, it's still there.

I need to see the perishing as perishing. It is so easy to walk past dying people and just be numb. Don't think about the eternity of hell. I thought, "Why did God do this, besides just for my benefit? Maybe he really wants to rally a prayer move for Liberty Avenue." Diocesan Convention was coming up, and I printed these little things to point to what was going on at Liberty Avenue, and to ask people to pray, to intercede for the pimps, prostitutes and the shameless sinners.

Often I find myself coming to a seige mentality and I think that we have got to break through somehow to get people to see sin, because there is blindness. Anybody who does evangelism knows that there is hardpan soil in many places in our country where people are unreceptive to the gospel. Their hearts are paved over.

As your heart begins to break for the perishing, it becomes a horrible thing. What God was beginning to show me is that the job description of the Holy Spirit is to convict the world of sin, righteousness and judgment. We can't do it. I have seen people come to the Lord with the lousiest presentation of the gospel you could ask for, and I have seen other people reject the Lord flat out in spite of an excellent presentation because you can't be convinced when you don't want to be. I am a believer in revival because I know that it is God's job to do the conviction of hearts.

When it is true national revival, I think that God will initiate revival in places of brokenness. He will come to places like Liberty Avenue. He is extravagant in teaching us to be intercessors. I have been praying with that group for a year-and-a-half. None of them are Episcopalians. They don't care whether I am successful or not. We are praying; we are not measuring ourselves. We confess using "we." We follow Isaiah's model: "Woe to me, I am undone, for I am a man of unclean lips among a people of unclean lips." We know that if we do not intercede for the sinner, who will? The guy selling condoms in Condom Nation isn't going to go home and ask the Lord to soften his heart. We are it. That is what intercession is, standing in the gap.

Program failure: I believe God has shaped this group so there is nothing we can humanly do to turn the tide. I just read 2 Chronicles, chapter 20, a big favorite, where Jehosaphat and the armies of Israel are surrounded; there is no hope. The wonderful thing about that story is that Jehosaphat knew there was no hope, there was nothing he could do, but he also knew to turn to God. God told him to stand and watch, this is my fight, watch me deliver you. After the whole city had fallen on their faces and looked to God, he delivered them, and they spent three days gathering spoils and singing praise. God is teaching us about our efforts. Yes, we have got to fight and labor, and get one and two and three against the tide. But if the tide is to turn, it has to come from heaven. The picture that I see is a picture of a sovereign God who has mercy on his people and does an incredible move that changes everything.

> I will go before you and level the mountains; I will break down gates of bronze and cut through bars of iron. I will give you the treasures of darkness, riches stored in secret places, so that you may know that I am the Lord, the God of Israel, who summons you by name. For the sake of Jacob my servant, of Israel my chosen, I summon you by name and bestow on you a title of honor, though you do not acknowledge me. I am the Lord, and there is no other; apart from me there is no God. I will strengthen you, though you have not acknowledged me, so that from the rising of the sun to the place of its setting men may know there is none besides me. I am the Lord, and there is no other. I form the light and create darkness, I bring prosperity and create disaster; I, the Lord, do all these things. You heavens above, rain down righteousness; let the clouds shower it down. Let the earth open wide, let salvation spring up, let righteousness grow with it; I, the Lord, have created it.
>
> Isaiah 45:2-8 (NIV)

As we pray, one of the things we confess is chiefly that the church is at fault. You can't blame the sinners for the mess we are in. What do we expect? Sinners sin, right? The church is to blame. The church has the burden today. We are the ones who hold the responsibility. We intercede for the whole church of Pittsburgh, cross-denominationally. We confess our failure to do it right, that we just can't.

Let me say one thing about positioning of salt and light and the sovereign Lord of the harvest. Salt has to be in meat to preserve it. It's great in the shaker, but if you are going to preserve the meat, you've got to be on it. Light is great, but under a bushel, it just doesn't help. We need to go into the really dark place for light to be light. Tie that to the idea that he is the Lord of harvest. The Lord has commanded us to pray the Lord send laborers to the harvest. But also pray that the Lord would raise up salt to put on the decaying meat and light in the dark places.

I have come to believe through this prayer group that God is tarrying to answer our prayers for revival for a very important reason: his nearness to the brokenhearted. Think about it. He releases his Holy Spirit in a powerful and special way; people become convicted of sin. But there is no one there to tell them the way of salvation, and they go weeping to their graves over their sin. He says, "Unless a preacher is sent, how will they know?" As we pray, we pray for the positioning of salt and light and for the Lord to send laborers to the harvest; we are asking him to bring the harvest workers together for the revival.

He sent Jonah to Nineveh, and the whole city repented. That was revival! If Pittsburgh did that, nobody would be ready for it! It would bust up everything. But there had to be a preacher there for that repentance to be turned into anything for God. He sent Jonah, who went reluctantly; we know it wasn't his delivery; it was that he finally got there to preach the simple message and they responded. Scripture really points to the fact that God loves those hurting places. Perhaps he tarries until we people of the Great Commission are obedient to do our part as co-laborers before he releases His Spirit. We stand on the edge of missing an opportunity and being under judgment for not taking that opportunity to go to those places open to the gospel. God has impressed on us to pray for the laborers. We also pray for those who are already there, the pastors of the churches and the apostolic leaders of the city cross-denominationally.

The last and most important element of what God has impressed on us is coming into God's presence. Sometimes when we get new people into our prayer group, often they are very anxious to jump right into intercession. Some of them want to start doing spiritual warfare, and binding and loosing things. I think God is speaking something very different to us in terms of the way we have normally prayed. He is telling us that he wants us to truly come into his presence. The thing that we say over and over in that group is: "God, we need you. We just need you. We don't need anything else. We need you! We don't want you to do anything, we just want you to be here."

Entering into his presence is what makes us come back. If you meet God when you pray, you will do it again. The key to why we have been a faithful group is that we don't rush past the throne. We stick around, and we don't ever leave it. Everything we pray is bathed in praise. In an hour-and-a-half, we may spend thirty to forty-five minutes doing nothing but honoring God for who he is. Not thanksgiving for what he has done, just honoring and praising God for who he is. What we have found is from that point on, he leads the prayer. We pray, "Let this prayer time be a time where Jesus leads us in prayer; and let it be his prayer that we pray today, so that we can be in agreement." He has prayed through us and we know it when it happens. One of the things we have prayed for Pittsburgh is that he would do whatever it takes to eliminate our pride. Pittsburgh has a history of steel barons and big money. Building a building that was three stories bigger than the other guy's across the street—that's the folklore of Pittsburgh. We pray our history. We pray for forgiveness. Our programs will never accomplish what we are asking God to do and that is to bring revival.

We need a sighting of Jesus. We need his face to shine. We need a sighting of Jesus in Pittsburgh now, and that's what we pray for. We haven't seen it yet, but God is leading us to pray, and we believe that that is what we are supposed to be doing regardless of when he answers.

SPIRITUAL WARFARE AND MISSION

The Rev. Edwin Stube

I once went on a retreat led by a Jesuit. He said that unless a work is begun in contemplation and carried out in the spirit of contemplation, it will not count for the Kingdom of God. His idea was that we need to get into the presence of the Lord and stay there.

We need to pray without ceasing. This means, first of all, setting aside times in our daily lives especially for prayer, preferably in the early morning. I am not naturally an early morning person myself, but I notice that Jesus had a tendency to get up before daybreak and find a quiet place somewhere to meet with his heavenly Father. Discipline is necessary in prayer. We need a daily routine of prayer including praying alone, corporate prayer, sacramental worship, and intercession for specific needs.

The Lord sent me to Indonesia where people by the hundreds gather each day at four or five o'clock in the morning to pray. I am convinced that was a major reason the attempted communist coup failed in 1965. It was miraculous. So was what happened afterwards. The government decided that anyone who did not believe in God was obviously a communist and must be killed. People had a choice, but they had to have a religion. A lot of animists did not want to follow the Muslim religion, which is the prevalent religion, because of the restrictions against eating pork; so hundreds of thousands of them became Christians. Most of them have improved their reasons for being Christians since that time. There has continued to be tremendous growth. The Lord is moving and it is a movement supported by prayer.

In addition to designated prayer times, we need to pray throughout the day in all our activities. This prayer needs to fit the situation and be under the guidance of the Holy Spirit. Saint Paul said to "pray continually in the Spirit." Prayer is not a set of gimmicks or systems, nor is it limited to endless repetitions. Attempting to pray on our own will cause the prayers to be too general and too monotonous. We need to have the kind of yieldedness to the Lord that goes on continually, and allows us to pray according to his will.

Let me share some of our experience on the mission field. My family and I knew that we were supposed to go into the mission field at some point. Near the end of 1964, knowing that the time was near, we started a prayer vigil in front of the altar in our church. We kept it going twenty-four hours a day for three months. My wife and I, her parents, my older kids, and some of our parishioners took turns praying for the Lord's guidance as to where we were to go, and what we were to do there. At our family prayers one day in December of 1964, the Lord spoke through my wife and said, "You are to go to Indonesia as soon as possible. You are to leave your two oldest children in the States and take the other five with you." The oldest was in college, so that was no great problem. We just had to arrange a place for him to spend vacations. Number two son was about to enter high school and we burdened the grandparents with him for the duration. We quickly sold most of our possessions, gave away what we couldn't sell, and within a month were on our way.

At that time, the Indonesians were having nothing to do with English-speaking people. The communists were in the ascendancy; the missionaries were leaving in droves, and we naively thought that since the Lord was calling us, we could go. Initially, we could not get a visa, but on the way, in Hong Kong, we were able to get a one-month tourist visa. We went, still trusting the Lord.

If you have heard from God, you will be tested on whether you trust him or not. I discovered that faith does not depend on feelings, because I was scared! I had a wife and five kids, no earthly goods, going halfway around the world with no idea of what was going to happen. Our tourist visa was extended a couple of times. Eventually the Lord allowed an error to pass in the immigration office in Jakarta, and we got a semi-permanent visa. It was illegal, but it happened. The Jakarta office had made a mistake and the local office did not know what to do about it. They debated all one morning while we sat outside and prayed like crazy. At noontime, they said, "All right, we will give you a semi-permanent visa." We had this visa for the duration.

The first part of prayer for guidance is hearing from God and knowing what he is saying. For that to happen, you have to be moving in the Spirit. The gifts of the Spirit must be in operation so that we can know what God is saying. The second part of the prayer is to trust him. The Lord has many ways of testing to see if we are really trusting him. It does not get easier; the tests get harder. When we were in kindergarten, they gave us simple tests. By the time we got to graduate school, the exams got harder. Ultimately, we have to pass the final exam.

Getting Started in Mission Service

In order to begin, there must be clear direction from the Lord which will come through prayer. When I began, the great advantage I had was a total lack of knowledge about the mission field. With no sense of what I was to do, I was totally dependent on hearing from God. I think that is a good principle. Seminary courses and missionary training can be good preparation. A knowledge of demographics and an understanding of the culture can be helpful. But ultimately, answers to the questions must come from immersion into the lives of the people and a day by day revelation of God's will. In our case, it was evident that God wanted "on the job" training for us. Jesus gave this kind of training to his first disciples. We need to see things as God sees them, and do and say what he gives us.

I discovered a couple of years ago that I may be an authority on Muslim evangelism. When I was asked to participate in consultations on the subject, I realized that many of the people we had led to the Lord were in fact Muslims. At the time, I thought of them as people who needed Jesus. It never occurred to me that we were dealing with "people groups." Being as naive as we were allowed God to orient us and learn the culture. Because we were in an attitude of prayer, God was able to guard our bodies and mouths and show us what he wanted. He graciously provided a young man who was very persnickety about telling me what I should and should not do: how to sit, how to move, what not to say. This young man and several others I worked with taught me a great deal about the culture and saved me from many disasters. I hated every minute of it at the time, but it was an act of love.

Understanding the Situation

God often has radical ways of getting things done. If we begin with prayer and ask him, he will provide understanding and direction. He will show us what he wants, when he wants it to happen, and what his ultimate purpose is in that place. If we are in tune with his purposes, amazing things will happen.

I knew about some evangelism theories. I knew that Episcopalians hold services in a church building and hope that somebody will drift in off the street. I had also participated in large open field evangelistic gatherings and had seen some spectacular results. But I wondered about what happens the next morning when the coffee is cold and the person is having a hard day. What will the results be in a week? I thought that the Lord must have something better in mind.

To find out what the Lord had, we started praying as a family. At the same time, we were learning the language and adjusting to the culture. Every morning I attended the prayer meeting at the church and slowly began to understand what was occurring. The Lord pointed out several young men who were to work with me. I did not approach any of them, but, one by one, they began to join our family for evening prayer. Since language understanding was still developing, we just praised the Lord, sang songs, and read some Scripture.

As time went on, we received invitations to homes where people were sick or demon-possessed or in some kind of trouble, and the Lord began to perform miracles. This brought more invitations, and wondrous things began to happen. In one home, a young man was unconscious from a spell put on him by his girlfriend. Unfortunately, it had not worked the way she hoped, and he had been unconscious for three days. The local witch doctor had also been invited. When we arrived, we said, "If the witch doctor is going to do his thing, we will not touch this. If you want us to pray, get rid of the witch doctor." He went away muttering threats. Despite the fears of the young men with me, we prayed and took authority over the situation through the power of God. The young man became conscious after we prayed, entered into the presence of God, and began to prophesy. His family were backslidden Christians. One by one, he had a word for them. They were convicted by the word and were converted. Naturally, word got around and the house began to fill with people. For three days and three nights, there were thirty or forty people there, and the young man had a word for each of them. Many people came to the Lord.

You will not find this in your books on evangelism. It is not a method. If we tried it again, it probably would not work. This was, however, God's method for that particular situation. When we are in God's Spirit through prayer, he provides the direction and the empowering. If God says something, do it. The results can be amazing!

Training Disciples

I was sent to Indonesia with the idea of establishing a training program that would set people on fire for the Lord. As I examined various models, I made some observations: the programs that were effective had begun with a vision from the Lord and lots of prayer. They had gone through hard times and struggles. At one point, it had been suggested to me that I should read my Bible a lot, so in a six-month period, I had read it through five times. It is pretty hard to fool me and tell me something is in there when it isn't. I noticed as I read that Jesus had never (1) scheduled a class, (2) given a lecture, (3) developed a curriculum, or (4) built any buildings. He gathered a little group of people and asked them to follow him. They started to walk and watched as he (1) performed miracles, (2) clobbered the Pharisees, (3) dealt with various kinds of people, and (4) raised the dead. I thought that maybe training was supposed to happen that way.

So that is our model. Since I did not yet speak much Indonesian, I just let the young people come along and see what Jesus was doing in the place where he was doing it. We were invited to churches and we would involve their young people in what Jesus was doing. When we left, they formed teams among themselves. Naturally, we encountered resistance, particularly from folks in established churches who felt that "young people should not be laying hands on people" or "miracles stopped in New Testament days." We got lots of "good teaching" from churches and had to counteract it with a lot of Bible study.

In Makassar, after getting kicked out of several churches, we were received at a church which had about twenty members. We were allowed to sleep on the floor of the church and hold services in the evenings. At first, things were really stiff and formal, but after several days, we had an all-night prayer meeting. A group of teenagers showed up, using this as an excuse to stay out all night. About 10 o'clock, I asked, "Who here would like to have an encounter with the Holy Spirit?" Those were the last words I spoke because the Holy Spirit took over. These young people fell on the floor, weeping and repenting before the Lord; they began to be baptized in the Holy Spirit, they sang new songs in the Spirit. One young lady began singing songs in tongues and translating them into Indonesian. Another, who they said had received all of her theological education at the movies, began to quote Scripture. She would quote a verse, and tell us what verse it was, and then give a wonderful teaching on the subject, without opening a Bible. All her friends knew she had never read a Bible. No one got sleepy that night!

As the word of this event spread, the same type of thing happened over and over again. We would go to a house meeting and the place would be crammed, with hundreds more outside. Street kids would come, initially making fun of what was happening. The next night they would be at the back of the room. When the prophecy started, they would repent and get filled with the Holy Spirit. Then they would prophesy. At the end of three months there, we baptized large groups of people. They formed teams who went to the interior of the island and other places. Everywhere they went, tremendous miracles happened, large numbers were converted and nominal Christians were soundly converted and filled with the Spirit.

All of this took place through much prayer and obedience and by the power of God.

Confronting Territorial Spirits

There is a lot of talk these days about spiritual warfare and territorial spirits. We were involved in this long before we had heard anything about it. As early as 1967, we encountered spiritual warfare on the mountain where we were living in East Java. Our village has one church and an orphanage. Before we moved there, miracles had taken place. A sick woman had been brought from another village for prayer. The young people at the orphanage had prayed for her. The woman died, but the children continued to pray. Towards morning, the children were all filled with the Holy Spirit, and the woman came back to life. At last report she was working at the orphanage and was doing fine. You can imagine that this was a powerful testimony for the young people, and they went off into the villages, evangelizing and doing miracles.

Up on the mountain was one Christian family in a tribe of about 300,000, all of whom were animists. They worshipped trees and rocks; everything had a spirit in it; they had to watch where they walked to avoid stepping on somebody's spirit. For twenty years, the one Christian family had been unable to defeat the spirits or make any new converts. Some folks who had become believers had fallen off a cliff and were killed. Praying for sick people only made them sicker. The Lord led us to go up to the top of the mountain where there was a large crater, the site of a previous volcano. In the middle of the large crater, was a cone which had blown, and smoke came from it continually. The people used to sacrifice their children in the volcano to the gods of the mountain to appease the spirits. The Lord told us that this was the spirit that held the mountain area in bondage. We spent ten days at the top in this cold, miserable place, praying and taking authority over the gods of the mountain. Then we began to move down the mountain into the villages.

In the first village, we made fourteen converts. In another village, a young boy had fallen into a charcoal pit and was burned over most of his body. He was on the verge of death; but, when we prayed, the Lord healed him instantly and completely. Another Christian family! In another hut, an old hag sat in front of the fire, rocking back and forth. She had not washed in fifteen years and her hair was a matted mess. A couple of the ladies from our village prayed for her, released the demons, took her to the river and baptized her. Now she was unafraid of water and could bathe. A few days later a nice looking young lady came to our village and threw her arms around the ladies. At first, they did not recognize her as the woman from the hut. She was delivered. Thirty new converts in that village!

Scenes like this happened numerous times as the gospel was taught and the people were discipled. Every area that opened to the gospel started with some warfare. Just as Jesus began his ministry with intense prayer, we did everything with prayer. Whenever he went to a new place, Jesus found a quiet place to pray. He taught and performed miracles. Then he moved to a new place and did the same.

Praying for Specific Events

When you observe what has been happening at this conference, you realize that people have been praying for months. It is important that every new ministry happen as a result of prayer!

At one time in Indonesia, we were able to have large outdoor campaigns (they are illegal now). The first one we had was held right in front of our house and was the result of months of fasting and prayer by our young people. They had a vision of the field filled with people. The entire setting was laid before them—a platform, the tent, sick people being healed, cripples walking, and even who was to speak from the platform. I was away when this began to happen and when I returned I found that they had been praying and fasting for a month and a half. They formed teams and took turns, one team praying for a day and then another team the next day. Sometimes a team would pray and fast for several days.

The campaign was not advertised in any way; but, each day, people started to come early in the morning. By afternoon, five thousand people were standing in the field. We gave out cards that were returned if the person was healed. We know that nearly nine hundred people were healed, we knew who they were and were able to follow up with these people in their villages. By going to the villages and gathering people together, we were able to form new congregations. The young people from our training center spent part of each week in the villages teaching them the basics of the faith. We trained the local Christians to receive and disciple new Christians.

Our training program involved gathering them together and involving them in prayer and Bible study. New Christians in Muslim villages are bound to experience severe persecution. We equipped them with the Scriptures dealing with the problem. We helped them learn to search the Bible to find answers for what they were experiencing. Once they grasped this concept, they were into the Bible, finding answers for themselves. Bible knowledge for them was a matter of life and death.

The life of a Christian comes equipped with unpredictable and insurmountable problems and opportunities. God, however, has an inexhaustible source of unimaginable ways of dealing with all these. It is important to hear accurately and follow his procedures.

Can This Happen in the United States?

Certainly, all I have been saying is difficult to apply in the United States. People have so many pressures; they are so oriented to programs and working things out for themselves. The pattern I am suggesting requires a whole new orientation. Saint Paul says that we "should be transformed by the renewing of our minds." This means that we have to exchange our stupid little natural minds for the mind of Christ.

The mission with which I have been associated is basically a prayer group that incorporated. We believe that in order to save our cities in the States, we have to use an approach similar to the one we used in Indonesia. That is, we need to get ourselves prayed up and out into the streets doing some miracles. That will gather a crowd. We need to be visible and you cannot be much more visible than in the streets.

Signs and Wonders

Miracles are an integral part of our ministry. The Lord seems to do things more spectacularly when we are invading the camp of the enemy. He does not seem to do this as noticeably in churches. Miracles are signs, but they are also manifestations of God's power. They are signs of the resurrection power of God. The resurrection cannot be effectively preached without "a demonstration of the Spirit and power," as Paul said. Powerful ministry cannot be exercised without much prayer.

Fasting and Prayer

Fasting is a form of intense prayer. Scripture tells us that Jesus fasted and prayed for forty days and afterwards he was hungry. This seems to imply that he was so intense in his prayer that he did not really care about food. Fasting should be done for a specific reason and not just for the sake of fasting. The burden to pray will come from God and it will be intense. We can also know when it is over, because that burden of prayer will be lifted.

Praying for Missionaries

Prayer for missionaries is a life-and-death matter. Any missionary can tell you whether or not people have been praying. They don't need a letter to tell them. As you pray for missionaries, pray in the Spirit. Let the Holy Spirit reveal to you what the needs are. You do not have to guess. If we pray and trust the Lord, our prayers will be specific to the needs of the ones for whom we are praying. If we ask anything according to his will, he will do it.

It is difficult to understand why God does certain things and why he does not do others. My wife was an invalid and spent full time in intercession. On occasions, she prayed for people to be healed during our campaigns. The cripples would get up and walk off, and we would wheel her back in her wheelchair. I think that God may just want us to know that he is God and we do not give him any instructions. Still, when we are operating in accordance with the will of God, we can expect great miracles.

EFFECTIVE TRAINING FOR
SHORT-TERM MISSIONS

Mrs. Edwina Thomas

In its first ten years, SOMA USA (Sharing of Ministries Abroad) has sent ninety-four missions to twenty countries. These mission trips have varied in length from about eight days to a nearby country such as Puerto Rico or Mexico to nearly three weeks for places like Pakistan or Africa. The differing time frames make it possible for people in all life situations to participate. SOMA usually recruits its missionaries from local U.S. parishes, asking that a church recommend those people who have been faithful to uncover and minister in the spiritual gifts that God has given them.

Short-term mission trips have a way of being life-changing, both for the individual and for the parish. As individuals go out to encounter different cultures, the global church, and the power of the Holy Spirit moving around the world, they grasp a wider vision of the church and their brothers and sisters around the globe. When that is understood in an experiential way, then there is a new message for individual churches. Both the missionaries and the parish come to understand in a deeper way that the church was not meant to be parochial and inward-looking, but that it has brothers and sisters worldwide, who also love the same Lord Jesus. There is a new vision of who they are, what they can do and how they can reach out and build relationships with people they might otherwise never have known. It takes time, at least four months or longer to prepare to go on a mission trip. There are a variety of practical issues related to putting mission teams in the field that need to be addressed.

The Invitation

A proper invitation from the receiving church is very important, since it assures that the team will be working under appropriate authority. If the team is working in the Anglican Communion, the invitation assures the bishop's blessing. Secondly, having an invitation assures that there is a host who is investing something in the ministry. This means that the host church is a participant in the mission and not merely a passive recipient of a gift they might feel obligated to accept. SOMA asks the hosts to provide food, lodging and transportation for the team while it is there. Although this may not always be possible, it is important because it brings the host diocese into a partnering relationship with the mission team.

However, there are places in the world where the Anglican Communion has no viable presence and where there is no Anglican authority to invite or to welcome a team. Since God most certainly intends for mission to reach beyond the Anglican Communion, adapt these principles to fit the situation you are facing.

Team Formation

It is very important that the team be carefully chosen and well trained. There are a number of ways this can be done. Discover the World, a ministry on the campus of Fuller Seminary, does cross-cultural training of parish teams. SOMA's teams are usually drawn from all over the United States, and they spend the first two or three days of any trip together in training and team formation.

Prior to that, time is spent in preparation which can take several months. Team members are asked to begin a spiritual journal, to commence the process of cleansing their hearts. A diary or journal, even a brief one, helps to show what God is doing in their lives in preparation for mission. Experience has taught that the most effective ministers in the field are those who are submitted to the Lord Jesus. That means preparing mentally and spiritually to move out in mission.

This is also the time when team members can begin to learn about the place where they will be going. Given the ease of getting information in our culture, different team members can be assigned topics to research on the country they will visit. Some may look up the country's political history and its current politics. Others may look at the general religious history of the area and at the history of the church with whom the team is partnering to see how it got there, how long it has been there and why it is where it is. Someone else could research the culture. (There are many resources for this including the annual CIA publication *The World Factbook* about the peoples of every country in the world; the Kennedy Center for International Studies (800-528-6279) publishes four-page briefings called "Culturegrams"; the nation's embassy can often supply information. The encyclopedia is always good.) It is also interesting to research the foods of the culture.

As you prepare to go, seek out someone from the country you are visiting who can function as a "bridge person." This may be someone who speaks English, who has traveled in the United States, or who lives here. (If there is a university nearby, one of the team could see if there are any students from the country and meet them. They would be thrilled to be asked about their country.) Ask that person to provide a briefing where you can ask questions and they can tell you about their culture and what they feel is important for you to know. Building relationships with someone from the country you plan to visit can be invaluable preparation.

Learn some words of the language. This is a way of saying, "I am humbling myself and honoring your language. I am not asking you to make all the effort to meet me." While this can be difficult, it is very valuable.

Team Selection

Team members need to be spiritually solid. A recommendation from the person who has pastoral oversight for them should be a part of the application process. This allows for screening so that if there is discernment that someone is not appropriate for a particular team, that can be presented in a loving way. Since SOMA teams move in the spiritual gifts of the Kingdom, team members who minister in the spiritual gifts God has given are ideal. The gift of hospitality is one of the most valuable to have on a team. That gift of love which cares for another person, makes them comfortable and at ease, and gives them a sense of peace transfers so well that even without language skills it is obvious that the same Holy Spirit is at work.

The size of the team is dictated by the purpose of the trip. Trips to do construction, conduct a Vacation Bible School or put on a conference require large teams. Each member of the team might be expected to perform in more than one capacity such as conducting workshops and also as a plenary speaker. If there is to be music, that means additional team people.

There are generally no age limits for team members, but it is necessary to be in good health. The age of team members is determined more by the type of mission and the people with whom the team will work.

Team dynamics change with the size of the team. Groups of six or seven can easily relate with one another. But once the group goes beyond that number, the natural thing to do is to divide the group into smaller units. These smaller groups can bond and seek God's will together. This gives individuals group accountability and also a place where there can be openness, honesty and the opportunity to share.

Team commitment is vital and, where possible, the team should come together for several meetings prior to the mission trip. This is where much prayer, planning, sharing of personal concerns and worship can happen. Teams especially need to learn to worship together and when team members come from different areas, it takes effort to meld the styles and find a comfort level for everyone. Finding that comfort level is important in order to be able to pray for one another as a group. Prayer partners within the group are also important. It is in the safety of solid team relationships and in the support you learn to give each other that you are able to reach out and minister. The team must learn to love, trust, nurture, listen, comfort, encourage, and be a sounding board to each other. When these basic needs that each team member has are met by various persons within the group, you are free to focus your attention on the work that awaits—the "ministry" God unfolds for you to do.

One of the greatest ministry gifts each of you is called to exercise is to see God's spiritual gifts in action and to affirm them in each team member. Pray for the discernment to see the intercession behind the tears or wisdom spoken from an unlikely person. God seems to choose the mission field to surprise his people with gifts they have never used before. They often need help identifying these and encouragement to continue to risk using these unfamiliar gifts.

Team Leaders

Using examples from the life of Jesus, the Reverend Michael Mitton, Director of Anglican Renewal Ministries, says that a team leader:

—knows and understands the world of his team members, and goes to meet them where they are (as Jesus did for Peter),
—goes for quality and a variety of gifts in his or her team, not for safety and ease of relationships (Peter, James and John),
—makes up his own mind about people and does not rely on others' reports; he welcomes those who have experienced the darker side of life (Levi),
—chooses his team in prayer, and continues to fight for them in this way—which means that he must make time to do this away from the bustle of the work place,
—blesses and encourages, as well as corrects if necessary, those in his team,
—does not allow power and responsibility to reduce his compassion,

—keeps the initiative, sometimes in unexpected ways,
—has a vision he keeps to, and so is not afraid of failures.

The team leader must be able to put the current mission into proper perspective relative to the sending organization and its strategy for this particular country at this time. The team leader needs to understand why the mission was planned the way it was and what the goals are in order that the team not be moved onto a detour by good intentions or other exciting ministry options. It is important to help the team value the work of others who have gone before and made their way possible.

Field Training

If a team is going to the field to perform a specific task, it is important that you know how to do that task before you leave. A bishop once shared that he had a bad experience with a missionary team who came to build a church, but did now know how to lay bricks. Knowing how to perform the task is no incidental matter. The way to prepare to go to the field and roof a building is to learn how to do roofing and to roof a building at home. Have a Bible school at home before you go to the field to conduct one. There may be experienced or skilled people on the team, but there may be some who are not, so some training is really important.

Plan for what is to happen on the trip. Make assignments so that team members can be prepared. Anticipate that programs may have to be rearranged depending upon the needs, but make plans so that the objective of the trip can be met. While always being prepared with a plan, be willing to submit your agenda to the Holy Spirit for endorsement or revision.

Intercessors

Intercessory prayer is essential for mission trips. Americans usually do not depend enough on prayer. God has taught me that without the covering of prayer when working in the Spirit, nothing is accomplished. In SOMA, we are now asking every team member to have a circle of intercessors around them. While on a trip, team members maintain contact with their intercessors through the wonder of the fax machine as much as possible. That way the prayer intercessors know what the needs are and how to pray specifically. There are many stresses associated with being on the mission field and team members find themselves without all their normal coping mechanisms. Prayer intercessors uphold the team and put spiritual wings under the team dynamics which helps maintain unity. At some point, every team member will probably experience a sense of use-lessness and unimportance; personal intercessory prayer helps to transfer the focus from oneself to Jesus Christ. In addition to the specifics for the mission, intercessors are asked to pray for protection, health, traveling mercies, discernment and unity.

Mission Romance

Persons in a ministry situation, living and sharing with each other on an intimate level, may have temptations. Short-term is both short and intense, heightening the need for closeness and bonding. Friendships are intensified by the pressure of culture shock, the long erratic schedule and by the loneliness that everyone feels.

It is important to steer clear from every potentially questionable sit-uation with the opposite sex regardless of their nationality. Romantic sparks divert attention and energy away from God's work, are spiritually destructive to the entire mission, and are a poor witness.

Preparation for Emergencies

Medical Insurance

There are some very practical considerations that must be addressed for team members. The first one is insurance. Many U.S. medical in-surance policies do not cover people outside the United States. Through SOMA's insurance provider, team members purchase a group medical insurance policy which includes a small life insurance policy with it. Should someone die overseas (in ten years SOMA hasn't lost anyone yet), returning the body is very expensive. For a minimal per day cost there is a small life insurance policy and medical coverage that extends for a period of time after returning from the trip to cover anything that may have started abroad.

Travel Documents

Be sure to carry extra documentation about yourself. I learned the hard way that it is very important to have a spare passport photo. We were once in Zaire when looting and violence occurred, the airport was closed, and we had to leave through Zambia. We did not have visas for Zambia and would have needed those extra passport photos if the Zambian authorities had not waived the requirement at the last minute. Another piece of documentation is a shot record. Different countries require different inoculations before you can enter and may require proof that you have them. The Center for Disease Control's Hotline for International Travelers is 404-332-4559.

Leave emergency information about yourself in a central location at home. Take with you the telephone numbers of people who can be reached day or night. Situations can arise where only one phone call out of the country is allowed and you will want to be able to contact someone. We were once in a situation like that and that one phone call started a powerful network all across the United States praying for our safety.

I also suggest that you photocopy the receipt for your ticket (so you have the ticket number). In the event that the ticket is lost or stolen, having the ticket number expedites replacement. Carry this photocopy separate from your ticket.

The United States State Department has a hotline for travelers. Before entering any country, it is a good idea to call for up-to-date information and warnings (202-647-5225). Just remember to keep these warnings in perspective when you hear them. This information will, however, tell you when it is unsafe to travel in any country and when Americans should not be there.

When you go into a foreign country with any instability, check with the consulate as soon as you arrive. My experience with these people is that they have always been very kind and helpful. They are there to serve us. They will record your passport number and ask where you will be going and where you are staying so they can reach you in the event of necessity.

Pack Light

The adage "pack light" applies to mission trips. Take a minimum of mix-and-match clothing. Three changes of clothing and a dress outfit (including appropriate shoes) should be sufficient. Remember to be respectful of the culture into which you will be going. Many cultures would be offended by what Americans consider modest. For women, dresses that are below mid-calf or longer with shoulders covered are appropriate. Slacks are totally taboo in many countries. Women's clothing that is modeled after men's fashions does not go over well either. Men can wear slacks and perhaps shorts in private, but never on the street. If people are offended by your appearance, they will not hear what you have to say. Researching the culture will help with wardrobe planning for any country. Observe how they dress, for dressing as they do speaks value to their culture. Also, do not take new shoes on a mission trip!

Some of our missionaries have taken suitcases of Bibles or other items to give to the host church before they leave. They then had a spare suitcase to bring extra things home with them. Another way to accomplish the same thing would be to pack a folding light-weight bag in with your luggage.

Other Considerations

Plan physically to go abroad. It has been suggested that team members participate in an aerobic walking program to get in shape. This is a good idea because it helps build stamina for the day when you may only be able to get four hours sleep.

Traveling with a group takes some planning. Having one person who does the checking in at the airport means that the ticket agent only has to deal with one team member. It also means that when the luggage is weighed, they will average the weight between the number of team members. This may save overweight charges.

Having a group banker helps expedite things at times. Every team member gives the banker a predetermined amount of money and the banker then pays for anything that is common to the team such as taxi fares, newspapers, tips, etc. When the bank gets low, everyone contributes again. This really helps to avoid confusion and prevent over-spending.

Responding to Requests Made Abroad

Expect that you will be asked to:

1. Exchange pulpits, if you are a priest.
2. Help someone get a visa.
3. Finance someone's seminary or college education.
4. Help finance a church building project.

It is easier if you decide ahead of time what your basic answer should be. If it is "no," then respond simply with "I'm sorry that we cannot do that." It is better to be up-front and honest than to leave persons expecting more than you intended by your vagueness.

Upon occasion, God has led a person or church, etc., to help with a project. You must be clear in your own mind that such help may be in God's plan for you or your church. Be prepared to make such decisions at home with the support and spiritual guidance of your own Body of Christ.

Be particularly wary when you are asked to provide something and then are told, "Please do not tell the bishop that I spoke to you." Our ministry is effective as we live the principles of the Kingdom of God. We must walk in honesty and integrity and encourage others to do the same.

Closure to the Mission

Coming back into your familiar world is as important as entering another culture. The goal is to provide the opportunity to reflect and share what has happened. The following questions are helpful when used in a team meeting, or for personal reflection on the airline:

—What was a personal highlight?
—At what point did you feel the lowest?
—What were the sacrifices you had to make to accomplish this
     mission (i.e. "count the cost")?
—Recount a time of ministry that was stretching for you.
—The most significant lesson God taught me was...
—What would I have done differently?

It is very affirming to have the team share the gifts they saw or experienced from each member. Take turns. Take notes.

Plan, if possible, a private time of good-byes; prayers, a favorite song, an opportunity for thanks to be expressed. Good-byes unsaid leave work unfinished.

Reentry

Everyone going on mission has made subtle but significant shifts in their worldview. Reverse culture shock is seeing your own familiar world through those new eyes.

Encountering culture closer and closer to our own at the end of a mission often brings the need for team members to affirm who they are in various ways—by spending money and/or wanting to eat at expensive restaurants. Perhaps this is an attempt to reestablish victory over the extreme poverty encountered. Sometimes the opposite reaction happens: there is an aversion to what now seems like excessive spending.

Some of the same personality changes that sometimes occur with initial culture shock—crying, sleeplessness, depression—can surface as persons struggle with the meaning of the encounters they have had. Often it is shrugged off as "jet lag."

Again, talking about problems one may encounter is effective. It is not unusual for team members to feel that life at home seems to have a superficial quality to it. It is hard to see family and friends less committed to the new priorities and excitement that you had as a team member.

You will find a balance between your new worldview and the familiar world of home. You should expect changes, however. It has been said: "If your short-term mission doesn't affect your Bible study, your finances and your social life, you may need to look at your slides again."

MISSIONARY TENSIONS
A Case Study from Africa

The Rev. Ian Douglas and the Rev. Titus Presler

Discussions of dilemmas arising in the Christian missionary enterprise can be helped greatly by the availability of case studies that offer narratives of real situations that have arisen in cross-cultural mission. Dimensions of mission embedded in the following case study include the relation between gospel and culture, church-to-church relations within the Anglican Communion, feminism as a cross-cultural movement, ecumenical cooperation, new forms of mission partnership, missionary training and support, and the legacy of Western mission in other parts of the world. The case is a useful point of entry in both parish and classroom.

This case study is based on actual incidents in the overseas experience of the Episcopal Church. Names of persons and places have been altered to protect identities.

* * * * *

Emily Morris felt stunned and hurt as she left the diocesan office building on Michigan Avenue. Her meeting with the Companion Diocese Committee had been so different from what she had expected. First, questions raised in Africa. Now, questions raised at home. Back in Chicago for Christmas, she had expected encouragement for the challenges she was facing in Uganda. Now she felt very far from the joy of the shoppers swirling around the doors of Marshall Field's. She wondered whether she should return to Uganda at all. She couldn't get out of her mind the question committee chairperson, Arlene McCormack, had asked her: "Emily, are you sure that you as a white woman have been sensitive enough to the culture?"

* * * * *

Before going to Uganda, Emily was director of St. Luke's Women's Rediscovery Center. As a psychiatric nurse, Emily had been deeply concerned about victims of domestic violence in the greater Chicago metropolitan area. With the financial and spiritual backing of her parish, St. Luke's Episcopal Church in Evanston, Emily opened Rediscovery. The center offered information and support services for women who were suffering from physical and emotional abuse. After seven years, Emily now was feeling that perhaps God was calling her elsewhere. She was single, middle-aged and felt free to travel.

Then Emily met Mrs. Mary Njai. Mrs. Njai and her husband, the Rt. Rev. Samuel Njai, were visiting St. Luke's as part of the Companion Diocese Program. For four years the Episcopal Province of the Midwest had been in a partnership with the Anglican Church of Uganda. The Diocese of Chicago was a companion diocese to the Diocese of Mitumba where Samuel Njai was the bishop. Emily had been interested in the program and had learned much about her African brothers and sisters in Christ. She remembered how surprised she had been when she discovered that the Anglican Church had been in Uganda for over a hundred years, and that today there are three times as many Ugandan Anglicans as there are American Episcopalians.

When the Njais visited St. Luke's, Emily had a long discussion with Mrs. Njai during the coffee-hour. Mrs. Njai told her about her plans for the Mitumba Women's Improvement Society. The society sought to provide a place where Ugandan women who had been mistreated or lacked access to economic power could gather for support and advancement. Mrs. Njai said the society had received encouragement from the Ugandan National Council of Churches (UNCC) and the Episcopal Church in the United States. The endorsement of the UNCC was very important since the Ugandan government required all religious organizations to be affiliated with the UNCC. Financial support for the Women's Improvement Society, however, was provided primarily by the Episcopal Church in the United States through the United Thank Offering and the Presiding Bishop's Fund for World Relief.

Mrs. Njai said she was still looking for a coordinator to help develop the society's program and Resource Centre. When Mrs. Njai said, "We need help from skilled Christian sisters like yourself—won't you come and help us?" Emily felt a rush of joy. It was just the opportunity for which she had been waiting and praying.

Emily had never thought of herself as a missionary. To her, the word conjured up images of imperialism and culturally insensitive Victorian men and women proselytizing defenseless natives. Through the Companion Diocese Program, however, Emily's ideas about mission had begun to change. She learned that there were no longer Anglican "mission fields" and today the twenty-eight provinces in the Anglican Communion work interdependently in mission. There had been several clergy exchanges between Mitumba and Chicago, and Emily felt that it was time for lay people to get involved. She saw the Women's Improvement Society and its Resource Centre as an opportunity to do some good at the grassroots where real people experience real problems. She wanted to see if her work with women in the United States could be used in Uganda. She decided to offer herself as a volunteer.

At Bishop Njai's suggestion, the Companion Diocese Committee recommended that Emily go to Uganda as a Volunteer For Mission (VFM). VFM is the Episcopal program that places American Episcopalians in two-year assignments at the request of overseas partner churches throughout the Anglican Communion. With St. Luke's, the Diocese of Chicago, the Diocese of Mitumba and the VFM Office all picking up pieces of Emily's support, it seemed to her that the churches in the United States and in Uganda shared equally in the project. Emily was very excited at the thought of being a flesh-and-blood link between the people of Chicago and the people of Mitumba.

* * * * *

After three weeks of orientation in the United States, Emily arrived in Uganda in early June. Immediately captivated by the people and culture of Uganda, she was swept up quickly into the life of the church. Women, especially, seemed to reach out to Emily and guide her through the complexities of living in a strange land. Although much of her first three months was spent learning the local language of Ganda, Emily still had time to make friends. At St. Cyprian's, a local parish on the outskirts of Mitumba, she found a welcoming community and a celebratory style of worship that immediately drew her in. Emily would often accompany the women of the church as they went about the routines of their lives.

As she sat for hours in the open-air market of Mitumba she began to get a sense of the struggles of the women—husbands taking additional wives, the threat of AIDS, abuse at home. Before long, Emily was being invited to weddings, funerals, and other family celebrations by the church women who lived in the country. Through her friendships at St. Cyprian's, Emily felt that she was beginning to understand Uganda, and especially the women of Uganda.

In mid-August, Mrs. Njai began to plan for the opening of the Women's Improvement Society Resource Centre. The center was to occupy a vacant building on the grounds of the diocesan headquarters and would serve to focus the work of the society. Many of the responsibilities for setting up the center fell to Emily as coordinator. She found herself painting walls, building bookcases, moving furniture, and waiting forever in lines to arrange for telephone and electrical service. This all seemed familiar to Emily as she recalled the early days of setting up Rediscovery. Mrs. Njai, however, was not always around, since she was often traveling to promote the Women's Improvement Society.

Through her work with the center, Emily made the acquaintance of a Baptist minister and his wife, John and Rachel Kataweire. Although there were not many Baptists in Uganda, Pastor Kataweire served as General Secretary of the Ugandan National Council of Churches. Often the Kataweires would invite Emily to have dinner with them and their seven children. They understood Emily's excitement about the Resource Centre, agreeing that such a facility for women was needed in Mitumba. Pastor Kataweire stressed that while the UNCC had endorsed the center, the Anglican financial investment meant his role in the center was limited.

In early October, the Resource Centre was nearing completion. The offices, library and common room were all furnished and painted. Emily worried that the grants from the United Thank Offering and Presiding Bishop's Fund were almost depleted, while the Women's Improvement Society had yet to run a program and the library was empty of materials. Drawing on her experience at Rediscovery, Emily felt that organizing women's support groups might be a worthwhile activity for the Resource Centre. Emily recalled the concerns of the women in the market and at St. Cyprian's—women abused by their husbands or women whose husbands had taken other wives while working away from home. She thought about mothers whose families had been torn apart by AIDS or war. She wondered whether Ugandan women talked openly about female circumcision. Emily believed that support groups at the center would enable women to discuss these concerns in a safe, non-threatening environment. When Emily discussed these ideas with Mrs. Njai, Mrs. Njai responded that she was not sure the center could address those kinds of issues yet.

By the end of October, Mrs. Njai was busy planning for a gala opening of the Resource Centre on November 15. Emily was pleased that the center would be open before she returned to Chicago for her Christmas leave. The first week in November, Mrs. Njai's sister died unexpectedly. She left Mitumba to attend the funeral and be with her sister's family in the small village of Bakavo, 350 kilometers away. As the eldest sister, Mrs. Njai was responsible for her sister's children and the care of their household. What worried Emily, however, was whether Mrs. Njai would return in time for the opening.

One morning, an Indian woman, obviously pregnant, knocked at the door of the center. When Emily invited her in, the woman, who looked to be in her early twenties, introduced herself as Shanti Rau. She looked worn and anxious as she poured out her story to Emily. She had become involved with a married Ugandan man, who refused to take her into his household. Shanti's father, an established Hindu businessman who was concerned about his reputation, sent her away from the family home. For the last three months Shanti had stayed with her sister and her husband, but she was no longer welcome there either.

Shanti pleaded with Emily, "I have no place to stay, I have no money, and now I have no family. May I please stay here at this women's center until my baby is born?"

Emily thought of Mrs. Njai. Communication with her would be impossible since there were no telephone lines to Bakavo. Taking Shanti in certainly seemed to be in line with the center's purpose. A brief telephone conversation with Pastor Kataweire confirmed her feelings that Shanti should be given space at the center. When Emily told Shanti, she was very grateful and moved her few belongings into one of the rooms at the center that afternoon. Emily spent a good deal of time that day and the next exploring possible directions with Shanti.

When Emily arrived at the Resource Centre for work on the third morning, she found Mrs. Njai but no Shanti. Mrs. Njai called Emily into her office. "Emily, I was very upset to arrive home last night and find that young woman staying here at the center," she said. "It is not your responsibility to take such actions. You have put me in a very embarrassing position, for people will now question what the center is about."

Emily responded, "I thought this center was established to respond to women in need. That's why I invited the Indian woman to stay here. It is the same reason I thought support groups would be a good idea. I know from the women's center back home that unwed mothers need lots of support."

"I saw that support groups are important in the United States," Mrs. Njai replied. "But you are not at home, and our ways are not your ways. I have worked with unwed mothers here and found the family issues to be very difficult and complicated. Our culture at this time needs to preserve the unity of the family. If you had understood Uganda and the church here, you would know that support groups for women who have gotten themselves in trouble are not the answer."

"Perhaps I don't understand," Emily said. "Maybe if I had a better idea of your plans for the center, I would know what my role is."

Mrs. Njai responded, "This center is to serve as the headquarters for the Mothers Union of the Diocese. Each month I will meet here with all the presidents of parish Mothers Unions in order to plan our activities. In addition, I hope to establish a craft shop at the center that will sell handicrafts made by women of our church. This will provide a source of income to women and their families. As the coordinator of the center, your role is to assist me in arranging the meetings of the Mothers Union and running the craft shop." Emily suddenly realized that her understanding of the Resource Centre was very different from Mrs. Njai's.

Emily said, "It seems to me the center should say something about who God is. God offers hope for the suffering and liberation for the oppressed. Even the newspapers here recognize that women in Uganda are not being treated fairly in marriage or in many other aspects of society."

"Yes that is very true, but our society is in trouble," Mrs. Njai answered. "God is also God of the family. With all the influences that have come in from the West, things are not as they used to be. Morals are breaking down. People no longer respect the family, which is so important for us Africans. God has standards by which people should live, and the church must uphold these standards."

"But what about compassion?" Emily asked. "Don't you think Jesus looks on the women with compassion first?"

"Yes, compassion is important, but as a foreigner you cannot know where compassion must come in and where discipline must come in." There was understanding in Mrs. Njai's tone, but also a firmness that let Emily know the dialogue had come to an end.

The next day Bishop Njai called Emily to his office. "It seems there is a problem with your work here at the center," he said. "You do not seem to be quite clear about the work of the Resource Centre and your role here. We have put a lot of work into this project, and it is important that it go smoothly."

After Emily explained her concerns, the bishop replied, "Our African culture is different from yours, and it is important not to move too fast. As a single woman, you do not understand the situation here. When you go home, I suggest you consider your position here very carefully."

That evening Emily called Betsy Moran, coordinator for VFM at the Episcopal Church Center in New York, and shared her frustration. "Try to work with the situation," Betsy said. "You have not been there that long, and, remember, you are under Bishop Njai's authority. If you have really got a problem, let's talk about it over the Christmas break." When Emily talked with Pastor Katawerie the next day, he was sympathetic but reluctant to intervene. "Mrs. Njai is a gifted person," he said, "and thousands of Mothers Union women look up to her. But you know, Anglicans are very concerned about the church and its position, which can make it hard to go out to the world."

The Resource Centre opened with a ceremony that included government and church dignitaries, and the few weeks before Emily's leave were fully occupied with coordinating arrangements for the many Mothers Union groups that began to frequent the center for Bible study meetings and crafts training. Their dedication and enthusiasm were inspiring, but Emily found herself still wondering about those who were not part of these groups.

When it came time for Emily to go home on Christmas leave, saying good-bye was hard. The Njais seemed distant and cold, while her friends in the market were so warm and loving. On her last Sunday, the people of St. Cyprian's composed and sang a special song to wish her a safe journey.

* * * * *

Back in Chicago, it was good to be home with family, friends and parish. When Emily called Arlene McCormack at her university office to get on the Companion Diocese Committee's agenda, the chairperson was welcoming but told her that Bishop Njai had written to Bishop Cranston about her situation. "The letter raises some questions," she said, "so I think this meeting on the sixteenth is going to be important. It will be good to hear how you see your experience."

Emily was nervous about the meeting. The people on the committee were intelligent, highly educated and dedicated to church work, but she didn't know how much international experience they had. After Emily shared her experience the chair read Bishop Njai's letter, which spoke of "misunderstandings," a lack of awareness on Emily's part of the African situation, and uncertainty whether Emily was ready to work under the Njai's direction.

"I don't question your intentions at all," said one committee member, "but we have to be careful about our attitudes. So many missionaries have gone out thinking they knew what was best for the 'natives,' and all they did was put down other cultures."

"I understand that," Emily said, "and there are lots of things in Ugandan culture I love. But women there have needs that are crying out to be met. Are you saying that feminism isn't a cross-cultural issue? That God is only concerned about American women?"

"Of course not," said Bob Willborn, a priest from the South Side of Chicago, "but it's going to be expressed in different ways in different places. What was appropriate at your women's shelter here may not necessarily be the best thing in Uganda. It sounds to me like this center is doing pretty good work. Why not just join in and help that effort get on its feet. Maybe later on you can move into some of these other areas of ministry."

"I think what is going on at the center is wonderful," Emily replied. "But it is only meeting the needs of those who already have their lives pretty well put together. Is that what the Episcopal Church had in mind when they gave money to start the center?"

The discussion went on, but seemed to go nowhere. "It doesn't look like we can solve this tonight," the chair said as she brought the discussion to a close. "From talking with the people at the Episcopal Church Center it's clear that we should be very sensitive to inter-diocesan relations. It is important in companion relationships that we try to put ourselves in the other person's shoes. Emily, over the next two weeks think about whether it is appropriate for you to go back, and let's meet again as a committee after Christmas."

* * * * *

"What am I supposed to do?" Emily asked herself as she headed into a deli for a cup of coffee. "Have I been too pushy?" The thought of returning to her working relationship with the Njais filled her with a feeling of heaviness. At the same time she felt pulled back to the women she had met, to the people at St. Cyprian's, to her friendship with the Kataweires.

"Where is God in all this?" she wondered. "God seemed so real to me out there, and that is where I feel called. What am I supposed to do?"

Discussion Questions

1. Before discussing the issues raised by the case, are there any questions of fact that you would like to have clarified first? Examples: What is the Anglican Communion and how do its autonomous provinces relate to one another? Where is Uganda? What is the situation of Indians in Uganda?

2. What issues of Christian mission are raised by this story? List them on a chalkboard or newsprint pad. What impact do these issues have on your thinking about this case? How does your reading of the case affect your thinking about these issues?

3. If you were in Emily's situation, what would *you* do? Would you seek to return to Uganda, would you stay in Chicago, or would you try to work out some other alternative? Explain to the group your reasons for your choice.

Lessons From Overseas for U.S. Churches

The Rev. Charles Long

I was sent to China just after the war and one day found myself on a very crowded bus going from my home to the mission office. Somebody started to pick my pocket. Since I was the only foreigner on the bus, I didn't dare ask for help. I reached into my pocket and held the hand of a young schoolboy. To my surprise, he looked up, and in perfect English, said to me, "May I have my hand back, please?" As we stood there looking at each other, he said, "I see you are a minister. Who is Jesus Christ and why is he so important?" The opening every young missionary dreams about! I had four minutes until we got to the bus stop and I had to give him an answer. That is the kind of situation for which we have to be prepared. Our answer needs to be clear and meaningful to witness Jesus Christ to someone with little or no Christian background.

A religious order in New York spent their annual retreat asking themselves how they would respond to the question, "Who is Jesus Christ?" At the end of the retreat, they combined their notes and came up with three answers. One answer was in the form of a litany, one was a

short story and the third was a one-act play. These people had been thinking about how they would be heard outside the church. Our world is becoming very secular and it is difficult to communicate. We realize that
we are very much captive to our own Christian sub-cultures and religious
language. Certainly this is true for missionaries working in the inner cities with other ethnic, racial or language groups. It seems so simple to just
start a Bible class, hand out a few tracts, get them reading *Forward Day
By Day,* and watch for folks to come. The huge cultural barriers soon become obvious. Others may have a totally different way of using the English language. Music has a different place in their lives. The cultural values, the assumptions about what is good and what is bad in human
relationships differ. The pamphlet "Learning from Africa" is the result of
putting this question to Stewart Lane, one of our missionaries in Africa.
What he wrote shows how to make contact, how to understand the influence of Africa on African-American culture, and some of the assumptions that are very different from our own.

The great missionary to India, Leslie Newbigin, now retired in England, began a series of books intended to deal with this question, but
aimed at the re-evangelization of England. English society is very secular
and although most people are baptized in infancy, only six percent of the
membership attend church, even on Easter. Less than thirty percent of
people interviewed on the streets of London knew what Easter was
about. Newbigin studied what could be learned from all the experience in
foreign cultures that would help develop effective evangelism for a secularized culture. Out of that developed a very creative and ecumenical
movement called The Gospel in Our Culture Network. A parallel group
has been developed in the United States. It is interesting that in England
they are dealing with a secularism that has developed over many generations. In America we are dealing with varying degrees of secular attitudes and religious pluralism as well. There is no one strategy that will
suffice for both countries.

One lesson learned from overseas mission that is applicable in the
United States is that care must be taken to identify the cultural and language differences in the group we are trying to reach. Missionaries must
receive training beyond that of a theological degree before they are sent.
When I was sent to China, I was the first one in several generations of
Episcopal clergy to be given any missionary preparation beyond a theological degree. I was actually given a year of full-time language study at
Yale and in Beijing. In Shanghai only a minimum knowledge of Chinese
was required, enough to shop in the markets or give orders to the cook. It
was possible to function in the great missionary institutions, universities

and medical schools with English alone.

Knowing the language opens the doors to an appreciation of the culture and its subtleties as well as Chinese values. The assumption was that Chinese students would come into the Anglican Church only when they could understand how to read the Anglican Prayer Book and the English Bible. We could arrange translations, perhaps, to help them and some students might find their way into Chinese congregations. The missionaries had little formal training in the Chinese language or the history of one of the world's great civilizations.

It was different for the pioneer missionaries of the early nineteenth century. China was then closed to all foreigners, so they went to the overseas Chinese community in Indonesia. They started to learn the language and the culture to be ready to meet the Chinese. The first two people to do this never did get into China. They started the basic translation of the Gospels and the Prayer Book. Bishop William Boone, the first missionary bishop sent to Asia, replaced them. His orders included organizing a printing press and getting the translations into print so that the printed material could reach beyond where the missionaries themselves were able to go. He was also to set up a school, if at all possible, to train a new generation of people to be bridge builders between the Western missionary and the Western church and their own culture and life. He was a physician as well and he established the first medical clinic run by missionaries in China. The great St. John's University in Shanghai grew from these efforts.

Having the printed word has proved to be of great value in reaching people outside one's own culture. It is much easier to study the differences that the words connote if they are in print. This has been tested and found to be true in the overseas mission of the church: whatever the target group for the gospel, that group is more likely to respond to the Word of God being interpreted in their own context and, if possible, in their own written language rather than to the spoken word.

Another lesson we have learned is the importance of missionary preparation. Historically, we have done very little of this. Missionaries were thrown into the job without any understanding of what the job required. Missionaries went to the field only to find themselves faced with problems of survival in an alien culture and ministry in existing congregations. The time for language and culture training came at the end of an exhausting day, with a tutor.

This lesson applies to the re-evangelizing of America today. We need to learn the language of secular America and some of it is not pleasant. People express themselves, not just in language, but through music and dance and the like. There is an assumption in certain circles in America that matters of religion are left for the mother to decide. Fathers do not discuss this. Culturally, it is important to acknowledge the prevalence of an unconscious, but very real, racist and colonialist attitude toward other people. In China I was accused of being an imperialist. This made me quite angry but I was an American and could not escape the fact that I was identified with the pressures of American economic and cultural imperialism. It is not possible to escape our own nationality and culture, and this is true whether we are working domestically or internationally.

Finally, it is important to examine the goals of a particular missionary undertaking and be very clear about them. A general statement about bringing people to faith in Jesus Christ is not an adequate statement of a mission goal. Our goal might be to plant a church or transform the society or set up a model Christian community. I have been told that Christianity spreads in one of two ways. Either it spreads like the scattering of seeds or it spreads like a drop of water spreads on a blotter. These describe two very different missionary strategies. Establishing a model church is one strategy. In Peking there was a marvelous Anglican cathedral with Chinese architecture. The service music was an adaptation of Chinese folk tunes. The whole congregation was the choir, lay and ordained Chinese took part in the service. There were wonderful schools for both girls and boys. Many resources had been poured into this model of what Christianity could be when transported from England to China. The intent was that it would catch on and spread like water on a blotter. It was beginning to happen, but it was slow.

The average Protestant missionary, however, was going from village to village handing out tracts, preaching the gospel, baptizing individuals and hoping these individuals would gather themselves together and continue to worship the Lord. This was the opposite "scattering seed" approach. The Roman Catholic method was to concentrate on the conversion of the leadership elements in society. The theory was that if the leadership was converted, the rest would follow. To some extent, any of these plans will work in the American setting today. The megachurches that offer something for everybody, that have a lot of excitement and energy, are building the model church. Many of them center on Bible study and prayer. There are other church planting situations that are more scattered, and some which work for the strategic conversion of leadership.

One of the chief critics of the traditional overseas missionary movement was a man named Roland Allen. One of his books is *Missionary Methods: St. Paul's or Ours?* His premise is that the reason for our lack of success lies in following our own methods and not those of St. Paul. He points out that St. Paul granted new congregations self-governance and responsibility for their own life from the very beginning, trusting them to the guidance of the Holy Spirit. He maintained no more outside control than was absolutely necessary, but he did not abandon the congregations.

Mr. Allen also points out that institutions beget institutions. Investing in education or the development of a new medical service for a foreign culture creates an institution with an insatiable appetite for more people and more money. Concentrating on building up educational and medical institutions does not plant and nurture independent churches.

A third observation made by Mr. Allen was that the devil had been very successful in inhibiting the mission of the church by making it dependent upon an ever-increasing need for money. Without money there could be no mission, no university, no hospital. The focus of mission and the sending church was to raise money to maintain the institutional process.

A significant American problem is that there are so many who know little or nothing about Christianity, or who are actually hostile to it. If the gospel story is truly culture transforming, how do we present that to a culture whose images and residual habits are Christian, but have been secularized? It may be easier to reach a completely secular culture than one in which all of the language and symbolism have been poisoned. My challenge is that each of us would take some target group of persons who would be within the reach of our home congregations, make an act of imagination and put ourselves in their places. Why are they not attracted to the gospel? What kind of missionary strategy can be developed for them that would not be dependent upon an endless supply of money or on responsible control from some outside person or agency? At that point, I believe we will be applying the hard-learned lessons from years of experience in foreign missions to missionary opportunities on our doorstep.

NEW MILLENNIUM, NEW CHURCH

The Rt. Rev. Roger White and the Rev. Richard Kew

The book *New Millennium, New Church* identified trends happening in the Christian church, particularly the Episcopal Church. Now we hope to take the trends we have seen and try to project out. We had the good fortune in 1993 to attend a symposium in St. Louis, Missouri, called *Shaping Our Future*. The word coming out of that symposium which described where we seem to be in our society, in the church and politically is "stuck." It is a word that seems to describe a sense of gridlock. This was expressed most clearly by Rabbi Edwin H. Friedman from Bethesda, Maryland. He has worked for a long time on religious family systems, how they work and how the church or the Jewish community can minister within the context of dysfunctional systems. Basically, he said that ours is a dysfunctional system as far as our society and religious communities are concerned.

Why is that the case? What is the reason for this sense of "stuckness?" The answer is that we are in the midst of a major chapter change in human history. We are at what some people call a plastic point, where things are beginning to meld and merge. We have reached the conclusion that this particular transition has a parallel in the Renaissance and the Reformation. These were major events which transformed the world in which we live and we are going through something like that now. This has profound implications for everything we do in the life of the church, from the way in which we gather for worship to the way in which we go into all the world and preach the gospel. The old has gone or is going; the new has yet to arrive. This helps to explain why there is so much stress and discomfort.

We live in a post-modern culture. Possibly the best way to define post-modern is to say: the ideas which emerged during the Enlightenment and which have shaped our culture now appear to have been pushed behind us. The idea of logically and rationally arguing a particular point from A to Z, the idea that God is a passé notion, that human beings do not need a spiritual dimension, is all being pushed behind us. We are moving into a world in which a friend of ours said, "The Great Spiritual Depression is over." This provides incredible opportunities for the Christian church, but does so within the context of the fact that Christians are, at least in the West, no longer the only kids on the block. There is everything, the old pagans, the sects, the Muslims and any group you can think of, fighting to provide the spiritual sustenance for which people are hungering.

The post-modern culture is also a homesick culture. We have lost our rootedness; we do not know where we have come from, which means we do not know where we are going. There is a sense of lostness in our culture. It has an impact on congregations, and in the workplace. We see it in the lives of the folks around us. People are scrambling to find something which will take away this sense of being cut off from home, from their roots.

The sociologist and marketer Faith Popcorn has written a book called *The Popcorn Report* in which she says the American response to this is "to cocoon," to build a haven in which to hide. If you notice, people are turning their homes into armored cocoons. They are attempting to find some safe place in the midst of the despair, the confusion, and the sense of fear. This comes out in our national and international life because America is becoming more isolationist. There is a "Fortress America" mentality in society which then plays back into the life of the church. The "America First" approach is understandable, but it is a projection outward of this idea of a cocoon. We want to make the United States into a cocoon where we can be safe.

How do we get beyond this particular position of stuckness? Rabbi Friedman told the story of Christopher Columbus. We have read three biographies of Christopher Columbus since that time, and he is a fascinating character. It is clear that his discovery of the New World, coupled with other things then happening, played a part in breaking the logjam in medieval society which in turn allowed the Renaissance and Reformation to flower. It required courage; it meant adventuring. Columbus did his homework very carefully before he went. He just did not get into a boat and and set sail westward. However after all his preparation, the point came when he had no option but to to launch out in faith and believe that he was doing the right thing, trusting that God would be with him as he ventured forth.

Abraham's situation was similar. God said to Abraham, "Go!" Abraham, probably having weighed the costs, went. He left the sophisticated, modern city of Ur of the Chaldees, took his camels and family and went to the land which God has promised to give him. That was a turning point in the history of salvation. When Abraham ventured forth, he opened the doors of possibility for God to use him. The church today is in a parallel situation, and we are convinced God is calling the church to be adventurous, to venture forth, to go out.

It is interesting that the secular press has not picked up on the radical growth of the Christian church in China. John Naisbitt in his book *A Global Paradox* spends one and one-half pages talking about the growth of the church in China which may now have as many as eighteen million Christians. When the missionaries left in 1950, there were one million Christians; this is an enormous expansion.

Perhaps the vision Hudson Taylor had in the 1860s for the China Inland Mission is behind this. The story is told of how he preached at a large church in Brighton, on the south coast of England, and the people seemed absolutely unresponsive. In despair he walked out of the church while the service was still in progress. He walked down the beach at Brighton, tears flooding his eyes, and he thought of the millions upon millions upon millions of Chinese who were never going to have the opportunity to hear the good news of Jesus Christ. It was out of that passion, that vision and preparedness to venture everything for Christ, that the China Inland Mission was born. Then the church began to spread inland.

The people in China who are coming to Christ today are the offspring, several generations forward, of the vision of those first Christian missionaries, and the first Christian Chinese who came to Christ through their ministry. This chain of events could change the course of the world. If the Christian church in China continues to grow at its present rate, by the time China becomes the next major superpower, which seems to be the trend at this point, the largest religious group in China will be the Christian church. What will that mean for the shape of the world in the twenty-first century and beyond? Even when we seem to be doing something which we think is rather small and insignificant, if we are prepared to adventure with God, listening to where God sends us, our work can have profound ramifications. Certainly, the implications are worth considering. Our task is to seek to frame a vision for the church, at a local, diocesan, national and international level, that is adventurous and follows the Holy Spirit's lead. Who knows what the implications will be. We can be assured that there will be a cost as well.

Leonard Sweet, chancellor of United Seminary in Dayton, Ohio, has written a recently published book called *FaithQuakes* in which he says:

> Does the church bring people up short of the needs of our time, smugly preferring rote religion, or are we daring to enter those moments when the fire of change will burn most searingly? Is our leadership willing to sacrifice and be re-invented, even to replace itself with more prepared, more skilled leadership if the church is to survive, or are we clawing for our best interests over God's?*

When we read that we couldn't read any further. Are we going to put our own interests first, and ultimately destroy ourselves, or are we going to put God's interests first? These are times of opportunity and times of insecurity. What we are seeking to do is to see what trends are

---

*Leonard Sweet, *FaithQuakes* (Nashville: Abingdon Press, 1992).

shaping the life of the church so we can exercise a faithful ministry within that context.

Trends are not predictors. We are not trying to predict where the church is going. Rather, we use trends in the life of the church as a sort of topography. We can get a sense of the direction in which the church is moving and the impact those trends might have if that momentum continues. It is our observation, as we pointed out in *New Millennium, New Church,* that we are now in a time in the life of the Episcopal Church where some tinkering or making minor adjustments will not solve the problems. We are in the time of major paradigm shifts. Change, at times like these, tends to be seismic, mammoth and sudden. It has always been the case that the church will react rather than be proactive. We really do not take planning for the future very seriously. What is happening in the life of the church is that the money is no longer there so we are scrambling for alternative approaches. This is reactive planning, not proactive planning.

Recognizing the trends, we believe, enables the planning process. Trends assist us in viewing the landscape to see where we are going. The Episcopal Church is a church that has plateaued. We have had an enormous decline in membership and now appear to be back on the growth track. That growth is small at the moment, but we are one of the few mainline churches that seems to have turned the corner and is beginning to grow.

What we are asking as we look at trends is, "Where is it that God would have us go? What is it that God would have us do? What are we seeing in the life of the church? How can we discern what God is doing with us as those people that he has called into his church?"

We believe that the renewal movements are having a major impact in the life of the Episcopal Church as they mature. These movements focus on God; they focus on being those who wish to discern and do the will of God in response to what God has done in a person's life, in a parish's life, in the church's life. Keeping the church theocentric, focused on God, is a significant problem for Christianity in the United States. As major denominations in the United States, we consistently tend to focus on ourselves and our own needs and as a result lose our focus on God. Renewal has brought the focus back to our relationship to God, to our relationship to Jesus Christ and to the inevitable response to that encounter. Renewal is about encountering God and encountering the person of Jesus Christ in our lives. It is a way in which the Holy Spirit has been inbreathed into a church where there are willing recipients for the presence of God, The result is revival out of which will come change. The movement is now over twenty-five years old in the life of the church. It is our estimate that it takes a generation from the seeding of an idea to the time when it has a major impact on the life of the church. We are now seeing a renewal in the life of the church, a reawakening to God and a renewed spirit.

There are some negative aspects to renewal movements. They tend to be anti-intellectual. They also tend to gripe but present no solutions to the problems, and disagree about where the church should go. The basic cry of renewal, however, is that cry made to Philip, "We would see Jesus." It is that sense of coming to know the presence of Christ in our lives that determines where the church goes.

Another trend that we see is the move of the church theologically to the center, the rediscovery of creedal faith; that we are a church whose basic teachings are summarized in the creeds. We also believe we belong to a church which we like to describe as theologically anorexic. We have an incredibly fruitful theological and spiritual inheritance in this church, and we ignore it. There is a huge richness in our tradition.

We recently had a conversation with a lady who had been a member of the Episcopal Church for two years. She felt her spiritual life would be enriched if we only had Scriptures to read and prayers to say each day. She had no idea that we had Morning and Evening Prayer and thought it was a wonderful gift. That is part of our rich inheritance which can nurture and nourish people in the life of the church. The trend toward a creedal faith in the Episcopal Church is the dividing line in the life of the church. The tension and division between those who hold to a creedal faith and those who do not is the real crisis in the Episcopal Church today.

One of the major trends in our church is the hunger for a deepening of our spiritual lives and for forming in the faith. There is very little in the Episcopal Church structure that addresses those two areas; a little catechesis, a little of the catechumenal process, but spiritual development tends to be abandoned to the seminaries. Eugene Peterson, a Presbyterian theologian, has written this:

> People begin to see that secularism marginalizes and eventually obliterates the two essentials of human fullness: intimacy and transcendence. Intimacy, we want to experience human love and trust and joy. Transcendence, we want to experience divine love and joy. We are not ourselves by ourselves. We do not become more human, more ourselves, when we are behind the wheel of a BMW or, when capped and gowned, we acquire another academic degree so that we can get a better job and do more and better things. Instead, we long for a hu-

man touch, for someone who knows our name; we hunger for divine meaning, someone who will bless us, and so spiritually a fusion of intimacy and transcendence overnight becomes a passion for millions of North Americans. For the most part, North Americans come up with a secularized spirituality which is no spirituality at all. Instead of being brought before God, "Oh come, let us worship and bow down," and led to acquire a taste for holy mysteries of transcendence in worship, we are recruited for church roles and positions in which we can shine, validating our usefulness by our function. Contemporary spirituality desperately needs focus, precision and roots: focus on Christ; precision in the Scriptures; and roots in a healthy tradition. Our culture has failed because it is a secular culture. A secular culture is a culture reduced to thing and function. Humans seek human fullness, intimacy and transcendence.*

We have emerged from the Great Spiritual Depression, where we have been without the nurturing nourishment of a deepening of spiritual life and formation in the faith. We have emerged with an enormous hunger in the life of our church for that development. There is a tremendous thirst in all levels of the church for this nourishment. We want to be servants of the Servant, which is a natural end product of developing the spiritual life and forming people in the faith.

Another trend we identified is the impact of stewardship in the life of the church. We have done very, very well in pledging in the Episcopal Church over the last twenty years. Now, however, there is a need in our church to address the whole of God's creation and our responsibility in caring for it. One of the great losses in our church is that we do not challenge our young people and we do not challenge our retired people. Statistically, a woman who reaches the age of 50 in the United States today without being impacted by either cancer or heart disease will probably live until she is 92. If she retires at 62, that leaves thirty years of usually healthy life. This is an individual who has experience and, hopefully, wisdom and energy and health. It is an incredible market where people could be challenged to spend five years in Haiti or five years in Uganda.

Our young people could be offered the opportunity to spend two or three years of their life, either before or after college, in service where the Lord calls them.

The stewardship of all our gifts, not only of creation, but of the gifts that we have, is closely integrated with spirituality. Faith is a response,

---

*Eugene Peterson, *The Contemplative Pastor: Returning to the Art of Spiritual Direction* (Grand Rapids, MI: Wm. B. Eerdmans, 1993).

and our response to the stewardship of the gifts that we are given is directly related to our response to Christ.

We also see new models of leadership. We believe that men and women with a passionate commitment to God's vision will be the ones who form the leadership of the church. Commitment is key. We anticipate leadership shifting from the clergy to the laity. We believe the clergy will be forced to look at new patterns of leadership within the church. Their role of nurturing the body of Christ will become more defined. These new paradigm leaders are likely to be people who venture, like Abraham and Columbus, folks willing to try new things. The unordained will be the key leadership of the church.

That is breaking the logjam. That willingness to venture involves, first and foremost, standing in the presence of God and knowing the presence of God. It involves prayer. It involves going to the Word of God, to reflect within Scripture upon what God is calling us to be. It involves discerning that vocation within the body of Christ, within the community of faith. Abraham, in the midst of his comfort and in his old age, gave it up and ventured because he knew that God would be with him. It was that venturing forth that enabled new things to happen and the new people of God to come into being. Without that type of leadership, that willingness to venture forth, we are going to remain "stuck."

Archbishop Carey has said, "The church dies from the top downward. Show me a parish where the leadership has no vision, and I will show you a parish that has no life." The parish that has visionary leadership, both clergy and lay, will experience growth in the Spirit and growth numerically. It is only as the leadership opens itself to the power and the presence of our Lord Jesus Christ, prepared to risk everything in the service of Jesus Christ, guided by the Holy Spirit, that new expressions of how God wants us to be his church will emerge.

Rabbi Friedman gave three characteristics of leadership. These three characteristics are to self-differentiate, be absolutely persistent and be ruthless. We have to be able to step apart from the emotions of events in the community. We must learn how to free ourselves and stand before God to see what God would have us be. Once we find that out, we have to be absolutely persistent. We also have to be ruthless in not allowing our family, our friends, anything to separate us from what God has called us to do and to be. Leadership is doing, but doing in the faith that God is with us.

We have asked the question, "Where is God leading?" How do we listen to what God is telling us to do? The church, through its people, is saying that we need to be gospel-centered in the whole of church life and in our community as church. That focus should be in the baptismal covenant that shapes our involvement both in mission and ministry.

According to the people in the dioceses, when asked by the Executive Council, the first priority by all the baptized of the Episcopal Church is mission, carried out most effectively at the local and diocesan level. The second priority, that of spiritual development and formation in faith, was discussed earlier.

The third priority is that we are one, united through the gospel imperative in the believing community. Even though we are a diverse and multicultural society, we find our unity in the person of Christ. We do not find our unity in what we do in our differences. Where we get rid of our differences is in the person of Christ. This would say that any real awakening in the church has to come with effort and an enormous outpouring of prayer. We say that the church needs to be drenched in prayer. If we do that, God will reveal through Scripture what this body is meant to be. Then we can venture out and do it.

In summary, we believe the following five points are key:

First, we need to address the spiritual crisis in the church. Unless this is done, the church will go nowhere.

Secondly, we believe missiology is critically important. God has called us to be missionaries, to be the proclaimers of the gospel.

Thirdly, we need to rekindle the church's theological vision in its preaching and teaching.

Fourth, we must show real concern for the pastoral implications at every level of the church's life. Both the clergy and the leadership of the church require nourishment and teaching to proclaim the gospel effectively.

Fifth, we believe that the first four have implications for the future structure of the church. That structure has to be based on effective mission and ministry for the church. After we have dealt with the first four, we will be able to see what that structure should be. Currently, we are in in-between times and it is critically important that we be the people who stand in the presence of God. As we pray and reflect, we will be able to discern what God wants us to be as individual Christians, spiritual communities, parishes, dioceses, and as the Episcopal Church. Our response to the call must then be obedience.

7

The Harvest Is White: Opportunities in Mission

CROSS-CULTURAL URBAN MINISTRY IN THE U.S.

The Rev. Duc Nguyen

I want to talk about urban mission and outreach to those people who live in urban areas, including a biblical foundation of urban mission, a theology of poverty, a role for the church and ministry to the urban poor.

America has become more urbanized. When I came to Los Angeles, San Diego was like a park with strawberry fields and orange groves. Now you see solid city from Los Angeles to San Diego. This is true in many parts of the world. In his book *From The City of God and The City of Seven,* Robert Lithecomb said that ninety-four percent of the population of Canada and the United States will live in cities by the year 2000. By that time, eighty-two percent of the people of Europe, eighty percent of the Russians, thirty-six percent of the Indonesians, forty-five percent of the Africans and seventy-three percent of all Latin Americans will live in cities. We are looking at urbanization, not only in America, but all around the world, although America has more. In 1950, Los Angeles had 4 million people, in 1990 it had 9.5 million and by the year 2000 it will have 14 million. The city of Paris had 5.5 million people in 1950 and will be at 10 million by the year 2002. By the year 2000, Mexico City will be the biggest city in the world and will have the biggest problems: no way to feed the people, no way to meet all the needs of a huge city.

There are many problems associated with urbanization. The infrastructure cannot cope with the growth of the population. Transportation is a major problem. I live in Orange County, California, and commute to Los Angeles. If I leave home at 5:00 a.m., the trip takes forty minutes. If I leave at 6:30 a.m. that same trip takes two-and-a-half hours. There are millions of people on the freeway using a lot of gas and increasing pollution. I work for World Vision and we are moving to Seattle to escape the costs associated with being in a large city. Every year we spend $100,000 to comply with smog regulations alone. Many companies are moving out of California because the infrastructure cannot cope with the population and the expenses of doing business. The sewer system was built to serve 4 million people and now there are 10 million. Costs for trash and garbage collection and other associated services are rising.

Another problem is unemployment. There are more people in the city than jobs. In Detroit, for example, seventy-five percent of the young adults are unemployed. The social problems of crime, murder, prostitution, gangs, drug addiction, and alcoholism all tax the cities and tax the populations who live in our cities. Homelessness is another problem that cities have to face. So many people are homeless. They have to be taken care of somehow or they create more problems.

The reasons for such urban growth can, perhaps, be explained by what sociologists call the "push and pull" of the society. The people who live in the countryside or in villages feel the pull to the city to find jobs, get away from the family, become independent, be themselves and do what they want. Refugees and immigrants want to come to America and they move into the cities.

Public transportation is another pull to the cities. Many refugees and immigrants cannot afford a car or the insurance and do not know how to drive very well. They prefer to take public transportation, and cities provide better public transportation than rural areas.

Education is another area of opportunity in the cities. There are colleges, public and private universities, vocational school programs and federal programs for employment training. Most refugees and immigrants have a good work ethic but they lack skills and a knowledge of the language. Once they have mastered these, they can do well. One problem is that in some areas they work so hard that their level of production creates tension with other workers because they produce more.

There are job opportunities in the cities that the residents are often not willing to accept. For a Vietnamese refugee used to making fifteen dollars a month, getting a job here paying five dollars an hour sounds like a lot of money. They are eager to work and because of the needs of the family they will work very hard.

The make-up of communities changes and with that change comes tension. The south end of Los Angeles used to be a black community, but now most of the people who live there are from Latin America, with Korean, Vietnamese and Laotian/Cambodian refugees coming within the last five years. The L.A. riots showed the conflict between the blacks and the Koreans. The community used to be totally black and then the Koreans started to come. The blacks feel that the Koreans are taking away jobs and business opportunities. This is not true but the misunderstanding is in the way the Koreans and Asians finance their businesses. They pool their resources and make loans. In Korea, the church has now come to the level of a social institution. If you want to be successful, you have to be a Christian, or at least you have to go to church. That is where all the business deals are made. There is a high level of trust among their people, so they loan money without any questions and without a contract. However, the competition between the blacks and the Koreans is very strong, making for a potentially explosive situation.

When we look at the problems of the urban areas, we have to look at who the people are that live there. First, there are the white ethnics. The first white ethnics probably came from Germany, Scandinavia and Britain. The second immigration, called the New Immigrants, were the people who came to America in the early twentieth century from Poland, Italy and Greece. Many of them are still there, but they are gradually being replaced by the blacks, Koreans, Vietnamese, Cambodians and Latin Americans, both legal and illegal. There is a change in the community. I have personally seen these changes taking place in a number of communities and have watched the tension grow because people feel that the new immigrants are taking over "our" city.

Where do the people of the community go when they move? Some of the blacks move to the suburbs. Some of them become middle or lower middle class. They move to an area where crime is lower. There has also been a move of professional people from the suburbs to the city to get lower-cost housing. There has been a program where a city home can be purchased for almost nothing if the buyer agrees to renovate and live in the home for a specified length of time. Then it could be sold. In some areas, the refugees have moved into an area in bad condition. Then they fix it up. The Vietnamese moved into area in Santa Ana in southern California when space could be rented for twenty cents a square foot. That same space now rents for three dollars per square foot. They have moved in, fixed things up, protected the property and now it is a very desirable business community.

When we look at the ethnic make-up of our cities, fifty-five percent of the black people live in the four cities of Atlanta, Gary, Newark, and Washington, DC. These cities are fifty percent black. The Census Bureau says that there were 14 million Hispanic people in the United States in 1980. In 1990, there were 22 million, an increase of fifty-three percent not counting illegal aliens. So we are now looking at between 25 and 26 million Hispanics in this country. In 1980 the Asian and Pacific Islander population in the United States stood at 3.5 million. In 1990 it was as 7.2 million. That is a growth rate of 107 percent. Very few of these people live outside urban areas, even if they are sponsored by a church when they arrive. Eventually they will move to a city where they seem to feel more comfortable. The United States has become very international with at least 100 different languages spoken around the country.

When these people move to the city, they have the opportunity to interact with many other groups. As Christians, we want to reach out to these people as they face all the problems of city life. How do we do that? What do we believe is God's intention for the city? It is very discouraging to look at an area such as Detroit or south central Los Angeles. The whole area is like Beirut with abandoned houses, children running around, the homeless people and addicts sleeping everywhere, just existing. What can we do?

As Christians, I believe we have to develop some kind of a Christian understanding of the reality of the city. What is God's intention? In both the Old and New Testaments, liberation and salvation are very important. We know that God wants to deliver his people if they are oppressed, if they live in slavery. We see in Scripture that God delivered his people from bondage in Egypt and we can see people in the cities from this perspective. Many, many people in the cities do not want to remain in their condition, but they do not see a way to escape. Somehow the church has to come to them with the message of salvation and liberation.

I believe that God wants to transform the city. God wants to bring peace into the conflicts between people groups and even within ethnic groups. I believe God wants them to live in peace and harmony with one another, to prosper, and I believe he wants us to commit ourselves to helping the people who have nowhere to turn.

It is interesting that Jesus, when he began his ministry, read from that portion of Isaiah which spoke of how he would come and bring deliverance to the people. Jesus ministered to the widows, the orphans, the sick, the weak and the poor. From cover to cover, the Bible is filled with commitment to and help for the poor. In many countries, poverty and debt are synonymous. In most countries, the people work hard and all they pay on their debt is the interest. They have never paid on the principal and they are always under a burden.

If we want to minister to the poor, we must understand them and their condition. There is a difference between the poor and the refugees in the cities. The refugee and the immigrant, even though they are poor, have a lot of hope and expectation for the future. They will work very hard because they have a first-hand knowledge of poverty from their countries. There is discipline in the family and the children do well in school. They are able to go to college on scholarships because the family has no assets. The problem is with the second generation, the people born in such countries as Vietnam or Korea, who came here as very young children. They did not experience the poverty of their home country and they do not appreciate their parents' hard work. It is very difficult to deal with these young people in this society because they have become so westernized. They have come to expect the Nintendo, the $150 a pair Nike Aire shoes, and they turn to crimes of stealing to get the money. They feel that their parents are crazy to work so hard. The work ethic is not the same for the second generation.

The young people also do not understand the pressure from the homeland. Many families, particularly those from Vietnam, Laos or Cambodia, send money home to support their family. They have a duty to support themselves here and help those at home. Often they work two and three jobs to do that. I have personally known two individuals who died right at their sewing machines because they worked so hard.

The young people also do not understand the fears of the elderly as they grow older. In Asian countries, they do not have Social Security. The parents have large families and expect that the children will care for them in their old age. Now they are here and they fear that they will have to go to a nursing home where they cannot speak the language and all the nurses speak English.

According to the 1990 census, there are nearly 20 million foreign-born residents in America and that may not include illegal aliens. The problem of illegal aliens creates a lot of tension in a community. The politicians, state and federal government officials and sociologists are unsure of how to deal with the problem. Financially, they are costing the country a lot of money. The solution to the problem is difficult, but if we do not help them, who will? If they are not helped, they become criminals and that will cost us more. It costs $25,000 to put a person in prison for a year. It will cost less to help them, but when we lack money and resources, what can we do?

Going overseas as a missionary is relatively easy. If the conditions in a country are unacceptable, it is not difficult to leave. However, the immigrant and the refugee are here and whether we like it or not, we have to deal with them. So the question is, where do we begin? We have to begin with ourselves by asking if we can help them. Do we want to share the faith with them? In the past many churches have been interested in ministry to immigrants and refugees, but they only provided help to make them self-sufficient. They did not share the faith and that left them with their religions of Buddhism, Confucianism and ancestor worship. A lot of people believe that all Vietnamese are Buddhists, which is not correct. Many of them are Roman Catholics and some are Protestants. It is very important to get to know the community, and networking with pastors and religious leaders is a place to start. What people believe is very important and once you understand what they believe, you will probably understand half of everything you need to know.

Network with the social service agencies. These agencies provide services to these people and know them fairly well. They can help you understand the different ethnic communities in the area. Information about the kind of populations in specific cities can be obtained from the local, state and federal governments. The Census Bureau can give you population reports as of 1993.

Network with businesses. Restaurants are a great place to meet people. People are very proud of their own culture, and food is one aspect of culture. People usually integrate more in terms of food than in terms of religion. Visit the Chinese, Indian, Korean and Vietnamese restaurants and become acquainted with the people.

Help the people organize the community and identify the leaders. It is very difficult to deal with community problems without leaders. Leaders are the ones with the information, the ones who can help deal with the culture. They know the problems and will help with understanding the people.

As a Christian, it is my goal that all immigrants and refugees should come to know the Lord Jesus Christ. All of us want them to become Christians. We can help them establish congregations and raise up their own leadership. The problem I am finding in many denominations is that Anglo pastors are very caring and loving, but they move on after a few years and then the community has no leaders. It is very important to consider leadership when we think about establishing ethnic congregations. Indigenous leadership comes from the people and stays with the people. Even if they move to another area, their people will see them as leaders.

Assist those who have leadership abilities by helping them to get training, go to seminary, and learn the American system so they can deal with all the social issues that are so different here. Establishing even a small congregation and providing them with leadership skills so they can grow is a wonderful ministry.

Congregational support in establishing a ministry is vital. There are risks in ministry to refugees and immigrants. There is the problem of language and culture. It is very difficult to have an ethnic congregation unless there is acceptance of them as a people group. Ethnic congregations require nurturing and commitment. It means involving everyone from the diocesan level down to the individual congregations.

Once ethnic congregations have been established, they can be empowered for wider urban ministry. They can work well together. By nurturing and assisting them to live in our country, helping them learn the American system and how to relate to the church at large and the community helps to strengthen the urban areas. They can save a segment of a city if they have the gospel and the skills.

REACHING MUSLIMS
IN THE U.S. AND OVERSEAS

The Rev. Don McCurry

There are a number of issues that I have heard surfacing that I believe need to be addressed. One is certainly the Black Muslim problem and the word angry. I have to be a bit autobiographical here. I grew up in Washington, D.C., three blocks from Lincoln Park. That neighborhood is totally black now. When I was growing up there were a few black people around the corner and the rest were far, far away. But there was friction between the races even then. I realized that I had a problem with blacks and it wasn't until I went to seminary that I had my first black friend.

Then after that the Lord led me into many racial situations, including Black Africa, where I had an apprehensive question before I landed there. I wondered if the love of God would flow as freely when I landed in Liberia as it did in other places. And, of course, it did. It was only five minutes before I felt at home. They don't all look alike. I was able to relate to them immediately without any internal fear or anything.

The love of God is universal, but in the case of Black Muslims, we are dealing with an injured people. They will throw the theological stuff in your face because they are covering hostility and they are actually feeding it, harboring it, and they are letting it grow. Unfortunately, there is a segment of Islam, the Louis Farrakhan variety, that feeds on hatred. The group called the Nation of Islam prides itself on blackness, divisiveness and hate. There are other African-Americans who have become orthodox Muslims, and they have gotten beyond what we call racist Islam. Others also have joined Islam because of their woundedness. This came home to me ten years ago when I succeeded in calling five of the leading black pastors together from downtown Los Angeles. I wanted to talk about how are we going to face the challenge of the Black Muslims.

We had scheduled two hours for this, and I never got in a single word. They unloaded on me, those five pastors, non-stop for two hours. They were hurting. Basically these are the things I remember. Brother Don, when we get through with you—they knew what they were doing—you go back to all your white evangelical friends and you tell them to come back into the ghettos and to link up with us, because the Black Muslims are telling us they are going to eat us up. They are saying the white man has abandoned us. They moved out and they just left us here alone.

The black pastors were intimidated by this very militant movement. They also were hurting, and they were pleading to the white evangelicals, their white brothers and sisters in the gospel, to come back and join hands with them to show Islam that we are united, that we are not racist. You could have knocked me over with a feather. I wasn't ready for that. I was expecting to have five leading, enthusiastic pastors expound on how to tackle this problem. What I discovered was we had another problem that had to be dealt with first. And that's food for thought for all of us. It's a grievous problem.

For myself, I have had to swallow the pride I have had, and start by apologizing to blacks when I meet with them. I have to say I am sorry. I haven't really done much, knowingly, against blacks except be in a couple of street fights between white kids and black kids when I was growing up. I had to go back to the Bible and look at the prayers of people like Nehemiah and Daniel and Moses, but especially Nehemiah and Daniel. These guys, as far as I can tell, are paragons of virtue and yet they began to confess the sins of their forefathers. I know when I first discovered that in seminary, I thought it was a little far out, a kind of affectation, that you really didn't need to do stuff like that. I didn't know that I had become a syncretized Christian, that I had been brainwashed by Western thought, secular humanism especially, and the hyper-individualism that exists in our society. When you are schooled in this hyper-individualistic, competitive, capitalistic atmosphere, you don't answer for anybody else's problems. You are out there to win; whatever that means. It usually means losing but you don't know it. But anyway, you never learn to think as a community, you never learn to think of communal sins, nor do you ever dream of apologizing for long-standing communal sins that the forebears in your community committed. And yet I think that is the only way we can start with our black brothers and sisters, especially if they do feel wounded.

There is no point in discussing theology with them; Black Islamic theology is absurd. Elijah Mohammed is God. God himself was black. And Armageddon is going to be the last war in the United States. That's absurd. But have we ever repented for our own sectarianism?

When we were younger in Pakistan, we practiced comity between the missionaries; it was very egotistical to do this. This area was Anglican, this was Scottish Presbyterian, this was American Presbyterian, this was Salvation Army, this was Lutheran. And then all these kids got educated, like in Lahore, the provincial capital of the Punjab. Let's say you have five young men there that get excellent education; they work in the government or the air force or whatever. And gradually because of their jobs they are dispersed around the country and they join the local church, because not all church denominations were in every city. Then at Christmas time, they come back home. One brother says, "Jamal, what church do you go to?" "I go to the Anglican Church in Multan." "Sadak, what church do you go to?" "Well, I go to the Salvation Army church in Shantinaga." You go around the circle of these five brothers who are all raised one way; they now belong to five different denominations. Their first question after they wake up to this discovery is, "What have these missionaries done to us?" A very interesting question. What do we preach? This is why I beg audiences everywhere to learn to preach the Kingdom of God as their primary note. Preach the gospel about Jesus Christ dying for our sins and being buried and raised again, under the rubric of the Kingdom of God.

Certain missionary leaders like Henry Venn of the CMS, the Church Missionary Society, popularized a slogan called the "Euthanasia of Missions." He meant that you would go over there, and as soon as you had planted a church and felt it would stand, you would withdraw. That was the euthanasia part. But then you would relocate. You don't go back home and say well done. You relocate and you start all over again. His point was you leave all of the local people to figure out what this should look like without you acting like ecclesiastical imperialists and imposing all the answers on them. That was the early Anglican approach to missions. Unfortunately around the turn of the century, a whole new breed of young people hit the mission fields and stepped into the places of these older leaders, and they loved power. They took the leadership of the churches and the cathedrals and the dioceses away from promising nationals. They became in charge of everything and didn't want to let go. Finally at the end of the Second World War, when the colonial powers had to retreat and everyone was talking independence, everything was rapidly turned over to national leaders. Some of them caught the missionary fire; most of them did not.

When I went to teach at Union Seminary where we were all cooperating in Gutenwala, it had been in existence for ninety-nine years, and I discovered they had never taught a course on missions there. They had never taught a local person that he or she could be a missionary, which meant that the missionaries functioned as patrons. Egotistically, it is kind of gratifying to be a patron, to be able to dole out stuff and manage things, but it doesn't build up a healthy church. Today, we are coming out of that, and what is happening is a new phenomena: the birth of latrification missions. I dislike using "Third World." So you put Latin America, Africa and Asia all into one word—latrification missions. Today we are watching the birth of hundreds of new mission societies. We are now learning to relate to them as brother and sister societies, which is perhaps the most healthy of all situations in the work of the Lord's Kingdom.

But about Islam, if I can go back to a phrase one of you used here—the last of the giants. Islam is somewhere around nineteen or twenty percent of the world's population. It is going through a renaissance, a rebirth. It is becoming more militant. Except for the terrorist movements, it is not an integrated or coordinated renaissance; it is spontaneous. It grows out of the early books and out of the present economic plight.

There is a book called *Operation World* that takes you through the whole world in one year. All the major countries of the world are listed there. If you look up the Muslim countries of the world, with the exception of the oil countries, they are all at the bottom of the economic power structure. They know where they are, they grieve over this, and they look at the West with admiration and jealousy. They want what we have, but they don't want the worldview that goes with it. In other words, they want the power. Among the militants—I am going to leave terrorists out of it, but among militants, the reasoning goes something like this. When we followed the original teaching of Mohammed, we succeeded in everything we did. We conquered the world. Through their military conquest, they reached almost to the English Channel by the year 732. They certainly reached Multan, Pakistan, by 711, one of the most phenomenal double armied expansions in opposite directions the world has ever seen.

The militants say the reason Muslims are not on top of the world is they have abandoned the teaching of Mohammed, they have become compromised. This leads to a mentality that they need to get rid of all secularized Muslim leaders and bring secularized countries like Egypt or Turkey back to Islamic law. They need to purify themselves of all non-Islamic elements and then they will be able to become the mighty power that God wants them to be. They will be able to exterminate all this godlessness. They use Western movies as the prime example of godlessness. They will be able to purify the earth of its corruptions, meaning Westerners. Then Islam will eventually become the religion of the whole earth, and God will be honored. That's how they will achieve God's honor, and Islam will become the all in all. When you ask a reformer like the late Mulduti of Pakistan, what the Kingdom of God is, he says the Kingdom of God is Islam on earth as it is in heaven. That's how he looks at it, borrowing a phrase from the Lord's Prayer.

We are living in a difficult age. The honeymoon is over, the easy days are over, the romantic days of going to mission fields are over. We are living in a tense time of growing confrontation. There is going to be more of it. The bombing at the World Trade Center is only one example. They feel God is on their side. Sheik Omar Abdel Rahman (from the New York bombing) wants to go on trial. He wants to go on public trial in the United States. He wants to defend himself, from the Koran, the last and greatest holy book of all the monotheistic faiths. He wants that pulpit, and he wants to prove himself innocent in the light of the last great holy book sent by God.

Interesting developments are going on here. How do you look at these people? I am just going to share a few things as quickly as I can to whet your appetite.

First of all, personally. I relate as a friend. I go as a learner. Islam is like a mirror image of Christianity. It has every kind of sect, every kind of division. It has the Protestant, Catholic division over apostolic succession versus democratically elected leaders. It has a charismatic movement called Sufism, which is not a real charismatic movement. It's got superstition, animistic practices where Islam didn't take very well. It has got secularism. So you need to become a learner and say teach me.

Teach me what you believe. You need to let them talk it all out, and find out where their need might be, where they are hungry. But you have to do that as a friend.

You have to learn to practice hospitality. I remember doing a series of studies at Bel Air Presbyterian Church where President Reagan used to go. A lady came up after my first lecture and she said, "I think I live next door to a Muslim." I said, "Great, what have you done about it?" She shrank back and said, "Nothing, of course. I am afraid of them." And I said, "Dear lady, would you do anything I tell you to do?" She got further away and said, "What are you going to tell me to do?" I said, "When you go home from church today, I want you either to buy, if you can't bake, or bake some kind of a sweet dish and I want you to go over and knock on the door of their house and I want you to say, "I am your neighbor. I really was a little bit afraid of you because I don't understand things, but I want to be your friend and I brought you this gift.'" I said, "Would you be willing to do that?" So she said she would do that.

The next Sunday she was up front waiting for me when I got there, just bouncing up and down, she couldn't wait to talk. She said, "It worked!" She said, "A nice young man came to the door. He spoke English. None of their ladies had those terrible black veils on. I was invited in and we had a wonderful conversation." It's one week later. And she said, "And now we are good friends." All that lady needed was a kick in the pants, someone to kind of nudge her to take the first steps in friendship.

Over all, we do have a very ominous challenge. There are five levels of activity that different ones of us need to be involved in. All of us can't do all of these things. The first level is deep, deep intercessory prayer. I believe prayer breaks down barriers like nothing else can. It releases God to create openings. I don't know how he does it, but apparently God waits to be asked for these things and then he moves. Apparently our prayers release God to move, something he probably wanted to do all along, but he was waiting.

The second level is at the highest levels of government, and that is the battle for human freedom, for religious freedom and human rights. Islam does not measure up officially, and they know it. When you talk to them, they say, oh, we are free in Islam, and you are free under Islam. When you press them, what they mean is you are free to become a Muslim. They are not free to become a Christian because it's the death penalty, according to the interpretation of the Koran, for them to leave Islam. We have never dealt with a religion like this before. It's a miracle that we are having so many conversions around the world in the light of this.

We have this high level of pressing Muslim countries to protect, if possible, religious freedom and human rights.

The next level is another unpleasant one, the battle for truth. Assuming the gospel is true, we are being slandered by these people. Some of our scholars need to answer these attacks because Muslims think they are right until they are challenged. This came home to me at Texas A&M. I had a former student call up and say, "Don, you have got to come down here and be on a panel discussion with a Muslim and a Jewish scholar." I said, "Mike, that is not my style. I don't like that stuff." And he said, "Will you promise to pray about it?" As I was praying, the Lord said to me, I want you to go down there and love those Muslims. I learned who my, shall we say opponent was, my fellow panelist. I read the book he wrote on Mohammed in the Bible. That was the topic, because they are trying to cop all the prophecies for Mohammed now. I knew all of his arguments. That was wonderful. He was quoting from Deuteronomy where Moses said God will raise up a prophet like me, listen to him. And Moses was married, Mohammed was married; Moses led an army, Mohammed led an army; Moses gave a law, Mohammed gave a law. They were finding all the points of similarity. So I shifted the whole ground to the miraculous, to the ten plagues, the crossing of the Red Sea, Jesus walking on water, Jesus feeding five thousand, Moses calling manna down from heaven. I dwelt on the miraculous and I dwelt on the sacrificial system and the blood and Jesus being the lamb of God. When we were through, the Muslim students rushed back to the Muslim panelist and they said why didn't you answer this point, why didn't you answer this point. The Saudi leader came to Mike and he said, "Okay, Mike, I am ready to study the Bible with you." I didn't seek that, but Mike and the Lord worked on me. And it worked. We got the chief of the whole Muslim student body studying the Bible. Somebody has to do that sometimes. That's what I call the third level.

Prayer, human rights, the battle of truth. The fourth level is one we are very familiar with: ministering to human need. These are the poorest of the poor, except for the oil states. We don't need to be reminded that Jesus said to remember the poor.

The fifth level is the level of personal evangelism, learning to sit with them to see that they are locked into fear. In Pakistan, if you have ever been to a Muslim funeral, it's something you will never forget; the screaming, the shrieking, the hysteria at the fear of death, especially among the women. You really see the fear of death out in the open there. And you see it in hundreds of other ways, in little things they try to do, in the prayers they pray for the dead, in the candles they burn, in the food they bring and the flowers, the reciting of the Koran on the seventh day, the fortieth day, the hundredth day, and one year later to make it easier for the dead relative in hell. They would like to know about salvation and we have to find the right way to share it with them because our common enemies are sin and Satan and death. They don't know how to escape from any one of the three. Their laws don't help them do it, just make them feel more guilty and more afraid. They don't know how to counter Satan, they don't know that Jesus broke Satan's back, broke his power. We have to find a way to relate to them and to bring them out of that kingdom. They have been deceived, enslaved, and then empowered in a negative way. That is what makes them so formidable, that terrific empowering through that lockstep mentality.

If you ever want to hold a local or multi-church seminar in your area, I am available to come.

* * * * *

Dr. McCurry has developed valuable materials describing what Muslims believe, what they practice and the kinds of Muslims in the world. A 112-page notebook as well as audio cassettes and videos can be ordered. He also conducts seminars to equip people to encounter Muslims and build friendships, counter Muslim philosophy theologically and through case studies, and pose questions which lead to discussion with Muslims. For information on this material, please contact Dr. McCurry at:

4164 Austin Bluffs Parkway, #357
Colorado Springs, CO 80918

SECULAR JOBS:
OPEN DOORS TO CLOSED COUNTRIES

Ms. Sharon Stockdale

No country, including those inaccessible to traditional missionaries, is closed to Christians with the right professional or technical skills. There are about sixty nations in the world where a secular skill or profession is the main way or the only way to gain entry. "Tentmaking" (a name taken from the example of St. Paul, the apostle to the Gentiles who supported himself by making tents) opens doors to such closed countries as Afghanistan, China, and Saudi Arabia. It opens doors to poor countries such as Haiti, Mozambique and Bangladesh. It opens doors to rich countries like Japan, France and Austria where a professional or business person has access to a different level of society than a missionary would. However, just going abroad does not make people tentmakers; they need to be committed to sharing the gospel with the local people. Some people from your church may already be overseas with IBM or another company. Do they have a vision for what they could be accomplishing where they are?

Abraham, Joseph, Amos, Daniel, Paul, and many others in the Bible served the Lord while they supported themselves with secular jobs. One of my favorite tentmakers in the Bible, besides Daniel, is the little Israelite girl who was taken captive by the Syrians and served the army commander's wife. General Naaman had leprosy, and the little girl told her mistress, "If only my master went to see the prophet in Samaria, he could heal him." This young girl was in the right place at the right time to have an impact for the Kingdom of God, and centuries later we have her story in the Bible, in 2 Kings 5.

There are many advantages to going as a tentmaker. Access to closed countries is the first one that comes to people's minds, but it's not the only one. The financial costs of sending tentmakers who earn a salary abroad are much less. Their costs of living are paid for. If we are going to reach the world, we need to have thousands and thousands of people involved. We cannot rely only on full-time Christian workers; we need lay people in all kinds of careers to do the work.

Modeling is another important advantage. Having a ministry while you are working to support yourself instead of being dependent on donations is a much more transferable model of ministry in many situations. It helps avoid creating "rice Christians," those who hang around the missionaries for their own financial benefit. If you are working to support yourself with your own hands, you are providing a model that many others can follow.

Tentmaking also gives you natural points of contact with the worlds of finance, education, government, commerce, fine arts, etc. You have the same problems as your co-workers. They get to see you every day. How do you respond in various situations? Does God really make a difference in your life? People can watch you. This can have a very sanctifying effect! When I was on a team teaching English in China to adults, we realized that we were being scrutinized, and people would see if we were different or not. We started praying that God would turn scrutiny into opportunity. As people see a difference, it sparks their curiosity and they begin to ask questions.

There are limits on what you can say in the classroom, but we asked God to open up opportunities. At Christmas and Easter, our students asked us about the holidays. People would also ask questions in personal conversations. If you are teaching literature, there are many references to Christianity that need to be explained. If you are a scientist, people wonder how somebody who is so logical and intelligent could believe in God! They cannot put that together. Yesterday someone told me their students asked them about family life and they wound up doing a skit of a wedding using the Book of Common Prayer! The students were fascinated with it. There are many ways to be creative. So tentmakers may have lots of opportunities to share, but you do work under a lot of limitations. You have to be as wise as a serpent and as harmless as a dove.

Another advantage that I really enjoyed was credibility. I wasn't being paid to talk about religion; my job was to teach. I was really glad that I worked with an openly Christian organization in China. At first the universities were very nervous of us as Christians, but now they welcome Christian foreigners more than non-Christian foreigners in China because we are more moral. We don't complain as much. We are more likely to fulfill our contracts and really care about our students. The welcome mat is out for Christian teachers, but not for missionaries.

All kinds of people are needed. Christianity is for the whole world. If the only Christians people see all have a white face, it's hard to argue with the idea that Christianity is a Western religion. Our fellowship included African students, African Americans, Hispanics, and Asians from several different countries who all believed. It has a very powerful impact demonstrating that the gospel crosses racial lines. Chinese Americans can face a lot of culture shock when they first go to China, but later on they have more opportunities just because they don't look foreign.

Retirees and people in mid-career will find that their experience and education opens many opportunities. There is often no upper age limit for people, as long as they are in good health. Age is respected in many societies. The cost of living is lower in many countries, so a retirement income can stretch farther. In many places, part-time work and consultant work are possibilities. Many countries would welcome the depth of experience and the feel for things that only come from having worked for years in a field.

The fields that are most in demand are agriculture, applied science, business, computer science, design, engineering, English language, journalism, law, science, technology, and translation, but there are many other openings. ECMC can give you information about a variety of agencies that place tentmakers all over the world.

Recent graduates may find doors open overseas that are not open to them in the USA. I would not want this to be the only motivation for someone to go overseas, but overseas experience does look good on a resume. We don't always have to come in as the experts. I know some Episcopalians who are studying overseas in countries where missionaries cannot go. The cost is often the same or not much greater than in the U.S. They have daily contact with their classmates. In some countries English is the language of instruction. You can also go as a language student. Having enough concern to learn someone's language immediately communicates that you care about their culture.

In terms of personal qualifications, good health, flexibility, teachability, friendliness, sensitivity, emotional maturity, good family relationships, being able to work on a team, and not being in debt are important. Good family and team relationships are a powerful witness. My team was very committed to each other. Our students could see that we were quite different from each other. One thing that stood out for them was that there was acceptance and forgiveness. Tentmakers also need to be people of integrity who are respectful and able to work under authority, which many countries value much more than Americans do. Wisdom, tact and having a servant heart are very important. Study the book of Daniel and look at how he related to the Babylonian officials. He was tactful, wise, and respectful. Some of the officials may be people we can reach for the Lord.

Tentmaking is very demanding. You do not have the support network you have here. How do you balance the demands of family, work and ministry? Spiritual warfare can be very intense, and we shouldn't be naive. It's not the government, your co-workers, or circumstances that are the enemy. One of the things that Satan loves to do is divide Christians. I have heard that the biggest reason missionaries come home early is because of problems with other missionaries. Being on guard can help you spot things when they happen. You need to have a growing relationship with Christ, be sensitive to the Holy Spirit, and be a person of prayer and perseverance. Obviously if God only sent perfect people, he wouldn't send any of us, but at least we need to be growing in these areas.

Professional qualifications are another major area. In most situations at least a Bachelor's degree is needed. For the honor of Christ and for the sake of serving the host country, it's essential that tentmakers do their work well. The job itself is a means of service. It can't just be a cover for a missionary work. It is very counterproductive to neglect the responsibilities that you were hired to fulfill; we need to be a witness in our jobs for the Lord. On the other hand, some jobs leave very little time or energy for ministry or building relationships. Some jobs can be quite isolating so there is little contact with local people. Just because you are in the country doesn't mean you really have access to the people. You need to look at that carefully when you consider various jobs.

If someone from your congregation wants to go, make sure they have the opportunity to get some training and experience. Don't send people out unprepared. Training in missiology can greatly multiply their effectiveness. What strategies have proven effective in that situation? What are some reasonable goals? How does this person's role fit into the bigger picture? People being sent out need to know the basics of the Bible, how to answer people's questions about Christianity, how to do friendship evangelism, and how to disciple new believers.

Training in cross-cultural sensitivity and cross-cultural communication is crucial. How do you affirm someone from a different background than your own? How do you learn a language outside of a classroom? There are many resources from which to draw. For example, *Language Acquisition Made Practical* (commonly referred to as LAMP) is a great book for helping people learn how to build relationships and communicate in another language. I highly recommend the one- and two-year degree programs in missions and evangelism offered at Trinity Episcopal School for Ministry.

Working with international students in the USA is some of the best preparation you could have for going overseas. Almost every college in the United States has international students from many different countries around the world. You need to be aware of basic ways not to offend someone and to express a real appreciation for another culture. For instance, if you have Muslims come to your home, don't serve them barbecued pork!

Get some basic orientation to the culture and the country you are going to, its history, and an awareness of the stresses of adapting to another culture. It can help you a lot. What things bother Americans about the country? What things bother the nationals about Americans? There are many things about another culture that are not better or worse, just different. An understanding of that can help you be a much more gracious and affirming person when you go overseas. A culture is not something that is just a pain in the neck to learn, there is something wonderful about the diversity of tribes, customs, languages, and nations.

We need to have a respect for the local Christians who may be in the country, not just assume that we have got it all. Some believers there may have suffered for decades and they really know something about following the Lord. We need to have the humility to listen to them.

Going with an agency provides accountability, direction, strategy, counsel from experienced people, pastoral care and fellowship. Otherwise, the isolation can be very great. I have seen too many people come back as casualties. It is both proud and foolish to think we can go off on our own without any support network. We need each other. Being on a team also gives other people the opportunity to see, "Behold, how they love each other." One of the criticisms of tentmaking concerns lone wolves who go off by themselves without any training or accountability and do a lot of damage.

Another thing that being with an agency does is help build long-term continuity in the ministry. In some places we have had teams for ten years, and there is a cumulative impact that no one individual could have brought about. That is really very important. One person laid a foundation for the next person.

What do tentmakers need from their home churches? I want to start out by recommending your church library get a copy of *Working Your Way to the Nations: A Guide to Effective Tentmaking* by Jonathan Lewis. You can order it from William Carey Library. This book has a tremendous number of helpful, practical suggestions.

Counsel is very important. We need help to discern God's call. We need people to pray with us and talk and think and dream and pray some more. Prayer support is vital from beginning to end, before you go, while you are there, and when you get back. It makes all the difference. We are not islands; we can't do it by ourselves, and we have to have people standing behind us who are praying.

Another thing tentmakers often need is some financial support, even if they get a salary overseas. Transportation to the country may be paid, or it may not. Medical insurance overseas, and the costs of placement, training, and orientation, need to be covered. Tom Telford mentioned a student who paid for her roommate's school debt so she could go overseas sooner. Sometimes people need help when they return. When I went to China, all our salary was paid in the local currency and we couldn't change any of it into U.S. dollars. So we came back with hardly anything. Someone who is home for the summer may need a car to get around. Sometimes needing more financial support means getting more attention, so the full-time missionaries get more of the spotlight. If a tentmaker doesn't need as much financial support, don't think that means they don't need your prayer support. They do.

Tentmakers need encouragement and communication with people from home. We need people to write to us. If you are writing to someone in a sensitive situation where the mail may be opened, be sure to follow the letter writing guidelines they give you, but don't be so paranoid that you don't write. Write about the high school football game or whatever, anything to let them know you care about them, and you haven't forgotten about them. If you can't write that you are praying for them, you can write that you want them to know you are thinking about them. Everyone knows how to translate that sentence.

Coming back home is often a difficult adjustment to make. When you go overseas, you are excited about all the new things you will experience. But when you come back, you want things to be exactly as they were when you left. The second year I was in China my mom moved out of the home that I grew up in. The third year when I got home for the summer I found out she had emphysema. After four years in China, when friends told a political joke, I didn't know what was funny. People were talking about songs, movies, and television programs with which I was totally unfamiliar. I had no idea what was in style. The high school students had purple hair. I felt as if I was on another planet.

Debriefing is very important. You would be surprised how many people never have an opportunity to share their stories when they get back. No one asks, or they want to know "How was it?" in twenty-five words or less. Give returning tentmakers opportunities to speak to the congregation. They can be a window on the world, and it can help inform your prayers. Ask them how you can pray for them and what the prayer needs in that country are. Questions like that can enable people to share from their hearts. It does not happen nearly as often as it should.

How can mission committees build a vision for tentmaking? First of all, include tentmaking in your missions policy as one of the strategies of modern missions. There are still too many churches that only have a vision for people going out in traditional roles. Include people who go overseas in secular positions as part of your church's outreach and pray for them.

Help the church learn about tentmaking. Invite a speaker from ECMC or Anglican Frontier Missions to your church. When you meet someone who has done it and hear their stories, it sets people's hearts on fire and they begin to get a big vision of what needs to be done in the world and the role they can play.

Is there somebody suitable in your congregation that your church could send? There is nothing like knowing a tentmaker personally to spark people's interest. Maybe there is already somebody overseas from your congregation who could be equipped for a more intentional tent-making role. Make sure they have a vision and get well trained.

Another thing your congregation can do is promote a healthy view of work. Do you have a vision of the people in the congregation as God's ambassadors in the workplace? George Pierce says he doesn't like the term "lay people" very much, he prefers to call us kingdom agents. How can you help people integrate their work and their ministry? You could have a forum for people in different professions to get together and talk about ethical problems they face, and meet with college students to talk about what is it like to serve the Lord in a particular profession, and the problems and opportunities they have. You can have people share testimonies in church from the workplace. Make it a point to build a healthy, biblical view of work in your congregation.

GOOD NEWS FOR JEWISH PEOPLE

The Rev. Alfred Sawyer

> "Behold, days are coming," declares the Lord, "when I will make a
> new covenant with the house of Israel and with the house of Judah,
> not like the covenant I made with their fathers in the day I took them
> by the hand to bring them out of the land of Egypt, My covenant
> which they broke, although I was a husband to them," declares the
> Lord. "But this is the covenant which I will make with the house of
> Israel after those days," declares the Lord, "I will put my law within
> them, and on their heart I will write it; and I will be their God, and
> they shall be my people. And they shall not teach again, each man his
> neighbor and each man his brother, saying, 'Know the Lord,' for they
> shall all know Me, from the least of them to the greatest of them," de-
> clares the Lord, "for I will forgive their iniquities, and their sin I will
> remember no more." (Jer 31:31-34, NASB)

When we read this passage and see the phrase "new covenant," most of us think of church, and the words that are used in the Prayer Book liturgy to celebrate communion. But notice with whom the new covenant is made: the house of Israel and the house of Judah. Speaking to Jeremiah, the Lord calls it the new covenant because he is referring specifically to the group of people with whom he made the old covenant.

The previous covenant was made with the Hebrews, the descendants of Abraham through Isaac and Jacob. Here God declares a new covenant.

We think of this term in relation to communion because during the Last Supper, Jesus took one of the cups of wine—probably the third cup, known as the cup of blessing in the Passover meal—and he raised it, saying, "This cup is the new covenant in my blood." He was specifically referring to this passage in Jeremiah. Everyone in the room would have known what he was talking about because they were all Jewish people familiar with the Hebrew Scriptures. They would have understood Jesus' declaration that what was about to occur would inaugurate this new covenant.

The differences between the old covenant and the new covenant are these: The old covenant was written externally, inscribed upon tablets of stone. The new covenant would be internal, written upon human hearts, allowing each person, no matter what his status or station, to be in a personal relationship with God. "They will all know Me, from the least of them to the greatest." No longer would the knowledge of God be something that came through an intermediary, through a priest standing in the gap interceding and offering sacrifice on behalf of the people to God. Each person would be in the position of that priest. The Lord was declaring here the priesthood of all believers, that we all would have open access to God. Jesus was saying that his death on the cross and the shedding of his blood would inaugurate this new covenant.

In the early church the big controversy was not whether a Jewish person could believe in Jesus and be incorporated into this new covenant, because the entire church was Jewish. The question was, could a non-Jew be a part of this new covenant? From the Jeremiah passage it appears that this covenant is made only with the houses of Israel and Judah. There was a big debate about whether a Gentile (anyone who is not a Jew) could follow Jesus as Messiah without first becoming Jewish. This is the raging controversy that we read about in Acts 15. The decision of the early church was that this promise is not just to the Jewish people. Going back for an overview of Scripture showed that the promise to Abraham was that through his seed the entire world would be blessed. The Lord did not select Abraham and his descendants in order for the Jewish people to keep the knowledge of God to themselves. A lot of people misunderstand this whole concept of "chosenness." They think that when the Jews say they are the chosen people, it means that they are just a little bit better than everybody else, and that they have the inside track to God. Not so! They are chosen to be the vehicles of the knowledge of God to the earth, to be a light for the nations, and to impart the glory of God to a world that did not know him.

Paul picks up the thread of this argument in Romans 9–11, when he said it is through the Jews that the Scriptures came, the promises came, the patriarchs came, and ultimately that the Messiah himself came. As Gentiles, we have been grafted as a wild olive branch into what was the covenant between God and the Jewish people.

So what happened? Why is it the exception rather than the rule today that Jewish people believe in Jesus? And why is this such a controversial subject? I travel a lot and speak to many different church groups, and there is nothing quite as provocative as talking about presenting the gospel to Jewish people. It really rattles a lot of cages. Why is this? We have to look at a little bit of history. The early church—all Jewish—made the decision to admit Gentiles and began to spread around the Mediterranean Basin into the non-Jewish world, with large numbers of non-Jews becoming believers.

In his letter to the Romans, Paul is probably addressing a mixed congregation of Jews and non-Jews. That is why he is careful to tell the non-Jews not to boast and exalt themselves over the natural branches simply because most of the Jews haven't accepted Jesus as Messiah.

In Israel, most of those who followed and believed in Jesus were Jews. We are told in the book of Acts that three thousand were converted in one day, and that there were numbers of priests obedient to the faith. There was never any question about the Jewishness of those early disciples of Jesus. Nobody was suggesting that by believing in Jesus, these people were ceasing to be Jews. The whole concept of Messiah is a Jewish one, promised by the Jewish prophets in the Jewish scriptures, so in their minds nothing was more Jewish than believing in the Jewish Messiah. It was the fulfillment of everything they had longed for and expected. They weren't converting to another religion; they were simply receiving the promise that God had made to their own prophets, that he would raise up a prophet like Moses from among them. He would be the anointed one who would bring redemption.

A Jewish rebellion against Rome in 70 AD resulted in the destruction of the Temple. At Masada, the last vestiges of that revolt were quelled. In 132 AD another revolt was attempted, led by a man called Bar Kokba. He was proclaimed Messiah by the chief rabbi of the day, Akiba, who encouraged all Jews to join in the revolt against the Romans. Jews who believed that Jesus was the Messiah didn't sympathize with the Roman occupation, but could not join the revolt because they would then be following a false messiah. At this point, Rabbi Akiba issued an order of excommunication, with two criteria. The first was anyone who "whispers over a wound," an interesting term indicating that the early Jewish church prayed for healing; and the second was anyone who reads the books of the "Nuheem," that is, the books of the heretics—meaning the emerging corpus of the New Testament. These people would automatically be excommunicated from the House of Israel. This was the beginning of the separation between those Jews who believed in Jesus as Messiah and those who did not. At this point, those who did not believe in Jesus and followed Rabbi Akiba were saying that followers of Jesus the Nazarene were apostates. Considered traitors to the Jewish people because they hadn't joined in the revolt against Rome, they were cut off from mainstream Jewish culture and religion. Also at this time, the Jewish religious leaders of the Sanhedrin were beginning to recognize the threat of "the Nazarenes" to the unity of the Jewish community and to their own position. Consequently, a polarization began to occur in the second century.

Jewish Christianity existed in the Middle East well into the fourth century, but finally died out. In that era, Christianity became legal for the first time. The first three hundred years of Christianity is a history of persecution. There were ten successive persecutions under the Romans, with the worst probably that of Diocletian, which was also the last. Then Constantine became a convert and it was suddenly legal to be Christian. Several things resulted. Before the fourth century, there weren't many church buildings, but now they began to be built. The clergy emerged as a different caste within the church. Clerics began wearing strange clothes, imitating the customs of the Byzantine court. Thousands of pagans came into the church with no real experience of Jesus—the emperor was a Christian; it was legal, respectable and even fashionable to be a Christian; so they became Christians.

With this influx of unbelieving, baptized pagans, the cult of the saints emerged, particularly surrounding the Virgin with the predominating influence of Hellenistic thought and philosophy. Some of the church fathers, such as John Chrysostom, said things like this: because the Jews have rejected Jesus, they have been rejected by God; they are a people under a curse; the church is the new Israel; all of the promises that God made to Israel have been inherited by the church, and naturally the Jewish people inherited all of the curses. Augustine said the only reason the Jewish people were still around was that God had preserved them in misery to show the truth of the Christian gospel.

The term "New Israel" is not biblical, never appearing in the New Testament. Paul uses the term "the Israel of God," which I think is something quite different, referring to the body of Christ, which is both Jewish and Gentile. His argument in Romans 11 is that the gospel is for all people, to the Jew first and then to the non-Jew. But the church began to develop a very triumphalistic, anti-Semitic attitude. We are the ones anointed and blessed by God; the Jewish people are under a curse. This attitude solidified during the Middle Ages and resulted in the deaths of thousands of Jewish people. First were the Crusades. As the crusaders rode out to the Holy Land, they stopped off in the towns of Europe to round up the Jews, put them in the synagogues and burn them down. Thousands of Jews died at the hands of people bearing the emblem of the cross. Then in the Inquisition Jews were given the choice of baptism or death, and thousands more died at the hands of the Christian church. There were successive pogroms in various parts of Europe as the Jews were blamed for everything from the plague, to natural disasters, to war. The blood libel emerged, alleging that Jews captured and killed Christian children to drink their blood. That may sound medieval, but just a few years ago in Eastern Europe that rumor was again being spread. Over the centuries the maliciousness of the blood libel resulted in the death of Jews in almost every country in Europe. Of course, the Jewish dietary laws strictly forbid ingesting any blood.

Here is the broad picture: what started out as Hebraic gradually became Hellenized; Jewish people who believed in Jesus became marginalized from their own community, gradually dying out; and the Christian church, which by now was predominantly Gentile, developed an attitude of hatred and antipathy toward the people from whom their faith came.

With the Reformation, you would think things would get better as people returned to the Scripture. Luther began with a very positive attitude toward the Jewish people, but when they didn't respond to the gospel, he changed his mind. Luther ended up writing some of the most vitriolic invective against the Jews ever penned, encouraging the burning of their synagogues and the persecution of their community. In fact, the Nazis used some of Luther's writings to justify the Holocaust. Granted, there was deeply ingrained anti-Semitism in Europe, and Luther was a product of his time and his culture. So, unfortunately, the Reformation did not impact the general perception of Jews by Christians.

The fruit of almost two thousand years of Christian anti-Semitism were the events that occurred in Europe in the 1940s. *Schindler's List* was abso-lutely the best film on this topic that I have ever seen. Although not easy to watch, it is something that everyone really needs to see.

Between 1942 and 1945, one-third of the Jewish people on the face of the earth were exterminated, not in the heat of battle, but simply because of who they were. It is an event that is unique in history. There have been a lot of people killed in wars over the centuries, but never before had people "with clean fingernails," in the words of C.S. Lewis'

Screwtape Letters, sat down and decided, we are going to systematically kill this group of men, women and children simply because of who they are. They set about their assembly line strategy with ruthless efficiency. At its height, 15,000 people a day were murdered. In the Jewish mind, this was done by Christians, and it is no use telling them that Adolf Hitler was not born again. To the Jews, Hitler was a baptized Christian leading a Christian nation in the heart of Christian Europe, doing his work while the world watched. To me, the ending of *Schindler's List* was the most powerful part because it pointed to what was really behind the return of the Jews to Israel. Nowhere on this earth can the Jews be safe except in their own land.

So, when Jews see Christian churches, Christian people and Christian symbols like crosses, they don't see religion, they don't see God, they don't see life and they don't see comfort. They see death! They see persecution, hatred and everything that has plagued them all of these two thousand years.

In modern times, trying to reach Jewish people with the gospel is a difficult task, and that is an understatement! What started out as Jewish has drifted so far away from its original roots, and the Jewish people are so alienated from what was their gospel, that it becomes very difficult to communicate the Good News to them.

Another problem is a very strong layer of Christian anti-Semitism which is just below the surface in a lot of people. A friend of mine was preaching in England a few years ago about the Jewishness of Jesus. A little old lady came up at the end of his talk, shaking with rage and red in the face, demanding, "Do you mean to say that Jesus was a Jew?" He said yes. She retorted, "Well, if I had known that, I never would have believed in him!" That may seem funny, but it's sad and true. This attitude on the part of a lot of Christians perpetuates the great gulf.

Christ Church was the first Protestant church built in the Middle East, and the first church of any kind built in Jerusalem since the Crusades. The Arab Christians of Turkish Palestine were predominantly Greek Orthodox, with a pretty significant Roman Catholic minority. If a Jew happened to be caught in the Church of the Holy Sepulcher, which is the main church in Jerusalem, built over the reputed site of the crucifixion and resurrection, it was an offense punishable by death. The atmosphere was not exactly conducive to evangelism. There was tremendous hostility on the part of the institutional church toward the Jewish people.

There have always been Jewish people in Israel; even during the Dispersion, there were always a few Jews who remained, and more started coming back in the Middle Ages. There was a Jewish community in Israel in the 1840s when we established this mission. Our mission was built specifically as an outreach to the Jewish people by agreement between the Anglican Church in England and the Lutheran Church in Prussia. A Protestant bishopric was created with alternating bishops. (By the way, this was the final straw for John Henry Newman, who left the Church of England to protest its alliance with a church not in apostolic succession.) The first bishop was a C.M.J. missionary named Michael Solomon Alexander. A rabbi who had come to believe in Jesus as Messiah, Alexander was ordained in the Anglican Church and sent out to be our first bishop in Jerusalem. He established an outreach to the Jewish people that by the 1850s resulted in a sizable congregation of 130 or so Hebrew Christians, including a number of rabbis. That ministry continued until 1948 when Israel became a state.

The Turks, who had ruled Palestine for four hundred years, were allied with the Germans during World War I. After the war in 1917, the British and the French divided the Middle East, with the British taking Turkish Palestine, Egypt and what is today Jordan, and the French taking Lebanon and Syria. The British operated under what was known as the League of Nations Mandate for Palestine. This resulted in a lot of Jews coming into Palestine. There had been a wave of immigration in the 1880s with the pogroms in Russia, but now that the Muslims were no longer in control of Palestine, numbers of Jews started immigrating, until the British, under pressure from the Arab world, shut the door in the 1930s, just as Nazism began to gain strength in Europe. In fact, almost all nations—including the U.S.—refused to take Jews who wanted to leave Germany. As a result, six million died.

After World War II, the British were financially exhausted. Tensions were great between the Jewish and Arab communities, with the Arabs naturally resenting the immigration of Jews into Palestine. Britain could not contain the troubles in the area, and turned it over to the United Nations. The U.N.'s partition plan gave part of Palestine to the Arabs and part to the Jews. The Arabs rejected the plan, saying they would settle for no less than all of Palestine. The Jews were not happy with the Partition Plan, but realizing it was better to have something than nothing, they agreed to it. The British pulled out on May 14, 1948, the State of Israel was officially declared, and immediately war broke out. Five Arab countries invaded Israel.

Israel today is a great military power, but in 1948 it had almost nothing. Yet in eighteen months, those five Arab nations with armies, tanks and airplanes were defeated by a tiny new nation of refugees. The story of that victory is too long to tell here, but to summarize, Israel's War for Independence was a miracle!

The Old City, however, home to Christ Church, was captured by the Jordanian Legion. No Jew was allowed to go into the Old City, and consequently the ministry of Christ Church to the Jews was put out of business for nineteen years. In 1967, in the Six Day War, Israel annexed the West Bank and East Jerusalem, and Jerusalem was reunited. The door was then opened for Jewish people to return to the Old City, and Christ Church was back in business.

Instead of the Jewish people coming back into Christ Church's ministry, we found that much of the congregation had gone abroad during the War of Independence. When I arrived there in the early 1980s, what I found was a very good evangelical ministry among nice English expatriates. Very few Israelis would venture into Christ Church at that time, but shortly after I came one happened to drop in. It was after Sunday service and I was dressed up in all of my regalia. In typical Israeli fashion, this man bluntly asked me why I was dressed like that. I thought for a minute and couldn't think of a good reason. Finally I said something about being Anglican, as if that would absolve me from all sins. He replied, "If you want to reach the Jewish people, you won't succeed dressed like that." I realized he was right. What they were seeing when I wore that outfit was the Crusades. They were seeing the Inquisition. They were seeing the Holocaust. They were seeing the persecution of the Jewish people by the church down through the centuries. They were not seeing the Jewish Messiah. I had no clue how in that slightly stuffy, English environment, we were ever going to reach the Israelis living around us. We were right on the edge of the Jewish Quarter; every day thousands of Jews passed the gates of our church.

So I gathered a group of people who felt similarly, and we started to pray, asking God to show us. The result of those prayers was that God started to draw in Israeli Messianic Jews, with the church gradually becoming a Hebrew-speaking congregation. Today it is the largest in the nation of Israel, with over 250 Jewish people worshipping Jesus in the Hebrew language on the Sabbath—Saturday morning. There is an active outreach as the congregation goes into the Jewish communities of Jerusalem. There are home groups all over the city. They go out in teams to witness and pass out tracts. We have a coffee shop attached to the church now, operated by the Hebrew-speaking fellowship, which has Arab Christians and Jewish Christians living, witnessing and working together. Believe me, that is a testimony in the Old City of Jerusalem. We have a bookshop right in front of our compound, facing the main street that leads down to the Jewish Quarter. Over the top of that bookshop is written in big, gold letters the passage of Scripture that we read at the beginning: "I will make a new covenant with the House of Israel and the House of Judah." That gets attention, as it is written in Hebrew. Israelis are intensely curious. People come in asking us what we believe. Many are being reached through the ministry of the bookshop. In addition, about seven thousand Israelis come through Christ Church every year because of its historical significance. They come in to hear the history, but we include the gospel. We begin with Genesis, go through the prophets and touch on Jeremiah 31:31, the new covenant. For the Jews, sacrifice was written out of the script with the destruction of the Temple: in modern Judaism there is no longer a concept of atonement in terms of blood sacrifice. Our presentation to the tourists concludes with what we call our Israeli altar call, because we ask the question, if since 70 AD there has been no Temple and no sacrifice, what is atoning for your sins today? This hits them like a ton of bricks, because it is probably the first time that they have ever heard the gospel, and certainly the first time they have heard it in Hebrew, with Jesus presented not as a foreigner but as one of them.

If you study pictures of Jesus in stained glass windows, almost inevitably he is portrayed with long, flowing blond hair, looking something like a Norse god, certainly not like a Jew. At a Catholic church in Israel, stained glass art depicts the betrayal of Jesus by Judas. Jesus has blond hair and looks as if he would have been a good Aryan member of the S.S. In stark contrast is Judas, looking like a caricature of the stereotypical Jew, complete with hooked nose and black hair. That window says it all: it depicts our attitude as a church toward the Jewish people. The Jews have never heard Jesus presented as one of their own. That's why the presentation in Christ Church is so powerful.

When I left Jerusalem there were three congregations of Messianic Jews, which have now grown to six. There are about forty congregations in the entire country, with probably close to seven or eight thousand Jewish believers in Jesus. This is the first time since the second century that there has been an indigenous Jewish church in the land of Israel. It's exciting, because in Romans 11 Paul makes it clear that the day is coming when Israel will acknowledge Jesus as Messiah, when all Israel will be saved. A hardening has come across the heart of Israel in part, says Paul, until the fullness of the Gentiles comes, and then all Israel will be saved. There are other clear predictions that the Jewish people will acknowledge Jesus. Notice the switch in pronouns in Zechariah 12:10: "They will look upon me whom they have pierced and they will mourn for him as one mourns for an only son." Not only is it one of the clearest examples of the plurality of the Godhead in the Old Testament, it is also one of the clearest indications that the Messiah we are looking for is the Crucified One. Many other prophetic passages talk about an outpouring of the Holy Spirit on the House of Israel at the end of day. I think that we are living in those times. The *Jerusalem Post* carried an ad this week which was taken out by an anti-mission group in Israel. The title was, "How to Refute Christian Missionaries," and the text asked, "Why have more Jews come to accept Jesus as Messiah in the past nineteen years than in the previous 1900?" These are the people who are trying to stop us from what we're doing, and they are acknowledging that more Jews are coming to faith today than in any other time since the early church!

I believe that we are now witnessing what Paul spoke about in Romans 11:15 (NIV): "If their rejection [of Jesus] is the reconciliation of the world, what will their acceptance [of him] be, but life from the dead?"

EFFECTIVE MEDICAL MISSIONS

The Rev. Dr. Don Youse and Mr. Keith McCaffety

DR. YOUSE: One of the great tragedies of medical missions in the Episcopal Church is that it is such a well-kept secret. We need to network enough so that when someone presents us with a problem, we are able to look to a resource for handling that problem. There is a great need within the medical missionary community, and all of our different gifts can be used in some way. The key is to persist in seeking the place where your particular gifts are needed.

A retired nurse-anesthetist I know spent four months trying to find out where he could do medical missions. The day he reached the end of his rope and decided that he was not supposed to do medical missions, he ran into a medical school friend who was in a medical mission in Haiti. He has now spent six months in Haiti. Be persistent in seeking where your gifts can be of use, because God really does have a place for you.

MR. McCAFFETY: There is something that we need to keep in mind when we consider ministering in medical missions. Do not become so overwhelmed by the size of the problem that you fail to be a part of the answer. When I made my first trip to Africa, what I saw bothered me so much that I wept and could not sleep. Then I remembered that even though I could not educate all the children of the world, one of the best education programs in the Third World operates twenty-four Episcopal schools in an area of abject poverty in Haiti. I cannot feed all the hungry in the world, but I know where Dr. Miller started a nutritional program in the middle of Africa that is feeding and teaching people. I know two Episcopal nuns who have a small clinic in a barrio in the Dominican Republic. These are places to start.

Christ's first commission sent the disciples out in pairs. He told them to enter every village, to preach the kingdom, to teach in the synagogues, and heal every manner of disease among the people. If mission is not addressing all three of those areas, it needs to stop and think. The Episcopal Medical Missions Foundation works to accomplish this by providing information, looking for volunteers, looking for equipment and raising funds.

Information

Episcopalians are basically ignorant concerning the mission work of their own church. We know more about the current religious scandals that we know about Dr. David McNeely, who does the finest medical work in the entire country of Haiti. Dr. McNeely is an Episcopal priest, an Episcopal missionary, and a physician doing a superb work.

What can we do in places of great need? At a mission camp and refugee center in Bangladesh, the children come each morning and we fill their cups with reconstituted milk. It isn't everything they need, but it will tide them over. I asked a Bengali lady there if these were Christian children, which was a very inappropriate question. She straightened me out. She said, "I do not know; they are hungry children." What we are doing in these areas is not because of what the children believe, but rather a commentary on what we believe and who we say we are. The children are hungry children, and I thank God for that Bengali lady who preached to me as I have never been preached to before just by answering my question.

In Haiti, women bathe, do their laundry and drink water from the same stream used by the pigs, donkeys and goats. Contaminated water is the biggest killer in the Third World. What one person in the village has, they will all get. So many children have bloated bellies because they have worms. They can receive medicine to kill the worms, but unless the cause of the worms is removed, they will be back in a year with a belly full of worms.

Dr. Seaton in India is a former surgeon who moved into primary health care and started going into the villages without his medical tools. He did not want the people to associate anything with the "magic" of medicine while he taught them. He said, "If I could do one thing in a village and one thing only, I would sink a tube well and get clean water." Clean water addresses eighty percent of the health problems in the Third World. In villages where the mothers have been taught that the worms will not come back if their children are allowed to drink only from the tube well, diarrhea-related diseases fell eighty-four percent.

Over the door at the nursing school at Daybonne, Haiti, is a metal relief showing a mother breastfeeding a baby, and it is there for a reason. Primary health care workers and midwives learn at the nursing school to tell the people to breastfeed their babies. They tell the mothers that their babies do not need formula; they do not need the bottle. Besides, formula is expensive and why spend precious money on something that you do not need? The Nestle's boycott several years ago came about because these ladies, who are unable to read the instructions, filled the bottles with creek water containing bacteria, germs and parasites. They had no refrigeration, so the bottle soured and they continued to give it to their babies. Finally, the babies got diarrhea and many of them died.

Babies with diarrhea are helped with a rehydration formula made of salt, sugar and water. Thirsty babies who drink from the creek only vomit more and become sicker. The rehydration formula is absorbed by the cells, which helps the baby get well.

Dr. McNeely is a physician in an area of 200,000 people in the mountains of Haiti. Also working there is an Episcopal priest, Pere (Father) Albert. There are twenty-four clinics, twenty-four schools and twenty-four churches in that area. There are few buildings, but the people meet. Primary health care workers are trained and they hear the gospel. Then they preach and heal. That is how Dr. McNeely can be a physician for that many people. (Dr. McNeely has now moved into Port-au-Prince to head the children's hospital.)

Father Albert looks after all the parishes and conducts as many services as it takes to allow everybody to worship. Church is such a big event that the people set up markets, they fellowship, play, eat and are in no hurry to get their turn to worship. The schools are doing an excellent job. The children would not come to school if they had to wear what they have, or don't have, so they wear uniforms that cost seven dollars. A whole cottage industry has sprung up around making the students uniforms using donated sewing machines and cloth.

If contaminated water is the first major problem in the Third World, diet is the second. Kwashiorkor, or lack of protein, causes skin to peel, hair to turn white and fall out, and swelling. Babies with this condition are called "good babies" by their mothers because they don't cry or make any noise and just sit all day. Children who should have black hair have orange or light-colored hair. It is easy to spot the children who are being breastfed, but when a mother has another child too soon, the first is taken off the breast and is denied this source of protein. From that point on, the mother feeds the child what she knows to feed him which is the pure starch of the casava root. These women are not stupid; they are ignorant about nutrition. They have never been to school and they do not know what protein is.

Children in the last stages of kwashiorkor are nothing but skin and bones. They have usually lost their will to live and food has to be pushed down their throats for two or three days before they regain their appetites. Then they eat everything in sight. The change in a child in a few short weeks is amazing. "When I was hungry, you fed me." "Those that would be dead are alive."

Medical missionaries go into villages and begin by weighing all the babies. The nurses are not only trained in medicine, but in agriculture because what you eat is what you are. The people in the Third World lack the right kind of food for good nutrition. These people are not dumb and they respond when they see changes.

A nutritionist trained at a hospital can go into a village and live for six to eight weeks and in that time the change in the children is miraculous. She will show the mothers how to make a mixture of corn, peas, soybeans and peanuts to make a complete protein to feed to the children. Then she will show them how to plant these crops in their gardens. By the end of eight weeks, the mothers can see the difference in their children. This is more effective than simply trying to tell them what their children should or should not eat and going away and leaving them in their ignorance.

It is so important to bring this training to the mothers. The brain begins to grow during pregnancy and by the time a child is born, ninety-eight percent of the neurons, those computer chips or smart cells, have been formed. This is the part of the brain that does all the thinking and stores all the information, rather like a library and file cabinet combined. By the time a child is two years old, the dendrites or telephone lines between the chips are in place. They are made of almost pure protein. The myelin cells and glial cells that glue the brain together are practically pure protein. By the time a baby is five years old, the brain has completed its growth, and an under-five brain that has not received enough protein has not had the building blocks to develop properly.

Water accounts for eighty percent of the problems in the Third World and diet accounts for another ten percent. The third element is sanitation. Making a bore hole latrine and letting the people build a thatch wall around it provides the people with a toilet. Our primary health care workers teach them to use this and not the bush or the stream. Add such simple sanitation techniques as hand washing and ninety-five percent of the health problems have been managed. This only leaves five percent of the people who really need to go to a hospital or see a physician. It is easy to see why primary health care is the biggest key to restoring health in many areas.

There are problems unique to certain areas. In Malawi, Africa, the women of the Chichewa tribe are small in the pelvis anatomically. This is a characteristic of the tribe and means that the women have difficult childbirth experiences. For centuries, their way of handling the problem was to stop eating protein when they became pregnant so their babies would be small and easier to deliver. This made for anemic mothers and anemic babies who were usually born premature. Training the people not to do this is complex. There are many cesarean deliveries here.

Always as our people work in the villages, they teach, they heal and they share the gospel. The gospel is preached to the poor all the time. Hospitals are in the poor areas in the name of Christ, and the poor know that they can go to the hospitals for the help they need. Education for the people is vital and we use every tool we can to communicate. Many people cannot read, so we use pictures to impress such messages as "Breastfeed your baby" or "Go the hospital and get regular checkups." The people can understand that. In many places, the nurses or healthcare workers teach using the oral tradition. They teach messages by singing them to the women and the women sing back.

We know that we fight against principalities. Those principalities are shamanism, voodoo, the evil that holds the people in fear, ignorance, poverty, disease and hunger. It simply is not true that the life of these village people is serene and at one with nature. In their minds there is an evil demon under every rock, behind every tree. Children with fevers have their feet plunged into hot coals to rid them of demons, and later the child's gangrenous feet have to be removed. We can minister to such a child and say, "In the name of Christ, get up and walk." But now we have a child who has no feet and where is this child to go for help?

Paul said that what you do will appear as foolishness to others. In Psalm 142 David says, "They lay snares for me everywhere. Nobody cares about me." Read that Psalm. "Take my soul out of prison, Lord."

The people's desire is to be dealt with fairly and to be surrounded by good people. They cannot look to their governments for help. Why is it that when the governments of these countries see us come with our donated equipment, they offer no help and instead, charge duty to get it into the country? They do not care about the people. There is no profit in giving leg braces to a poor child. There is no profit in providing protein for malnourished children. The child with no feet can only go to a mission hospital to get the help he needs to walk. The hospital and the mission put there in the name of Christ will make the braces and teach the child to walk.

Another tragedy in the Third World happens to women. Women are to have babies, babies and more babies. Men do not assume any responsibility other than to father the children. We once saw a woman who had given birth to three children by cesarean section. Two C-section births are all one woman should experience and the doctor recommended that this woman have a tubal ligation. The law, however, says that the woman must have the permission of her mother-in-law, who does not want her son married to a "useless woman."

All of our hospitals are involved in family planning, birth control and child spacing. The women are very eager for this information and even the Catholic missions in many areas are asking us to come and put on programs in their villages. We foster among our nurses the concept that as women they have value. They have as much responsibility in deciding how many children they will have as their husbands. We try to teach them that they are not the property of someone like their mother-in-law. We are seeing results in changing attitudes.

Girls are housed at Little Roses Orphanage in Honduras, where we care for them. A physician examined them and found them to be the most healthy children in the country. Many of the girls in such homes in Latin America are not orphans; they are brought there by their mothers to protect them from their fathers who would put them to work as prostitutes.

As Westerners, we must recognize how we contribute to the poverty that exists in some parts of the world. The island of Roatan, off the northern coast of Honduras, is a vacationer's paradise. What tourists do not see in this paradise are the eighteen thousand Miskito Indians who live on this island in poverty. They live in places like Brick Bay, located down on the muddy flat where water comes in every night and raw sewage is all over the ground. They cannot move out of this area because they would be mistreated, so they build a place and live there. The church is there in the midst of all this poverty.

Tourism contributes to their poverty because goods are priced for the tourists and the Indians cannot afford to pay that price. The Episcopal Church has the only clinic there for the poor and it is attached to one of the resorts. The resort provided the building and pays the utilities because the clinic has a hyperbaric chamber for divers who get into trouble. The resort uses this in their publicity and they charge the guests for using it. Guests pay two dollars a day for insurance so they can use it if they need it. On the other hand, the Indian divers are abused by being urged to dive repeatedly into very deep water to get lobsters for the fishing industry. They stay down too long and their equipment is not in good condition. They, too, can get help from the chamber. There is a health care nurse and a physician on duty at this clinic and the agreement with the resort is that care will be provided for their guests, but care must be given to the poor.

Looking for Volunteers

Most people can serve somewhere at some time. For example, the St. Luke's Clinic building in the Dominican Republic is in need of plumbers and an electrician to complete the facility. We need physicians, nurses, dentists and some lay people who will do what is needed to get the clinic in shape.

Eye care is another critical need. Dr. Landers is an ophthalmologist who heard about the need twenty years ago. For the next seventeen years, he went to Haiti twice a year and did cataract surgery. Because of him, thousands of people see. Three-fourths of the blind people in the world today could see if they had medical care. China, for example, has 800,000 people with cataracts and very few physicians who can remove them. They are being trained, but there are not enough ophthalmologists.

Looking for Goods and Equipment

Hospitals and clinics in the United States discard enough equipment every year to outfit every mission hospital in existence. We try to get our message out to hospital administrators, physicians, medical and dental folks and nurses. We ask if we can tour their basements and storage facilities to see if they have things we can use. We may find a perfectly good x-ray machine replaced by a later model. We ask them not to dispose of unused packages of supplies, even though they are not supposed to use an opened package. We contact large companies with pharmacies to send us medications.

We have already gathered enough equipment to outfit St. Luke's

Clinic with a complete two-chair dental facility. We have enough equipment for an eye clinic; we have all the examination tables we need and beds are coming. When K-Mart changed its pharmacy, they gave us all their old pharmacy shelving. Now we can set up a complete pharmacy.

We look for implements and goods to help the people care for their families. With sewing machines and materials, mothers can learn to make clothing. We receive kits that contain everything needed to complete a garment. When we can do this, we are saying to the people, "Once you were no people; now you are God's people."

Raising Funds

There is no question that we raise funds. When one of our physicians has a need, Episcopal Medical Missions Foundation targets that need in our fundraising efforts. Churches help by funding special projects. A church in Louisiana has funded a mobile dental unit to be sent to Honduras. Another unit has been sent to the Dominican Republic, so teeth can be repaired and saved, rather than just pulled to alleviate the pain.

When I speak to groups in the United States, I contrast the primary needs of diet, water, and sanitation with the things that are killing Americans. Here, the problem is mostly self-inflicted. It is what we are doing to ourselves that is doing us in. We need dental care because we neglect our teeth, we need medical care because we abuse our bodies. The seven deadly sins of health maintenance in the United States are: cholesterol, sugar, alcohol, salt, tobacco, saturated fat and lethargy (lack of exercise).

The leading cause of death in the United States is heart disease. We used to believe that the heart wears out, but we know now that it does not. The heart succumbs to the cholesterol and saturated fats that we consume over time. Our diets, in a place where proper diet is so readily available, lack what our bodies require to maintain health and we do not eat what we should.

Involvement in medical mission is the church's exercise in compassion. It is a part of the preach, teach and heal command of the Lord Jesus. Is this what we ought to do? John the Baptist had the same question. When he was in prison and about to be beheaded, he asked two friends to go to Jesus and ask him, "Are you the one or not? Should I look for another, or are you it?" The friends came back and told John what they saw Jesus doing. Based on that report, John was satisfied that Jesus was the Messiah. My report is the same as the one John received. Take into your mind and into your heart what I have shared after visiting these places.

"The blind see, the lame walk, the deaf hear. Those that would be dead are alive. The lepers are cleansed and the poor hear the gospel." I hope you, like John, will say, "That's it!"

TEACHING IN
A CROSS-CULTURAL ENVIRONMENT

Mr. Stewart Wicker

"Then you will know the truth, and the truth will set you free."
John 8:32 (NIV)

This verse, I believe, is key to cross-cultural teaching. Jesus is speaking to the Jews who had become believers, talking to them about his teaching and how people will *know* they are his disciples.

As teachers, we have a responsibility to convey truth. Certainly there are many ways to do that, but as the absolute truth is conveyed, we can lead people and encourage students to grow in the Lord or come into a relationship with him.

Paramount to teaching cross-culturally for the Christian is the strategic role teaching as a vocation plays in the Great Commission. It is important to look at how the gospel can be communicated through teaching, the ways in which teaching in a cross-cultural environment differs from mono-cultural teaching, and where the gifts of teaching can be used to contribute to sharing the gospel in all the corners of the world.

First of all, who gets involved in cross-cultural teaching? Experiences from many people indicate that teaching credentials are not a high priority. What is important is having a sense that God is calling you out of the particular place where you are to become involved in missionary service. Secondly, having a gift for sharing information, teaching a Sunday School class, training people or teaching informally are all talents and abilities that God can use. There are many schools which are eager to have volunteers come for a period of time to teach in a variety of capacities. It is worth mentioning that in any area of missionary service, the opportunity to be a teacher is always there. Holding small Bible studies, helping students to learn the English language, community health projects, the list is as endless as the opportunities.

Try to learn from the experiences of as many people as possible, because so much of cross-cultural teaching is experiential. There are a number of theories relating to cross-cultural teaching and it is good to study them. However, be aware when entering a new culture that what we know is not nearly as important as the willingness to learn.

If we are going to communicate the gospel, we must be functioning in the body of Christ. Working in conjunction with a local body of believers will probably mean involvement in a very different environment. In a closed country that may mean the local body is made up of only one or two other people who may be teaching with you. In these situations, support from a sending body is particularly helpful. Knowing that there is someone at home who is praying for you and for your circumstances will provide strength and peace.

Where possible, we need to take advantage of the opportunity to draw on the wisdom of local Christians. It is especially easy, as teachers, to think of ourselves as "experts," particularly in our field. The people within the community where you are trying to build bridges have tremendous wisdom they can share, particularly within the context of the Christian body. Sharing with them to learn also provides the opportunity to be an encouragement of their vision and involvement perhaps in the local educational institution where you are serving.

Living the gospel so that students and people around us see that there is something different in us will give the words we speak greater meaning. In many situations, the gospel can be taught directly; perhaps in a Bible class or in a Sunday School. Vocational teaching, however, is often done in a setting where living the gospel is what will provide the opportunity to share the gospel. Sharing the reality of the gospel in students' lives, to be able to pray with them about a family member, or about a problem they are having, and to see God work in their lives can really make a difference.

Sharing the gospel in the lives of students opens doors for going into their homes and being with them in their community. To be with students where they are living, and not just in the classroom is an opening to seek and pray about in any context in which you are teaching. Seizing the opportunity to share the gospel in students' lives, to encourage students to become a light to their particular community, to disciple students and to help them grow in the Lord so they can reach out to others will live on long after your temporary time with them has been concluded. The crowning accomplishment of these efforts comes when we are able to reach those who are able to continue our role and exceed what has been begun. To see a discipled person step out in the vision to which God is calling them will multiply our efforts to complete the mandate of the Great Commission.

Teaching cross-culturally can be different from monocultural experiences. The first difference is that the teacher becomes a learner. The students have so much to teach the teacher. If we allow ourselves to be vulnerable by not being the expert, doors will open into people's lives. Allowing students to share important aspects of their culture can result in deep conversations. Conversations may develop with students about such things as why relationships are so important in their culture, when in ours, time is so important. These times show students that we have an interest in their culture and help us become more sensitive to the students. At the same time, it is important to be culturally sensitive so that credibility is not lost. In some cultures, the teacher is the expert and in order to be credible it is important to maintain that perception.

On a personal level, as a teacher in Honduras, I had to realize what my cultural baggage was. Was I trying to communicate through my teaching what I thought was important? The baggage that we carry is not necessarily bad baggage, but it is different and we need to be sensitive to how that is reflected as we work with people of other cultures. One of the greatest calls of the teacher is to be a communicator and we need to be careful that our own baggage doesn't compromise that call.

Another difference in cross-cultural teaching has to do with our view of discipline. In the classroom environment in the United States, in particular, we expect people to sit in their seats and listen. Other cultures may allow more creativity, with students moving about and doing other things. The entire atmosphere may be much more relaxed, with students not expected to conform in the way we have come to expect. Discipline in that environment can be very different.

Respect and submission to national colleagues can be very important as a witness to students. Taking on a superior attitude can eliminate effectiveness and make entering into relationships very difficult.

As much as we would like to be an insider in the culture where we teach, it is not possible. This concept is often difficult to accept, but it is very real. We can build bridges, but we have not lived the same lives as they have, we have not experienced what they have, and we never can. In my own situation, I had to realize my own natural limitations and trust the Lord to overcome them. I made it my goal to try to establish respect by striving to glorify God through the work I was doing, by being professional and trying to do a very good job. I felt that this was an important part of my witness.

Building relationships is key to ministry. That can often mean saying "I'm sorry" many times. But asking forgiveness is a very important part of building relationships. A teacher is a "conduit of knowledge" and can serve as a bridge from one understanding to another. In the case of cross-cultural teaching, the understanding is from one people to another. If there have been difficulties in the relationships between that culture and ours, we may find ourselves in the position of seeking forgiveness for our own people. This can be tremendously healing and allows for being a bridge builder to the truth, as we walk together, pray together, study the Bible together and grow in the Lord together.

Finally, be a friend as demonstrated by the love of the Lord in our own lives. To be able to quietly lay down your life and make a sacrifice without making it known, and to walk away with both tears of sorrow and joy knowing that God has through our individual weaknesses borne fruit makes all the lesson plans and cross-cultural frustrations worth it in the long run.

OUTREACH TO INTERNATIONALS IN YOUR COMMUNITY

Mr. Leiton Chinn and the Rev. Paul Frey

Reaching out to internationals in a community and building relationships is exciting global missions at home and provides training for cross-cultural ministry. The general principles used to establish such a ministry are not limited by church size and the opportunities may be more available than anyone might think. The thrust of such a ministry may be to temporary residents such as international students, but could also be to immigrants and refugees. Not every area is so situated that there is a community of international students accessible.

In Fairfax, Virginia, the experience began before the realization came that the demographics were changing. With a growth rate of over 200 percent for Hispanics and Asians, the community was in the early stages of "browning" in the area, comprised mostly of immigrants and refugees. Since this area is also close to Washington, DC and many colleges and universities, there are many international students as well. The idea that God might be raising up some people for local cross-cultural ministry was the spark that ignited an outreach to internationals.

The vision for such an endeavor became reality with the support of the rector and the leadership of the church. A small number of people began to pray for those who were to form the nucleus of the team and God responded by bringing together a small group with a heart for such a ministry. From the very beginning, the group determined that their planning would include publicity, program and provision, and praise.

Publicity meant informing and involving the church as this was the base out of which would come the volunteers and the financial support. Publicity also meant spreading the message throughout the area to those places where international students would be likely to see the information. In an area with colleges, universities, junior colleges and English language institutes, there were many avenues through which to distribute the information. Surprisingly, response to notices posted on student bulletin boards has been quite positive. Whether the students were lonely or adventurous, they were willing to come to an event sponsored by a Christian church.

Since the focus of this ministry was to be to international students, the initial planning centered on what could be offered as programs and provision. Hospitality and opportunities to get acquainted with other students, both foreign and American, was high on the list. The programs were planned with an eye to looking at the felt and real needs of international students. Some programs were designed for friendship and social interaction, such as potluck suppers. Other events were planned to be enriching and provide mutual learning opportunities. All programs were intended to promote cross-cultural understanding unless advertised otherwise. Certain holidays, such as Thanksgiving, are conducive to discussing history. Christmas and Easter, however, are times when the events are publicized as being from a Christian perspective.

International students can have any number of needs with which a caring community can provide some assistance. One of the easiest ways to develop a friendship with an international is to offer to dialogue with them in English. Success in their classwork depends on their skill with the language and helping with English conversational skills requires little training for most Americans. Discussion questions are provided for the volunteers. There may be a need for a more structured English as a Second Language program but an easy starting point is to talk together. Having international students share some of their language simply shows that there is an interest in that student. Once a friendship has been developed, sharing of faith and life can be done very naturally.

Sensitivity to the physical needs of students who may have come from a climate which does not include winter could include such things as gathering winter coats and allowing the students to select one that fits. Volunteers assist with other practical needs such as helping to find appropriate housing, learning how to drive a car or how to use public transportation.

Culture shock is very real, both coming and going. The most crucial points in the international sojourn are entry and re-entry. When students come to this country, they are usually eager to learn and explore. Events which help students do this with some guidance are very welcome. Opportunities to get to know people socially help with the transition. Invitations to homes are very welcome. Awareness of those times of school holidays when American students go home to be with their families, leaving the international students alone, are great times to invite them to dinner.

When students have been in this country for a long period of time, they adopt our ways and adapt to our culture, and returning home can be another shock. Awareness that this can be an unexpected development for international students and providing assistance here can be especially meaningful. Engaging students in discussions about what changes may have occured in their lives will help to make them aware of what to expect when they return home.

Certainly, a program of social outreach to individuals from another culture may also have a goal of being able to introduce that person to Jesus Christ in appropriate ways. It is important to always maintain integrity and honesty. If a program is to be presented from a Christian perspective, it should be advertized as such. There are times, such as Christmas and Easter, which are natural opportunities for sharing the Christian message. Caution must be exercised, however, to avoid arm-twisting. International students, in particular, are receiving a lot of information quickly and trying to rush them into Christianity can be counterproductive and very frustrating. A long-term friendship relationship is what will lead another person to Jesus Christ. Opportunities for retreats and short breaks in the school schedule are ideal times when discussions can happen in relaxed surroundings. Be aware, however, that most students have limited financial support, so time away events should be very economical, free or have partial sponsorship available.

Often when doing social outreach with internationals, there will be those individuals who request assistance with immigration issues. Directing them to someone with expertise in this particular area is the wisest type of assistance. Having a resource who is knowledgable in this area and who has integrity will be very helpful in these instances. Some people who come to this country are very well educated but cannot speak the language and need help to find appropriate immigration connections. Many people have come illegally and may decide to stay that way, even when we encourage them that the gospel is quite clear about obeying civil laws. One of the ramifications is that people who have come here for a better life, who have watched their children starve or who are in danger of being shot if they return home, will find that aspect of the gospel difficult.

When ministry reaches out to immigrants, refugees and internationals, meeting the needs that they have, some will begin to come to the church. It is important that such a ministry have the support of the leadership and that culturally these people can and will be included. Such things as reading the Scripture lessons in another language can be upsetting for congregations that have not been prepared. Moving out in ministry to internationals, be they immigrants, refugees or students, is a ministry that has to be covered with prayer, publicized openly and the praise and thanksgiving returned to the Lord.

* * * * * * * * *

For additional resources and practical ideas for initiating or augmenting an outreach to internationals, please contact

Leiton Chinn
International Ministries Fellowship
14712 Calvary Place
Centreville, VA 20121

or

Truro Episcopal Church
10520 Main Street
Fairfax, VA 22030

PARTNERS IN MISSION WITH NATIVE AMERICANS

The Very Rev. Ronald A. Campbell

Before the Civil War, as early as 1840, the Presbyterians, the Congregationalists, the Roman Catholics and the Mennonites came as missionaries to the Indians. The Episcopalians came some time later. By this time along the Minnesota River, the Indian tribes had been broken into small bands of from two hundred to four hundred people. In 1861 there was a Civil War going on in the South and an Indian war in the Northwest. The Indians were fighting for the food which the army would bring, but that Indian agents would take and sell to shopkeepers in settlements. Unfortunately, this led to much fighting and killing between the white man and the Indian. In 1861, as a result of fighting over food, thirty-eight Indian men were hanged in Mankato, Minnesota, an aftermath to a war that started over the theft of some chickens. Prior to the hanging, a Presbyterian wrote a song in the Dakota language, the translation of which still remains in the Episcopal hymnal. It is an indication of how the language works because the hymn as written had seven verses in the Indian language and only two remain in our English hymnal. Translating from the Dakota language to English is much more difficult than translating from English to Dakota.

In 1890 at the time of the massacre at Wounded Knee, the Indian people in the region of South Dakota and Minnesota were farmers, using oxen to plow gardens, raising cattle and shipping them to Chicago. The people on the reservations farther west were not as advanced because they lived on closed reservations. The reservations in the Minnesota region had been opened to settlements with Indian and white men having land side-by-side. The Indians learned to live the way the white man lived.

By 1861 there were many Indian people who were half-breeds. My name is Campbell; my mother's family name is Robertson. The French also came into the area, so there are Indians with French blood too. In fact, one of the men hanged at Mankato was named Baptiste Campbell, probably a renegade relative of mine!

I grew up on the Sisseton Reservation in the upper northeast corner of South Dakota. I left the reservation when I was fourteen years old to attend boarding school, where I met my wife. I graduated and joined the army. This was during the Korean War and the worst thing I ever did was volunteer for that place. I will never do that again! After I got out of the army, my wife and I were married. That was forty-one years ago and we have nine children and twenty-nine grandchildren. We lived off the Sisseton Reservation for almost thirty years.

My ministry at Pine Ridge began when I was sent there by the bishop. Twenty-six years ago, when the bishop told you to go to a place, you went, and when you went to work on a reservation, you were a missionary. So, I am a missionary. When I arrived, Sister Margaret Hawk, a member of the Church Army, was already there working as a teacher. She also served as a very good teacher to me, initiating me in the way things were done at Pine Ridge. While I was serving at Pine Ridge, I was ordained into the diaconate and priesthood.

I learned a great deal at Pine Ridge. I was in charge of nine churches in which services were held. On one Sunday, services were held in three churches, the next Sunday there were services in three different churches, the next Sunday there were services in two churches and on the fourth Sunday, a single service in a church fifty-five miles away. This put an average of three thousand miles on the car each month.

One of the best lessons I have ever learned, I learned at Pine Ridge. When people start to do things, sometimes they think they are real good and they think too much of themselves. Well, it seemed that was what I was doing; I had the blackest shirt, the blackest suit, the blackest shoes and the blackest socks. I was a deacon! One of the Indian traditions is to give gifts and have food when someone is new. This was happening and the food was laid out and I was about to bless the food when there was a knock on the door. My daughter, Rachelle, answered the door and the man standing there said, "Hello, little girl. Is your father a minister?" Little Rachelle said, "Yes, sir, but before that he used to be a human being." Boy, I dropped to the floor. I am not as good as I think I am; I am only a human being.

The bishop gave me a church building that had to be moved and repaired. A friend of mine from Colorado offered to bring fifteen white kids up, to be joined by fifteen Indian kids, and we were going to repair this church building. We learned a valuable lesson from that experience. Not every kid is an outdoors person and there were three girls in this group who wouldn't use the outhouse. After three days, I took them to the public health hospital where they all got enemas. I wanted to send them home after that, but they cried and cried, so I gave them each a job. We had four outhouses and every morning they each had to take a pail of water, a scrub brush, a mop and clean them. They got used to it and it turned out to be a very good experience.

I return to Pine Ridge every chance I get, because I have a large extended family there. There is an Indian tradition where you never run out of a mother, father or cousins. I was adopted into a family there, to take the place of their son who was killed in World War II. So I have a family at Pine Ridge, with a mother and two sisters. Every time I go, I get a big meal and they treat me just like I am their real brother. That is one of the things that is traditional, or cultural, with the Indian people. If someone from the family dies and they see someone that could take that person's place, they are adopted into the family.

A lot of people wonder about the Indians on reservations. They think that the Indian people receive money from the government, and if that were true, I would be out spending mine. Some Indian people do own land, which they lease, and receive money from the farmer who leases that land and uses it for agricultural purposes.

There are nine reservations in South Dakota and there are similar problems on all of them. Alcohol, drugs, and gambling are on every reservation and the problems, I believe, are due to the educational level of the people. When my wife and I left the reservation at Sisseton, we noticed the education level of all the people, especially the kids. When we came back to the reservation, the education level had declined. It is hard to tell that to the tribe, because they live there all the time and they don't see it like we do. My wife is a teacher and does substitute teaching whenever she can. What she has noticed is that the decline in the educational level of the kids seems to be related to fetal alcohol syndrome. Some things are being done about this, but it is not strong enough to make much improvement. There are places on the reservations where people can go to get help, but the people giving the help also have the problem.

The Indian women are now trying to work with young mothers to tell them how to care for themselves if they are going to become a mother. In the Indian culture from years ago, when a mother was carrying a baby, their mothers and grandmothers would help educate them. They would keep the young mothers away from the hard work and send them out to pick berries and talk to their babies so the baby would be educated when it was born. The women today are trying to use that type of psychology to tell the young mothers to stay away from alcohol and cigarettes.

We need missionaries to come to the Indian people. We need someone like Bishop Hobart Hare, who was the first bishop of South Dakota. I wish I could have known him, because he apparently was quite a go-getter. For a man small in stature, about five feet, eight inches, he came into Niobrara when it was Dakota Territory and his influence reached from Sioux Falls, Yankton and Santee areas all the way to Pine Ridge. He went from there to the other Sioux reservations and sent a representative to Sisseton to begin churches in that area.

Bishop Hare was tough and he had to be to survive visits to reservations where he faced guns, bow-and-arrows and lances. Often he needed the protection of soldiers to get to his own people. Bishop Hare called the first meeting of all the Indian churches, the Niobrara Convocation. These continued annually for five years. At one time there were eighty-seven Indian congregations in South Dakota and five thousand Christians attended one of these events. The *Yankton Gazette*, a local newspaper, sent reporters to see what was happening with these Christian Indians. The reporters arrived at night and had to sleep in a teepee, unaware of what surrounded them. When they got up in the morning and looked out, all they could see for a three-mile radius were teepees, tents and wagons. All this was a result of the work of Bishop Hare.

There hasn't been someone that tough among the Indians in South Dakota in a long time, and we need someone to come who is like that. It is very difficult to be an Indian and work among the Indians. Unfortunately, there are too many relatives and a native is not taken seriously. A stranger can come in among the people and say the same things the native has been saying and the people will listen. I can tell people dying from the effects of alcohol what is happening but they feel it is all right because they are Indian. We need someone to come who is strong and can talk about Jesus, tell the people the good things and help them forget the bad. That would be a very good friend for the Indian people.

It would be a great help to people like me to have someone that would be able to take my place. Young, energetic people who are able to work hard and work with the young people can make such an impact in the life of Native Americans.

Not too long ago a young man, younger than I, came from Charlotte, North Carolina, with his wife and two children. Boy, did we have fun working, working hard. He liked it and the kids liked him. In fact, they liked him so much that when a mother in one of the churches had a baby, he was asked to be a sponsor for that baby at baptism. Now he has ties to St. John's Church in Lake Traverse. This young man had such a good experience that, after he left, he wrote that he was considering leaving his own denomination and becoming an Episcopalian. The next time I spoke with him, he had done that. We need many, many people like him to come and work among the Indian people.

On my own reservation, Sisseton, there are ten thousand Indian people. They may all be baptized, but that doesn't mean they are all really Christian. Some of them have joined the Jehovah's Witness or Mormons, or they are practicing the Indian religion. Often the only time people come to the church is when they have a baby and want to have the child baptized. The lure of money and food will entice Indians into different religions, and there are groups that use that as a means of getting the people to come. If I had to estimate, I would say that about eighty percent of the Indian people would call themselves Christian.

On my reservation in South Dakota, it is the young people who are practicing what they call Indian religion. The young people seem to want to be Indian so badly; they have long braids with beads all over. However, I tell them that if they want to really be an Indian, they should walk straight, hold their heads up and their shoulders back. That's not exactly what they want to hear. Unfortunately, in their pursuit of an Indian religion, there is no one around who knows what that would be. My grandfather is the son of a priest and he grew up on Standing Rocks Reservation. He doesn't know anything about Indian religion and he says we would need someone at least 150 years old who could tell us! What is coming back through these young people is the wrong thing.

The needs in the area are great. Personally, it would be helpful to have someone to administer the office while I am away. In order to meet the needs of the people, I am on the road so much and not able to receive phone calls and perform clerical duties. Someone who could answer the telephone and help the people with such things as making up baptismal certificates from information that is recorded so they can get their Social Security. Priests who could conduct worship services would be helpful because of the number of congregations. Right now, I have four well-trained layreaders and they can do everything but hold communion services, but I could use more help from the ordained.

Education and training for leadership are both needed. There is a program through Vancouver, British Columbia, in which a professor will come down for a week and then we send students to them for a week. This is going to take a long time because it is only done once a year. But Indian people respond to and respect strong leadership. For instance, they expect to always see me wearing my clerical collar and they have embarrassed me at times when I have had visiting clergy who do not have their clericals on by asking if they are ashamed of their uniform.

There are groups from West Virginia or Virginia who have been coming to Pine Ridge for the last several years to conduct summer camps and Vacation Bible School. The Brotherhood of St. Andrew holds a junior camp for our young people. But we need missionaries to come to South Dakota and commit long term to working among the Native American people.

CHURCH PLANTING AMONG HISPANICS IN THE UNITED STATES

The Rev. José D. Carlo

The most important decision about doing Hispanic mission and ministry is *not to do it* unless you are sure it is the Lord's special calling for you. Too many clergy or laypersons get involved in Hispanic outreach because they have time, energy, funds, want to help and see an opportunity for church growth. All of these are great and necessary but unless it is the Lord's doing we strive in vain. Our enthusiasm and commitment must be tempered by our waiting upon the Lord and the guidance of the Holy Spirit.

Effective mission and ministry to, with, and for, the Hispanic community demands that we clarify and expand our Christian vision of them and of ourselves. All of us have stereotypes about the majority and about the minority. Sooner or later we must accept the fact that we are all *ethnics*. We all carry about some *ethnic baggage* and this will influence how we do Hispanic mission and ministry.

Roughly one-half of the Christians in the world speak Spanish, and Hispanics have been in the USA for close to five hundred years. Soon, almost twenty percent of the population of the USA will be speaking, eating, listening to music and celebrating as Hispanics. They come seeking the "American dream" and fleeing from problems in Central and South America, the Caribbean, Spain and many other parts of the globe. Hispanics are impacting our *economy* (tortilla sales will soon surpass bread sales); *social structure* (bilingual education and the increasing number of Hispanic baseball players and political representatives are a reality), and *culture* (our music, films, food and dance are feeling the pressure and the energy from south and east of the border).

A stereotype of Hispanics would define them as Roman Catholics and mostly illegals, poorly educated and poor, having large families and undisciplined or lazy. Admittedly, they are hospitable, excitable, colorful, and God-fearing with an inborn capacity for overcoming adversity through a faith based on popular piety.

All of this is partially true, of course, but there is so much more. Many of them are Protestant, born-again Christians, and third- or fourth-generation citizens. Increasingly, more are graduating from universities and becoming professionals with well paying jobs, small families and "WASP-like" priorities. They remain hospitable, excitable and colorful but many are experiencing a "cultural and spiritual dry spell" as they seek out and question their roots and compete in a nation where the majority is not Hispanic.

They are not, as we might mistakenly imagine, a people with no familiarity or background in the church. Latin America is home to over 400 million Christians and even though some would argue that at most fifteen percent are active Roman Catholics (this percentage is surprisingly similar to the percentage of active Christians in Europe), the fact is that religion permeates all facets of their lives. In one form or another, though they may not have been inside a church in many years, Hispanics have been impacted by Christianity.

The syncretism of Christian and pagan beliefs and rituals; the naming of cities and streets and great festivals after some saint or biblical story; and the celebration, within the church, of the important events in their lives, all witness to the important role the church plays in their lives. We are not talking of an unchurched people.

The family, the church, the school, the government and the economy all work to form a tightly knit support system for the individual and his/her family, faith and beliefs. This support system is one of the main things that Hispanics leave behind when they come to the United States. They come seeking a better life for themselves and their children but quite often they must pay a great price.

The extended family is no longer at hand and commitment to the same can be a drawback. Language, skin color, lack of appropriate education and job training, and what at times is seen as a "highly traditional or medieval" church experience, are stumbling blocks. Their whole support system becomes wobbly and is under lots of stress and pressure to change. Given these conditions, it is not surprising that a sense of loneliness and a spiritual void quickly develops. These can only be healed with a renewal of their Christian faith and an ongoing, life-giving religious experience.

Mission and ministry to, for and by Hispanics must be rooted in a faithful response to the teaching or our Lord Jesus Christ, and in the very nature of the church, as expressed in Holy Scripture. Numerous biblical passages may be quoted and the following are but a small sampling.

Christ has broken down the cultural dividing wall between Jews and Gentiles and hence any cultural dividing wall (Eph 2:14,17-22). The Lordship of Christ supersedes all cultural, social, economic and sexual divisions (Gal 3:26-29). In Christ we belong more to one another than to any cultural group. The new creation in Christ abolishes all human divisions (1Cor 12:12-13, 26-27; 2Cor 5:16-20). The mission of the church is to all peoples and nations and we have all been called out of darkness into God's marvelous light (1Pet 2:9-10). Christ takes on our human nature in order to save us.(Phil 2:5-11).

Numerous Old Testament stories and New Testament parables emphasize the need to care for the stranger and the needy. Matthew 25:31-40 highlights the importance of these actions when we appear before Christ on the Day of Judgment.

In summary, Hispanic mission and ministry must not be another program or fad but rather:

—a positive response to the Great Commission of our Lord Jesus Christ (Mt 28:16-20), and our need to live in him, not only for ourselves but for others.

—a prayer, asking God to breathe into our corporate and individual lives a new spirit so that we may be inspired and enabled to give of ourselves in creative, effective, humble and forceful actions for the benefits of Hispanics in our communities and to our mutual growth.

—a following of Christ's example to "love by incarnation" by putting ourselves in the other person's shoes, adapting our particular Anglican/Episcopal heritage to meet the needs, struggles and aspirations of another people, and identifying with and for Hispanic culture and language without losing our identity but rather rediscovering it and being enriched with this new dimension to our life.

—a willingness to be open and involved with Hispanics in a dialog of word and action which will help us enlarge our vision and fulfill our Christian calling to follow Christ

—death and resurrection experience in Christ with our Hispanic sisters and brothers.

The challenge is to respond in a well-planned, long-term commitment to this mission and ministry.

You might ask, does the Episcopal Church have anything to offer Hispanics? The response is that to isolated and alienated Hispanics as well as to integrated and successful Hispanics, who are struggling to define their new identity and maintain their dignity, the Episcopal Church offers what it offers to us and to all peoples:

—THE FAITH: Catholic and Protestant. Holy
                                Scripture and the universal

	Creeds in a framework of reason and dialog.
—THE FELLOWSHIP:	Inclusive, pastoral and familiar. A democratic institution offering multiple opportunities for lay commitment, decision making and stewardship at all levels. Many and varied opportunities for corporate and personal spiritual growth.
—THE SACRAMENTS:	A varied Liturgy with Apostolic Orders and all the sacraments enhanced by active lay participation and a structure allowing for creativity.
—THE PRAYERS:	Prayer Book order and dignity with room for evangelical spontaneity and charismatic spirit.

If this is true then the following question is—what's in it for us? A very legitimate, human and biblical question. Indeed Hispanics have much to offer the Episcopal Church and specially to our established congregations.

—THE FAITH:	A sharing in their daily re-living of the Exodus and the "wandering Aramean" experience. Their joy in times of adversity and thankfulness in the face of extreme necessity.
—THE FELLOWSHIP:	A rediscovery of the "base communities." Their spontaneous personal warmth, the extended family and the "abrazo" (bear-hug).
—THE SACRAMENTS:	A lively liturgy. The celebration of life with color, dance, drama and fiesta within the walls of the church and beyond in the streets and the homes.
—THE PRAYERS:	A profound personal piety and devotion intermingled with a deeper sense of sacrifice and the meaning of the cross.

In Holy Scriptures, when the people respond faithfully to God's call, the benefits are incomparably greater than the sacrifices. The benefits to our Episcopal heritage of entering into a faithful relationship with Hispanic people who have different, yet equally profound, religious experiences and traditions will be a greater fullness and growth in our life in Christ. Sociologically, through the involvement of the congregation, church members will experience the realities of the Hispanic presence and hopefully respond positively. All will learn to better cope with cultural diversity.

The church must regain the skills which St. Paul so ably possessed: the ability to transmit the faith in multi-cultural situations. What we will learn by accepting the Hispanic challenge will spill over into many other areas of the church's total mission and ministry.

Two other questions must still be answered. Since they are in the USA, shouldn't they learn English and come to our English worship services? The reality for Hispanics is that they must, for the sake of survival, learn English. Yet deep personal relationships, feelings and spiritual experiences are best expressed in one's mother tongue. Worship and adoration come from the heart in the language one knows best. For the Hispanic this is Spanish. On the other hand we have the opportunity of choosing to learn another language to broaden our mission and ministry and to help our neighbor.

Then again, by using Spanish, aren't we just promoting or extending the life of the ghettos? In reality the ghettos are already formed—both theirs and ours—and the walls of separation are already in place. The ghettos are formed not so much by language as by misunderstanding, fears and a feeling of being abused or not being wanted. We can help to break down these walls and facilitate the process of mutual understanding and compassion by knowing some Spanish.

So, how do English-speaking Episcopal congregations go about planting Hispanic congregations? The following are five basic steps which must be fulfilled to define the vision and scope of the mission and the participation of the whole congregation in the ministry. Completing these steps will take a minimum of six months and, unless a major problem is encountered, they can be fulfilled in from twelve to eighteen months. This may sound like a long time but if we remind ourselves of how long, and with what patience, the Lord has been calling us it will help us to be patient in our preparation. The plan presupposes that the rector or vicar is, at least in principal, in favor of searching out the possibilities for this mission and ministry and will be supportive of these steps.

Step 5: Prayer This is the most important step and must be continuous throughout the six to eighteen months. *Pray for discernment:* Is this really a call for our congregation? Why not be involved with other groups? Why Hispanics? Don't we need more time and evangelism with our actual congregation? Aren't there other more pressing needs? This step requires that a prayer committee be formed. The committee would be composed of some who favor this outreach; some who are doubtful, with many questions, and hopefully, some who are skeptical, if not outwardly against the whole idea. The commitment for each committee member would be to pray daily for discernment. The prayer committee, as a whole, would meet every two weeks to share insights, questions and study and discuss the Acts of the Apostles. *Discernment* is the key word.

Step 4: Bible Study As the committee continues to pray and study they would develop a biblical and theological basis for this mission and ministry. The emphasis may be outreach, or unity, or servanthood but in all cases a biblical grounding must be developed for present and future actions. God's call and blessing of Abraham, (Gen 12:1-3); Jesus' Parables of the Kingdom in Matthew 13; the Holy Spirit's intercultural evangelism on the Day of Pentecost (Acts 2) and many other biblical teachings need to be studied and applied to the congregation's present situation. The development of a vision and a proposed mission statement is crucial.

Step 3: "Seeing" the Hispanics Few of our churches are neighborhood-oriented churches. Quite often church members drive or ride public transportation some three to ten miles to attend services. Rarely do they "see" the people or the neighborhood with whom they now want to do mission and ministry. Who are these Hispanics? Are they migrants and poor or are they middle class and English speaking (which would involve us with Hispanic-sensitive ministry and not with Spanish-speaking ministry)? What are the statistics on the economics, health, education, and growth of this particular group? Are there other denominations involved in doing Hispanic ministry? Can we work together? Answering these and many other questions will help the committee to define and be specific when they report on the proposed Hispanic mission and ministry.

Step 2: Involving the Power Structure This step recognizes the fact that, in the Episcopal Church, if anything is to be accomplished it must have the blessing of the "godfathers and godmothers" of the congregation together with that of the clergy and the vestry or bishop's committee. How will the existing groups in the congregation be impacted? Where will the funds come from to cover the additional expenses in the budget? What will it cost, in time and resources for the clergy to learn the basics of the language or for additional staff? How will this change the time and space use of the buildings? How about Spanish prayer books and hymnals? Who will celebrate the additional Eucharist required or will we try bilingual Eucharists? Are there Hispanics among the actual church members? What are our resources of time, talent and treasure which can be directed to this mission and ministry? The response by the clergy, vestry and other leaders of the congregation to these questions will be a measure of their commitment, or lack thereof, to this new mission and ministry. This must not be seen as another program, one among many, of the congregation. The new mission statement, and the commitment to the same by the church leaders, must now be in print and ready for distribution.

Step 1: Involving the Whole Congregation Somehow the whole congregation must gain a sense of participation, ownership and commitment to this new mission and ministry. This is the time to do the kinds of events and celebrations that help the whole congregation understand that this is their ministry. The results of the efforts in the four previous steps, which may have been briefly reported in the congregational newsletter, now get major coverage. Church members may have heard about something being planned but now they see it legitimized through the newsletter. A series of sermons on mission and ministry and, in particular, Hispanic outreach would be initiated. The choir would present new Hispanic hymns (there is a Christmas hymn in the 1982 hymnal). Tacos and enchiladas would be an option at the next congregational supper. This, together with background Hispanic music (leading to the invitation of a Mariachi band at some future function), and a Hispanic folklore dance group would add to the sense of celebration. Hispanic friends and neighbors would be invited to these events. If there is a Hispanic worshipping group in the area, some interchange would be in order. Getting the two ECW's together enhances the relationship. This would be the time for the rector or vicar to go south of the border for two to three weeks and take a crash course in Spanish. One or two bilingual Eucharists should be presented during this period. It is important that the congregation see this new mission and ministry as a positive spiritual experience, as a celebration of life within the Body of Christ and as an expression of their total stewardship. What talents do we have to offer i.e., tutoring, ESL classes, and so on? Which of our existing programs could be expanded to help, i.e. food pantry, AID's ministry, citizenship classes, etc.?

Step "0": Launching Our New Mission and Ministry If all has gone as planned and the previous steps have been essentially fulfilled, we are now ready to officially launch our Hispanic mission and ministry. The following three suggestions are crucial.

Publicize the New Service. In an Episcopal church in downtown Los Angeles a large sign was hung at the front of the church saying: "Bienvenidos. Misa los Domingos a las 12:30 p.m., Bienvenidos" (i.e., "Welcome. Hispanic Eucharist at 12:30 p.m. on Sundays, Welcome"). A few "welcomers," some ushers, some Hispanic prayer books, a lay reader and a priest were ready. The first week six persons attended, then fifteen, twenty-five and after two months fifty persons could be expected. Music, baptisms, first communions, and Bible study were quickly added.

Fill a Need. In another congregation the food pantry was expanded but, and this is the important addition, as the food was distributed, the recipients were asked if they had any special prayer needs (i.e., for someone sick or for guidance, for thanksgiving, etc.). Notepaper and pencils were ready and the recipients were told that the food pantry group would be praying for them and their specific needs. This quickly led to a short intercessory prayer service (and later to a Eucharistic celebration) before the food was distributed.

Set a Day and Time which is convenient to the group being served and when there is no rush so that a "cafecito" and socializing time can follow. This is key to the building of community and allows a time for questions and future educational efforts. Another congregation has its parish hall entrance across the street from the exit of a mostly Hispanic public elementary school. Parents, mostly mothers, seeking shade from the hot afternoon sun, would wait by the parish hall door for their children to come out of classes. Some parishioners started serving lemonade to the group, making friends and initiating a dialog. Soon the questions were about this church and "Is it Catholic?" and "Can we look inside?" etc. This process is lovingly called "lemonade evangelism."

As can be seen, ministry began simply by observing what was happening and what was needed and showing a concern and a willingness to serve with prayer and in the name of Christ. The spiritual hunger for a deeper relationship with Christ and greater knowledge of the Holy Scriptures is there. Quite often we are dealing with "lost sheep" who may have been Roman Catholics or Pentecostals but are now essentially nowhere. One must be ready to answer their questions with an upfront: "We are Catholics, but not Roman Catholics, and we differ in the following ways." The news will spread quickly and if what is presented in the name of Christ meets their needs, spiritual and otherwise, the Hispanics will come. This might involve celebrating the Eucharist in their homes and the development of "base communities."

We offer the familiar structure of liturgy and the sacraments. Language may present a challenge (actually, half of our Hispanic ministry will be in English), and sensitivity to culture, history, holidays (i.e., When is Mother's Day for them?), and deep spiritual feelings is vital. We will have to be patient as they teach us about themselves and be ready to receive their help in doing this ministry. Eventually, this mission and ministry must be carried on by and through Hispanics and we will be "depending" on them. This may be difficult for some to accept, yet it is the beauty of being part of the Body of Christ. As Hispanics become familiar with the Episcopal Church they will value what we offer and we will learn from the gifts they bring to the Episcopal Church.

On page 855 of the Book of Common Prayer, "An Outline of the Faith," it reaffirms that "The mission of the Church is to restore all people to unity with God and each other in Christ" and that "The Church pursues its mission as it prays and worships, proclaims the Gospel, and promotes justice, peace and love." A commitment to Hispanic mission and ministry will require a sensitive balance of those actions seeking to incorporate Hispanics into the life and worship of the local congregation and those actions seeking political rights and social justice for Hispanics. This commitment must be based on prayer and sound biblical and theological teaching and respond to the reality of the Hispanic presence.

Our resources and creativity will be stretched as we reach out to serve the poor and the increasing number of educated business and professional Hispanics, the recent immigrant and the long-time resident or citizen, and those who speak only Spanish, or only English, or combine both into Spanglish.

We can and we must become ever more deeply aware and respectful of each other, Anglos and Hispanics, so as to love each other as we love ourselves, or even more as Christ loved us. It is difficult to transcend one culture and very easy to imagine one's culture as God-given. Demanding that Hispanics take on our culture is both patronizing and demeaning. Simply taking on their culture and values lacks integrity. The answer to the problem of conflicting cultures is neither synthesis nor acculturation by one side or the other, but redemption. And redemption, through and in Christ, is the mission and ministry of his Body, the church.

In conclusion I'm convinced that God is calling the Episcopal Church to increased and effective mission and ministry to, for and with Hispanics.

A DYNAMIC STRATEGY FOR
CHURCH PLANTING IN LATIN AMERICA

The Rev. Canon Tom Prichard

A vision for church planting that started in Lima, Peru, is now sweeping across the world. There is great potential in this vision that we, as Episcopalians, can be a part of to win cities around the world in the name of the Lord. We were introduced to the Encounter With God church planting strategy by Christian and Missionary Alliance Church missionaries. It has within it some principles that are totally different from the traditional goal of Anglican church planting. One CMA missionary told us that his experience of being involved with the Encounter With God program was like trying to change the tire on a moving car. Our own experiences have made the meaning of that statement very clear.

The first principle is that the goal is so different. When I went to Bogotá, Colombia, in 1983 as a missionary with the South American Missionary society, my goal was to plant a church that would one day stand on its own. The intent was to plant a church that would be self-sustaining and self-governing. The CMA people had a very different goal. They wanted to reach the city of Bogotá for the Lord so they could reach all of Columbia for the Lord. The concept of building, equipping and inspiring a church that would be prepared to plant daughter churches to reach the entire city was a wild, new idea. They were not simply trying to plant a self-sustaining church.

The second principle involves the way in which they communicate that goal in their stewardship. From the moment a church is started, ten percent of the offering is set aside to establish a special, revolving fund to be used to build a daughter church. Beginning with the very first meeting, a portion of every offering is set aside for that purpose. They are always giving with a vision. Amazingly, the members of the congregation all understand that the goal is to reach the city. This is so different from our concept of contributing to a building fund as our church grows, build a church and spend the next few years paying off a mortgage.

The third principle within this strategy is the emphasis on team ministry. The first instance of this that I observed in Bogotá involved fourteen missionaries. At their first service they had those fourteen missionaries and two Colombians. The make-up of the team was international, with five nationalities represented. So the glue that held the team together was not a common culture, but the common love of the Lord Jesus Christ.

Another significant fact about this team was that it had no "star." We are all aware of instances where there is a senior pastor or rector who is an incredibly gifted, articulate person around whom the church just explodes. Then when that person moves on, the church is really shaken. These teams were built in such a way that there was no one person who would stand out. With this team strategy, allegiance to a person is avoided.

Another facet of the Encounter strategy involves the way resources are dispersed. Many mission organizations, the Episcopal Church included, tend to spread their resources around in an attempt to be fair with everybody. The end result is missionaries are spread around establishing lots of small congregations who will always remain dependent. This creates a situation that can become very complex and making the churches independent is a struggle. The Encounter strategy concentrates the resources with a focus to building up congregations that will have over one thousand members. These congregations then concentrate their resources on planting daughter churches.

Another issue is a focus on the middle class. The socio-economic identity of the Episcopal Church in Latin America is the reverse of what it is in the United States. In many cases, the Episcopal Church is essentially a blue collar and lower-class church. Praise God for that, because that is where a lot of people are. The unfortunate side of that, however, is that the church has not reached the middle class in Latin America. That does not bode well for future leadership. It is very difficult for the people to make a transition to national leadership and to have leaders who can continue the work and plant daughter churches. For example, the Diocese of Peru has been searching for a bishop. The best candidate is a wonderful godly man, but he only has about a sixth- or seventh-grade education. His ability to reach Peruvian professionals has to be considered if he is elected bishop. The advantage of working first with the middle class is that it forms a group of people who can assume the leadership and then mobilize others to reach their city in the name of the Lord. They are given a vision, discipled and trained. The later generations of the church can then reach down to the very poorest of the poor. This Encounter strategy has been very effective at planting Christ-centered churches in very poor neighborhoods.

Approximately three years ago the Encounter people started a church-planting effort targeting the upper class, the most difficult to work with in Peru. In Monterico they secured a very nice house in a nice neighborhood and started holding services there. Within a few months they were packed. They had a number of evangelistic outreach efforts appropriate to that cultural group. One such effort involved having a Peruvian art show with an art critic. The critic explained the art and the message behind each piece which often was a communication of despair. He then wove that into his own testimony of how the Lord had changed his life. This type of evangelistic event was effective and appropriate to that socio-economic group.

Another very intentional church planting effort targeted the worst neighborhood in the city. This was the pornographic district where the drug addicts and prostitutes are—a real center for crime in the city. They rented a striptease theater and turned it into a daughter church. This is very different from our idea of church planting which seems to follow where our members are.

This church planting strategy often works in a cycle. Using the Bogotá Encounter strategy as an example, they began with fourteen missionaries and a couple of Colombians. This is the most difficult time because there is no momentum base with which to begin. Experience has shown, using this particular strategy, that the period of time to grow from zero to two hundred takes longer than growing from two hundred to one thousand. Once the church has grown to one thousand, they begin their daughter church with a "year in the womb." Some key pastoral leaders and two hundred key committed members of the church will begin to worship in the parish hall. They will begin to build their identity as a congregation. Their stewardship will be separate, and they pay their pastor's salary and develop their congregational life. After about a year that congregation moves to the particular area of the city that they are trying to reach with the gospel. They begin by either renting a facility, or purchasing a plot of land and erecting a temporary building. Successive expansions to the temporary building are added until they are ready to build the permanent Christian Education building with space for about five hundred people. When they are filling that twice, then they build the mother church which may seat as many as 1,500 people. Once that is completed, the energies of the congregation are turned to planting another daughter church and the cycle begins again.

Our first effort at using the Encounter With God strategy is taking place in Tegucigalpa, the capitol of Honduras. This is a city of 800,000 or more people with a substantial squatter settlement on the outskirts. We started with a team of about a dozen missionaries who rented a house with a seating capacity of about sixty people.

The church is called Cristo Redentor (Christ the Redeemer) and is located on a fairly busy street about a block off the main thoroughfare. One of the critical aspects of the Encounter With God strategy is to find visible and accessible facilities. The church initially attracted a high number of children but not many men. So the team made a deliberate effort to target events that would draw men into the church. Recently Fred Fetterolf, the retired president of ALCOA, addressed a businessmen's luncheon. He shared with them how it was that he, as a successful businessman, had become convinced that the gospel is the truth and how it made a difference in his life.

Evangelistic campaigns have been a part of the fabric of this strategy. We had an evangelistic conference this January followed by another in February. The people converted in January brought their friends and family members in February. One man got up before the whole congregation and gave his testimony. "I asked the Lord into my life four weeks ago. God has changed my life, and I am excited. My cell group is almost ready to multiply now. Great things are happening, but the thing that really pleases me is that today my son and daughter-in-law have asked Jesus into their lives."

The idea is to have a regular, flowing series of evangelistic events where those who have been converted have a place to bring their friends to hear the same message.

American congregations often would like to do something in mission but are not sure what it is that they have to offer. SAMS's short-term mission program helps congregations to use what they do well in a way that will make a difference. One such congregation had a strong Vacation Bible School. We invited them to come to Honduras to do a one-week Vacation Bible School. We advertised that it would be totally in English for children to beef up their English and get Christian education at the same time. Forty children attended, thirty-one prayed to ask the Lord into their lives and it gave the team eighteen families with which to follow up. SAMS is enthusiastic about short-term missions when they are coupled with long-term missionaries. The short-term team can do something which will give the long-term team a breakthrough they can follow up. The important thing about short-term mission trips is to make them count. It is important to share with people the reality of the gospel and relate to them on a spiritual level. They need to hear about what Jesus has done in a believer's life.

Other aspects of our strategy in Tegucigalpa involve building relationships with people. We have spent two years becoming acquainted with people in our target area—real estate people, people who have driven us around the area, anyone that we can meet that will speak up in the community. Then we get names and addresses and when we have an event, we invite them. The invitations are hand delivered which makes it very personal. We have now built a nucleus of Hondurans who do the inviting and it is really taking off. We advertise the speaker and the topic and try to make things relevant so the people will want to come.

One area where we are actually holding back the SAMS missionaries is the area of social ministry. SAMS has significant social ministries everywhere we are serving, but in this instance we want the church to grow and social ministries to grow out of that congregation. What we are trying to avoid is having an idea hatched by gringos, financed by gringos and then turning it over to the Hondurans when we leave. We would like it to grow out of the life of the congregation with the vision and finances for the ministry coming from the Honduran leaders themselves. This has been frustrating, but we have seen some terrific examples of social ministry in the Encounter model. One church in Llima is feeding 300 children breakfast each morning. In another church, a pastoral team is going into the parks to build relationships with the boys who live in the streets. There are between 100,000 and 200,000 children living in the streets of Lima. Once they have built relationships, they ask the boys if they would like to live in a home. They have an intermediate step of families who will take these boys in and help them prepare to live in a family. Then they are finding permanent homes for these boys.

We continue to pray and God moves and provides the resources. Newcomers to the faith need instruction as to what faith is all about, how to face temptation, what repentance is and why the Bible is the Word of God.

There is much to do, but God has provided the people, the strategy and has opened our eyes to his desire to reach entire cities and countries with the good news of Jesus Christ.

LESSONS FROM CHURCH PLANTING IN SINGAPORE

The Rev. Canon James Wong

The Diocese of Singapore includes six countries: Singapore, with 3 million people; Thailand, with 60 million; Vietnam, with 75 million; Laos with approximately 4 million; and Cambodia, with almost 8 million. These total 150 million. Finally, there is Indonesia with 195 million, which brings the total to about 345 million people. Our diocese incorporates more people than live in the entire United States.

Let me begin with the tragedy of the Anglican Church. Anglicanism has been in Singapore for 150 years, because all those years we were under England. There has been only one Anglican church planted in Bangkok in over one hundred years. There was one Anglican church in Vietnam, but, of course, after the war it was closed. The communists took over the land and now it is used as a bar and a dance hall.

The so-called missionaries from America, England, and Australia who came here and worked for 100 years had no vision. They made themselves very comfortable by transporting English culture into Bangkok. For instance, a missionary would drink cocktails at parties, act as a diplomat, christen babies, and enjoy a lot of diplomatic privileges. He was seen as a chaplain to the English or American embassy. That was the condition of the Diocese of Singapore.

Recently, a lady challenged me, asking, "What right do I have in Singapore to start converting the Muslims and the Buddhists? Why don't you leave them as good religious people? These people have their own religions, why do you need to bother them?" They say when I convert them I am proselytizing, and that's bad, bad, bad.

That is also the current view of some missionaries, I am afraid. But God is doing a new work. The new wine had to be in new wineskins, and that is why there is a whole new spiritual upsurge in Africa and Asia now. I am sure it is also happening in Latin America, although slowly, where the nationals have to take the responsibility of bringing the gospel to the nations. In God's goodness, the second wave of mission endeavors over the last forty years has been much more evangelical in nature— strongly gospel-preaching, Bible-oriented, and much more clear in their evangelistic goals. Part of the new work that God is doing in the second wave is through what we call the "faith mission"—groups such as Youth With A Mission (YWAM), Operation Mobilization, Campus Crusade, and Navigators. These parachurch movements, led by lay people, are having a significant impact all over Asia, including in our Diocese of Singapore. They have filled a tremendous vacuum.

I still remember that in the early fifties, we were a liberal, traditional, and very English church. Anybody who lived in England could come to Singapore, worship in the Anglican cathedral, and not even notice that they had left their country. But when the Holy Spirit began to renew our diocese from 1970 onwards, things changed dramatically. God is transforming the church from being inward-looking, with little spiritual life, into a dynamic church!

The point I want to make is: take heart! There was a time when I was in despair, feeling like a voice crying in the wilderness. Most of the senior clergymen in the Diocese of Singapore were missionaries from America, England, and Australia who had no concept of the gospel. For them, good works, social justice, and maintenance were the mission of the church. There was no gospel preaching, Bible teaching, or evangelism, and certainly no mission! That was the situation until 1972, just over twenty years ago. Then the Holy Spirit came! Thank God!

My bishop went to the World Council of Churches as a nonbeliever. When he was in Bangkok, a young Fijian Anglican, who had been affected by the renewal from New Zealand told him what God was doing in the Diocese of Fiji. My bishop was a little impolite; he did not quite believe all this. So the Fijian priest gave him two books: *Like a Mighty Wind* by Mel Torre about the revival in Indonesia and *Nine O'Clock in the Morning* by Dennis Bennett.

My bishop read the books, but he didn't know what to make of them. He went to sleep and later woke up speaking in tongues. It was really a work of the Holy Spirit!

Peter Wagner was at the same conference in Bangkok. He was the first one to tell me that something had happened to my bishop. He said, "When he comes back, you will have a new bishop." I said I would believe it when I saw it for myself. The bishop had rebuked me only a week earlier, saying that I was arrogant to believe in salvation. He didn't even believe in God. But when he came back, he was a transformed man! He had discovered Jesus as his own personal Savior.

Since we had both received the baptism of the Holy Spirit, the bishop and I began to share our experiences through preaching and teaching. Interestingly enough, the Singaporean clergy were very receptive. Guess who resisted us? All the missionaries! They were upset with the bishop, saying he was undignified praying in tongues and laying hands on the sick.

The bishop opened up the cathedral for a healing service. We thought maybe fifty or one hundred would come; the cathedral was never filled. But one thousand people packed the cathedral! The people there were non-Christians—Indians, Muslims, and Buddhists. They were unbelievers. When they heard that there was going to be a healing service, all these non-Christians came into the cathedral for the first time. I still remember that during the service one person went into a trance and did Kung Fu as that demon spirit came out of him. When God's Spirit began to work, the manifestation of evil spirits came up. We began to pray for these people. And when we made the altar call, three quarters of the congregation came forward—people on crutches and wheel chairs. We didn't know what to do! So the bishop said, "Let's lay hands on them and pray." Miracles began to happen! A revival broke out in 1973!

Of course, the non-Christians who were healed, delivered, and saved were delighted! They knew Jesus! But the ministers and the missionaries who were American, Canadian, English, and Australian were so upset with us. In two years, our whole diocese was emptied of missionaries. The missionaries just packed their bags, saying that they could not work in a diocese that was too fundamental, too emotional, and had too much fantasy. We lost many clergymen overnight. When they finished their contract, they didn't want to renew it. They said, "We don't agree with this kind of ministry! It's not Anglican. This is not respectable. How can you turn the cathedral into a circus?" It did look like a circus. When non-Christians come in, they are not used to Anglican worship. They don't say, "Holy, holy, holy," and then keep quiet. People made noise. They screamed because, when the power of the Holy Spirit came, the evil spirits manifested themselves. So the missionaries and clergymen who were against the Holy Spirit's work were suddenly gone.

I received a vision as the renewal came into our diocese. The vision that was given was that of a ship in dry dock. When a ship is in dry dock, you have to do a lot of scraping of the carbuncles and everything that is stuck to it. You have to clean and polish it. When the cleaning process is over, the water level rises. Suddenly the lock has to be opened so the ship can sail. The Lord was saying that God was renewing the Anglican Church in Singapore. It had been dry, and he was in the process of cleaning and purifying the church. Now there was a spiritual high tide coming. While we didn't know it at the time, we were in the early stage of the renewal.

The vision showed me that God wanted our church to launch out into the deep. God gave my bishop a similar vision. He saw a dry well. Then God told him that this was a dry season. When a well is dry, a lot of weeds and dirt accumulate around it. God said that this was a time for cleaning up the well. When the well was clean, then water would rise up.

In the meantime, beginning in 1965, Singapore became independent. The British government gave us semi-autonomy, so we began to self-govern. Three problems were addressed by the new government; housing, education, and employment.

People need to live in houses. When the British were ruling, Singapore had backward, filthy, inadequate housing. In Chinatown, for example, they didn't rent rooms, but rather bed spaces. A bed was rented three times over, and people slept by shifts. Everyone slept an eight-hour shift and paid by hours, using one bed. The British colonial government is a backward government that takes everything from the country without giving anything back. That is why God is judging Britain today. They are economically depressed and are reaping what they have sown. They have exploited the wealth of Africa, Asia, and South Africa and they never put it back.

From 1970 onwards, God brought about a change to our national development, and the church had an opportunity to reach the masses living in the new high-rise apartments. Unfortunately, the Anglican Church was not equipped for this task because, like the British government, we were just as backward in the church. We were comfortable in our very middle-class, suburban churches. The government was building twenty to thirty-story high-rise apartments very fast. At one stage, they were building one new flat per hour. When I found out that eighty percent of all our churches were not in the midst of a high-rise but in the middle-class, comfortable suburbs, I suggested to the diocese that we needed to change our mission strategy and to build churches in the high-rise housing estates. Of course, before the renewal, the churches were not ready for that. I made this proposal to St. Andrew's Cathedral. They voted it down so I left. But remember the vision of a ship in dry dock? After the cleaning up, the repainting and scraping, the water would rise and the lock would have to be opened so that the ship could sail out. I began to ask for the interpretation. God said the church needed to reach out to people rather than asking the people to come to church. Now, we had a congregation of only sixty people, but, fortunately, it was in a high-rise housing estate. The average age of the membership was only eighteen to twenty years old. My wife and I were the oldest people in the church! They were all converts who were eager to learn the Bible. It is easiest to work with people who have no Anglican tradition.

Almost fifty percent of our young church became renewed in the Holy Spirit overnight. We had an overnight retreat, and Ed Stube, an Anglican priest we knew nothing about, was present there. After I finished speaking, I thought, "Well, let's have supper and go to bed." But all our leaders, instead of going to bed, went into a nearby field. Ed was laying his hands on them and praying. Every one of them was baptized in the Holy Spirit! So the church came into the renewal experience.

I reminded them of the vision, that God told us to launch out. I said, "Let's take the vision from God seriously, find the new housing, and plant a church." But they all didn't want to go. They were too settled in the church. Although they were young, they were comfortable. I said, "Who will go?" Six young persons, ten percent of them, said, "We will go with you." So eight of us went to a new housing estate about two miles away. We found, fortunately, that my wife's sister was moving into this estate. She was a backslidden Anglican who had already stopped going to church. We met in her home, starting one Sunday with ten of us. It went on Sunday after Sunday in the living room. We worshipped, preached the gospel, sang, took an offering, and challenged the people to evangelize door-to-door. When this became successful, we began to grow, and we became twenty, thirty, forty, fifty. Interestingly enough, the six who left were soon replaced by new converts in the mother church. So they didn't miss them.

The first success led me to plant a second church. The same thing happened. It took another six to ten people, who were quickly replaced by new converts in the mother church. A third extension church was started, a fourth one, and a fifth one. During the period between 1974 and 1979, five years, there were eight new churches. Don't forget, it started with only sixty people. With the renewal, the church grew. During that time between eighty and one hundred people actually left the mother church for church-planting purposes. But what you give away, you never lose. I am telling you this principle. Clergymen, don't be afraid to give away people in church planting. God honors giving. When people were sent forth in mission, the mother church grew from sixty to over three hundred in five years. Of course, as the one hundred people went out, they didn't stay one hundred. Every one of these daughter churches also grew.

There are two types of growth: quantitative growth and qualitative, or deepening, growth. I knew some church growth theory from Fuller, but there is nothing like testing out a thesis. Churches grow in a number of ways, the easiest being quantitative growth. I think every pastor wants a church that grows from zero to one thousand. That's quantitative growth, your membership growth. I believe that God wills his church to grow. You may start with a small church, but it can grow through prayer, the renewal of the Holy Spirit, the faithful teaching of the Word, training, shepherding and discipling. In other words, quantitative and qualitative growth must go together.

I learned there is a third thing to do if you really want growth. You have to organize for growth. This is where management for growth, planning for growth and having a vision for growth are so important. This cannot come from the vestry or a church member. It has to be from the leadership that God has raised up. That doesn't mean it is a one-man job; it will have to be team work with the senior warden, elders, vestry, and others in leadership. I call this "organic growth." One of the weaknesses of most Anglican churches is lack of management for growth.

Now let me suggest that before you grow, expand your leadership base. As you expand, you create room for growth. As you expand your leadership base and release more lay people, your church will grow bigger and bigger. This is organic growth. It is your ability to equip, train, and release people for the work of the ministry: evangelism, outreach, witnessing, and church planting.

Now in all my church planting work, we never hired people. All the pioneers for growth were laypeople. The lay evangelists, the lay pastors, the lay workers still had professions, but they also had a fire for God and a zeal to serve him.

The key is leadership training. If your church doesn't have this foresight, it will not have healthy growth. A lot of churches want quantitative growth but are not willing to release some of their leadership into outside ministry. Let me tell you this: if you only have one set of worship leaders, one preacher, one organist, one choir, one set of ushers, that's all you will ever have. But when you plant ten churches, you have ten sets of leadership; you expand the Body of Christ. That's good management. So as you grow big, grow wide also.

Every parish must plan extension growth, church planting. My target now is not to start with six or ten, but with twenty. Twenty is an easier number with which to start. Of course, if your congregation is only one hundred, maybe you must start with ten percent. And never despise fifty—send five of them! Using the tithing principle, you should tithe the manpower too. Build it into your spiritual plan. By sending them out, you are releasing men and women to the work. You trust the Holy Spirit to mature them and give wisdom. But at the same time, you, as the equipper, are always closely enabling, equipping, and teaching them.

Does your church have a vision statement? It is very important that you begin with a vision. The vision statement of The Chapel of the Resurrection, our current church is:

> To build a caring community committed to evangelism, discipling, and church planting.

So to anybody who joins the Chapel of the Resurrection, it is very clear who we are. And the way we work toward our vision is through small cell groups of ten to twelve people. Now, home cell groups are not very common in the United States, especially in the Episcopal Church. It is a pity. All over the world, especially in Asia, the growth, the strength is in the home cell units where there is a lot of caring, pastoral care, ministry, and prayer. If you have fifty people in your church, you have five home cell groups. If you have five hundred, then you need fifty, that's all. A home cell should be committed to evangelism because its purpose is to witness and multiply. We give them a target; once a year the group multiplies. So we begin with ten people; by the end of this year, we should have twenty, and we should have two cell groups. That is a faith goal.

Our second goal is to plant twenty churches in Singapore by the year 2000. This was launched in 1990, the beginning of the Decade of Evangelism. In other words, our parish will plant two new churches every year. At the moment, we are on target. When I return to Singapore, our eighth church will have been planted.

What is our strategy? We emphasize personal evangelism, the 5-3-1 approach. We encourage testimonies by new Christians because they are the best evangelists. We ask them to share in public how they became saved so the congregation is encouraged. They are reminded they need to go and witness. Also, we develop stronger and more creative youth programs. Now in my visits to England, Canada, and the USA, one thing I notice is that your churches have no young people. You have no future in your church. If your church is fifty adults, do you know how many young people you need? One hundred, a two-to-one ratio. For every adult in your congregation, you must aim to have two youths in it to make it a healthy church because as the young people grow up, you allow for the dropout rate. And as the adults die, the young people will rise up into leadership. If your church has one hundred adults, you must have two hundred youth; otherwise you have failed your future. In our churches, we have a lot of young people.

Young people are the greatest evangelists. Build youth churches. Don't integrate them into the adult service. Once in a while that is okay. But regularly have something more dynamic, music that is more lively, and a program that is suited to young people.

So start youth churches, strengthen and enrich home cell groups, focus on receptivity. Industries have R & D departments, research and development units that look at the population to develop methods of "evangelizing." I think every church must have an R & D department. Do you know what 5-3-1 means? We encourage each member to pray for five unsaved persons during one year. Then each member prays that God will prepare the way so that he or she can do a one-to-one witnessing to three. Finally, the member believes that one of them will be saved by the end of the year. So a church of 100 will have 200 on-fire Christians at the end of the year. And a home cell group of ten members becomes twenty. That's evangelism.

The only way to disciple converts is in the home cell groups, not in the big Sunday service. The Sunday service is a time of celebration, inspiration, and instruction. But the real caring and work is done in the home cell groups, where spiritual maturity and growth continue with the strong teaching and application of God's word.

I am a Bible teacher. From 9:00 a.m. to 10:00 a.m., one hour before our main service starts, members come for one hour of solid Bible teaching. This includes the adults, new converts, youth, and children. We felt that Sunday was best, because it is hard to get families to come on a weeknight. But you have to educate your people. If you want a strong church, teach the Word of God. The people love it. There is no singing. I open with prayer and teach the Bible. At the end, they have a few minutes' break for coffee, and we start our worship service. That is discipling.

Finally, every congregation aims for twenty percent growth in converted adult baptisms. In other words, a church with twenty members can expect four new converts every month. We have a lot of adult baptisms through conversion growth. Then we establish two new churches each year. We are on target.

What I have shared with you is an Episcopal/Anglican model. Over the last twenty years, it has transformed dead churches into living testimonies. In Singapore, all the churches are like that. The whole diocese is growing.

Only then go from evangelism into mission, because we believe if we are not successful at home, going overseas doesn't make us successful. If we don't know how to reproduce in Singapore, at home, going to Indonesia won't make us reproduce. So our rule is this: if you want to go overseas, plant a church at home first. When you are successful, you can use this principle in any part of the world and reproduce. Don't take your mistakes overseas. Overseas, it is more difficult because of cross-cultural factors that involve added pressures, misunderstanding, discouragement.

I shared my testimony to encourage you. Remember, I was just one man in the diocese who believed in the Word of God. They criticized me for bringing the Bible to church, saying, "We Anglicans don't need the Bible; we have the Prayer Book." I didn't oppose that, but I stood faithful, preaching and teaching the Bible. The Holy Spirit came with renewal, and God did the rest.

More people in Singapore are being released into ministry from money given to missions than ever. Our diocese gives three million U.S. dollars a year to foreign missions. We have Singaporean missionaries in Japan, the Philippines, Thailand, North Africa, Central Africa, South Africa, Bolivia, Indonesia, India, and Sri Lanka. They are entirely supported by the parishes. When people's hearts are touched by the gospel, there is joy in giving.

8

Bear More Fruit: Enabling Others

NATIONALS AND MISSIONARIES: LESSONS FROM KENYA

The Rt. Rev. Dr. David Gitari

Are missionaries still needed in Kenya and can they make a contribution? The answer to that question is yes; missionaries can make a contribution. That may mean that they will not be doing mission work in the traditional way. There may still be some places where that pioneering work is still necessary. The church in Kenya, and perhaps in other areas as well, can use people with certain skills that they are able to share. There is always a need for skills in carpentry and construction, teaching, business and technical skills. The church is one big family of believers and I think we need to remember that the mission of the church is not our mission. It is the mission of God. Sometimes we make the mistake of thinking that the mission is ours. As a result we say that we can use this or that, we don't want this or that because this is my mission. That is a mistake. If people feel called to make a contribution to a certain mission, they should have the opportunity.

There are many areas where no trained people are, and having someone come to start something new and train people is most welcome. In fact, the government requires that when someone comes and asks for a work permit, they must give the government the name of the person who will work under them. That way when the individual leaves, there will be someone to carry on the work. There is always that kind of emphasis.

In the Diocese of Mt. Kenya East, we have a communication department, with a print media department, electronic media department and so forth. But we need more personnel. The people who work in that department are paid by the diocese, but they also generate their own income. The print media publishes books which we sell; the electronic media people do video filming in church and they earn money.

When missionaries come, we hope that they would have their support provided by those who have sent them. Of course, we would also want to feel that we are making a contribution, and our contribution might be to give the missionary housing or fields to sow.

So, how does one go about becoming a missionary? In Kenya, we have had more experience in partnership with the British, especially with CMS and BCMS. Our procedure with them is that a bishop makes a request for a missionary. The bishop identifies the type of missionary that is needed. These agencies have lists of people who have been inquiring about opportunities to come overseas. From that list the right person is identified, that person undergoes from ten to twelve months training in Birmingham, England. Then, when they come to Kenya, they spend another three months in our language school studying the language. It is always recommended that any missionary coming to Kenya should know Swahili. It is quite possible to learn Swahili in three months and be able to communicate. If the missionary is going to other areas, they may have to study another language in addition to Swahili. After that, the missionary is under the direction of the bishop and works for as long as the bishop requests.

The biggest challenge for any missionary coming to Kenya from the United States concerns support. For someone who is qualified and planning to stay for some time, and making a comparison with what the CMS missionaries earn, it may mean the equivalent of 15,000 Kenya shillings per month. That is approximately $300 U.S. a month. The bishop is on that kind of salary not including his housing and transportation. Housing and transportation would be an additional 15,000 shillings, so it would be about $600 U.S. per month.

Another challenge that missionaries can face is in the area of tensions. It is best to come with simplicity. Naturally there are things that missionaries will have that Kenyans might not. A missionary might have a car and if it is used to help others, it isn't a problem. Living a lifestyle that is very different from the people in the area can create tensions. It is important to be sensitive to the culture and not place a lot of importance on possessions.

The church in Kenya has faced tensions internally. For instance, discussions about the ordination of women began in 1978 and it was not accepted until 1986. The province did not accept it until 1990, but the agreement was that those dioceses which did not want to ordain women did not have to comply. About fifty percent of the dioceses have accepted the ordination of women. The other fifty percent have not really rejected it. They just do not think it is a problem worth their time. The women are being accepted and some of them are exceptionally fine clergy and pastors. But male chauvinism is everywhere and sometimes I get letters from parishes complaining about the women priests. When I investigate, I find that it is only because she is a woman that they are showing prejudice. As they continue to experience the women in ministry, I am sure even that kind of tension will come to an end.

Another area of internal tension is with the government. As long as the church preaches prophetically, the government will never be happy. The government is always keeping an eye on me, for instance. Just recently I challenged the government officials for grabbing land away from poor people. Within the context of a service, I exposed the officials who had taken sixty acres from a group of people who had been cultivating it for thirty-six years. I did not give names, but said that some civil servants had grabbed the land. I was called upon to substantiate my allegations, which I did and gave the names of those involved to the commissioner. One of those involved was the commissioner. Then higher officials became involved and they wanted me to come to the police station and write down the names, which I had already given them. They said that if I did not do that, they would arrest me. I refused to go so they sent their criminal investigator to my house. He wanted me to write a statement saying that I refused to write a statement. I refused to do that and they did not arrest me. The district commissioner has said, "The bishop will be taken care of." I do not know exactly what that means. It could be another raiding of the house or anything.

Before I left to come to the United States we had a big service, thanking God that the land had been returned. The clergy read a statement signed by eighty-three clergymen saying that if anything happened to the bishop, they would hold the commissioner responsible. So that is where the situation stands just now. I had a telephone conversation with the commissioner before I came to America. I told him I was coming to

America and when I come back we shall have a battle. This could be like being at the top of the mountain where you have to descend and cast out a few more demons.

That is what the relationship between the church and the government in Kenya is like. The bishops speak, they are threatened but they will speak. We are not worried because, as a result of our ministry, we can see changes. The church in Kenya has been courageous and taken a strong stand and the church is not in turmoil.

Kenya is affected by what is happening around it in several ways. The problems of Somalia mean an influx of thousands of Somalis to Kenya. Refugees come, bring guns, and maraud and kill people. When there is trouble in Ethiopia, the Ethiopians flee to Kenya. Many refugees from Rwanda have gone to Uganda, to Tanzania, to Zaire and a few have come to Kenya. Every day on the news we see that people are being killed. We know that we have fellow Christians there. As soon as I heard of the turmoil in Rwanda, I tried to telephone my fellow bishops and all I could hear were voices in French. This affects the church very much and we must pray that there comes a resolution and peace.

Another big challenge is AIDS. Unless God does miracles and scientists find a cure, that thing is going to kill millions. In Uganda, some villages have already been wiped out. In 1986 there were about twenty-six known cases in Kenya; now there is about one million. Within a very short time every family has lost someone to HIV.

The challenge to the church is to provide programs for AIDS awareness, to care for the orphans, to teach people who are affected how to handle it and to extend care to the sick and families affected. It is having an impact on family life because women are fearful of their husband if the husband has worked away from home for a period of time. We pray for a cure, but, in the meantime we know that we must teach fidelity and AIDS awareness for the young people.

Before the end of the century, the greatest challenge for the church will be Islam. The rest of the Christian world may not realize the impact of this. In Kenya where the Muslim population is only ten percent, compared with seventy-three percent Christians, the Muslims are pouring in millions and millions of dollars from Arabia, Iran and other places. They are building mosques in every little town, whether there are Muslims there or not. They are inviting people to come in. They have forced the government to give them time on the radio so that now it is about half Christian and half Muslim. You have to pay for the programming and they have money to pay for the programs. They are doing a lot of aggressive evangelism and they are gaining ground. They reach areas of un-reached people first.

I would call this one of the greatest challenges of all times, not just in Kenya, but in Africa and even in the United States. The refugees coming from Somalia to settle are missionaries. We must do something about reaching Muslims here, in Europe and in other places.

THIRD WORLD MISSIONARIES: A CASE STUDY FROM INDIA

The Rev. Dr. Andrew Swamidoss

India is made up of several states, each with a different language. From tip to tip, India spans seven thousand miles and the major mode of travel is by train. The trains are very congested; food or drink is only available from the platform when the train stops. Traveling in first class may be tolerable, but second class is very difficult. Unauthorized people easily get on and off at various stops. Traveling by truck or car is very difficult because it is impossible, due to language differences, to read the signs.

Even a modest trip in India can bring one into contact with fifteen different languages, the major non-religious problem in the country. Hindi became the official language of India after independence, and it was hoped that it would have a unifying influence on the people, but it has not happened. About 200 million people speak Hindi, 70 million speak Bengali, and 50 million speak Tamil. Most people in India have three languages, English, Hindi and the mother tongue. This is very difficult, especially for the children.

Very few people in India are land owners and the only opportunities for the villagers are to sow the land and be a worker for the landlord. Urbanization is centered around such cities as Bombay, Calcutta, Delhi and Madras; people move to the cities to get jobs where there are none and they live in the street. They survive by picking up food at restaurants. Teenagers work all day picking up papers which they bring to dumpsters and will get, perhaps, ten rupees—a very meager sum.

India grows by almost one million people every year. Although there is a program of family planning, India is now at 900 million people. Middle-class people can understand family planning, but it does not mean much to the slum dweller. The men, in particular, are drunk most of the time, they do not care for their wives, they will go with anyone, causing the population to further increase, and when they get money it is used for drink. There is no medical or health care for the poor.

Many, many people in India have remained in the villages in the rural, tribal areas because they know that they can at least earn a modest living and have some pride in life. By remaining in the village, they can have their own house, a small hut, and not have to live in the street. There are water buffalo, facilities, and some equipment to help with agriculture, so these villagers have not rushed to the cities.

Food production is not sufficient and rice and wheat are imported, due in part to the increase in the population. Also, the farmers are dependent upon the monsoon. If there is a monsoon, then there is flooding and they cannot cultivate. If there is no monsoon, then there is drought.

There are insufficient quantities of everything in India. Such commonplace articles as paper towels, for instance, are very costly. There is not a lot of electricity and we use some gas lamps, but the gas lines leak. My children take candles to their schools to have light to study.

Because each state in India has a different language, it is like placing Europe into one country. Among the 850 million people, sixty-five percent are Hindus, fifteen percent are Muslims and 4.6 percent are Christian. People of other religions such as Buddhists, Jains, Sikhs, etc., comprise about twelve percent. Saying that four percent of the people are Christians means that about 42 million people are Christians. Half of this 4.6 percent is Catholic, because the Catholic missions started in the fifteenth century; whereas the Protestant missions started (realistically) with William Carey in 1793. Before that, one other Protestant missionary came from the Lutheran Church in Germany, but he was not effective. Then several denominations from the United States, England and other places came. The Church of South India (CSI) and the Church of North India (CNI) is made up of this two percent, predominantly Anglican, group. The Church of South India has twenty-one dioceses. It is the oldest united church and the first to bring together Episcopal and non-Episcopal traditions. After twenty years of negotiation, the Church of South India was inaugurated in 1947, bringing together constituents from the Anglican, Methodist, Presbyterian, Congregationalist and Reformed traditions. The church was predominantly Anglican, with the Methodist, Presbyterian, Congregationalist and Reformed numbers being small. So the Church of South India is Episcopal. It is a hierarchical church with a bishop and a diocesan council. The liturgy is from the 1611 Book of

Common Prayer. The Church of South India also has a Book of Common Prayer for Communion and other rites.

In one sense, it is not a united church. It is the Anglican Church, but because it is united with one or two others, and at the time of uniting did not have the blessing of the Archbishop of Canterbury, they have made us the United Churches. So there is the Church of South India and the Church of North India. South India is actually only four states. I am in the Church of North India, but I am from the Church of South India.

The second thing I would like to tell you about is the church's involvement in missions. The individual parish determines mission involvement. It depends upon their commitment to Christ, to the Word of God and to mission. If the bishop is strongly mission-minded, if the priest is strongly mission-minded, then the parish is strongly mission-minded; otherwise, it becomes rather cold. In many places, the church is cold. This can be because of the priest or the bishop, but generally it is because of liberal theology.

The blessing in disguise, however, is that the people are joining together and forming missionary societies, such as happened with the Episcopal Church Missionary Community in the U.S., supported by people who have a commitment to mission.

Priests and laypeople form the societies and the support comes from individual Christians in India. Both parishes and individuals provide financial support to individual missionaries. The bishop may not officially recognize an individual, but they are sent out from a parish that has made a commitment to support one missionary. There are many of these societies and that is why the gospel is progressing. The Friends Missionary Prayer Band has 350 missionaries fully supported by individuals in India. During the 1960s, when overseas missionaries were not allowed to come to India, many, many Indians went into the field. People have said that India should be reached by Indians and we from the South where there are more Christians, were given the challenge to go to North India. Missionaries from overseas are unable to come, so we have to go because of the gospel mandate, the Great Commission.

In fact, I am one such product. I taught senior high school for nine years, from 1961 to 1970. Then I got the call for missions in the South. I could not resign my job because my parents were getting older and in India it is the obligation of the children to support the parents until they die. In 1970, I married; my wife, who was a junior high school teacher, remained at home. I went to seminary in North India at the Union Biblical Seminary which had 200 students.

This seminary moved and left behind a large campus with buildings, chapel, dining hall, playgrounds and dormitories. They were trying to sell it to a Muslim foundation to be used for a medical college, but somehow God intervened. A few of us joined together and called for a consultation on missionary training known as the Yavatmal Consultation on Missionary Training. We talked about three things: the specific nature of our program, who would operate the program, and the property. We met in August, October and December of 1983 and in February of 1984. We divided into subcommittees and discussed whether we would buy the property, would they give it, or would we build our own program and they would own the property. The Lord did a miracle and all three things were resolved. In February of 1984, a two-year Certificate in Missions program was inaugurated. The property committee set a price in Indian rupees the equivalent of $1 million in U.S. money; we bargained and the U.S. dollar value continued to rise. We paid between $560,000 and $600,000 instead of $1 million because of the rise in the U.S. dollar. The Lord did a miracle and that was the way we were able to get the property. We owe gratitude to the Episcopal Church Missionary Community for their involvement and assistance in completing this purchase.

In 1989, while I was in the seminary, there was an election for bishop in another diocese, the Free Methodist Church, to elect the first Indian bishop. Both the Registrar and the President at the seminary were Free Methodists and each offered himself as candidate for bishop. Obviously only one could be elected. The Registrar became the Bishop, and the President left the seminary to become the President of another Bible college. The board invited me to become President of the seminary and my wife and I initially declined. However, the Spirit of God would not leave us and that is why we are at Yavatmal College for Leadership Training. I am the Director, and God continues to confirm us in this place. Our two main goals are missionary training and the education of missionary children. We have a college, a school, and a hostel. Presently we have seventy-two candidates in the college and we graduated forty candidates in March of 1994. There are thirty-five students in the hostel, a beautiful eighteen-acre compound. There are more than one thousand children in the school. The local children come and stay. We are able to teach them Scripture. In morning assembly we teach a song, have a prayer and a Bible reading and the Lord's Prayer. When opportunities come, we are able to talk to them about Christ.

We have moved from support of missionaries to training and then to outreach. From the vision of the 1960s to send out missionaries, the arrival of actual workers in the 1970s, the training of missionaries through the 1980s and into the 1990s, the emphasis continues to be on training so the result will be more missionaries, the vision will be sustained and the resources of the Church will not be wasted. When missionaries come for training, six months is spent studying language so that it is done systematically and is not hit or miss.

Conversions happen when missionary societies send these trained missionaries to receptive areas which are primarily among tribal people. I have been there, and it is within these tribal groups that mass movements to Christ are happening. The missionaries go to the tribal groups, two by two, either as single people or married couples. These people learn the language and identify themselves with the villages. They live as the villagers live and interact with them in everyday life. If they wait for a bus and it does not come, they walk back to the village with the people and, while walking, they talk about Christ. This is sometimes called walking evangelism. As the missionaries continue to do this, the village people start to ask questions about why these people from South India have come to live in their village and learn the language. They begin to see the light.

Power encounters also make church growth happen. For example, in one village a lady was about to die. All the traditions and black magic had not worked to heal her. Finally, the lady was brought to the missionary. The missionary touched her and prayed and there was a healing. When this happened, the people felt that God was working and the entire village became Christians.

In another place, I personally baptized 190 people. It happened because the missionary leader told the missionaries that as soon as they had evangelized a village, they were to talk to the villagers about the mandate of preaching the gospel. They were to tell the villagers that they should go from one village to the next and talk about Christ. A power encounter happened when a leper in another village was healed. Then he became an evangelist and talked to other people about Christ. One lady made the observation that it is among the tribal people that the miracles and healings are happening.

The accusation is often made that the tribal people convert easily because they are illiterate and uneducated and that we are using money to influence them. Actually, the tribal people are animists and worship spirits and have a fear of black magic. When the person of Christ, the Jesus of the Synoptic Gospels, is presented, the people understand that here is God, the God for whom they have been waiting. When they see miracles happen, when a missionary student comes to them and prays with them and healing takes place, they see the power of God.

An example of how this happens occurred in one village where a missionary had talked about Christ and people had been converted, particularly one family. Following this conversion, a group of people was traveling a distance to market with carts full of goods and the converted man was among them. Suddenly one of his two bulls just fell down. Everyone stopped and the people told the man that because he had become a Christian, his bull was going to die. This simple man, a new convert, just kneeled down on the road. He said, "Lord, my bullock is about to die and these people are mocking you. My missionary friend has told me that you are a living God. Right now, I want you to kindly heal my bull that it might get up." Lo and behold, the prayer of a few minutes from a poor ignorant man who does not know Christology was answered, and the bull got up. These people, who had tried to get the bull up, were amazed. The group became Christians. Conversions happen because of miracles, just as in the New Testament days.

Opposition to the gospel comes from anti-Christian elements and Hindus. There is a revival of Hinduism and the Hindus think India belongs to them; therefore the Muslims and Christians should not be there. These groups are quite militant and want to establish Hindu nationalistic village governments. The Hindu high caste families reject God. In 1947, India gained independence. The missionaries were unwelcome and were not given visas. At that time, when the Hindus were approached with the gospel, they rejected it because they were rejecting colonialism.

An important man in Indian history, a man named Ambetka, a low-caste man, studied in England and received a doctorate. He was a very influential man, a freedom fighter, the framer of the Indian constitution, who rejected Hinduism because Hinduism did not help the untouchables. When he did this, he was seriously considering becoming a Christian. But Gandhi, Nehru and the political leaders warned him against becoming Christian because the colonial British people were Christian and that was who they were fighting against. So Ambetka became a Buddhist and all the untouchables identify him with Buddha. Now Buddhism is coming in India and where there is a statue of Buddha, there is one of Ambetka also. They do not know the teachings of Buddhism, but they have done this because of Ambetka. If this man had become Christian, forty percent of India might be Christian by now.

We have experienced opposition at Yavatmal, most recently directed at the principal of our school where the local students go. The principal was seven-months pregnant and a particularly rough student had misbehaved, ending the day, along with a group of his friends, making fun of her. She did not do anything that day because school was over and she wanted to remain calm. The next day, however, when the boy came to school, she told him to go get his father. The boy did not bring his father, who was a widower. The next day the principal told him again that she wanted to speak with his father. The boy became very rude and shouted in the class that he would cause the principal a lifetime of trouble. Then the boy went out and committed suicide, leaving behind a note that said it was due to the principal that he had done this. The police came and arrested her without any proper inquiry. Because of the harassment she suffered, she lost the baby. Had it not been for many donations of blood, the lady would have died as she was critically ill.

The point of this is that suicides are very common in India, about five hundred per day in a population of 850 million people. This one, however, was given much attention in the paper saying that it was all the fault of the seminary. The school went on strike and the children would not come. We decided to take drastic action so I announced that we would close the school indefinitely. The parents went to the education officer, who came and told me that we must open the school and he would see that the students did not misbehave. They gave the principal a three-month maternity leave, and they wanted to dismiss her. This is a good case study of the type of opposition we experience.

Persecution is continuous and those who oppose us use every opportunity to cause problems. As a country, India bleeds with corruption and materialism. Our campus has been vandalized, I have been thrown in jail and police officers have been bribed to prevent them from speaking for us. It is important that we all pray for these groups every day; pray for the church in India and also Yavatmal where missionaries are trained and where we care for and educate missionary children. The staff numbers some fifty to fifty-five people with approximately 1100 students in the entire facility. Pray for our school and the hostel; pray for the staff who teach and work there. Pray that opposition will be overcome.

WORKING IN PARTNERSHIP
WITH THIRD WORLD MISSIONS

The Rev. David and Mrs. Rosemary Harley

DAVID HARLEY: In August of 1993 my wife, Rosemary, and I left All Nations Christian College because we were excited about what God was doing in the world with the development of missions from Africa, Asia and Latin America. We heard church leaders from those continents say training is extremely important to successfully send out missionaries, and a number asked if we could come and help. So we left the security of a college job in Britain to be available to encourage missionary training in the Two-Thirds World. We are missionaries of Cross-Links, an Anglican mission in Britain that used to be called the Bible Churchmen's Missionary Society. We are coordinators with a group called Evangelical Missions Resources International Network, which is part of what is called Fellowship of Witness here. We are also training associates of the World Evangelical Fellowship Missions Commission, which links a broad spectrum of evangelicals of many denominations across the world.

I suppose the most significant development in world mission in the last thirty years has been the rapid deployment of missionaries from Africa, Asia and Latin America. However, it began long before that. There are stories going back 150 years of missionaries from various Two-Thirds World (non-Western) countries being involved in mission. But the growth has been quite phenomenal from 1972, when it is estimated that there were just under three thousand missionaries from the Two-Thirds World, to 1988, when there were nearly thirty-six thousand. These figures are from the *Handbook of Two-Thirds World Missions* by Larry Pate, published by MARC in time for the Manila Lausanne II Congress in 1989. He updated the figures in the April, 1991, issue of *International Bulletin of Missionary Research*.

Projected growth forecasts these figures rising up to 162,000 by the end of this decade, meaning there would be more missionaries from the Two-Thirds World than from the West. But those are projections, not predictions, and we cannot be certain that this rate of growth will be sustained.

But if one asks why this missionary movement has grown, three things stand out. First, there is the growth of the church. Where the church has grown and been blessed by God, missionaries are being sent out. Some of the leading countries in the sending of missionaries are the ones that have seen the greatest church growth.

Second, we see churches that have caught a vision for mission. At a conference in São Paulo, Brazil, I was amazed to hear four thousand Latin American Christians saying: we have a responsibity for mission; it is time that our countries stop receiving so much and begin to give; the baton of world evangelism has been carried by our brothers and sisters in North America for two centuries, and now it is coming to us. The Christians from Latin America feel responsible to carry the torch for world mission.

A third reason for the growth of Two-Thirds World missions is the result of greater political stability and economic strength. That is particularly true of Korea and Singapore, which are now sending out more missionaries.

Many missionaries are now from indigeneous missionary societies of the Two-Thirds World. In 1980, these societies numbered 749; by 1988, they had risen to nearly 1,100.

The Evangelical Mission Society of Nigeria now has 450 couples, most working within Nigeria, but a certain proportion in West Africa or further afield. The total budget for 450 missionary couples is $40,000. Amazing! Until recently, they were paid only about eight dollars a month. That represented half their monthly support; they are meant to get the other half by farming in the communities they serve as missionaries. They seem to manage. One of the problems is that once they have actually established a church with seven families, the missionaries have become dependent on their farms, making it difficult to move on to a new place.

We had the privilege of meeting one couple, from the Diocese of Sokoto in the north of Nigeria, who have started two missionary societies and two training agencies, and now have the responsibility within the Association of Evangelicals of Africa for developing missionary training in each country in Africa. They are a key couple who are training people to go and be missionary trainers.

The Bishop of Ibadan, the second largest city in Nigeria, has a broad vision for reaching others in the diocese. In the last four years, fifteen new Anglican churches were planted in the city, averaging between five hundred and one thousand members each. I spoke at the dedication of one, called Jesus Christ's Ambassadors Evangelical Anglican Church, started among the poor.

A number of bishops in Nigeria have a real vision for outreach and an awareness that the church must be more flexible. They are allowing the worship to become more truly African and are seeing their churches grow as a result.

The churches of South India and Northeast India, where the Christian church is strong, are now supporting five thousand cross-cultural missionaries. One man, who finished his Master's degree, had a chance to do a Ph.D., but turned it down because he felt the Lord calling him to become a missionary. Having served as missionaries, they are now leaders of a school outside Bangalore, training missionaries of the India Evangelical Mission.

In Korea, one man had a concern to reach students and young professionals. He began regular worship meetings which very quickly attracted four thousand every week. He has filled the Olympic stadium in Seoul with 100 thousand young Korean men and women, and it is most moving to be at their meetings and to see them worshipping God. It is exciting to see the many young people whom this man is influencing to go out into the world.

ROSEMARY HARLEY: There are some natural advantages for Two-Thirds World missions and missionaries. First, they have natural contacts and links. Koreans can move into China and learn Chinese more easily than a Westerner can, because there are links between the languages. They also have links with the peoples of Central Asia. Koreans have opportunities in Mongolia, where they can meet needs quicker and more easily than Westerners. South Americans can go to Portugal, Spain, Mozambique and Angola more easily, because they have the language. Also, because of the Islamic influence in Spain before the Spanish Americas were founded, they seem to have a natural affinity with Islamic cultures. Indians, of course, can go to Bhutan, Nepal and the neighboring states more easily. Nigerians can go into other West African countries without visas and work permits. They can also relate to North Africans more easily than those of us from the West, so they have tremendous advantages. Korean and Indian engineers, Filipino maids, and others with appropriate skills can go into the Middle East to work. Many times there are others of their families already there, so Asians, Africans and Latin Americans can go to expatriates from their countries in some of the least evangelized countries of the world, as well as to the U.S.A. and other Western countries to work among Koreans, Nigerians, Indians or Hispanics, and so on. These are some of the natural links and contacts that the Holy Spirit can use.

Second, they tend to be less of a threat. They do not have a colonial imperialist past like the British. They are not known as a superpower like the United States. On the whole, they are not expected to come as the technical experts and whiz kids who know everything, and therefore cripple the growth of the local church. They can come in and be less threatening. We read about some Protestants in Russia who said they would prefer people from Asia and Africa rather than from the States and Europe because of this factor.

Third, in many areas, they don't stand out physically like many Westerners do. I have heard frightening stories about blonde British girls going to South America, being followed and mugged, because they stood out like tourists. In Africa, there is no way those of us from the West could be Africans; we stick out like sore thumbs. However well we learn the language and identify with the culture, there are certain things we cannot change. There are some parts of Asia now where the church is growing rapidly, and it is much easier for Christians from those areas to go into unreached parts of Asia because they're not a threat and fit in more easily. Many Latin Americans have dark hair and lighter skin and can fit very naturally into the Middle East. One resulting problem for Two-Thirds World missionaries can be that sometimes they look so much like the local people that they are expected to speak the language fluently, and they're not forgiven in the way we Westerners may be.

Fourth, as a generalization, missionaries from the Two-Thirds World are more willing and able to accept a simple lifestyle. Most of us from Europe and America arrive on the field with our crates, our barrels and our boxes. How many North American and British missionaries live in mud huts, as the people do in many rural areas? Yet to reach these un-reached rural people groups, you need missionaries who willl go and live alongside them, accepting food and water from them.

We know of three young Nigerians who went to a people of the Central Plateau state where there were no Christians. The people had said, "If Christians come first, we'll become Christians, and if Muslims come first we'll become Muslims." These three went and within a few months there were eighty being prepared for baptism. They encountered amazing openness. How did they live? The chief simply put them in a hut. (I don't think that I could do that.) They were only given transport there; they weren't given any money. They just had to trust the Lord for three months. And that in turn made them dependent on the people.

This is true of Indian missionaries, too. Many are graduates from the cities, but they are willing to live on fifteen to twenty dollars per month in order to serve Christ. So a willingness to live simply is another advantage of Two-Thirds World missionaries.

Fifth, they tend to understand people of the Two-Thirds World better. The cultural jump is not so great. In Africa, the thought is, "We are, therefore I am." But this is not true of us in the West. We are individualists; our homes are our castles; our territory is mapped out; our religion is private. For us, it is such a big cultural jump, whereas for them, they understand community, they understand family, and they understand the need of the local people to provide for others. We cannot comprehend the pressures of life there or the best ways in which to evangelize. They are much better at that.

Sixth, some are more used to learning languages than we are. Many Two-Thirds World people speak a tribal dialect, plus a trade language, and also a little English. They are accustomed to coping in different languages. They do not have that awful psychological block that many of us have.

Finally, they are more aware of a spiritual dimension. They have missed out on rationalism and the Enlightenment, and they actually believe in a spirit world. When they see people possessed by demons, they know that they are possessed by demons. We stop and think, now, is this mental illness? I think they are more aware of the whole spiritual realm than we are and treat things spiritually. Therefore, they see the need for prayer and trust God in a more real way than we often do.

DAVID: We are not saying there is no place for missionaries from the West. We are pointing out the tremendous potential of this great new mission force that God, by his Spirit, is leading out.

There are difficulties, and here are six problems that missionaries from the Two-Thirds World face:

First is pressure from families who don't want them to go. Particularly if they are the eldest child, or if they've had higher education, they may be expected to stay at home to support the wider family.

A second problem is discouragement from their pastors. When we asked Nigerian missionary candidates what was their most difficult problem, they replied, "Our pastors didn't want us to do this. If we want to be involved in Christian work, they tell us to stay in the church and help them there."

A third problem is caused by culture shock. Even when missionaries work in their home nation or an adjoining country, they may find that things are very different. We have heard of missionary candidates from various parts of India who had heated arguments about the proper way to cook rice. We know of one Japanese missionary who worked in Thailand and faced quite a lot of animosity because of Japanese aggression in the war.

A fourth obstacle is financing. We have met many Brazilian missionaries in Europe who said, "Our church blessed us and said they would be right behind us, but they haven't sent us anything." We met one young family who came to the U.K. as missionaries and had to live in a room in a church. It is a serious problem. Within Nigeria or even within West Africa, Nigerians can cope financially. But if God calls them to work further afield, many cannot do it at the moment because they do not have the financial resources.

A fifth problem is the education of children. What do you do about your child's schooling if you're a Christian missionary working in an Islamic area? You can't send them to the local Islamic school. You want them to attend the nearest missionary children's school, until you realize that a term's fee will be about five years of your whole salary! One couple we know, the Famonwes, have a vision to start a school for the children of Nigerian missionaries. This is a real need.

The sixth hindrance is a lack of training. Hundreds of missionaries have gone out from Brazil in recent years, but many are returning home after a relatively short time. Many are disillusioned because they find that Portugal, Angola or other countries are not the same as Brazil. For example, although Portugal may have the same language, the culture is very different, and the people are not as responsive or as enthusiastic as Brazilians.

Koreans have a real potential in world mission, yet they are strongly monocultural and find it difficult to understand other cultures. Such problems can best be overcome by the provision of adequate cross-cultural missionary training.

ROSEMARY: How can North American churches cooperate with Two-Thirds World missions to maximize their effectiveness? One instant reaction is the easy way out: "They're taking up the battle and carrying the torch of mission. Great! We can sit back and watch it go by. They can do it, therefore we can give up." In the past they didn't send missionaries because we seemed to teach that it was our job. Now, simply because others are shouldering the task of the Great Commission does not mean that we can lay it down.

Another reaction is that if it is so much cheaper to send someone from the Two-Thirds World to an unreached people group, then let's stop sending North American missionaries and just subsidize the local people in their efforts. Simply to send money is a very abbreviated, abridged method of participating. Without personal connections, the blessing of being involved in mission is going to be taken from us.

One danger is dependency. If we send the money, they are doing what we want. We are directing and encouraging them to think that they can't raise the funds to do their projects.

Maybe that isn't even as bad as the loss of credibility which may result. Indian Evangelical Mission and Friends Missionary Prayer Band both will not accept money from Western sources for evangelism at all. They hear Hindus say, "You're bringing a foreign religion. We've got our own." They reply, "No, Jesus was born in Asia." Next, the Hindus counter, "You're being paid by foreigners to come." They are able to respond, "No, we're not; Indians gave the money." And this is when the

Hindus start to listen, when they realize it's other Indian Christians who are sponsoring the team. When you go to people of other faiths, they are soon going to ask where you get your resources.

One way for North American and British churches to interact is to request literature from some of these indigeneous missions and then ask, "How can we pray for you?" These people are going into real spiritual warfare. One group went to a Hindu town, was stoned and sent away, just like Saint Paul. Yet one of the team—who had nearly been killed—said, "I feel that the people there were ready for the gospel. I must go back." He went, and there is now a church in that town. In another area, the Hindus said, "Either you leave or we kill you." They took all the team's possessions and put them at the bus stop. Christians going into these situations need our prayers. It would be good to be "yoked" with a particular mission, keeping informed about its activities, and praying regularly for its needs.

As we learn about Two-Thirds World missions in a more personal way, we're being challenged to find ways to cooperate. Some are joining international missions because they wish to go to other countries, such as from Nigeria to Ghana, or Ghana to Zambia. CrossLinks, our Episcopal mission, is paying for a Christian from the Middle East to live in Spain to be involved in media broadcasting across North Africa, and she's much better at it than we could be. They are also supporting an Indian teacher in Tanzania, and other Indians to work among Asians in the U.K.

There is a dilemma about how to fund Two-Thirds world missionaries in Western missions. The North American system depends upon each missionary raising his or her own support, but how can you help people who are unable to do this? Our mission, generally, has run on a more Episcopal line: the churches send money to the mission and it is then shared out. But, are we willing to take that risk? Some of these people won't be bringing their own money in and will need to be subsidized by others. Are we willing to work together?

We have got to organize. For example, we might need a church in Washington, D.C., to support Joseph from Nigeria to go to Morocco, even though he is not one of their congregation. Often churches will only support their own people, giving to individuals instead of missions. Are we willing to make the sacrifice to support somebody else?

DAVID: We really need to facilitate greater partnership. In the future, we should be saying that part of the vision of a particular mission is to partner with our brothers and sisters in the Two-Thirds World; therefore we want to build a fund whereby we can finance them as well. I suspect that people might really latch onto this concept if they understood it.

ROSEMARY: Multi-cultural mission sounds good, but when you cannot talk to your fellow missionary because he only speaks Urdu, do we conclude that everyone needs to learn English, which is what usually happens in international missions? Do we think we're superior because we come from the West?

There are basically four areas in which the West can subsidize indigeneous missionaries without compromising their evangelistic efforts.

First: capital expenses. Although Indian Evangelical Mission and Friends Missionary Prayer Band do not want money for evangelism, they will take funds for necessary buildings, especially for training centers. ECMC has raised money for Yavatmal College for Leadership Training.

Second: medical expenses. The salaries for Indian and Nigerian pastors and missionaries are so low that if a wife must have an operation, or a child needs medical treatment, they can't afford it unless there are special gifts for the purpose. Special medical emergency funds could receive money from overseas.

Third: children's education. The Indian missions have set up schools for missionary children. They were sending educated missionaries to tribal areas where there was no education for their children, necessitating the use of boarding schools. These schools indirectly support evangelism by keeping those missionaries on the field and are worthy of support.

Fourth: training. We have had experience in training missionaries for fifteen years, so this is why our mission has released us to be available where needed in the Two-Thirds World to encourage missionary training. Don McCurry would come into this category, as he is available to travel and train people for Islamic mission. There is a general need for help in training, and also for books and literature. At the Nigerian mission we visited in November, the library was a funny little storage room off a garage, with tattered, old books on a rundown bookshelf next to a motorbike.

These people are actually getting on with the job, so one does not want to spoil it all by giving them missiological degrees. A lady who set up a training center for East Africa said her non-graduates tended to be better missionaries in the rural areas. It could be a different story in the cities. But because they are trying to evangelize unreached people groups, higher education is not the most necessary thing; it's the ability to live simply. So, training and libraries need to be appropriate. Big books and tomes are not essential, rather basic biblical teaching and simple books giving an overview of the history of missions from a world perspective would be helpful.

DAVID: *Perspectives on the World Christian Movement* by Ralph Winter is being published in Nigeria at a fraction of the cost, and it has been very helpful. That is one way that the U.S. Center for World Mission is helping.

One of the greatest witnesses of the gospel is when there are international teams, such as Nigerians working with North Americans, and Koreans working with the English. This clearly demonstrates that mission is not a Western thing. The church is an international body, and that is what the Lord's vision is.

RECONCILIATION: A COMPELLING MORAL VISION FOR EASTERN EUROPE

The Rev. Brian Cox

All of this is from God, who reconciled us to himself through Christ and gave us the ministry of reconciliation: that God was reconciling the world to himself in Christ, not counting men's sins against them. And he has committed to us the message of reconciliation. We are therefore Christ's ambassadors, as though God were making his appeal through us. We implore you on Christ's behalf: Be reconciled to God (2Cor 5:18-20; NIV).

One of the things I like to do is to take informal polls. Some years ago I took one in which I asked people what they thought the message of Jesus was. I asked this of people both inside and outside the church. The answers were very interesting. The most common answer was that the message of Jesus was about love, in terms of "Do unto others as you would have them do unto you." The second answer was that the message of Jesus had to do with salvation. Certainly the Bible talks a lot about love and salvation. But as I read the New Testament, I find that the primary message of Jesus had to do with the Kingdom of God. The message of John the Baptist, as the forerunner of the Messiah, was that the Kingdom of God is coming and is near. The message of Jesus was a little different. His message was that the Kingdom of God is upon you. It is here.

The question becomes, "What is the Kingdom of God?" As I read the Bible, and particularly the New Testament, the heart of the Kingdom of God is the experience of reconciliation with God, self, and others. We have something unique to offer people because they cannot find reconciliation anywhere except through Jesus Christ. The church may try to be a social organization, but in many places private enterprise does it better and more efficiently. Our primary job is not to be a social organization. Our primary job is to talk about the Kingdom of God, the heart of which is the experience of reconciliation.

This is something that I have come to see more clearly as I became involved in the work of the kingdom in east Central Europe. My involvement in the work of reconciliation began with a watershed experience when I did a sabbatical in South Africa in 1984. While I was there, I began to reflect on the gospel in the context of society. Without realizing it, I was becoming more sensitive to the biblical message of reconciliation.

Sometime later I attended a meeting in northern Virginia with a group of renewal leaders from the United States, the United Kingdom and South Africa to talk about establishing a ministry called SOMA in the United States. What was unknown to me at the time was, they had invited me because they had decided that I was the person to do the pioneering work to establish SOMA in the United States. It took three days of my being with them before I could come to that realization for myself. In 1985, I began pioneering the work of SOMA, Sharing of Ministries Abroad, as the first National Director. Our primary focus was spreading renewal throughout the Anglican Communion. Teams of clergy and lay people were taken to Latin America, Africa, Asia and the Middle East to conduct renewal conferences for clergy and lay leaders.

In February 1989, a colleague in Atlanta called saying that he felt that the Lord had laid it on his heart that he and I should take a SOMA team to East Germany. That really came out of left field because SOMA had not had any involvement in the Eastern Bloc. I said to him, "There is one problem. Nobody is inviting us. Without an invitation, you cannot get a visa, and without a visa, you cannot get in." What I sensed, however, was that the Holy Spirit had prompted the phone call, so I said, "Look, today is Tuesday. Why don't you and I agree that every Tuesday we will pray for East Germany? We will pray that God will open doors and knock down walls." I was speaking metaphorically. I did not think God would take it so seriously as to knock down the Berlin Wall! So often we are exhorted to pray for missions and what happens? God begins to change our own hearts and us as individuals. So I began to pray for

East Germany. A couple weeks later, I remembered a man by the name of Paul Toaspern. Paul was the leader of City Mission for twenty-eight years for the East German Lutheran Church, and also the head of the East German charismatic renewal. We had met in England in 1984 but had had no further contact. I began to pray for him, all the while not knowing what his circumstances were at the time.

In June of 1989, at an international meeting in Jerusalem of about 100 leaders, the group was in prayer, focusing on renewal, world mission and world evangelization. There were extended sessions of praise and intense prayer into certain areas of the world. Two areas were identified as major areas into which the gospel needed to penetrate; one was the Eastern Bloc and the other was Islam. On one particular afternoon, the group was in prayer and doing spiritual warfare for the Eastern Bloc. During that time, the Holy Spirit impressed upon me a particular verse. It was Habakkuk 1:5, "Look at the nations and watch—and be utterly amazed. For I am going to do something in your days that you would not believe, even if you were told." I shared that aloud with the group. Larry Christiansen, who was sitting right in front of me, turned around and said, "I really want to confirm and affirm that Word. I really feel that the Lord gave you that Word." I had no way of knowing that something big was about to happen.

The next thing was seeing a news clip on November 9, 1989, of the beginning of the dismantling of the Berlin Wall. I remember that I began to cry because I felt as if I had been a part of that; small, but nevertheless I felt that God had begun to bring me into the situation in terms of my heart and my emotions.

The next major event for me happened on December 10, 1989, during an 8:00 a.m. worship service at our church. In the Episcopal Church, as we all know, God does not attend an 8:00 a.m. service. However, there was a sung prophecy, one of those abiding prophecies which you only hear perhaps once in ten years. It electrified that worship! Even more interesting was that our diocesan bishop was attending the service and he heard all of this. The prophecy had such an effect on the service that we stopped it right there, pondered that word and we prayed into it. Basically, it was a Macedonian call that said we were to go to Eastern Europe. That morning I knew that God was speaking to me personally. At lunch, the bishop confirmed my feelings by saying, "I think God was really speaking to your church this morning. I do not think you can ignore it." I realized that we had to begin to take this seriously.

I began to wrestle with what Israel did before they went into the Promised Land. They sent out a scouting team, so we began to ponder the concept of a scouting team. Once we felt that this was what we were to do, I asked two other men to accompany me, and we were the scouting team. We settled on the places: East Germany, Czechoslovakia, Hungary and Romania. Our plan was to drive from Berlin to Bucharest on a pioneering mission. Before we left, we tried to establish whatever contact we could. We knew of a Reformed pastor in Hungary who had a ministry there called the Community of Reconciliation. I wrote to him to establish contact, but I never received a reply. A Romanian woman in the congregation was establishing a contact for us with the Evangelical Brethren Church of Romania. I was pursuing the one contact I had in East Germany, a Lutheran church in Leipzig. I had visited Bonn recently and had dinner with a member of the German parliament who told me how the revolution actually began in this Leipzig church. He felt strongly enough about my going there to send me the address of the senior pastor and the superintendent. I wrote to him and, again, received no reply. As for Czechoslovakia, we had no contacts at all.

When it came time to go, we had such a very sketchy idea of what we were going to be doing that we even considered canceling the mission. We decided to step out in faith. My seat on the plane was in a row of five and there was only one other gentleman in the row. As I was waiting for the plane to get on the runway, I was reading my briefing book on Czechoslovakia and the gentleman leaned over and said, "That's my country." In our discussion, he told me he had fled to Los Angeles in 1953, had become a prosperous businessman and that his uncle was the Provincial of the Franciscan order in Czechoslovakia. He asked if I was planning to go to Prague and the purpose for my visit. I explained that we were actually on a scouting mission for our church and that it was our intent to establish friendships and begin to understand the need and the situation there. Then he said, "Who are you planning to see?" I thought about that for a minute and then I said, "Well, I don't know." I was not sure how he would respond to that, but he said, "Would you be interested in meeting leaders from the underground Roman Catholic Church?" That was the beginning.

Three days later, when we arrived in Prague and checked into the hotel, there was a letter from this gentleman waiting for me. The letter said that in an hour we would be picked up by a Brother Filip from the Dominican Order! For about the first hour-and-a-half it was like meeting someone from another planet. I have had a great deal of overseas international cross-cultural experience, I am comfortable relating to people from other cultures and am familiar with the initial discomfort and awkwardness, so this was normal. During the conversation, Brother Filip shared the fact that some years previously he had had a tremendous conversion experience where he had been filled with the Holy Spirit. It was as if a light had suddenly been turned on; I realized that we had everything in common. We began to share with Brother Filip about the purpose of our visit, which even then we knew had something to do with reconciliation. He was excited and arranged for us to see his Father Confessor, who was the deputy to the Archbishop of Prague. The next day we found ourselves in a meeting with a priest who was the leader of the Roman Catholic charismatic movement in Czechoslovakia. Next, Brother Filip took us to see the provincial of his order, Father Dominic, who had been in prison for two years and shared a jail cell with a man by the name of Vaclav Havel, who had become president of Czechoslovakia. God just began to open doors sovereignly. All we did was show up.

In Leipzig, it happened again. We arrived on a Saturday night and attended a service the next morning. We were approached by a young man who spoke very good English. He took us around, introduced us to other people and that evening we were in their homes having fellowship with them. Years later, he told me that on the night of our arrival he had dreamed of three Americans coming to the church. In the dream he was told to welcome them into the fold. God had been preparing our way. Over and over similar experiences were repeated as God opened doors. I have now been to east Central Europe twelve or thirteen times.

As I have spoken to leaders and groups in east Central Europe, a five-point message has evolved which is what I believe God has called me to impart to them. The first point of the message is that east Central Europe needs a compelling moral vision. Most Westerners do not understand that Marxism was a moral vision for society. Westerners tend to think of Marxism simply as an economic system. It was much more. It was a moral vision for society. Even dissidents against Communism say that Bolshevism gets into the blood. It affects the way people think, their values, the whole way they approach life. As I listened carefully to people, I began to see that from both a spiritual and a political side, something truly historic had happened. One moral vision for society had collapsed and there was now a vacuum throughout east Central Europe. A new moral vision for society had not yet been born. In other words, Marxism as a moral vision for society had collapsed, but there had yet to be born a new moral vision.

The second point is that reconciliation is the name for this compelling moral vision for society. It is a single word, but I find that the word *reconciliation* is a powerful word in any language. I don't know what it is about that word reconciliation, but it brings out powerful feelings wherever it is discussed. In 1993, I gave a speech in the Czech parliament about reconciliation and it evoked a heated discussion amongst the parliament members. I spoke in a high school gymnasium in Bratislava, Slovakia on reconciliation and, again, a heated discussion in the class. In August 1993, I was in Zagreb, Croatia, and as we began to speak about reconciliation, as you might imagine in a nation at war, it provoked quite strong reactions. There is something very powerful about that word. The fact is, reconciliation speaks of the importance of personal relationships, whether between two individuals or two nations. It speaks of a society in which everyone is included, and diversity of thought, expression and personality is allowed.

Reconciliation speaks of a society that is open and allows for cultural integrity and social mobility. Reconciliation speaks of a society that is able to resolve conflict peacefully. That is an important thing in east Central Europe. Reconciliation speaks of a society that places importance on the healing of relationships and on forgiveness. Reconciliation speaks of a society that respects the dignity and human rights of every person. Reconciliation speaks of a society that can look openly and honestly at its past, so that the emotional and spiritual wounds of its victims can be healed. The current situation in South Africa is, I believe, entering a very difficult time. As South Africa moves toward political justice, there must be a healing of the spiritual and emotional wounds in the black, the colored, and the Asian communities from what they have suffered. The sins of apartheid are not over yet; there is still much to be healed. Society has to be able to look openly and honestly at its past. President Havel of Czechoslovakia has a great heart and a desire to be a reconciling force in the nation, but he made a key mistake early in his presidency. In a public statement, he said that he felt it was time for the society to move forward, for there to be healing, to put the past behind and forget it. The people who agreed with him were the Communists. But for the people who had suffered because of the crimes of the Communists, there was no acknowledgment of the pain and suffering that had been caused. I have come to realize that there cannot be true and full reconciliation unless the pain and the suffering have been acknowledged.

Reconciliation speaks of a society that recognizes and values the spiritual hunger within all of its people and gives them the freedom to find peace with God in whatever way they choose. Reconciliation is a vision that is clear, easy to understand, easy to articulate. It is a vision that is people oriented. It says, "We put people first in our society." It is a vision that ultimately glorifies God. Reconciliation is not just a spiritual word; it is an inherently political word because it talks about how, as people, we are going to live together.

The third point is that reconciliation has many facets. Reconciliation is the building of bridges, of understanding and creating unity in the midst of diversity. The goal of reconciliation is unity, not uniformity. Our own society is experiencing the tension of multiculturalism as a heated issue currently. What we are really struggling with is, how can we learn to find unity in the midst of diversity within our society and to value the diversity of different people? What are the limits of diversity? As a society, we have not answered that yet.

Reconciliation has to do with demolishing the walls of hostility between people. Sometimes walls will grow up between people over irreconcilable viewpoints. As an example, the people in the Pro-Life and Pro-Choice movements in our country have irreconcilable viewpoints. Often what happens is that people tend to personalize their feelings about an issue. A person who is Pro-Choice becomes a sort of Darth Vader to someone in the Pro-Life Movement. Irreconcilable viewpoints within a society can become the means by which walls of hostility grow between people. Sometimes it has to do with personality conflicts; people simply do not like each other. In the political movements in east Central Europe, two political parties may basically agree on all points, but they have split over personalities.

Inherited prejudice creates walls of hostility and we all have inherited prejudice. I do not believe people who tell me that they are not prejudiced. Either they do not know themselves very well, or they are just not being honest. To one degree or another, we all have prejudice, which can get in the way and create walls between people.

Another facet of reconciliation has to do with conflict resolution. This is a process of peacefully resolving open conflict between two or more parties. The goal is to bring about a cessation of hostilities and a non-zero sum gain solution.

Yet another facet of reconciliation has to do with the healing of relationships so that two parties can come to a place of forgiving each other, removing the cause of the conflict, being willing to bear the pain of that which cannot be changed, and being willling to acknowledge the pain and suffering caused to each other.

Reconciliation is also about social justice, that process that establishes justice in the heart or soul of a nation. Some key words to aid in this understanding are respect, human rights and equity. The goal of reconciliation is a just society in terms of its political, economic, and social structures.

When I was in South Africa, conservative, white Christians could be heard saying, "I really do not understand what the problem is in the black community. Why can't we just be reconciled and get on with things?" The black Christians were saying, "There can be no true reconciliation until there is justice." They were right because true reconciliation cannot be found in the reality of injustice. Until that injustice is addressed, full and complete reconciliation will not be experienced.

Reconciliation has to do with the healing of old wounds. Throughout much of east Central Europe, there are many people who have suffered as a result of the crimes committed under Communist rule. There is a large community of former political prisoners who need spiritual and emotional healing. When I first began to talk about this concept with some of the leaders, it was a new concept for them. I spoke of the need for spiritual and emotional healing for former political prisoners because it is not possible to build a nation on a foundation of bitterness. Bitterness is something that is passed from generation to generation.

The fourth point of this message is the basis of unity. There is no ideology or institution that can bring unity to people. In my world travels, I have had the opportunity to interact with almost every major ideology in the world and I have yet to find one that unites people. There is also no institution of which I am aware that unites people. Even the church as an institution divides people. My question is, "Can we come together in the name and spirit of Jesus Christ?" I believe that Jesus, the person of Jesus, is the real basis of unity and reconciliation. This has to be stressed over and over again. When Jesus is removed from the process of reconciliation, only the illusion of reconciliation is left. It looks like reconciliation, it sounds like reconciliation, it smells like reconciliation, but it is not the real thing. In Bratislava, Slovakia, I was handed a publication by a Dutch group. They had started out as a Christian group, but they now say they are an interfaith body of people committed to reconciliation on the basis of a commitment to non-violence. Being committed to non-violence sounds good and there certainly have been some tremendous examples of that in this century. The basis of reconciliation, however, is not a commitment to non-violence. That is not going to reconcile anyone. As I read the New Testament, the basis of reconciliation is Jesus and only Jesus, and what he did on the cross.

Finally, the last part of the message that I bring to east Central Europe is a challenge. The challenge is for people to become instruments of reconciliation in their own society. I can bring the vision; I can impart that vision into the lives of individuals, but ultimately God has to raise them up and use them as instruments of reconciliation.

I believe God is doing something in our day that is truly phenomenal. I believe he is preparing for the great catch to come, but the way he is building the net is relationally, not organizationally. I believe that what is happening in our day is that God is building a net which has to do with linking together his people across denominational, city and international lines. At one level, these relationships appear to make no sense, to have no logic to them, but what God is doing is linking the Body of Christ together for the great catch of fish that is coming. Jesus promised that the harvest at the end would be greater than anything that had been experienced in the first century. Are we in the earliest stages of that great harvest?

THE BENEFITS OF
SHORT-TERM MISSION TRIPS

The Rev. Bill Francis

During the last thirty years, there has been a significant explosion of short-term missions. Not only are people being sent from our own nation to other parts of the world, but short-term missionaries are being raised up in other nations and are going out into the world. In 1975 there were six thousand missionaries sent from the United States, a number that increased to sixty thousand in 1987, just twelve short years. Churches, as well as parachurch organizations and missionary organizations, are involved in short-term outreaches. Classically, short-term mission outreach can be for two weeks or can be for as long as two years. Short-term outreach involves all sectors of society and denominations, inter-denominational and non-denominational churches, as well as people of all ages.

When we look to Scripture for a precedent to justify what is happening with short-term missions, we look to the Lord himself. The ministry of Jesus lasted just three years. That was one year more than what might be classified as a short-term mission experience. Of course, we are talking about the Son of God with great power and authority who was totally focused on his mission. Nevertheless, it was a relatively short period of time that changed the world forever. During his ministry, Jesus sent his twelve disciples to different towns and villages for short periods of time going door to door, witnessing to the Kingdom of God. Later, he sent out the seventy to various towns, villages and cities. He said he would follow them later. These short-term outreaches were to prepare for his coming to these locations. Paul's missionary journeys were also relatively short-term. The purpose of his journeys, of course, was to plant churches, but the short-term outreaches helped to prepare the way toward this end. Thus we see with both Jesus and Paul scriptural precedent in justifying short-term missions.

It may very well be that in the last half of this century there are more short-term missions than at any other time in the history of the church. This is very encouraging because short-term mission is highly strategic, not only for the cause of world evangelization, but also for the strengthening of the individual, the church, and the family. Let's consider now how these four areas are positively affected through short-term missions.

Having been involved in Youth With A Mission for twenty years, I have seen firsthand that short-term outreaches have strengthened the existing mission or church which the short-term outreaches served. During the time that I directed the YWAM work in El Paso, Texas, and Juarez, Mexico, we hosted some 1000 to 1500 people a year, who would come for outreaches to help our work. Our work included an orphanage, a medical outreach team, training schools, building houses for destitute people and various other programs. We greatly appreciated the help provided by these outreach teams. For example, we were able to renovate our office building in a matter of weeks instead of many months with their help.

This same thing happened on YWAM's University of the Nations Campus, situated on approximately sixty acres of land in Kona, Hawaii. Most of that campus has been built by church groups who have come to work for short periods of time. Church teams from all over the world have built an entire university campus which now trains and sends missionaries all over the world.

One of the most difficult nations in the world to reach for the gospel is Spain. SAMS missionaries John and Ninfa Dixon had labored there for three years, working very hard to produce a church. At the end of three years they had three people attending their church. Then a group of twelve people from Indianapolis helped them for two months on a short-term outreach, and now they have a church of fifty people. This number is highly significant for Spain.

Secondly, God uses short-term missions to strengthen the family. Our family witnessed this firsthand with a group called King's Kids, a ministry of Youth With a Mission. Our oldest daughter and son went on a King's Kids outreach to Leningrad before the Soviet Union had disintegrated. The group of kids ranged in age from ten to eighteen years. They worked with a church of sixty members for two weeks, doing street work through drama presentations that would draw a crowd. After the presentation the pastor would preach a sermon and then the church members would minister to individuals who expressed interest. In a period of just two weeks that church went from sixty to six hundred with the help of a group of young people who, supposedly, cannot be used of the Lord because they are too young. The ongoing work of this local church was definitely strengthened by this short-term outreach, and the kids grew in their walk with the Lord which in turn strengthened their families.

Short-term mission outreach produces long-term missionaries. A study done several years ago found that eighty percent of all long-term missionaries are in that position because of the inspiration and the call that the Lord gave to them on a short-term outreach. Operation Mobilization, over the years, has done extensive outreach into Italy. Currently the estimate is that fifty percent of all long-term missionaries in Italy have come from short-term outreach as conducted by Operation Mobilization.

Long-term mission organizations are born out of short-term outreach. This is how Youth With a Mission came into existence. It began primarily as a short-term outreach organization, but evolved into a full-time missionary movement. Today there are over 7200 full-time workers in YWAM, the vast majority hungry to do more than what the typical local church was able to provide.

The work we were doing in El Paso and Juarez was born out of a short-term outreach. In 1989, a group of three hundred YWAMers plus many local churches gave out, door to door, some 55,000 New Testaments covering the entire city and placing God's word, free of charge, into homes which had no Bible or New Testament. Not only was a New Testament placed in every home, but this outreach brought the Body of Christ together in a way that was unique and special. Relationships were built as they learned more about one another. It also gave the YWAM outreach credibility. We were able to do what we said we felt the Lord wanted us to do. A year later, when YWAM went in with a permanent mission work, there was established credibility and solid relationships, which made establishing permanent mission work much easier. Short-term outreach produces long-term missionaries and it produces long-term mission organizations.

How does it affect the individual? The Lord has given us the mandate to go. Actually, that was the last command Jesus gave to his disciples, and to us. It is something that all of us, as Christians, should be serious about doing. In Matthew 28:16-19, we see how Jesus means this to happen. When he gave that last commandment, the Great Commission, he didn't just tell his disciples that this was what they were to do and to get on with the work. The disciples came to Jesus as he was on the mountain. They met with him there, saw his resurrected body, his glory and all of his majesty. They fell down before him and worshipped him, praised him and gave him glory for who knows how long. It was then Jesus gave them the commandment to "go." The "go" is definitely a mandate, but it is so important that it proceed from a context of worship. As individuals, we must be in that right relationship with the Lord that comes through worship, prayer and preparation before him. Only then can we reach out to the world.

What are some of the benefits to the individuals who step out of their own comfort zones? The "go" of the gospel requires that we step out of those comfort zones, but once we press through we are able to meet the Lord who is waiting for us. It can be something of a fearful time because we find ourselves in unusual, and sometimes uncomfortable, situations. Taking the risk to venture out of our particular comfort zone allows the Lord the opportunity to meet us as individuals in a way he otherwise cannot. What a wonderful blessing we have as Christians to meet the Lord in new and fresh ways day by day. For the individual who does step out, there is a new sense of confidence, strength and blessing.

While we were in El Paso and Juarez, we had a discipleship training school for Mexican nationals. Traditionally, the Mexican people have been on the receiving end of missions, but they have something unique to give to the rest of the world through Jesus. People groups everywhere have a certain aspect of the Lord that can be revealed to the world through their culture and these Mexican young people in our training schools were an example of this. For instance, one school went to Minnesota and Michigan on their two-month outreach. They were able to preach in several public high schools, something which would have been impossible for Americans. In Michigan, they taught people in a Lutheran Reformed Church how to evangelize by going out with them day by day. They also worked with a Hispanic congregation of fifty or sixty people. This church grew to around 150 people. When these young people came back from evangelizing "the great white brother," they had a healthy confidence about them that they did not have before. They had been strengthened in their walk with the Lord. They also had the benefit of being exposed to other cultures and people groups and the opportunity to see how God works through them.

There is also that aspect of short-term outreach that allows for testing the ground. If anyone believes that he or she may be called into full-time missions, there is nothing better than being involved in one or two short-term outreach opportunities to provide a foundation for making that decision.

How does short-term mission outreach affect the family? Over the years, my wife, our four children and I have had opportunities to participate in outreach together. It has brought us closer together as a family and enabled us as individuals to grow closer to the Lord. During the summer of 1993 our family went with a King's Kids outreach into Mexico. The times of worship and mission that we experienced were powerful with such a sense of the presence of the Lord. When we are about what is on God's heart, when we worship him and share him, we can sense the power of his presence. During one time of worship and prayer at an orphanage in Juarez, two or three older teenagers said that they had spiritual needs. My eight-year-old son, along with two or three other kids his age, went to these teenagers and began to minister and pray for them. As a father, this blew me away!

Going on outreach together as a family is not always comfortable or easy, but the blessings far outweigh the discomforts. When our two oldest children were ten and thirteen, they went on a well-chaperoned, well-organized outreach trip to Jamaica for six weeks. They ministered in churches and witnessed in the streets and had a marvelous time. I was out of the country when they returned and my wife met them at the airport. When they got off the plane they were both crying and my wife thought, "Wow! They really missed us." That wasn't why they were crying; they wanted to go back to Jamaica, not because it was such a pretty nation, but because, for the first time, away from Mom and Dad and in a way they had never before experienced, they were used in ministry by the Lord. They wanted to go back and get more of the blessing. Imagine the effect that had on us! Since then either our children individually or all of us together have gone on short-term outreaches during the summer.

Finally, what does short-term outreach do for the local church? For the local church that is supportive of the outreach, there is great blessing. It is so very important that there be good communication between the pastor, the members of the outreach team and the congregation. To strengthen the relationship between the outreach team and the congregation, the support should be visible by commissioning the team. It is also vitally important to prepare the team with much prayer and clear and regular communication with one another. It takes time to learn about the culture, to communicate with the mission organization with whom the team will be involved and to make practical preparations. It is my recommendation that a year of preparation be set aside and after six months no new members be accepted on the team unless there are extenuating circumstances. It takes time and preparation to build relationships. Once that team has completed an outreach mission, there will be strong relationships that will have bonded as a result. That can only bless the church because the stronger we are in our relationships with one another, the stronger the church will be. This also helps the church to become more ministry-oriented because of the realization of how the Lord can use people as never before. New-found ministries can be applied to the local church as discovered on the short-term outreach and that can only add strength to that body.

It also takes time to raise the funds necessary to make the trip possible. There are a number of ways to raise the needed money and some good reasons for doing them. Young people, in particular, may not be able to raise enough to cover all their costs, but the experience of working to raise money teaches them what hard work produces, and it builds up their faith that God will provide.

Every outreach team needs a debriefing time when they can look at what the Lord has accomplished through them. They also need the opportunity to share their experiences with the congregation. This will be a real encouragement for both the team and the congregation and continues the enthusiasm for missions.

There are a few guidelines that I believe are important to keep in mind when making plans to do mission outreach. First of all, keep the expectations high, but under control. God undoubtedly wants to do marvelous things through his people, but his people should be going on outreach because they have a servant heart. An attitude of learning from the people being served is, I believe, indicative of a true servant and an attitude God will bless. It is also important to understand that every gift we have, or even no gift except a willingness to serve, can be used by God to increase his kingdom. Our gift to God is to be available; he will build the work because that is his business. Our business is to be available, contribute whatever it is that we have and allow God to use and bless our offering. With that understanding, outreach will be meaningful to us in whatever capacity we serve because the Lord will make us aware of that.

There can be pitfalls to doing short-term outreach but many can be prevented by doing good preparation. Generally short-term outreach is a great strength and blessing to the mission organization being served, the one doing the serving, the local church supporting the outreach and any family that is involved.

Finally, because mission is so central to God's heart, blessings seem to flow. Churches which are involved in reaching out beyond their walls receive spiritual and other blessings. God will pour out his blessings on those who are willing to reach out to the world in missions.

PARTNERS WITH RUSSIAN ORTHODOX

The Rt. Rev. Roger White and the Rev. Richard Kew

Two churches, the Church of England and the Episcopal Church USA were invited to participate in a special relationship with the Russian Orthodox Church as it emerged after seventy-two years of persecution. Throughout those seventy-two years of persecution, the Archbishop of Canterbury and the Presiding Bishop of the Episcopal Church in the United States had maintained contact and even made visitations to the Patriarch of Moscow. Because of the support given to the underground church through that period, when the Russian Orthodox Church emerged and was looking for friends, they came to the Anglican Church, specifically to the Church of England. The Bishop of Oxford, as the appointee of the Archbishop of Canterbury, and the Rt. Rev. Roger White, as the appointee of the Presiding Bishop, were assigned the task of establishing a team that could be of practical assistance to the Russian Orthodox Church as it came out of this period of persecution.

The additional team members are Canon Dr. Robert Wright of General Theological Seminary and Suzanne Massie from The Harvard Russian Research Center. Ms. Massie wrote *Nicholas and Alexandra* and *The Firebirds*, is an authority on Russia, speaks fluent Russian, and is an honorary citizen of St. Petersburg. There is a counterpart team in Russia with Archbishop Kliment of Kaluga and Borosk, a diocese just outside Moscow. He is second-in-command of the Russian Orthodox Department of External Affairs, the department which deals with all affairs with government and with other churches and the Russian Orthodox Church. The head of the department is Metropolitan (Cardinal) Kyois. The other members of the Russian team are a layman who has long been associated with the External Affairs department, Valeri Chukoloff, as well as a female staff member from that department. These two committees form a coordinating committee that meets twice a year, once in Moscow and once in the United States.

An exceedingly warm relationship has been established with the Patriarch of Moscow, His Holiness Alexi II. In the hierarchy of the Catholic world, the Pope is the head of the Roman Catholic Church; in the Orthodox Church the Patriarch of Constantinople is number one and the Patriarch of Moscow is number two. He is an incredibly influential person in Orthodoxy. It is quite unusual for the patriarch not to be a Russian, but this gentleman happens to be an Estonian from that tiny country to the West.

After so many years of persecution, the basic structure of the Orthodox Church has survived; namely, a patriarch and the Holy Synod. In the Russian Orthodox Church everything is done by the Holy Synod, made up of eleven metropolitans and the patriarch. They appoint all the bishops and give consent for everything. In Rome, the Curia, a much smaller group of individuals, is the decision-making body. What has emerged in Russia is a very primitive church totally out of touch with the rest of Christianity. It is somewhat czarist in structure and background, because that is where it came from. It is a church that went underground during the Communist regime and emerges now with a liturgy in the archaic language of Old Church Slavonic that is not understood by modern Russians, rather like using Latin for the Roman Catholics. It also is a church with very few clergy and only three functioning seminaries (Note: Nearly fifty seminaries by 1995).

To get a perspective on the condition of the church, it is thought that during the Communist regime in Russia more than 70 million Russians died. Almost all the Orthodox priests and also many believers simply disappeared off the face of the earth. Under Stalin, there was reportedly a time when only 600 churches were left open in the whole Soviet Union. For sport, Kruschev used to send army units out to blow up village churches. During the Kruschev years, 20,000 Orthodox churches were destroyed and most of the other churches and their buildings were taken over by the government and used for whatever purpose they felt was appropriate; they were turned into bakeries, garages for storing school buses, for maintaining tanks and other uses for thirty, forty or fifty years. In the first three years after the end of Communist rule, 30,000 church buildings were returned to the Russian Orthodox Church, along with the monasteries and all the lands belonging to the monasteries. All of a sudden this church, which has very little structure, few priests and only three seminaries finds itself with all this property. At the same time, the monetary system has fallen apart. The ruble is worth nothing and here is this emerging church with no money, all these churches and all this property. Yet, churches are being restored all over Russia by the village people as they begin to feel safe enough to state that they are, and have always been, believers. Russia probably has 60 million Russian Orthodox believers. There is a very large number of emerging Christians; some of them surprising ones that no one ever knew were Christian.

In that three-year period, the Russian Orthodox Church went from three seminaries to thirty-two, and now the number is fifty. Those seminaries are full and are producing priests. The seminary in Minsk, which is in the country of Belarus, will graduate 184 priests in June of 1994. The church, and the graduates themselves, admit that they are poorly prepared, but the need for priests is so desperate that they are getting them through the seminary as rapidly as possible. There are presently more than a thousand students at one of the Moscow theological institutes and four hundred at the seminary in St. Petersburg. Convents have been returned and there are newly established religious communities where nuns and monks are coming in large numbers.

Persecuted people, as they emerge, are ultra-conservative, very suspicious and elitist. To them, a test of Christian faith is in how long an individual has been persecuted and remained faithful. This becomes evident when the Russian Orthodox asks of all those Americans pouring into the country trying to convert everybody, "How many years of persecution have you endured? Is your faith soft, or is it really firm?" Because as Americans, we must reply that we have never been persecuted, the Russians are very skeptical. They have come forth as a church where everybody knew who the believers were because their very lives depended on it. They are suspicious not only of other Russians, but also of other churches. There is enormous hatred in the Russian Orthodox Church, and in Russia generally, for the Roman Catholic Church. That is seen clearly in Yugoslavia, between the Croats and the Serbs. One reason for that is that the Pope, for the first time ever, appointed an archbishop for the mission in Moscow. This is interpreted as a direct affront to the Patriarch of Moscow, so there is animosity between them. This further aggravates the long-standing rift which has existed since the Great Division between the Eastern and Western church. Unfortunately, in ecumenical affairs, Rome still says that when the Orthodox people become Catholic there will be unity; the Orthodox Church says that when the Catholics become Orthodox, there will be unity, resulting in a logjam.

In 1993, 220,000 Americans were bringing their brand of Christianity to Russia. Every kind of sect imaginable was pouring into the country without any control. The attitude was one of "Let's convert the Commies." No one gave a thought to the fact that some of them might not be communist, but rather Russian Orthodox. In an attempt to put some legislation in place that would clarify the issue of who could enter Russia as missionaries, the government asked the churches to formulate a policy. The Orthodox Church asked a Baptist leader, a Roman Catholic bishop, an Orthodox archbishop and a member of the Protestant churches in Russia to survey Western countries for their policies for missions. They found that it is very difficult to get into the United States as a missionary unless a church here provides sponsorship. It is impossible to get into Italy or Spain because of the influence of the Roman Catholic Church on those governments to disallow visas. Britain is becoming more difficult because of the threat of Islamic terrorist groups.

The Russians decided to go the way of being as open as possible and suggested legislation allowing anyone into the country who was established in their home country as a church. That meant that in the United States for example, an entity recognized as not-for-profit could get a visa. There was misunderstanding of the legislation in our press and, in particular, by the Southern Baptists, who felt that the Russian Orthodox Church was trying to prevent Baptists from entering Russia. Interestingly, the Patriarch had said, "The Russian Orthodox Church does not see itself as the exclusive church in Russia," and Metropolitan Kyril has said, "The Russian Orthodox Church has always been and remains persistent in its pursuit for religious liberty for all people." However, pressure was put on President Clinton who called President Yeltsin and asked him to veto the legislation, saying that to pass it would be disruptive to the relationship between Russia and the United States. The Russian Parliament ultimately overruled the veto, but nine days later shells were going through the parliament windows and it was all for naught.

The point is, however, that there was a desire for some control to protect the people of Russia from every conceivable sect pouring into the land trying to proselytize everyone, including the Russian Orthodox. The Russian Orthodox Church has always been a very active member of the World Council of Churches and there is an agreement among the members of that council not to steal members from each other. The Russian Orthodox folks are particularly incensed because one group that is really trying hard to establish itself there is the United Methodist Church, and they are trying to convert everybody—Russian Orthodox included.

This very primitive, very basic church bases most of its teaching on icons so people can understand the story of Christ, the story of the Trinity, and Scripture. This church does not understand the well-financed Western church and its use of radio and television that have inundated their country with modern technology. For all those seventy years of persecution, these believing people have been "non-people," who in the eyes of existing authority simply did not exist. A known believer was not allowed to have any land in order to grow vegetables, and in Russia, two-thirds of the food is grown on private plots, not in communal farms. A believer could not get any food that was distributed in a village; a believer's children could not go beyond the eighth grade in school. A believer was a "non-person" and simply did not exist. This Russian Orthodox Church that has emerged is comprised of poor and uneducated people, and that was very intentional. They are not a sophisticated group of people and they do not understand the intricacies involved in Western evangelism.

The current fiscal situation in Russia is such that it could soon be bankrupt and this will impact the United States because we will have to bail them out. As an example of what things are like for the Russian people, the man who is head of communications for the Russian Orthodox Church earns forty-five dollars per month; his father, the dean of a very large engineering school in Moscow, earns forty-five dollars per month and his mother, who is a professor, also earns forty-five dollars a month. Their apartment rent is $110 a month, so he lives with six adults in order to exist in Moscow. This is devastating for the life of the church. There is growing antagonism toward Western culture, especially to Americans, because of the belief that what is being imported is not appropriate, not helpful to family life, and not helpful to Russian life, giving rise to growing pro-Russian sentiment. Also, the country is being overtaken by gangs and ethnic mafias. Thirty percent of the Russian economy is controlled by gangs of Mafiosi. This did not exist under Communist domination.

The programs established at this point basically have to do with the exchange of people. There are five dioceses in the United States that are linked to Russian dioceses. There are also parishes linked to parishes and bishops to bishops. Seminarians, mainly from Russia, are doing exchange visits and attending seminary in this country. Laypeople and numerous young people and groups are participating in exchanges, and tours of laypeople from the Episcopal Church in the United States to Moscow, St. Petersburg and other areas offer the opportunity to share expertise. Such areas as communications skills, social outreach, how to do ministry as a church in a local community, evangelism and Christian formation, and the whole area of Christian education are where the needs are great. There are thousands of church schools and Sunday schools emerging for the first time in the Russian Orthodox Church with hundreds and hundreds of kids involved. The need is great for practical assistance in these areas.

Work is being done with the World Council of Churches to assist in such areas as social and educational work, hospital development, ministry to aging people, and the development of schools from kindergarten to college. They want to establish Christian schools. In Russia, Christian education is required in all the secular schools, but the Russian Orthodox Church wants to establish their own schools, colleges and post-graduate colleges so they can involve their own young people.

The Russian Orthodox Church has requested theological dialogue. They have been in the backwoods and out of touch for so long. Some theologians from the United States went to Moscow and were joined by theologians from both Moscow and St. Petersburg to have our first discussions. The conversations, at their request, centered on episcopacy and we discovered an enormous amount of commonality, both in the practical aspects of being a bishop and in our theological understanding. They have asked that these discussions continue and touch on other theological areas. While they do not ordain women, they are very interested in discussions on this issue. There are many women in Russia in significant positions of leadership in the life of the church, but they do not ordain women. They also question the ordination of homosexuals.

St. Xenia's Hospital in St. Petersburg was established and is now operational with major assistance from the Presiding Bishop's Fund. They have a great need for agricultural development expertise. The monks in the monasteries, who now find themselves with two hundred acres of land, do not know anything about farming.

The Russian Orthodox Church has survived through a very rough time under the Communists. The harassment that started under Stalin continued into the late 1980s. There was, however, freedom within very small parameters to minister and exercise pastoral care. Many people think that the church has been compromised by the KGB and the truth of that depends on how we interpret "compromise." Any priest or bishop attempting to do the work of God had to keep the KGB relatively happy, because there was always at least one KGB informant in the congregation. The priests were not allowed to wear their robes in public, a priest could not wear any distinguishing garments, and the clergy were the only people to pay taxes, so they have carried an enormous burden. Inevitably they had to strike up some type of working relationship with the KGB in order to minister to the people. If that is compromise, then that is what they did. Now every barrel has its bad apples and some clergy did become total KGB informants. There were also those who were prepared to make the necessary sacrifices in order to care for the people God had entrusted to them. The dissidents are the ones who made no compromises at all and they could be tools in the hands of the KGB by spreading rumors. It is important now that new leaders be trained who have not been in the priesthood or in church leadership throughout the Communist period. The KGB is still in existence, although in a different format, and still able to pull the strings that make life difficult.

There are many reasons to work with the Orthodox Church. It is the dominant religious group within Russia. As Anglicans and Orthodox, we are very close to each other. The Orthodox are creedal Christians, affirming the Father, Son and Holy Spirit. They believe that the Holy Spirit regenerates people, they stand firmly on the authority of Scripture, and they are a church which has been shaped by and shapes Russian culture. God has given us this as a gift so that we might share some of our riches with them and they might share some of their riches with us. In June of 1992, Metropolitan Juvenaly, the number two man in the Orthodox Church, said that in our relationship they would like a partnership in charity and catechesis. The Russian church provides a tremendous amount of care for people in the area of charity, particularly since the demise of the government that had provided a very crude form of cradle-to-grave welfare.

SPCK is involved in catechesis teaching and has been one of those agencies in Britain which the Archbishop of Canterbury used to maintain the relationship with the Orthodox Church, making the involvement natural. The need for leadership was mentioned earlier. Over 20,000 churches have reopened since 1990 and there is a need for at least 15,000 priests, not only for parishes but for university, hospital, prison, and military chaplaincies. The Orthodox Church lacks monetary resources and the collapse of the currency has been a great burden. Two bishops from the United States consulted the Episcopal Church to provide support for one hundred seminarians. The Adopt-a-Russian Seminarian program has been very successful in providing support for seminarians by having parishes here provide sponsorship. A Russian seminarian can be trained for six hundred dollars a year and these are the men who will be the key leaders in the years to come.

The shortage of Christian literature in Russia is mammoth. The Russian people are highly literate, but Christian books were not allowed under the Communists. Twenty miles from the center of Moscow is St. Nicolai Kuznelsky Church, a parish that has become a center of thinking people who are being converted to Christ. Even though the Christians were kept deliberately uneducated, there were intelligent men and women feeling after God who found their way into the church and gave their lives to Jesus Christ. The rector of this parish holds a Ph.D. in Applied Physics from Moscow State University and the leader of the laymen is the head of the computer science department of Moscow State University. They established a little publishing house that is crucial because they are doing not only reprints of Orthodox classics, but also books on how to read the Bible, prayerbooks and devotional materials. The most important publications are the educational materials which we take so for granted. In 1991, religion could not be discussed with a child; now they have thousands of children in Sunday School. The children bring their parents to church and the parents are converted and baptized. Since the cost of publishing material in Russia is so low, seemingly small amounts of money can put a lot of material into the country.

The St. Tilchon Theological Institute was established to take these educated people who are coming to know Jesus and form their minds so that instead of thinking and functioning like Communists, they think and function like Christians. They are being taught how to study the Scriptures and to know the history of their country from a Christian point of view. The St. Nicolai publishing house is producing textbooks for the St. Tilchon Institute and these books will be duplicated and copied all over the country to provide good Christian education for others.

We in the Episcopal Church are able to help provide much-needed resources by producing Christian literature for education and devotional life. The Russian people are now receiving the Scriptures and the need is for supportive materials so that people can grow as they read and study the Bible. The most important thing, however, that can be done for the Russian Orthodox Church, and for ourselves as well, is to pray for one another. There is a real recognition that the American church needs prayer, the Episcopal Church needs prayer, and the Russian Orthodox Church as it emerges needs prayer. The exchange program has brought life to this because we can now pray for a brother or sister in another parish by name. Through prayer and God's grace, the Russian Orthodox will become a strong witness in that country. Through our continued dialogue and work we can look to more and more opportunities to be supportive to our Christian brothers and sisters in Russia.

COMMUNITY DEVELOPMENT IN THE U.S.

The Rev. Antoine (Tony) Campbell

To begin, the first thing that I would like you to do is think of two favors that you would like to ask somebody to do for you. Your two favors could be such things as: I would like you to call home for me; I would like you to wash my car; I would like you to give me a ride to the airport; I would like for you to give me your American Express Card. Ask the person you know the least to do one favor for you. Remember your second favor for use a little later.

This is a workshop on Christian community development. Community development is creating a Christian atmosphere within an entire community, not just in the community of the congregation, but the community in which you live.

Christian community development, I believe, begins with the incarnate Word. John 1:14 says, "And the Word became flesh and made His dwelling among us. We have seen His glory, the glory of the One and only who came from the Father, full of grace and truth." It is because of this Word, this Word that was made flesh, that we can live in hope. It is because this Word was made flesh, that we can live in peace. It is because this Word was made flesh that we can live in joy. It is this Word that transforms our lives and makes us into new people, makes us into people of joy. It makes us into people of hope. It makes us into people of mercy.

We didn't gather here just because we wanted to come up to the mountains of North Carolina. Instead, we came here because somehow Christ has touched all of our lives, somehow Jesus has made a powerful impact upon who we are, and that has brought us together making us one band, one body, one family, one body in Christ, because we have beheld the glory of Christ. It is this love that makes us one people, one person. It is the Holy Spirit that binds us together and makes us one. It is this Holy Spirit that makes us a family.

We are called to share this joy, this light, the knowledge of the Word made flesh that we have seen. It has brought joy and great happiness to our hearts, enables us to love one another, care about one another, to be a special people. When you share love it grows, when you share faith it grows and when you share the Light of Christ, it grows.

Not long ago, a friend of mine and his wife had twins. He called me at 3:00 in the morning and said, "Tony, Tony, Tony, I've got twins!" I could just feel his excitement. That is the kind of excitement we have in the life of Christ. I remember, when my first son was born, I was so happy and proud. Later, when Ben was sick all night, throwing up all over the place, with Julie and me walking the floor with this little baby, it finally dawned on me that, "Somebody did that for me!" Somebody loved me when I couldn't love myself. Somebody cared for me when I couldn't care for myself. Somebody got up in the middle of the night and walked the floor with me. Somebody loved me that much and I was able, because of that love, to share that love with somebody else. That is what Jesus has done for us. Because of that love we are able to share that love with somebody else. It makes you want to run down the street and shout, "I've got this! I know this person who has redeemed my life and saved my life and healed my life!"

I remember feeling so good at 4:00 that morning for what my Dad had done for me that I called him. When I got him on the phone, I said, "Dad, I just want to thank you for all that you did for me. I want to thank you for caring for me when I couldn't care for myself. I want to thank you for holding me in the middle of the night. I just want to thank you, Dad." My Dad said, "Son, that is fine but next time could you call me at 8:00 please."

Sometimes, in life, there are people who cannot hear the gospel because of the torrents of pain and hurt in their lives. Sometimes people are struggling so hard just to exist that they are unable to recognize or reach out to life and hope when it is offered. The Word incarnate will not become real unless the people of the Body of Christ incarnate their lives into the pain and hurt-filled lives of these people and lead them to safety.

The history of the church can be divided into four ages. The first is the Post-Apostolic Age, from about 30 AD to 311 AD. It was characterized by persecution. There were household churches where people met in small communities and supported one another. The interesting thing about it was that it was a contrast community, radically different from the people around it. People lived differently, cared about one another and contrasted so much from society that people were willing to join even at the risk of losing their own lives.

Then from 311 AD to 1789 AD, Constantine came in and we had the Age of Christendom where the church and state became united. It was an age of Christian domination when people were forced to become members of the church and the risk was in not joining. The whole notion of being a contrast community, people that care for people in the surrounding world, was lost.

The years between 1789 and 1960 can be called the Age of the Establishment Church. Protestant norms and values dominated society. There was an informal alliance between the state, education and the social and business world. There was prayer in schools and in order to succeed in business it was important to belong to the right church. The church was the center of community life. In small towns in the South there is a town square with a courthouse, surrounded by the local Baptist, Methodist, Presbyterian, Episcopal, or Pentecostal churches. Protestant norms and values dominated and not to join invited social disapproval.

The Post-Establishment Church came in 1960 with the election of

John Kennedy, and approval of being other than a Protestant to make it in society. American society is now marked by increasing specialization, increasing individualism. Church life has become marginalized. Efforts have been made to reestablish the 1950s church but now we have the great opportunity, once again, to become the contrast community. We have the opportunity to bring people in because we live in a manner so radically different from other people.

This is the time for us to do this because it is a time of church crisis. Between 1960 and 1980, together the Presbyterians, Lutherans, Methodists, Church of Christ and Episcopalians lost three million members, and ten thousand congregations. There is evidence of spiritual hunger because these people did not just disappear. During that same time the Assemblies of God grew by seventy percent: Jehovah's Witnesses grew by forty-five percent; Seventh Day Adventists grew by thirty-six percent; Southern Baptists grew by fifteen percent. Even the Roman Catholics grew by five percent.

There are other reasons why I believe we have a crisis now, an opportunity to reach out and really create a Christian community in the places where we live. I want to give you some statistics about how hard life is for children. If these don't make you cry, I don't know what will. There are 65 million children in America, 14 million of whom live in poverty. Of those children, twenty-four percent are under the age of six and fifty-five percent live in female-headed households. Over 100,000 children go to bed homeless each night; thirty percent of all first graders will not graduate; fifty-one percent of all African-American males will not graduate, at a cost of $250 billion a year in lost wages and taxes.

It is also a moral crisis because we have one million girls (one in ten) who will become pregnant this year. One million, four hundred thousand teenagers use drugs. Each day 100,000 children go to school armed, and 125,000 will not go to school because they are afraid. By the time children graduate from high school, twenty-five percent will have contracted some sexually transmitted disease. Between the ages of twenty and twenty-four, 9500 adults have been diagnosed with AIDS, which indicates exposure by the age of thirteen. This one is, I think, particularly damning to American society: thirty-four percent of all thirteen-year old children report that they have had sex with six or more partners. Jesus said, "The harvest is plentiful, but the laborers are few." One in four girls are sexually abused by the age of thirteen, and one in seven boys are sexually abused by the age of seventeen. We have a crisis in America and the church must step forward to build coalitions and ministries that will create community.

These statistics have a human face. We have a summer camp on Pawleys Island for abused and foster kids. I had talked about the presence of Jesus in our lives. Later one of the kids grabbed me by the sleeve, and said, "Rev, I want you to tell me where Jesus is in my life." I said, "What do you mean, son." He said, "Well, Rev, I am sixteen years old. I lived with my parents until my mom died. When my mama died, my father was an alcoholic and couldn't take care of us. I haven't seen my brothers and sisters in two years. I don't know where I am going to go when I leave here because the foster home I am in can't take me. I am sixteen years old, all I own is what I have on my back and I can't even read. So where is the presence of your Jesus in my life?" A young lady, thirteen years old, came into my office because she was pregnant. She said, "My mother and father have gotten a divorce, my mother hates me, I am pregnant with a child now, what does God have against me?" We have an opportunity as Christians to witness to the love of Christ. This means that we must be the arms and hands and feet of Christ. We must show the mercy of God in Christ.

Now, think about asking that second favor and asking it of the person you know the best. Which favor would be easier to ask, the first or second? The second, of course! The reason is because of the relationship you have with the person. This is the key to building Christian community in the church and the community. It is in relationships; it is in knowing people. It is in caring about people. It is in incarnating our lives into their lives and building relationships so we can lead them to safety.

The church often makes mistakes in building community. First, we don't seek out the call that people have on their own lives. Christian community cannot be built unless we know where each person's call is in their own life. A major mistake is in asking people to do things they don't want to do and are not called to do. We ask people to volunteer to do things forever. I am an athlete, and people just assume that I want to work with children. I do want to work with children, but I don't always want to work with children. The church often does this and the product is two fruits, guilt and anger, neither of which is in the list of gifts of the Spirit. Either a person is going to be angry because they are going to do something they aren't called to do and don't want to do. Or, they are going to feel guilty and just stop coming or not do the job.

The key to building Christian community is in building relationships among people, knowing their hopes, their dreams, their aspirations. In order to build community, find the cross in that community. Find the pain and need and bring people around these. Discover where their hopes and dreams are, what talents they have, what gifts God has blessed them with. Discover where they want to be good stewards with the resources God has given them. Discover where the call of God is in the midst of a congregation and people will become involved and active in responding to that call.

One of the things I like to ask churches is, "How big is your God? Is your God just big enough to handle the four walls, or can your God handle the entire community?" In Pawleys Island we believed that God was big enough to handle the entire community. Initially, we had a budget of about $60,000 a year, about $50,000 of which was given by the diocese. An average Sunday worship service had between five and sixteen people attending. There was about a $200,000 deficit in buildings that needed repair. Six years later there were between forty and fifty people at worship on Sunday morning, with a budget of $1.5 million and a staff of about twenty. Over three thousand homes had been built or repaired in the community. A new climate of hope had been created in a community where hope had been lost.

Community development happened in areas where there was pain, hurt and need. A summer program for children at risk had 160 kids from broken and foster homes throughout South Carolina. Children came and spent eight weeks in the camp learning language arts, math, reading, art, vocational training in auto mechanics, welding, data processing, hotel/motel management and golf course technology. A comparison of test scores done at the beginning and end of the camp showed a forty percent improvement in language, twenty-four percent improvement in math and seventeen percent in reading. Aptitudes were identified, providing these young people with hope and determination to work toward a more successful life.

A dental program was developed because so many children had never had dental care. An adult day care center was opened to care for seniors who were not having hot meals or socialization. Often the hot meals literally meant the difference between life and death. One elderly gentleman was observed dividing his food in half. He would eat half and take the other half home. On Fridays he would divide his meal into fourths. He had a wife who was an invalid and unable to come to the center and he was saving part of his meal to take home to her.

A medical clinic was opened using the services of a retired doctor who wanted to provide some service to the community. There is a Seeds of Hope program that assists poor farmers in selling their produce to the community.

Every program was tied to worship. There would be Christian devotions, Christian education or evangelism. All too often the church throws away the best it has to offer. People need the ultimate hope that is in the gospel: to develop social programs and exclude the gospel is totally out of balance.

The housing ministry built almost seven hundred homes in the aftermath of Hurricane Hugo. There was a kitchen where, at one point, two thousand meals a day were prepared. These efforts drew in people from all over the United States who were from every station in life, rich and poor alike. The beautiful part was that these people worked side by side to address the needs and pain and hunger and loss together in God's name.

The problem in America today is not that we don't have adequate laws. We have the laws on the books to say that we are supposed to be able to live together. The problem in America is that black, white, Chicano, elderly, young people don't know how to live with each other anymore. We have become a violent nation. It is only the church of Jesus Christ that has the answer. It is the only place that can teach people how to live with each other from the heart, because rules can't force that to happen.

One of our projects focuses on young people working on homes and building community with them and teaching them Christian values. Generally, the young people work on homes where there are other youngsters. There was one instance, however, where an elderly gentleman lived in a house that was so bad that we bent some of our own rules and brought in some young people to help. While they worked, this gentleman just sat on his porch and rocked and said nothing. The young people had grown accustomed to receiving some tangible expression of thanks for what they were doing, something to eat or drink or some comments from the homeowner. This gentleman said nothing and the kids got quite discouraged and wanted to leave. They were persuaded to remain for another day and, in a time of sharing, one young lady told about how she had decided to watch the man. She first noticed that she never saw him eat so when she went back to get lunch, she made him a sandwich. When she gave him the sandwich, he thanked her profusely and she realized that he did not have anything to eat so he couldn't offer the workers anything to eat.

She continued to observe the gentleman and late one afternoon his sister came to visit. He took her all over the house showing her the running water that had been installed, the first in his seventy-six years. He showed her the new windows and the repairs to his bedroom and living room ceilings to stop the leaks. Finally the old gentleman took his sister into the living room, dropped his cane and holding both her hands, with tears in his eyes, said, "Today I know my God is not asleep in heaven because today my prayers have been answered."

The young woman had to stop several times during her testimony because she was crying uncontrollably. Every young person who had worked on that house was crying uncontrollably. These young people had witnessed as powerful a proclamation of the gospel as any sermon or sacrament. Now they understood and were participants in Christian community and the key was in the building of relationships.

In our parish, we have claimed every problem in the community and we have claimed every resource in the community. It is like investing in the stock market. If we invest, then at year's end we get a dividend. If we don't invest, we get nothing. If the church erects walls and separates itself from the community, then when the community thinks about where to go and where to send money, it will not be to the church.

There is a housing project in South Carolina called St. Elizabeth's Place that was built with grant money. People in the area pointed out that in the seventeen years since Fritz Hollings had become a senator from South Carolina, no one had received this particular grant on the first try. The anticipated wait for this grant was five to six years. So, to get the project started, I set about organizing a board and I sought out people from the community who had a strong interest in the elderly and in housing. The first recruit was a doctor who "just happened" to be a friend of a gentleman by the name of Strom Thurmond. Another recruit was someone who was socially acquainted with Senator Hollings. The final recruit was a man with a deep concern for the elderly in the community and, just by coincidence (?), the father of the governor of South Carolina. Each of these people was made a member of the board for St. Elizabeth's Place and the application for the grant was submitted. It was the most amazing thing. When the application got to Washington, a call came back asking how much money was needed and how soon!

In order to do community development, whether it is housing, a medical clinic, a school or Christian education in your church, find out *what the need is,* find out *who wants to address the need* and *who has the talent to address the need.* Build relationships with people, find out what their hopes and dreams are, their aspirations and find out what their family connections are. Scripture tells us that "The light shines in the darkness and the darkness will never overcome it." Darkness won't overcome light because the Spirit of God blows through and in his people. He is constantly calling us to new life and new hope.

I was once in the company of a group of seminarians when one member of the group stated that he believed that sometimes God called us to fail. Most of the group nodded in agreement. I had not seen that in the Bible, so I told the group, "I don't know which book you are reading, but I can't find anywhere in my Bible where God causes people to fail. God may call his people to suffer. God may call his people to hardship. God may call his people to difficulty, but God never, ever calls his people to fail." If God calls us to a ministry, if God opens up a hurt or a pain in your community or congregation, and if you feel the call in your heart and step out on the water, God will carry you through. There is an old Irish blessing that says, "The will of God will never lead you where the grace of God cannot keep you." A newer saying is, "Never fear to trust an unknown future to a known God."

We have a new opportunity to be the contrast community; a new opportunity to bring hope and the light of Christ into the world. It is time to seize that opportunity and do mission for Christ. Let people know the glory and the joy that we feel in the hope that is in our Lord and Savior. This is the hope of the gospel, and this is our promise through God's salvation.

COMMUNITY DEVELOPMENT OVERSEAS

Mr. Kerk Burbank

Community development begins, I believe, by asking questions. Where are you? What are your interests? What kinds of needs do you have? We need to understand what community development is and what the theology of community development is.

For me, the starting place with development was that I was a business man, running my own advertising and public relations agency. A young Presbyterian lay lady there persisted in talking to me about Jesus Christ. To make a very long story short, I came to the place where I asked Jesus to come into my life—and he did in a startling way. It was a real power encounter. Also in my office were people who were talking to me about what we would characterize as "New Age" today. There was some real spiritual warfare going on in our office in Paoli, Pennsylvania.

After I came to Christ, I vowed I would never go back to the Episcopal Church because it was a wonderful Presbyterian lay lady who had led me to Jesus. I said, "Well, the Episcopal Church really doesn't understand the gospel, because I have never heard a clear cut call asking me to give myself to Jesus. I have never heard the promise that he would forgive me, cleanse me, change me and come and dwell inside of me." Now, I am sure there were priests that had said that to me somewhere along the way I mean, I think there were—but I never heard it. Perhaps that was just me!

I became involved with a parish church that was Episcopal, was turned on for Jesus and I became involved with the charismatic renewal. I discovered that Jesus was alive and well in the Episcopal Church. After three years of discipleship and evangelism training and being in prayer groups, I offered myself to the national church. I was praying those "Here am I, send me" kinds of prayers that Isaiah prayed. One day in the prayer closet I said to God, and I said it just once, "I will go where you want me to go. I will do what you want me to do. You know I have been saying that over and over, but now I will tell you what I would like to do, where I would like to go, because maybe you want to know. I would prefer to go to Kenya and I would prefer to be working in organizational development."

The fellow who was the missionary director for 815 was then on the field. With my resume in hand he came back and said, "I have a missionary call for you to the Diocese of Mt. Kenya East, to work with an on-fire bishop by the name of David Gitari. He wants you to come and build a development organization." After I was told a little bit about it, I shared it with people and I went. I was totally unencumbered by knowledge. I was absolutely dependent upon the local people and upon the Holy Spirit.

I have no idea why I selected Kenya. Another possibility mentioned was Zaire and my French was rusty. I preferred to go to Kenya. I had never really wanted to go to Africa because it was rather a threat to every American businessman. This was the greatest job that I have ever had. I have never had so much fun, been so fulfilled, worked longer hours, prayed longer and harder and had so much happening.

The Africans really got to me in great ways. One of the things that they got at me with was my worldview. When I went to Kenya, I was going there to evangelize. I got a more holistic worldview as I was there.

When we think about development we tend, in our good Western, Greek worldview, to separate the physical from the spiritual. We think of social science, economics, management and education as development. We look at theology, religion and ethics as evangelism. We tend to draw these fairly concrete categories. Some of my students from the Third World say, "You have these wonderful categories that we do not have."

The African worldview says that in tribal religion there is a supreme being, or force; you have a god. There is also a middle realm that includes the spirits, the ancestors, the deceased and the saints. They are either a bridge to the supernatural or they are alongside, depending on the worldview, but they are humans. Part of this also includes barracca, astrology, mana, dreams, sacred objects, and the whole realm of magic and witchcraft. For the Africans, this is a part of life they deal with on an ongoing basis. What often happens is that missionaries come into this culture with our "Greek split" view and they do not even think about angels and demons. Few in our Western seminaries teach much if anything about angels and demons, yet they are throughout the Bible. To add to this is this other world of humans, animals, plants and matter. The Westerner who comes into this culture may say, "Well, I never thought of myself as a missionary. I thought of myself as a Christian." This was my perception when I went to Kenya. I considered myself a Christian, but I was going there to work in this very single, physical area. I discovered that in the Hebraic worldview there are not the dichotomies that we have in the Greek worldview. It is a whole, with God's creation, angels, demons, humans, plants and matter there as the created order. God is all around it, over it, above it, but also present within it. Think of how David expressed this in Psalm 139: "Where can I go to get away from your Spirit?" For David, God's Spirit was ever present. The Old Testament did not make the kind of differentiation we do, and this may be something that requires some change in our worldview. It certainly was changing for me. Charts 1 and 2 highlight the differences.

We find in the gospels that Jesus talks about the Kingdom of God being over and above anything else. If you were to do a word count, you would find this to be the single most talked-about topic in the gospels. Jesus is always talking about God's Kingdom! What was it? What was it like? He says, "Repent, for the Kingdom of God is near." In Hebrews, chapter 12, we read of thousands of holy angels. We also see the communion of saints and the cast of witnesses that surround us. In our Western theology we do not think about that, but in African theology, the dead are always there. They are part of the community. They have never left. We have this God and his people, the church, who are in the world warring against principalities and powers, the world and the flesh to save fallen people and reinstate God's rule and God's Kingdom. We have a big separation here, then below we have Satan's kingdom and the notion, as Jesus said, that there is another kingdom. Jesus talked about Satan's kingdom and saving people from that kingdom. Unevangelized people, Jesus tells us, are part of that kingdom. They are doomed, they are fallen and we are to help them recognize that and come into God's Kingdom.

CHART 1

TRUNCATED CHRISTIAN WORLDVIEW

WORLDVIEW ASPECT	SCRIPTURE REFERENCE
TRIUNE GOD (Father, Son, and Holy Spirit)	John 14--16
. . . .	
God in His people (the Church) in the World	Colossians 1
Warring Against Political Powers, the World, and the Flesh	Ephesians 6 I John 4
Saving suffering, Fallen People Physically	Matthew 25, Luke 9 & 10
Spiritually Making Disciples	
Reinstating God's Rule	Matthew 28
Impoverished and Enslaved Humankind	Romans 1 & 6
Subject to Evil and Death	Colossians 1
. . . .	
Animals	Romans 8:19-20
The Earth (?)	Romans 8:19-20
Universe (?)	Romans 8:19-20

CHART 2

HOLISTIC CHRISTIAN WORLDVIEW

WORLDVIEW ASPECT	SCRIPTURE REFERENCE
TRIUNE GOD (Father, Son, and Holy Spirit)	John 14 - 16
. . . .	
GOD'S KINGDOM Thousands of Holy Angels Communion of Saints	Revelation Hebrews 12
. . . .	
God in His people (the Church) in the World	Colossians 1
Warring Against Principalities and Powers,	Ephesians 6
the World, and the Flesh	1 John 4
Saving Suffering, Fallen People Physically	Matthew 25, Luke 9 & 10
Spiritually Making Disciples Reinstating God's Rule	Matthew 28
Satan and his kingdom	
Evil Spiritual Principalities and Powers (with Specific Geographic and/or People Group Authority?)	Ephesians 6
. . . .	
Impoverished and Enslaved Humankind	Romans 1 & 6
Subject to Sin and Death	Colossians 1
. . . .	
Animals The Earth (?) Universe (?)	Romans 8:19-20 Romans 8:19-20 Romans 8:19-20

We need to bring God's Kingdom to all the rest of creation. Bishop Gitari helped me to understand this holism. Jesus came to save everything and everyone. He came to save all of creation.

Why Do We Have Christian Community Development?

First, I would define Christian community development as bringing God's Kingdom not just to individuals, but to entire communities; not just to the realm of the spirit in evangelism, but to the whole person in the realm of their physical, spiritual, emotional, social, intellectual and economic needs. In our Western worldview, we tend to put these things into those categories that are difficult to pull apart inside us into separate categories.

Scripture commands us in Matthew 5, John 14 and 1 John 4 to love in "word and deed." First John 4:17 has been my greatest motivator. John says, "Do not love just in word and thought, but love in deed." St. Francis used to say to his people, "We must proclaim the gospel everywhere and sometimes we must use words." God loves the whole person, and as witnesses to God's character, we are to love the whole person.

Often in Western theology we have bypassed the social commission clearly expressed in Matthew 25 that precedes the Great Commission. We will be judged on whether we took care of the hungry, the poor, the sick and the needy. As evangelicals, we have tended to differentiate and say that there is a difference between the "social commission" and the "Great Commission" or evangelism as described in Matthew, chapter 28. Missionaries have found universally that when they go to the field it takes from one to three years to learn the language and the culture. How can that time be used effectively? Make friends.

Bishop Gitari discovered that the missionaries who knew technical skills could be of immediate use. In order to do that, however, we need to know the community needs. It is important to listen to the people. Some wonderful Christians in Malawi had a hospital and found that people were coming twenty miles past a government hospital to them for care. When they asked the people why they would do this, the response was, "The medicine is the same but the hands are different." With that healing hand, the presence of Jesus, they were able to use their technical skills to work for the immediate benefit of the people.

Theologically it is important to remember that we are told to free the oppressed. Isaiah, in chapter 58, talks about people who fasted and prayed continually. Isaiah tells them they are not being heard by God because they had not freed the oppressed, they had not shared their goods with the poor. Ephesians, chapter 4, continues this thought where it talks about enabling and equipping the saints for ministry. Our experience in the Diocese of Mt. Kenya East confirmed this for us. The ministry was limited because of a lack of transportation vehicles. By assisting them to get a number of vehicles and by setting up a health clinic, with the introduction of some technology, the people were free to do things.

Certainly in these areas, there is spiritual warfare. St. Paul said we would not do battle against flesh and blood only, but principalities and powers as well. The advantage that Christians have over secular groups is that while we work in the physical realm, we deal with the spiritual realm. Behind lots of sickness and poverty are spiritual forces that want to maintain their hold. As Christians, we can pray about that and we know the Lord gives power and will give us victory. God told us to take dominion over the whole earth in Genesis 1 and 2. I can testify that the Lord provides a kind of personal renewal and is very, very present among the poor. I have seen him, felt him and understood him palpably in ways with the poor that I have not in other places.

Development or Relief, or Both?

Is there a difference between development and relief? Actually, it is a continuum. We have relief; we have rehabilitation; we have development; we have the building of self-sustaining institutions. Relief brings to people the basic needs of food, water and shelter. This is immediate and done to sustain life. Rehabilitation gives people basic skills. The objective is to rebuild, repair or cope with a loss. This involves a longer time period as well as training.

Development takes much longer and it allows people to experiment with new ideas. They often lack the political skills to make the system work to help the poor. They lack such technical skills as found with health care workers. They do not have seeds, equipment or the knowledge of what would make their crops grow better and faster. Moving development along to the point of a partnership where there are self-sustaining institutions takes even longer—generations perhaps.

Imperialism or Unemployment?

The Apostle Paul was the quintessential missionary, or church builder. If we look in the New Testament for his example, we find that he never spent more than three years in any missionary situation. Paul believed that if the people were filled with the Holy Spirit and knew Jesus in a personal way, Jesus could direct them personally. Paul trusted that the local people had skills and talents and they understood their own situation better than he did. They really did not need him an awful lot. Essentially, he worked himself out of a job.

It is critical that as we move into the development area, we remain sensitive to the culture. Our approach needs to be one of learning from them. Relief is important and immediate, rehabilitation is training and development is moving into the future. Imperialism says, "It cannot be done without us!"—but it can be! It is important to assess the situation, what the needs of the people are and where the skills and talents lie. Change will come when the community determines the need and becomes involved in meeting that. That is the point at which we can move on.

When I was preparing to go to Africa, my bishop, who had been a missionary to the Philippines, called me to his office. His one piece of advice to me was, "Kerk, God was at work in Africa long before the white man came or even now before you get there. Long after you are gone, God will be at work there. If you remember that, you will be a good missionary." That was very good advice.

So Who Changes, Them or Me?

Change happens! Entering another culture and living with the people is a wonderful way to gain their perspective. Missionaries see life very, very differently when they do this. As an outsider, our understanding of the insider deepens. Getting in contact with the people moves us from theory to knowledge. We see and live with the needs. We can see what affects the people. They have sick and dying children, adult health is poor, food is inadequate and the people do not know how to get the help that may already be available.

It is important that we shed our preconceived ideas. Our worldview is so different. What would work in our own area is not applicable halfway around the world. Development has been a failure when people have a preconceived formula that they attempt to make fit in a local situation.

No matter how long we live in another culture, there are facets of that culture that will never be ours. I will never be an African. I am just the wrong color. African males go through a public circumcision and I have not. This means that they had certain shared experiences that I never had, and never will have. A lot of our past is different. My friend, John Stewart, uses a wonderful term, "not an outsider, not an insider, but an alongsider" to express how we can be considered a friend.

If we can enter the culture and be seen as a good friend, someone that the people really trust, they will share what it is they really want to do. That trust starts when they know we truly hear them. Listening to where the people are and helping them with what they consider to be the most important things in their lives opens a relationship. They will begin to consider other alternatives and think in a wider perspective. We can then begin to share ideas instead of being a boss or a director. The nature of good Christian community development is to allow them to make the decisions.

It is so important that we pray and ask God to lead us. I went to Kenya as a businessman with no development experience. I came back and went to Cornell for a degree in development. Guess what! I discovered that everything we were doing was on the cutting edge of what people considered the clever things in community development. Thank you, Holy Spirit!

HOMELESS FAMILIES, SECOND CHANCE

Mr. Mike Wurschmidt, the Rev. Toni Stuart, the Rev. Anne Halapua

MIKE WURSCHMIDT: Nine years ago, I had a computer business in three states, and I thought life was grand. I was three weeks away from being ordained in another denomination and I thought, "Lord, this is great!" Literally overnight, the business was lost. A large, large company basically stole it from us. My wife, Tina, and I were left holding all the liabilities of running a business in three states and we lost everything. We resigned from the pastoring that we were doing, moved to Denver, Colorado, and tried to start over. This was merely the beginning of our life struggles. Over the course of the next year, it went from bad to worse. On Friday, April 22, 1988, with Tina pregnant with our second child and a daughter eighteen months old, we became homeless.

Both Tina and I have undergraduate degrees. We both come from very good families and were raised in Christian homes. This sort of thing is not supposed to happen to people like us; but it did. I stood in food lines, I stood in shelters asking for help, I delivered newspapers in the middle of the night and I knocked on doors to see if people would let me clean their computers. I did what it took to care for my family. It wasn't until we had been homeless for eight weeks, totally dependent upon others to survive, that I really realized how much Jesus Christ really did when he died for me, how much he loved me. I had a faith in him, but I did not really understand the magnitude of what he went through for my sins, my mistakes, my pride, that as a Christian, I had taken for granted.

Project Home Again began a month after we got off the streets and out of homelessness. I received a phone call from someone who had heard that World Vision was hoping to train churches in the United States to adopt homeless families. They had heard about my situation and what we had done. My response was to tell them that I had nothing to offer them except what I had learned. In July 1988, World Vision flew me to Los Angeles and Project Home Again began, based upon my experience and the experience of three other individuals who had worked with homeless families and individuals. Project Home Again began in Fresno, California, and Denver, Colorado, with training in churches. Six months later, World Vision decided to make the program national. In early February, 1989, Project Home Again really took off.

The Rev. Toni Stuart and the Rev. Anne Halapua work in the Diocese of Los Angeles, training Episcopal churches to adopt homeless children and their families. They heard about Project Home Again and were trained by coordinators in the California area. They have become experts at working with homeless families and Project Home Again would not exist throughout the United States without them.

Homelessness in America is a very serious problem. While this fact may be well known, it is difficult to maintain a perspective on the magnitude of the problem here in the United States. There may be as many as three million homeless people, depending upon how the 1990 census figures are interpreted. Many of us who work with the homeless believe that number is probably low. We say that because it does not include what we call the "hidden homeless," or those families that live with other families. The Census Bureau figures are only projections of people in the shelters, the streets, the hotels and in cars. There may be more than 500,000 homeless children in the United States. Toni and Anne can attest to at least 65,000 homeless children in Los Angeles County alone. The average age of a homeless child is six years old. The number of homeless families is expected to rise twenty percent or more this year alone. Eviction and the high cost of rent will displace over 2.5 million people this year. There are 13.8 million children living in poverty in the United States; fifteen percent of American children are born into poverty. When we talk about missions our minds tend to think of missions overseas, but missions in the United States is very, very important. There is a very large group of unreached people who may have heard the gospel and the name of Jesus Christ, but they know nothing of who Jesus Christ is, other than his name.

Is Project Home Again really mission? Acts 1:8 says, "But you will receive power when the Holy Spirit comes on you; and you will be my witnesses in Jerusalem, and in all Judea and Samaria, and to the ends of the earth." My attention is drawn to Jerusalem because I know that missions to such places as China and India are absolutely vital, but so are missions in the United States. How many times have we seen the homeless families, the wino, the vagabond or the bag lady in our own streets? There was a time in our not-so-distant past when we would have cried; now we have become hardened.

Many are called to be missionaries overseas, but many are also called to stay home. It is difficult to understand a church that will engage in only one form of missionary activity. Project Home Again provides practical hands-on mission experience, not just for one person or one family, but for the whole church. It is a direct cross-cultural experience because going into the inner cities in the United States is a cross-cultural experience, big time. Involving a church in Project Home Again can be the launching pad to mission experience overseas. Doing evangelism through the giving of oneself in simple and practical ways without traveling a long way from home is very effective mission involvement.

The basic premise of Project Home Again is that one church will help one family. The children in the family should be sixteen years old or younger. A team of from eight to twelve volunteers is formed to walk beside the homeless family, loving them, assisting them to find furniture, a job, and a place to live, all in the name of Jesus Christ. The money that is raised does not go to some organization with gigantic administrative overhead but directly to help one family. Lord willing, the family may even come to know Jesus Christ. Perhaps the family might join the helping church or they are helped to find another. However, joining a church is not a prerequisite for adoption.

The prophet Isaiah rebuked the religious leaders of the day who were standing on street corners, fasting openly, saying the "woe is me" stuff. The Lord told Isaiah to let them know what true fasting was.

> Is not this the kind of fasting I have chosen: to loose the chains of injustice and untie the cords of the yoke, to set the oppressed free and break every yoke? Is it not to share your food with the hungry and provide the poor wanderer with shelter—when you see the naked, to clothe him, and not to turn away from your own flesh and blood? Then your light will break forth like the dawn, and your healing will quickly appear; then your righteousness will go before you, and the

glory of the Lord will be your rear guard. Then you will call, and the Lord will answer; you will cry for help and he will say: Here am I. If you do away with the yoke of oppression, with the pointing finger and malicious talk, and if you spend yourselves in behalf of the hungry and satisfy the needs of the oppressed, then your light will rise in the darkness, and your night will become like the noonday. The Lord will guide you always; he will satisfy your needs in a sun-scorched land and will strengthen your frame. You will be like a well-watered garden, like a spring whose waters never fail. Your people will rebuild the ancient ruins and will raise up the age-old foundations; you will be called Repairer of Broken Walls, Restorer of Streets with Dwellings (Is 58:6-12; NIV).

In our lives as Christians, we see many broken and hurting people and we do nothing because we think there isn't anything we can do. We hope that these people will make it and that there will be a dramatic change in them. Scripture, however, states very clearly that when we give of ourselves we are quickly healed ourselves. There are changes in our own lives when we give away what God has given us. This principle applies as well to the whole church when, as a Body we give, God will restore and heal that which has been broken for years.

ANNE HALAPUA: Currently I am the director of Anchor House, a homeless shelter in San Clemente, Southern California, that is a part of the Episcopal Service Alliance in Orange County, California. I came into this position as a result of field work I did among the homeless in Los Angeles while a student at Berkeley. I determined that if I lived at the shelter I could learn about homelessness much more quickly; now I don't know what it would be like to live anywhere else. I don't own anything anymore except a car which is a necessity in my job. Everyone who knows me knows that anything they give me will be given away. I do not believe you can give away a bed or bus passes without giving away the love of Jesus Christ. I believe that the homeless family sees Christ in the eyes of parish members who are involved in this ministry.

Besides the work of managing Anchor House, I also work with people who want to volunteer to help homeless people and have no idea how to do it. To work with the homeless through a parish is similar to watching the spread of a wonderful contagious disease. It is as if the Holy Spirit just throws love all around. Parishes that have been able to minister to a homeless family are incredibly encouraged, minister more to each other, and move out in other areas of ministry. Project Home Again opens doors to overseas missions, and locally as well. Project Home Again teaches a congregation to look without fear at their neighbors, to look with trust and be willing to risk, because there is risk. A homeless family may not think it is wonderful to be involved with these Christians, but as long as they know that they have received the love of Jesus Christ, the rest is up to God. The congregation's job is to be the Body of Christ in that place, with that family.

TONI STUART: My function is as a site coordinator for Project Home Again to assist parishes to become involved in adopting a homeless family. First of all, it is important that the program be presented to the rector or vicar of a parish and be assured of his or her support. A site coordinator can then be invited to a parish to present the program either by preaching or speaking to the largest possible group of people. Once the parish has made a commitment to the program, a commitment form is signed by the priest and the vestry which limits the amount of time the parish will be involved with the homeless family. A strategic part of Project Home Again is that there is a limit to the time involvement, usually six months for each family.

The first task of the parish is to raise enough money to cover two months' rent, utility deposits and a little extra cushion. There are many creative ways to raise money. One team with which I worked asked each household on the team to pledge an amount and then find another household outside the church to match that amount. They use this as an evangelism tool to tell people about the project and what their particular parish is doing.

Once these funds are raised, teams of from eight to twelve people are formed; they receive training and participate in Bible study provided by a site coordinator. Each team is divided into four task forces of two members each, using the biblical example. Team members are each assigned a specific task, taking into consideration their unique gifts and skills, with a job description to guide them. The task force responsible for helping with employment will research available community resources. Another will have the responsibility of finding the necessary furnishings for a home. Stocking the kitchen with staples and filling the cupboards is the responsibility of yet another task force.

The site coordinator will visit nearby shelters, build rapport with the managers and seek out a family for resettlement. The size of the family can vary, but should be a family with a minor child and at least one adult. The family should not be addicted to any substance and should be one that will be able to make good use of this opportunity. This is where shelter managers are key, because having lived with them, they know the families better. There are some very good reasons for being so specific in the selection of a family. Many churches have no experience ministering to someone who is homeless. If the first experience the church has is with a family just coming out of some type of addictive rehabilitation, it will probably not be positive and they will never work with a homeless family or person again. The key to continued involvement is to build a history of success—and we want success because success means more room in the shelter for the homeless. Parishes can elect to become involved with high-risk families once they have experience dealing with the homeless and have also some successes to which they can look when they need encouragement.

Certainly every plan has its exceptions. Not every family will have an employable adult. Some long-range planning may be involved if the family is a single mom with a child. Finding mom employment may not be best for her or the child; getting her back in school to complete her GED or completing her college education may be wisest. That means that she may be on welfare for a period of time, but the way off welfare is through education. The church does not fund education, so the team may find that it will need to research carefully the resources available for someone in this situation. We have had successes with this and have a young woman in Denver who has graduated from college and is now employed as a teacher.

Next, the task force conducts an in-depth intake interview on the family and a check of the references they have provided. The reference check is done to determine that the information that has been provided is accurate.

Once a family has been selected, the site coordinators and the ministry team meet with them to complete the planning agreement. This is where the family set their goals for the next six months. Some goals may seem to be very obvious: get into affordable housing, find jobs or even get their teeth fixed. Then the ministry team indicates how many of these goals they are willing to meet. If the team and the family agree, they have a partnership. The church team is not a group of social workers, but is a safety net of trained friends who are going to work with the family for six months.

Once the agreement has been completed, things can happen quickly. The team task force with the responsibility for finding housing accompanies the family to look at what is available. It is important that the family be able to afford the rent once the first and last months' rent has been paid by the parish so, by necessity, it is going to be very inexpensive housing.

Moving-in day is the time when the entire parish should be involved. There may be a special day when donated items are brought to the altar during worship so that everyone can be a part of prayer for the family. The actual moving-in day can be quite a day of celebration. We really encourage teams to make it festive and involve as many people as possible.

Once the family has moved into their home, different task forces help the adults to find work, the children to enroll in school and assist the family to deal with any medical or legal issues that might come up. Then the church gradually pulls back and allows the family to struggle to live on their own, living their own lives in their own home with the assurance that they can call on the church team if they need help with unanticipated problems.

While all of this very practical work goes one, there is also something spiritually happening. From the family's viewpoint, they may never have been loved in this way before. To have someone not related to them spend time with them, spend time in prayer for them, spend money to help them or time to get to know them is a new experience. This is a real gift of God. For some members of the team, there is a real bonding that takes place.

However, certain expectations about the family may not be met. Little disappointments can develop if it appears that the family is not grateful or doing something right. The gift in this for us is that it makes us look at those parts of ourselves that we have wanted to keep hidden. Inevitably, a family member will do something that will make us angry, and the reason it makes us angry is because it represents a part of ourselves we have not wanted to face. This is the time when God is growing and developing us spiritually.

MIKE: Project Home Again is a simple, effective way of helping a church help one homeless family at a time and it works! Thousands of families have been helped.

9

Wineskins for New Wine: Episcopal Mission Societies

ANGLICAN FRONTIER MISSIONS

The Rev. Tad deBordenave

Are you aware that today twenty percent of the world has never had the chance to understand who Jesus Christ is in a way that they can believe in him and follow him as their Lord? They need our attention.

To illustrate that point let me tell you about a missionary couple who traveled to western China for the first time. As the only Westerners there, they drew a crowd. This scene was repeated several times. The Chinese people wanted to use English words with these English-speaking Westerners, so they would say, "Coca-Cola." The missionaries would smile. The Chinese would smile in return. Then one of the couple would say, "Have you ever heard of Jesus Christ?" This time the return look would be blank. No one there had heard of Jesus Christ.

A few years ago, I was trekking with some friends in one of the most popularly traveled areas in Nepal. I heard that a Tibetan Lama, a sort of Buddhist bishop, was there. We hunted him down, took him to tea, and talked to him about his religious beliefs for about forty-five minutes. Then I said to him, "What is your impression of Christianity and Jesus Christ?" He had a blank look. He turned to his friend and said, in English, "I have no impression of Christianity. I have never met a Christian, and I do not know who Jesus Christ is."

It takes extra effort to think of those who are out of our sight and out of our mind—1.2 billion people in "World A"—those who have never heard the gospel and have no access to the gospel. Anglican Frontier Missions reminds the church of the least evangelized, and of our responsibility to make sure they hear the gospel of Jesus Christ.

AFM began in 1990, when about twenty mission leaders from the Episcopal Church met in Richmond at the Global Strategy Room of the Foreign Mission Board of the Southern Baptist Church. Many of us felt that there ought to be an Episcopal response, a vehicle into World A. That began on All Saints Day, 1990, the same month that the Decade of Evangelism began. This served as a reminder to the Episcopal Church that the vision of the decade should be farsighted enough to go to those who have not heard. A group from northern Virginia, including myself, was formed as a result of that meeting and we met monthly. With significant support from the Overseas Missions Committee of the Diocese of Virginia, we gradually put together Anglican Frontier Missions. In the spring of 1991, as I was reading Stephen Neill's book *The History of Christian Mission*, it became very clear to me that frontiers were broken by people who were willing to say, "I will cut my ties and I will go out there." I heard the Lord saying to me, "Cut your ties and go out there." I borrowed a line from Moses that I do not think many of you can use. "Lord, you have got the wrong man, you know I stutter." Well, the Lord had heard that before, and he said to me the same thing he said to Moses, "I will be with you." My wife said, "I will be with you." So I left St. Matthew's Church, where I had been for seventeen years, and Anglican Frontier Missions began in the fall of 1993.

We have borrowed from others as much as we can; we are in no sense reinventing the wheel. One of the things we have borrowed is slogans—inspiring slogans that will stir us to World A. Dwight L. Moody used this line a hundred years ago, as he tried to stir the students to go the ends of the world and complete world evangelization by the year 1900. He said, "It shall be done. It must be done and it can be done!" I was in Dr. Barrett's office a week ago, and I mentioned that I would be using that line. Dr. Barrett said, "Moody should have added 'and it wasn't done.'" Things have changed and we hope that by the year 2000, we can present, as a birthday present to the Lord, an entire world that has heard the gospel.

I would like to use Moody's slogan for the basic structure of this presentation. "It shall be done." When Moody said that, he was not expressing optimism. He was describing a certainty that he saw in Scripture because he had read Revelation. It describes how some from every nation, tribe, tongue and people group will be around the throne and will sing, "He is worthy. Worthy is the Lamb."

To understand Moody's certainty, we must begin near the beginning. In Genesis, chapter 11, there is the description of the dispersal of the people groups to the four corners of the world. In the conversation that God has with Abraham, in Genesis 12, we find out what God intends. He said to Abraham, "You have seen the way in which all these nations have been dispersed, how they have refused me and are pursuing other gods. I am going to bring back to me, before history ends, all of the nations of the world." Abraham said (respectfully), "It's a little late for that, isn't it? You have got to be kidding! I mean, they are in the desert; they are in the mountains; they have hostile borders; they are not going to let you in by denying visas; they are going to kill you if you say you are there to plant a church. I mean, it's a little bit late, isn't it?" God's response was, "Here is what I am going to do. I am going to make for myself a people, and I am going to train and disciple them. They are going to bear my imprint and have my aroma. They are going to be like a tilted mirror. Light is going to come down from heaven and hit that mirror to reflect my glory. I am going to send them to the nations, and I am going to bring the nations to where they are. That is how I am going to do it." Abraham said, "Who do you think is willing to do something like that?" God replied, "I am starting with you! And I am going to make a great nation of you. When you and your descendants go into the four corners of the earth, I will bless you and you will bless the nations." This is what God has been up to ever since Genesis 12, when the first Great Commission was given.

How are we doing? Let's ask the Apostle Peter. He can answer for many of us. Peter is a typical Christian. His response typifies the response of the church. He was the first leader of the church in Jerusalem and God knew that Peter had to get it right. So God had a conversation with Peter in a vision. This is how it went from Peter's point of view. God said to Peter, as the leader of the church, "You are doing a great job with the Jews who are in Jerusalem and Judea and some in Samaria, from all the corners of the Jewish world—you are doing a great job. And now I want you to go to the Gentiles." Peter said, somewhat respectfully, "Are you sure you want us to get into that? You know, we have really got our plate full: Heresies?—We have heresies right here in Jerusalem. We have the law-watching Pharisee Jews who are converted and telling us one thing, and we have the law-liberated people telling us another. We have heresies right here among the Jews. Squabbles?—We have squabbles. We have the Hellenistic women mad at the Jerusalem women. We have more than we can handle right now. And besides, I am not really sure those Gentiles are all that interested in you right now. Maybe, if they were to come knocking on my door..." The knock that Peter heard at the door at that moment was the servant from the Gentile centurion Cornelius, saying, "Will you come and preach the gospel to us?" Peter got the point, and the unevangelized have been knocking and asking for the gospel ever since. But Peter's reluctance typifies the response of the church.

We have said, like Peter, "We have too much on our plate, Lord, to go into World A. Maybe later. Heresies, you want to read heresies? Read some of the resolutions in diocesan conventions! Squabbles? All the Presiding Bishop asked us to do was see that there were no outcasts—nobody inside our church who felt like an outcast—and we have been squabbling about that for six years. Mind you, Lord, we have put our best energy into renewal, to make sure that we are really doing well by ourselves as the church. And when we have a bishop on the other end of the telephone overseas inviting us to go, we go." Basically, however, our attitude is, "It is a little late, and we have too much on our plate to get anything going among one *billion* people in places we have never heard of."

How good it is that we are out to see that there are no outcasts inside the Episcopal Church. It would appear, though, that God wants us to also have as a rallying cry, "Let there be no outsiders to the church." He is pleased, I am sure, with our partnership principles in the Episcopal Church which say that we will not go where the church exists unless the church there invites us. We only go in partnership with the vision of the bishop in the field. But God wants us to see that there are limits to the logic of partnership. There is no bishop in Lhasa, Tibet, Marakesh or Ankara. How are we to respond to those people who have no bishop to do the inviting? The Lord says, "It shall be done." He loves the Muslims in Marakesh; he loves the Buddhist in Lhasa and the Hindu in New Delhi just as much as he loves Billy Graham. He has sent his Son that they, too, will know the forgiveness and hope that lies at the heart of God. It shall be done.

Moody then said, "It must be done." What do we gain as a church by committing ourselves to world evangelization? I will give you two answers, two ways of seeing how God uses missions to further his purpose for us, his purpose that we shall be changed into the likeness of the glory of his Son, Jesus Christ.

First, consider the impact on us as we go to China. I heard a great missionary scholar for China say that he and others believe that the number one priority for the church today ought to be the evangelization of China. Take that seriously. There are a number of reasons that suggest it is so. The first is, we know God loves the Chinese more than he loves anyone else—because he made more of them! There are Chinese dispersed to almost every country of the world today. If the Chinese are evangelized and mobilized, then every country of the world has a force for evangelism.

Fully 500 million unreached people live inside China. If 400 million Chinese do not have access to the gospel of Jesus Christ, that is fully a third of all the unreached people of the world, inside China. The numbers are staggering. If the church in the West were to mobilize and go in to evangelize China, we would meet a church we would not recognize. God has purified them in a way that very few churches in history have been purified through suffering and persecution. The Chinese call it "opportunities for blessing." They have grown because of their prevailing prayer, and a hundred years of sacrifice. The Chinese are a church committed to witness no matter what the repercussions. Those repercussions for the Chinese who witness to their Lord are awful, yet they do! They cannot be quieted.

I heard a Chinese leader recently talk about the eighteen years he spent in a prison camp during the Cultural Revolution. He said he would not trade those times because he had such sweet communion with God. Because he was a scholar and a leader, he got the worst job in the camp—emptying the cesspool. That was how he got his time alone with the Lord. No one would go near him while he was doing his job, and he would sing and praise God. There are ways that Western Christians can evangelize China. First, though, we must be humbled so that we have been worked on in the same way that they have.

Second, there is a long line of missionaries and missionary agency staff who are waiting for an invitation from you to go into your churches to speak about prayer and financial support for them. More than they need these churches, however, these churches need them. Church pulpits need a missionary to describe the global perspective of what God is doing. The prayers of church people need to hear strange accents. Church budgets need controversy and line items—not just between paint and salaries, but paint and salaries and missionary support for people who represent them in the field. Church folk need to talk with missionaries who have stories of valor and need. Through missionaries, we have the opportunity of drawing closer to the heart of God. It must become real to the person in the pew that they accompany a missionary when they pray and give. It must be done.

"It can be done." How is it that the world can be evangelized in our lifetime? We are hindered by such barriers as difficulties with visas. We are overwhelmed by the staggering numbers, 1.2 billion—twenty-two percent of the world's population. That question, "How can it be done?" has many answers from God. The Foreign Mission Board of the Baptist Church came up with what is called "non-residential missionary" as one answer.

Let me tell you about my non-residential missionary work to the Qashqa'i people. These people are called "the most unevangelized people today." There are one million of these semi-nomadic people living in southwest Iran. There is no Scripture in their language. There are no radio programs, no pastor, no church, and, as far as is known, no Christian missionary agency assigned to work specifically among the Qashqa'i. When I began, it was like walking into a stadium where the contest was going on for the eternal destiny of the Qashqa'i and being told that I am not permitted to go to the field of battle. What do I do? Were all the options closed off? No. I walked up the stairs to those large glass boxes that surround many of the stadiums today. My first stop is in the press box. I have begun to use media and publicity methods to say to the Christian church, "Won't you pray for the Qashqa'i of Iran, that God will begin to open up ways for them to hear the gospel in a way that is relevant and meaningful to them?"

From the press box I go to the communications command post where people wear those funny headphones. They are not Qashqa'i, but they are other people inside Iran. There is a lot of static, but there are ways to find out what is going on inside Iran and how some of that can be brought to the southwest corner of Iran where the Qashqa'i live. I know that by pressing on, I will be able to find out if there are Qashqa'i refugees in other parts of the world, or Qashqa'i students that Christians can work among and mobilize. I can discover what the openings are. From what countries will Iran allow people to enter? What are the needs of the Qashqa'i? What Christians could be permitted to live and work among them?

I then moved to the broadcast booth—to ways that I can be in connection with every part of the Body of Christ worldwide. We have unparalleled resources today. One of the resources is the ability to communicate worldwide with the Body of Christ—a way to connect with the worldwide Body of Christ. I might find a Pentecostal veterinarian in Argentina who is willing to go to the Qashqa'i. I might find a Presbyterian nurse in Korea willing to go. I might find a Roman Catholic teacher in Uganda who is willing. I know it is going to multiply.

Three years ago, Greg Muffleman began working with an unreached people group of several million people. No missionary was assigned there before the Mufflemans and another non-residential couple. They went to the pressbox and the communications post, and after only three years, there are more than two dozen Christians from all over the Body of Christ living in the area with the intent of planting a church there. It can be done.

We need to remind ourselves that the church is nothing more than a servant. The Lord says to us, "Your job is to do what I tell you to do. Here is your list. It is for you to go out and start; it is for me to make sure that you have the resources of my Spirit to see that it is accomplished." Our work is to do the work God gives us.

The movie *Schindler's List* gives a remarkable metaphor for the ministry of the church among the unevangelized people of the world. God laid the destiny of about four hundred Polish Jews on the heart of a wealthy German industrialist. Schindler maneuvered around barrier after barrier on behalf of his people. He orchestrated events with amazing resourcefulness and creativity. He persevered in spite of so many others around him who really did not care. This pilgrimage changed him to where he counted it a privilege beyond all else to be able to stand beside, on behalf of and before these Polish Jews whom he loved very much. It cost everything that he had, yet he was glad to do it and wished he could have done more!

The church has been given a list of about twelve thousand ethnic groups for whom the gospel of Jesus Christ is not within reach. These are the people "at the ends of the earth." We are called to help plant churches among them. It can be done. God will show us ways and will supply the resources. It will change us, but it will change us into the image of our Lord Jesus Christ. We will find it a privilege beyond any other privilege to have been involved in that ministry. It will cost us, but it will give us a glimpse into the center of the heart of our missionary God, as we go where he calls us to go.

Anglican Frontier Missions reminds the church of the least evangelized, and of our commission to make sure that they all hear the gospel of Jesus Christ. Because he has said, "I will be with you," some from every nation will be with us when we sing that hymn, "He is Worthy."

EPISCOPAL CHURCH CENTER

The Rev. Canon Patrick Mauney and Mrs. Dorothy Gist

Due to the many changes in mission policy made at the General Convention of the Episcopal Church in August 1994 we have included these two articles by the Rev. Canon Patrick Mauney and Mrs. Dorothy Gist which explain the situation as of Fall 1995.

THE REV. CANON PATRICK MAUNEY

The Domestic and Foreign Missionary Society of the Protestant Episcopal Church in the United States of America was organized in 1821 and remains the corporate and legal entity of the national church. The membership of the Domestic and Foreign Missionary Society was then and is now every baptized member of the church. The Protestant Episcopal Church (PECUSA) itself (also called The Episcopal Church and commonly known by the inaccurate acronym ECUSA) became, in 1789, the first autonomous church in what was later to be known as the Anglican Communion. The Episcopal Church today consists of ninety-nine domestic dioceses and twelve dioceses in the central region of the Americas and in Taiwan. Former dioceses in Brazil, Liberia, the Philippines and Mexico now constitute (or are part of) autonomous provinces in the Anglican Communion. (The former PECUSA dioceses of Cuba, Puerto Rico and Costa Rica remain under the metropolitical authority of PECUSA's Province IX, as does the more recently constituted Diocese of Venezuela.)

In 1994, the active baptized membership of the Episcopal Church was slightly in excess of two-and-a-half million. Although there has been a small increase in numbers for the past three years, the present baptized membership is about thirty percent less than it was several decades ago. This diminution in numbers is a feature shared with other historic Protestant churches in America and may be attributed largely to demographic reasons. Although relatively small in numbers (we make up about one percent of the population), the Episcopal Church remains one of the most influential churches in the nation. A recent study undertaken by Purdue University found Episcopalians "seven times more likely" to be found in powerful positions as in the general population (Jews are the next most likely). While still largely a church of the white upper middle class, the Episcopal Church has significant and visible minorities in the Hispanic, African-American, Asian-American and American Indian communities, as well as a wider distribution than formerly in lower income groups.

The term *decentralization* may be key in understanding recent movements and events in our church. At the recent triennial General Convention of the Episcopal Church, the national Executive Council recommended significant cuts in the national program budget and staff. This was in response to declining income from the dioceses (while overall giving continues to increase) and a "listening process" that indicated an apparently widespread desire for a less powerful central bureaucracy and more partnership with and among the individual dioceses and internal provinces of the church. A reorganized national staff and budget are intended to support the desire for greater involvement of all members of the church.

This movement toward decentralization, if it can be called that, is society-wide, with manifestations of the same spirit occurring in government, business, large charitable institutions and religious denominations. The more disciplined and thoughtful of our members are asking the pertinent questions, "How can we be the best stewards of our considerable resources in furtherance of the mission of the church? Can x program best be carried out in the local congregation, by the diocese or by the national church? Or by a broadly based partnership?" In any event, it is clear that large, centralized institutions created in another day, in all sectors of our society, are undergoing fundamental changes.

How does this societal shift affect the world mission of our church? The legal name—Domestic and Foreign Missionary Society—is significant. The whole church, not only voluntary societies, is to be the missionary agency. Ecclesiology determines missiology. For most of its history, this has been true of the Episcopal Church. Missionaries have been sent and financial grants made in the name and under the auspices of the national church. Even so, the past decade or so has seen the formation of several voluntary missionary societies, whose express purpose has been to recruit, train, send and support missionaries. The rationale usually given for this is that the national church has been derelict in its task.

In fact, the number of missionaries sent by the national church has declined significantly in recent decades. At the same time, financial grants to overseas dioceses and other partners in the Anglican communion have increased apace, so that where there were once American missionaries there are now resident church workers, often supported by grants from the Episcopal Church. In the budgetary triennium 1995-97, some twenty million dollars in grants to overseas partners are foreseen. In addition, partner churches will benefit from grants through the United

Thank Offering (UTO) and the Presiding Bishop's Fund for World Relief.

The tension between the national church ideal and voluntary societies is recognized by most Episcopalians, on reflection, as a healthy one. Still undefined is the matter of how one relates to the other. This is, of course, one aspect of the larger question about the proper role of large institutions in society, as noted above. One of the recommendations before General Convention was a major cut in national program support for missionaries (among many other cuts recommended). This recommendation was rejected decisively by the General Convention, leading us to believe that the national church as a missionary society is still a reality.

General Convention also budgeted for a triennial study "to develop new strategies and structures through which the Domestic and Foreign Missionary Society of the Episcopal Church will continue the Church's work of sending and receiving missionaries in cooperation with parishes, dioceses and existing voluntary mission agencies." This study will be done cooperatively with the Episcopal Council on Global Mission, a broadly based association of groups interested in world mission awareness and outreach.

In summary, then, the Episcopal Church is a venerable institution whose corporate name signifies its understanding of the missionary nature of the church. As an integral and even influential part of its civil society, it experiences tension and engages in debate over the proper role of institutions in its congregational, diocesan and national expressions. It remains, in almost all ways, a vibrant and growing church that acknowledges its place and responsibilities within the larger Anglican and ecumenical community.

MRS. DOROTHY GIST

Following an extensive "listening process" throughout the Episcopal Church and with the ecumenical partners, the Executive Council voted in February, 1994, to change the support of programs and to restructure and reduce the national staff. Included in the Executive Council's changes was the shifting of the deployment of missionaries and volunteers from the national level to dioceses and parishes with the national staff serving in more of a consultative role.

Concurrent with the Executive Council's action on the mission program of the church, we faced another downsizing. As a result, the Mission Personnel Office was reduced from three management and two support staff to one management and one support staff.

Following the Executive Council's action, Bishop Grein, Diocese of New York, and Bishop Thompson, Diocese of Southern Ohio, immediately took action to insure the continuation of mission efforts. Michael Kendall, Archdeacon for Mission, Diocese of New York, and Judy Gillespie, former Director of World Mission, carried on dialogue to insure mission at the local level. Before the convention's vote on mission, several bishops, or their designees, expressed the need for the continuation of the global mission program of the church. As a result the Global Education for Mission (GEM) was created to serve as the channel to enable mission engagement at the local level.

In August 1994, General Convention voted to maintain the mission program at the national office, to restore the mission budget and to increase the budget for the Volunteers for Mission (VFM) program. In this process, the networks and groups of the church are to be used as a channel to strengthen mission engagement. The convention also approved a resolution for study and reflection on mission as the parishes and dioceses were encouraged to provide more education on global missionary work.

Another major action of General Convention was the approval of the change in the funding formula for dioceses. While the convention voted to restore mission at the national level, we had to await information on the financial response to the new diocesan funding formula. As a result, this moved us almost to the end of 1994 before we were able to seriously begin the recruitment and placement of missioners.

In order to quickly move ahead with the recruitment and screening of missioners, Melba Larson (former Associate in Mission Personnel), whose position was eliminated in the downsizing, was hired as a consultant for five days per month to process applicants from inquiry to placement. A temporary staff person assists with the overall clerical responsibilities of the office.

In the interim between the vote of Executive Council and the action of General Convention, Mission Personnel focused primarily on maintaining the personnel already on the field. We recruited, screened, and assigned only a few new missioners. Since many volunteers serve for only one year, the hold on new volunteer appointments resulted in the significant reduction in the total number of assigned volunteers. During 1994, approximately four hundred inquiries were received from persons interested in mission service. With the hold on new assignments, inquirers were referred to their priests and bishops for direction in terms of their mission interest. During 1994, nine volunteers and two missionaries were assigned as new appointments.

To bring the national church's focus on mission in line with the actions of General Convention, several full-page ads were included in *Episcopal Life* and *The Living Church* to highlight mission service and to encourage persons to consider service. For those who volunteer their services, Mission Personnel provides for cross-cultural orientation, financial assistance when the volunteer's insurance doesn't provide for pre and post medical examinations, language study, and medical/dental/life insurance. For newly assigned missionaries, the sending and receiving dioceses are encouraged to join with the society, whenever possible, to assist with the funding required for the assignment.

In the first eight months 1995, with the clarity of the new diocesan funding formula, Mission Personnel has received and processed 1,171 letters, telephone calls or visits from persons inquiring about mission service. This significant response can be attributed to several factors: the ads in *Episcopal Life* and *The Living Church* which focused on the assignment of new missioners, mission discussions throughout the church, mission interpretation by returned missioners, and the assistance of returned missioners in our recruitment efforts.

Racial/Ethnic Exposure Program

Currently the Office of Anglican and Global Relations is involved in a number of programs designed to further mission participation. The Racial/Ethnic Exposure Program (REEP) which celebrates the diversity of the Episcopal Church was created to encourage persons of color to explore missionary and volunteer service. Since very few persons of color apply for mission service, the REEP provides a short mission exposure with the expectation that some might consider long-term service. Additionally, we look to the REEP participants to assist with the recruitment of other persons for mission service. In the debriefing as they compared notes on experiences and as the commonality of being Christians in diverse settings clearly emerged, one volunteer reported that the overarching mission message is: "We are all children of the same God."

A total of thirty-one persons have served through the program since its creation in 1991. Following participation in a summer exposure program, Virginia Doctor was assigned to serve as Lay Missioner, Diocese of Alaska; and Lita Killip is teaching English and Bible in China. We remain hopeful that other persons of color will step forward for long-term mission service.

Seminary Internships

In the past four years, we have been encouraged by the number of seminarians who have served through the Volunteer for Mission program: Keith Yamamoto, General Seminary, is presently serving with the Episcopal Church in Cuba; Michel-Jean Szczepaniak, Episcopal Divinity School, served with the Diocese of Christchurch, New Zealand; Angela Ifill, Virginia Seminary, is assigned to Bishop Tucker College, Mukono Diocese, Uganda. Through the REEP: Alan Smith, Yale Divinity School, served in the Diocese of Cape Town; Carole Robinson, Virginia Theological Seminary, served in the Diocese of Panama; Ruth Anne Garcia, General Seminary, assigned to work-camp in Russia. Seminarians from the Office of Spanish Ministries in the Diocese of Los Angeles: Mario Gonzales, assigned to the Diocese of Alaska; Ramiro Rodriguez assigned to the Diocese of Belize; Isidro Gonzales, assigned to the Diocese of Panama; Michael Kim, Yale Divinity School, assigned to the Diocese of the Dominican Republic; and a seminary aspirant, Terry Star, was assigned to the Diocese of Alaska. We are hopeful that this is the beginning of an ongoing exposure for many other seminarians.

South to South

We have sought to identify nationals from one overseas diocese to be assigned to another overseas diocese. We use the phrase from the World Council of Churches: "South to South" to define these appointments. In most cases, the "South to South" placement is with a missioner who has some understanding of the culture, country and the language where assigned.

Through the "South to South" placements, the Rev. Santiago Garcia from the Diocese of Guatemala initially served in the Diocese of El Salvador and most recently has been transferred to the Diocese of the Dominican Republic where he serves as Dean of Theological Studies. Other "South to South" appointments are in the pipeline and hopefully all components will be completed and we will be able to move ahead with the placements.

Mission to the USA

Herbert Arrunategui, Staff Officer for Hispanic Ministry, assisted us with the arrangements for the Rev. Carlos Lopez-Lozana, Episcopal Church in Spain and his wife, Ana, to serve as missionaries to the USA, February–May 1994. They served at St. Paul's Church, Westfield, New Jersey, and this provided an excellent assignment for their ministry as missionaries to the Episcopal Church. On Carlos's return to Spain, he resumed his duties as rector, Church of the Redeemer, Salamanca. In November 1995, Carlos was consecrated as the new Bishop of the Episcopal Church in Spain. Through the assignment of Carlos and Ana, we experienced how reverse mission informs us of life in another culture while they were missionaries to us. This enabled us to look at similar and different concerns.

Mission Associates

The most valuable resource in the recruitment endeavor is the network of missioners who have completed mission assignments. The mission associates provide additional support with the recruitment and initial interview of potential missioners, and they greatly assist with mission interpretation, cross-cultural orientation, re-entry programs, and the Racial/ Ethnic Exposure Program.

Ecumenical Work

In the annual ecumenical meeting of denominational people to assess the candidates to teach English As a Second Language through the Amity Foundation, National Council of Churches of Christ, we had three qualified Episcopalians, but did not have the funds to enable their placement. As a result, the United Church Board of Higher Education in Asia (UCBHEA) and the United Church of Christ (UCC) responded with funds to enable the assignment of: Elease Eleazar, Diocese of North Carolina; Jane Fladd, Diocese of Los Angeles; and Lita Killip, Diocese of New York. Early in 1995 with clarity on our funding, we assumed the major portion of the funds for the three China educators; the UCBHEA and UCC asked to continue with a small percentage of their financial support.

Other joint appointments are those with the Anglican Church of Canada where the Rev. Santiago Garcia, Diocese of Guatemala, was initially assigned to serve in the Diocese of El Salvador as Theological Educator, and more recently has transferred to the Diocese of the Dominican Republic where he serves as the Dean of Theological Studies. Keith Yamamoto, seminary intern, is serving with the Episcopal Church of Cuba. Conversations are underway for other joint appointments with the Anglican Church of Canada.

We benefit from cooperation with the Anglican Church of Canada and our ecumenical partners and will seek ways to enhance these relationships.

Exposure to Mission—Panama

I served as co-leader for the "Exposure to Mission" sponsored by the Episcopal Council for Global Mission which provided an opportunity for persons to participate in a cross-cultural experience in the Diocese of Panama. The learnings from this pilot project have to do with entering into the lives of another people who are conditioned by traditions other than our own. These learnings require us to listen with our hearts and to place much importance in developing relationships with the sisters and brothers with whom we minister and not to transport an American solution to all concerns. The evaluations of the nine participants provided an in-depth reflection of their experiences which will be lifelong. Hopefully, there will be many other opportunities for an "Exposure to Mission" throughout the church to inform and strengthen persons who are interested in mission and in some cases may serve as chairs of missions committees.

The Future

As the GEM group develops its strategies for mission in the life of the church, we are working together to determine where and how we will relate, and what shape the relationship will take. We are faced with the need for sensitivity and responsiveness to different approaches yet to be determined which will lead the church in uniquely responding to mission challenges. In so doing, it is imperative that we look afresh for emerging new forms of mission and test them against our best sense of mission and what it is that God calls the church to be.

We look to expanded and creative ways to enable persons to serve in mission. One illustration was the dialogue with the staff of the Committee to Assist the Episcopal Diocese of Honduras (CAEDH), where the discussions resulted in an agreement where CAEDH will focus primarily on the recruitment of educators for the mission schools in the Diocese of Honduras. Using our common screening guidelines, Mission Personnel will assign a specified number of applicants each year following their successful completion of the cross-cultural orientation program and medical clearance. In this arrangement, Mission Personnel will focus on other mission needs in Honduras and from other parts of the world. As a recruitment channel, CAEDH is included in the "Mission Opportunities List," along with the independent voluntary agencies in the Episcopal Church who provide training and assign missionaries and evangelists.

In a meeting with the Rev. Pierce Klemmt and the Outreach/

Missions Committee, Christ Church, Alexandria, Virginia, they shared information on their challenging ministries which include their VFM educator in the Diocese of Honduras. Their other ministries include Our Little Roses Home for Girls, Diocese of Honduras; Chernobyl Crescent which focuses on children ravaged by radiation from the Chernobyl disaster; Mengo Hospital in Uganda; and their South Africa Partnership ministry. These mission engagements reinforce the fact that local parishes are actively engaged in mission and doing a fantastic job. The Outreach/Missions Committee shared: "We are heartened by the lovely stories of lives changed—of those who called out, and of those who answered." "Then I heard the voice of the Lord say, 'Whom shall I send? and who will go for us?' Then I said, 'Here am I. Send me.'"

As GEM's strategies unfold for mission engagement, it becomes clear that we must share our expertise and utilize GEM as a vehicle to increase the numbers of assigned missionaries and volunteers of the Episcopal Church in comparison to other mainline denominations. The following statistics emphasize this need:

Episcopal Church: missionaries - 28; volunteers - 29
Presbyterian Church: missionaries and volunteers - 669
United Methodist Church: missionaries - 423
United Church of Christ - Disciples Church (Christian Church):
                                       missionaries - 163; volunteers - 25

Margaret Larom has returned to the Church Center as the World Mission Interpretation and Networks Officer in the Anglican and Global Relations Cluster, and will be engaged with the mission networks of the church in determining ways for us to work together more effectively. Additionally, she will seek to discover channels to bring a greater understanding of mission engagement to the church.

The Mission Personnel Office is charged with the recruitment, screening, and placement of qualified missioners in response to the requests from overseas and USA bishops. In responding, we share in a "partnership" where missioners say they receive more than they are able to give. In their assignments, we aim to assign missioners who will support and enable the nationals with whom they serve in partnership.

As active partners with GEM, we will explore ways of cooperation. While we are not certain what shape the partnership will take, the sharing of personnel requests ("Mission Opportunities List") from partner churches throughout the world is one possibility. Other possible areas for joint collaboration might be to sponsor cross-cultural orientation events, provide counsel and information, continue to enable the racial/ethnic participation, and provide a channel for ecumenical appointments.

The mission staff responsibilities are among the most exciting, fulfilling, and challenging. We feel we are involved in the loving service of Christ's mission and witness, having as our fundamental task, to proclaim Christ's concern for the total person and the total community in the worldwide mission of the church.

As we chart the future course for Mission Personnel, we are committed to insuring a global mission program in which all persons are called and empowered to participate fully in the mission of Jesus Christ. We are committed to increasing the concern and involvement of every member and every parish in Christ's mission to the world. In faithful obedience, we will respond to the inquirers' appeal: "Here I am! Send me!"

EPISCOPAL CHURCH MISSIONARY COMMUNITY

Ms. Sharon Stockdale

ECMC started the New Wineskins for Global Mission conference with two ideas in mind: the ECMC Board of Directors wanted to celebrate ECMC's twenty years in ministry, and we wanted to provide a catalyst for missions in the Episcopal Church. There are so many different mission efforts in the Episcopal Church which the average Episcopalian a) hasn't heard of, b) would be greatly encouraged to know about, and c) could work with to impact the world for Jesus Christ. Perhaps ECMC could bring all these organizations together and help put missions on the map for Episcopalians!

Praise the Lord, he has blessed New Wineskins, and the conference succeeded "above all we could ask, think, or imagine!" ECMC is planning to continue putting on a New Wineskins for Global Mission conference every three years, bringing Episcopal mission agencies together with speakers from around the world to inspire, motivate, and give practical help to Episcopalians who care about world missions. That is what ECMC's purpose statement is: "ECMC is a voluntary society enabling Episcopalians to be more knowledgeable, active, and effective in fulfilling our Lord's Great Commission to make disciples of all nations."

As I said, 1994 is ECMC's twentieth anniversary. We are the sponsoring organization of New Wineskins, but New Wineskins is only one of the ways ECMC has been working to fulfill our purpose. We have four main ministries:

ECMC produces resources to raise mission vision in your parish.

At your invitation, ECMC staff can present a Mission Awareness Seminar in your parish or diocese to help equip you for outreach locally and to the ends of the earth. God's kingdom is growing and expanding around the world today in ways that are unprecedented in history. What part can you play? An ECMC Mission Awareness Seminar will give you an opportunity to have your vision and awareness of mission around the world expanded. What are God's priorities for the world and the church? We can give you a glimpse of what God has been doing from biblical times until the present. We can introduce you to avenues for work as partners in mission with developing national churches and take you to the frontiers where Christ has never been named. We can help your church set priorities and enable you to plan the next steps to a growing ministry in the US and overseas.

Mission Awareness Seminars can be adapted to fit your needs. We can focus in on new strategies in missions, developing a missions committee, Episcopal missions agencies, effective holistic ministries, reaching out to international students, or unreached people in the U.S. and around the world. Call us!

Another mission education resource ECMC produces is the *Reach-Out* bulletin, with inspiration and information about what Episcopalians are doing in missions in the USA and abroad. We do six issues a year, which are sent to ECMC supporters and by request.

We also have produced workshops and videos on topics such as the role of prayer in renewal, evangelism, and mission, how missions fits into the life of your congregation, ministering to internationals in the USA, Jesus' Style of Evangelism, etc.

ECMC trains mission committee members and missionaries-to-be.

ECMC has given orientation, counsel, and debriefing to hundreds of Episcopalians who have served in cross-cultural ministries in the USA and overseas. When Walter and Louise Hannum started ECMC in 1974, there was no formal training for Episcopal missionaries. Since that time, they have given orientation to more than three hundred Episcopal missionaries who have served as Volunteers for Mission, appointees of our national church, with the South American Missionary Society, Episcopal World Mission, Anglican Frontier Missions, as well as with a number of interdenominational agencies.

The ECMC Missions Clearinghouse provides up-to-date information on Episcopal and interdenominational missions agencies and missionary training programs.

Once or twice a year, ECMC staff teach an Introductory Course on World Mission, a one-week course on the world from God's perspective and what your role could be as a missionary or as a sender. ECMC moved from Pasadena, California, to Ambridge, Pennsylvania, in 1990 to help Trinity Episcopal School for Ministry (TESM) get a missions department started. Walter and Louise Hannum are adjunct professors at TESM, and they have taught mission courses during the regular school year as well as during TESM's January and June terms.

ECMC equips Episcopalians to reach unreached people groups around the world.

ECMC counsels "tentmakers" who use their professional skills to go share Christ's love in countries closed to traditional missions. We can tell you about Episcopal and interdenominational avenues to reach those who have never heard. ECMC members helped raise funds for the Yavatmal College for Leadership Training (YCLT) to train Indian nationals as missionaries going to villages, tribes, and people groups in India with no church. Through ECMC's Anglican Frontier Fellowship Fund, ECMC members have supported Episcopal missionaries reaching unreached people groups in the Middle East, Central Asia, and around the world. One hundred percent of the donations from checks made out to ECMC marked "for YCLT" or "for Anglican Frontier Fellowship Fund" are used for those ministries. ECMC does not take any percentage to cover our overhead for administering those funds.

ECMC encourages prayer and care for Episcopal missionaries.

The ECMC Prayer Calendar is included in the *ReachOut* with prayer requests from Episcopal missionaries and mission agencies. It is updated every two months. We can also help you know how to nurture, encourage, and support Episcopal missionaries from their first inklings of a call to cross-cultural ministry, to seeing they get good training and counsel, to helping them on the field, to when they return home.

You can help!

ECMC is a voluntary society, supported by donations from individuals and parishes, not our national church's budget. We would value your partnership with us in prayer and financially. ECMC exists to enable Episcopalians to be more knowledgeable, active, and effective in fulfilling our Lord's Great Commission to make disciples of all nations. Let us know how we can be of service to you!

EPISCOPAL COUNCIL FOR GLOBAL MISSION

The Rev. Richard Jones and Mr. Tyler Zabriskie

ZABRISKIE: In order to give you an overview of the formation and future of the Episcopal Council for Global Mission, three of us who have participated in the leadership of the Council are present. Two years ago, I was the convener of the Episcopal Council for Global Mission. Richard Jones, Professor of Mission and World Religions at Virginia Theological Seminary, is the council's convener this year. Titus Presler, who will convene the council next year, is also with us. Titus is a lecturer in Anglicanism, Globalism and Ecumenism Studies at the Episcopal Divinity School in Boston, and co-rector of St. Peter's Episcopal Church in Cambridge, Massachusetts.

The Episcopal Council for Global Mission was born in 1989 as an outgrowth of the annual mission conference in Sewanee, Tennessee. The Sewanee mission conferences were sponsored by four organizations: South American Missionary Society, Episcopal Church Missionary Community, the National Church Mission Office, and the University of the South. Over the ten years these conferences were held, it became increasingly apparent that two agendas were emerging. One agenda was to educate and raise mission awareness in the larger church. A second agenda was to meet with other leaders to share their experience, visions and challenges. Because there were few opportunities for communication about mission policies and theological perspectives among the sponsoring groups, tensions began to build. Eventually, these tensions threatened to impede the larger task of mission education.

In an effort to work together, fifty representatives of Episcopal mission organizations gathered in 1990 to try to answer two questions: "Can we work together for the glory of God? Can we agree to disagree on certain things, yet focus on common goals?" Four covenants were drawn up which represented commitments that all the participants were willing to make. We decided to meet annually to discuss what God was doing in each of our organizations. We agreed to look for ways that we could share information and resources so that all together we could build up the work of the Episcopal Church.

We developed a council that operated on a consensus model, sometimes called a circular model. There is no administrative hierarchy. Each year a convener is chosen, along with a co-convener who will become the leader in the following year. People who wish to serve on a steering committee offer their names, and then names are pulled out of a hat. As we have met over the last four years, issues of misunderstanding and mistrust that previously restricted common action were, to a large extent, resolved. Today, there is more communication and trust, and creative ideas are developing. ECGM has developed a forum to gather together, pray with one another, and find common ground.

Each year ECGM meetings have a focus, in addition to sharing news about our various organizations. In our first year, we held the meeting in conjunction with a conference on unreached peoples called Anglican Frontiers. ECGM asked the question, "Can we recognize a place in the larger mission of the Episcopal Church for taking the gospel to ethnic groups and communities that have never heard it before?" It turned out to be a very successful initial conference. Partners from overseas participate in each Council meeting. These Anglican partners are invited to raise questions, critique and speak to the way they perceive what we were doing.

In our second year we decided to openly discuss the differences in our theologies of mission. We invited two speakers, one from Trinity Episcopal School for Ministry, and another from St. Michael's College, Toronto, Canada, who represented a broad Catholic theology. They addressed the issue of Christology and what it means to proclaim the gospel to people of other faiths or no faith. Although Christology and evangelism can be polarizing issues, we found that discussion and debate yielded greater understanding. While differences of opinion abound, we are seeing greater respect for other ways of understanding God's call to mission.

During 1993, ECGM met with the Standing Commission on World Mission, the body that shapes legislation between meetings of the General Convention. Among the topics was the autonomy of new provinces in the Anglican Communion. This year, the Council will concentrate on forming proposals for mission structures at the national level.

JONES: Our statement of purpose describes the Episcopal Council for Global Mission as a network of Episcopal organizations involved in global mission, "committed to meet and communicate, in dialogue with our Anglican partners and each other, in order to promote the unity and effectiveness of the mission of the Body of Christ." This is not a body that has authority to divide the world into comity zones. This is not a body that is, at least thus far, doling out funds, nor the place to come to for the funding of your organization. We are not, ourselves, deploying people. We are a network of organizations that are doing all of those things. We are committed to meet, believing that face to face, much truth will emerge and conflict can be dealt with. The dialogue is meant to be with each other, which is to say, US-based Episcopal Church organizations, with the help of visitors from outside. In 1991, Bishop Kauma of Namirembe Diocese, Uganda, was a great breath of fresh air as he candidly told us that every time he leaves for a tour of the US, he is given a shopping list from his orphanages and organizations. He was equally candid in his observations about our circle.

The covenants were worked out in 1990 and new member organizations are asked whether they in good conscience can subscribe to the following articles:

First, in theology, recognizing that God is truth, we discern truth through dialogue in community, desiring to avoid untested assumptions about one another. We seek to understand various mission theologies by committing time and resources to listen and talk together with honesty and mutual respect.

Second, we have acknowledged that it is a legitimate and important part of an Anglican understanding of mission to promote a vision throughout the Communion to work for the extension of the church among groups where the gospel of Christ is not known. That may mean that work needs to be done among unreached peoples within existing Anglican dioceses, or it may mean work is to be done in areas where the Anglican Communion has not heretofore been historically present.

Perhaps most controversial is the third item, on partnership in mission: that "in a spirit of respect and cooperation within the body of Christ, we covenant to accept as a norm the receiving of appropriate invitation/permission." The idea is that we agree not to violate the jurisdiction of existing Anglican authority.

Last, information sharing is an easy one; well, maybe it isn't. "We covenant to share mission information on projects and procedures relative to recruiting, screening, selecting, training and placing missionaries. We further covenant to explore ways of coordinating our activities in order to encourage healthy cooperation and discourage unhealthy, competitive attitudes in the world mission field." To share our mailing lists and financial sources—now that's the real test of trust. Do you introduce your fellow mission agency to your donor? We have not done very much about creative fund raising, but it's a topic with which we need to deal.

In our conception of this council, membership could be open to any agency, whether incorporated or not, a parish, a diocese, a program of a university, and others. In the past, a number of large parishes with sizable budgets or significant engagement in global mission have been a part. Membership is not open to individuals; the Episcopal Council on Global Mission is an organization of organizations. Organizations who are not comfortable signing our covenant, are still welcome to participate in observer roles. They can be a part of the sharing, but in terms of having representation, they are not voting members. We are not normally a voting organization, but that was the distinction made.

ZABRISKIE: If you want to be more involved in mission, there are several things that you or your parishes can do. The first is to pray. Pray because all mission depends upon prayer. Second, if you know of local groups in your parish or diocese that want the resources of these member agencies, or if you are looking for a particular type of resource, write to us. Each organization in ECGM handles different aspects of training and orientation, and has special relationships with different parts of the world. Generally speaking, this vital information is not broadly known in the Episcopal Church. Your priest or bishop may not be aware of many of these organizations and the resources they have. Third, you may want to form a link between your congregation and some missionaries that are already on the field. Finally, all of these agencies are able to accomplish their goals because individuals, parishes and dioceses believe in what they are doing and contribute to their work. We encourage you to explore being financially committed to a mission if something it is doing is close to your heart. Your involvement may help your parish to grow in its commitment to mission.

The Episcopal Council for Global Mission does not have formal authority in the national church. Nevertheless, we are pleased to provide a place where networking and conversation about global mission are happening in a constructive way.

EPISCOPAL WORLD MISSIONS

The Rev. J. Eugene Horn

First, I want to discuss what I believe is the context of the time in which we are living. Second, I'll outline some past history of Episcopal World Missions, identify the most dramatic results that the Holy Spirit has reaped through us to date, and sketch a little bit of the new EWM that is just emerging.

The context of the times is very clear to those paying attention to what the Holy Spirit is doing in the church—Jesus is renewing his body in many ways. God is doing some extraordinary things in the world that are fulfilling the prophecy given in Joel and in Acts:

> In the last days, God says, I will pour out my Spirit on all people. Your sons and daughters will prophesy, your young men will see visions, your old men will dream dreams. Even on my servants, both men and women, I will pour out my Spirit in those days, and they will prophesy. I will show wonders in the heavens above and signs on the earth below...The sun will be turned to darkness and the moon to blood before the coming of the great and glorious day of the Lord, and everyone who calls on the name of the Lord will be saved (Acts 2:17-21 NIV)

We Anglicans don't have a very good eschatology; in fact, for the most part, we don't have one at all. But God is pouring out prophetic anointing on the church that has been absent for a long, long time. God is doing what is necessary to cause the hearts of people all over the world, including unreached peoples, to have a hunger in their hearts for the Creator of the world to be revealed to them. Almost every people group to which we present the gospel has a folktale or legend about the day that will come when the God of the universe will reveal himself to them. Part of our strategy must be sensitivity to the Holy Spirit so that when we go to these people we will be prepared to best present the gospel.

The Lord is also giving strategies to the church. People prophesied for years in advance that the doors of Russia would open for a very short period of time, and then they would close again. When those doors did in fact open, the church was not prepared to mobilize in response, and now I believe we have missed one of the great mission opportunities in our lifetime, because the Mormons, Jehovah's Witnesses, pornographers and New Age folks made it into Russia almost immediately. Now we believe the doors of China are about to open, and unless the church changes its heart and begins mobilizing now, we are going to miss China just the way we have Russia. As we enter new arenas, there are real twentieth-century power encounters occurring between the forces of darkness and those who serve the living God. Unless those of us who serve God have the ability to pray, to intercede and to wage spiritual warfare, we are going to blow it again. It seems that the way we have done missions for the most part was to figure out some kind of a program, rather than tapping into God's plan and being able to proclaim the gospel with the power of the Holy Spirit, which is the only effective way to do missions or anything else in the church of Jesus Christ.

God is calling and restoring the church to prayer. There is a great, worldwide intercessory prayer movement throughout the body of Christ. It is happening all at once in every place the church exists where people are willing to be submitted to the lordship of Jesus. People are hungering to learn how to pray, and it is only by effective, fervent and prevailing prayer that the work of God can be done.

Another thing that the Lord is doing in the context of the times is to make networks of people. In the Anglican Church we have isolated ourselves from the rest of the body of Christ in many ways. And now God is growing the church with people that we respect the least: people that he has poured out the Holy Spirit upon, who may not be educated or academic, and don't have all the resources that we so proudly proclaim. In fact, the reality is that in eight of the ten largest churches in the world the pastors have no education beyond high school, not even any formal Bible school training. Of those ten churches, the largest is over 800,000 and the smallest is over 60,000 in a single congregation. Perhaps we ought to re-examine the old ways of doing things.

It is only as we enter into a personal relationship with the Holy Spirit, learning how to walk in the Spirit and live by the Spirit, that we will be effective in doing what God has called us to do.

Episcopal World Missions is now about ten years old. We have survived a relatively rocky beginning. In 1990 we discovered we were in serious, significant debt and had to decide: do we go bankrupt and close the doors, or do we spend the time, energy and resources to pay the debt and continue the ministry that had begun? We have worked very hard to retire the debt, and once that happens, we will hire an executive director. We have four salaried staff. I am a parish priest serving as the board member with responsibility for supervising the administration of the mission, but it's all done by telephone and fax.

Up until now, our strategy has been to ask people to commit at least six years in a foreign field and preferably be career missionaries. We have sent people to work only in settings where the church is already established so they could work under Anglican bishops. We now have a dozen missionaries who are, or have been, located in the following countries: Kenya, Singapore, Japan, Jordan, Israel, Cyprus, the Solomon Islands, Zaire, Malawi, Bangladesh, Pakistan, Madagascar, Russia and Spain.

Some dramatic results have been achieved. I will share two extraordinary stories. Recently we sent Esther Miller, who received her one-year lay certificate at Trinity Episcopal School for Ministry, to the Diocese of Lake Malawi. A widow in her fifties, Esther is an anointed evangelist who has never met a stranger in her life. She found the condition of the church in Malawi to be an Anglo-Catholic 8:00 a.m. church setting. Everything was very cold, with no warmth in the church. It was simply the tradition that you did not sing with joy, you did not smile, and there was no humor whatsoever. They were evangelized about a hundred years ago by an Anglo-Catholic portion of the Church of England.

Esther, being who she is, began witnessing to people and leading them to the Lord. A number were baptized in the Holy Spirit. She began praying for people as opportunities arose, and God healed nearly everyone for whom she prayed. Living in the same compound at diocesan headquarters was the provincial treasurer. His oldest son died. About a half hour after his death, Esther came in, and the Holy Spirit instructed her to lay hands on him, pray, and command him to come back to life. He did! That really got the attention of the Bishop of the Diocese of Lake Malawi. A few days later he asked, "Esther, how did you learn to do all of these things?" She replied that with the exception of raising someone from the dead, this is what anybody in her parish at home would do. He asked her, "Who taught you?" She answered, her parish priest. So within a few months her parish priest came and spent six weeks in Malawi.

At his first meeting with the bishop, the priest was given a very troubling and stern prophetic word from the Lord, regarding some issues in the bishop's life. This encounter lasted for several hours, resulting in the bishop's repentance over these issues to the Lord. Up until then, he had been very antagonistic to three young priests in his diocese, two of whom had been trained in America and met Jesus as Baptizer in the Holy Spirit. He had been hostile to them and moved them around the diocese, but now he came out of the confessional praying in other tongues.

A few days later he opened a conference with his clergy by confessing his sin, asking the priests to forgive him as the Lord had. He then announced that it would no longer be business as usual in the Diocese of Lake Malawi. Nearly half of the priests had not met Jesus personally as

Savior and Lord, and during the eight days of that clergy conference they were born again. More than two-thirds of the clergy and their wives met Jesus as Baptizer in the Holy Spirit.

On a Sunday morning during the conference, the visiting priest from America had the responsibility for preaching in a very large church that holds over three thousand people. At the end of the Communion, he had permission from the bishop to extend an invitation to the congregation to meet Jesus as Savior and Lord. This is the first time in living memory that this has happened in any Anglican church in Malawi. Over two hundred people responded and thus began a great outpouring of the Holy Spirit. At the final meeting of the clergy conference the bishop told his clergy, "When you go back home, I don't care if your elders get upset with you; I want to hear reports that you are proclaiming the gospel, and that the fire of the Holy Spirit is falling upon your congregations."

Since August of 1993, over 100,000 people have come to Christ in the Diocese of Lake Malawi. There are now over 150,000 Anglicans with only forty-three clergy. Each priest is responsible for fifteen to thirty individual churches with no transportation but their feet. The bishop has not only released the priests to proclaim the gospel in a new way, but as he notices parishioners empowered by the Holy Spirit who begin sharing their faith, he commissions them as lay preachers. The Holy Spirit is reaping tremendous and dramatic results.

A second story is about a missionary of ours we have seconded to another agency. For security reasons I will identify neither the missionary nor the organization. This man is a priest, also a graduate of Trinity, who is working in the Muslim world. An entrepreneur, he is extremely energetic, bright, and in love with the Lord. His agency is implementing some of the most creative ideas I have ever heard about how to work in the Muslim context in order to lead people to Christ. The ministry is moving forward in a dramatic way; thousands of adult Muslims have turned to Christ and been baptized in water. Indigenous leadership is developing in indigenous churches called messianic mosques which remain in the Muslim cultural context, but for whom Jesus is Savior and Lord. They call themselves "fulfilled Muslims" or "messianic Muslims," very much in the messianic Jewish style.

The Lord is leading us at EWM to examine what we are doing now, and to seek his will about where we are supposed to head in the future, and what the organization should be like. At a vision strategy meeting, one of our board members said it sounds as if we have already made the decision that we are going to color outside the lines. While moving through this process we have made several policy decisions. We are going to concentrate our primary resources on reaching unreached people groups. We are going to send missionaries to plant churches where there are no bishops. We want to do everything possible for the Great Commission to be realized in our time using entrepreneurs, tentmakers, short-term missions and career missionaries.

We are using teaching English as a Second Language as an access into closed countries. Right now that is the primary tool available for Christians to get into China, because the Chinese government is asking for teachers of conversational English. They will pay your stipend for a three-month stint or longer, and it's a ripe opportunity that the church needs to take advantage of as soon as possible.

We are going to continue strategies as we have in Malawi to use established relationships and missionaries to bring revival and renewal to the church. One of the fruits of the ministry in Malawi is that the bishop has gotten a heart for missions, and he desires to develop a missionary-sending and training program in order to send Malawian Christians all over Africa, if not to other parts of the world. To enable that effort is a part of what we believe we need to be about. We are going to do everything possible to send not only Americans, but to become a mission agency sending Episcopalians and Anglicans from any place in the world. We want to take them from their country, culture and climate, and send them where they are being led by God to proclaim the gospel, in a different culture, clime and geographical location. There is a whole file folder full of requests for missionaries from different parts of the world which we are currently unable to fulfill. We are targeting every part of the world that is not Spanish-speaking.

The way we do it is that all of our missionaries have responsibility for securing all of their own prayer and financial support from family, individuals, churches, and so on. We have a very effective training program for accomplishing that, and we have all of the administrative systems in place to be able to make it possible for them to go nearly anyplace in the world that we and they together believe the Lord is calling them. The most important ingredient is having a group of people that you can trust will pray for you, upholding you before the throne of grace, and that you can count on to be available to deal with any kind of difficulty or emergency that comes along in your life and ministry. In normal life emergencies arise, but on the mission field they are often more acute, the crisis is greater, and the threat to life is significantly more severe.

I have a parish which is deeply committed to mission. We have sent out four missionaries from our own congregation and support five others.

We are primarily a home cell church, and every one of our home cells has responsibility for providing support for an individual missionary. When I first arrived nine years ago, their total giving for everything outside of themselves was $17,000. Last year, this church of 120 members provided over $60,000—more than half our total income—for missions.

Jesus says in Matthew 24:14, "And this Gospel of the kingdom will be preached in the whole world as a testimony to all nations and then the end will come." That is the charter of Episcopal World Missions: to do everything that we can with the responsibility that the Lord entrusts to us, to do our share as effectively, rapidly and efficiently as possible, under the leading and empowerment of the Holy Spirit.

NORTH AMERICAN MISSIONARY SOCIETY

The Rt. Rev. Alden Hathaway and the Rev. Jon Shuler

Let us hold fast to the confession of our hope without wavering, for He who has promised is faithful; and let us consider how to provoke one another to love and good deeds, not neglecting to meet together as is the habit of some, but encouraging one another; and all the more, as you see the day approaching. (Heb 10:23-25)

HATHAWAY: This conference is a gathering of people to encourage and provoke one another to love and good works, because he who has promised is faithful, and we desperately need to respond in a faithful way.

Jon Shuler and I met at an Episcopalians United conference in Baltimore last September, where he gave his testimony. I was deeply moved to hear how Jon resigned from his parish in order to devote the rest of his ministry to the Great Commission in the Episcopal Church. It dovetailed with a long-standing challenge in my own life: how to get our church unstuck from where it has been over the last many years. We seem to be solely engaged in issues of our own interior life, rather than seeking to understand how we are to exercise our ministry beyond ourselves to the world, which is our true mission. One of the reasons we are at such odds, and why we are tearing each other apart, is because somewhere along the line we forgot that the mission of the church is what we should be all about.

These are the four basic premises. First, the unequivocal gospel of

Jesus Christ is the best message for the world, and it is absolutely essential that this message be heard.

Second, unless people have a missionary heart, they are incomplete Christians. I came to learn this as the rector of a congregation. I thought we were all pretty good in terms of our life together; we had all kinds of good organizations and lots of life going, although our stewardship wasn't so hot. But then a priest from Africa came into our midst and put upon our hearts the plight of the church there, and all of a sudden it unlocked us. People who went over to be with this man in his context found their lives changed, and this caused other people to go. We became a sending church, and that began to mobilize us all for the mission that we had across the ocean and across the street. We were only partially Christian until we gained a missionary mentality. So if you really care for your people and their maturity in Jesus Christ, you must impart a missionary perspective.

Third, in the United States today we live in a missionary situation. We no longer have a Christian culture in which biblical ideals, values and principles are reinforced by our surroundings. Society is a foreign place, and the culture will literally suck the Christian faith right out of you unless you are well-fortified.

I think about kids in some Pittsburgh neighborhoods with pistols in their pockets, ready to blow each other away because nobody has ever shared with them that their lives are worth anything. They don't know that they are made by God, he has a destiny for them, and that their lives are precious. These Pittsburgh kids are an unreached people, as far away as a tribe in Iran. There is plenty of missionary work right across the street, in the slums and in the boardrooms. Many top business executives, if asked to describe who Jesus Christ was and is, would not have the slightest idea of how to answer. This does not take away from our need to be involved in foreign missions, but our life as the Episcopal Church includes mission to the United States.

Fourth, the most effective agencies for evangelism and mission for us as Episcopalians are viable parishes: congregations that are alive to the gospel of Jesus Christ, where people are growing up in the faith, and are themselves becoming agencies of mission. That's the way we as Episcopalians do mission work the best.

I have come to realize that traditionally the most effective agencies for renewal in the church are independent, spiritual societies. Churches are very seldom renewed by their own established organizations. We here in the United States are indebted to those private societies for the establishment of the church in this country. I am also thinking of the formation of some missionary societies, including the South American Missionary Society, the origin of which was really part of my conversion.

Therefore, the thought is, what about a North American Missionary Society: an independent society that would gather together resources and individuals who have a heart for the mission of evangelism, outreach and missionary work to North America? Its purpose would be to proclaim the gospel for the ongoing conversion of American society, employing a strategy for the planting of a specific kind of missionary church. From the very beginning the church would be conceived, organized, and intended to become a viable parish that would grow to a certain size and then spin off other viable congregations, and do that perpetually, therefore creating the next generation of the Episcopal Church. I believe that there are both the people and the money to respond to that initiative.

Until last fall, Jon Shuler was the rector of Church of the Ascension in Knoxville, Tennessee, a church that had become a viable, vibrant congregation built on the basis of small-group ministry. It was the fulfillment of this man's dream to have a vital outreach congregation for Jesus Christ. Then in the last year or so in the Diocese of East Tennessee, there was a movement to restructure General Convention, to completely change it. The bishop bumped that resolution over to this man, and so, being an obedient Episcopalian, he took the bishop's directive and decided to organize a conference called "Shaping Our Future," which met in St. Louis in the summer of 1993.

SHULER: I would like to share with you what has become the guiding passage for my life and ministry. This passage so perplexed me in the early days after my conversion that I told an older saint of the church that I couldn't understand it. He looked at me very piercingly for a moment, and said, "Son, it's the central verse of the New Testament." It is Ephesians 3:7-13, and Paul wrote it.

> Of this gospel I have become a servant according to the gift of God's grace that was given me by the working of his power. Although I am the very least of all the saints, this grace was given to me to bring to the Gentiles the news of the boundless riches of Christ, and to make everyone see what is the plan of the mystery hidden for ages in God who created all things; so that through the church the wisdom of God in its rich variety might now be made known to the rulers and authorities in the heavenly places. This was in accordance with the eternal purpose that he has carried out in Christ Jesus our Lord, in whom we have access to God in boldness and confidence through faith in him. I

pray therefore that you may not lose heart over my sufferings for you;
they are your glory. (NRSV)

When that verse and its context came into my heart, after four years
of evangelical theological training and twenty-six years as an Episcopal
Christian, I was plunked down by the grace of God into an Anglo-
Catholic parish in England. Soon that parish was caught up in charismatic renewal. So I found myself in the middle of an evangelical, catholic
and charismatic thing, and I thank God for that. I formed the impression
that what God was doing in that little parish in Durham was showing us
what he meant Anglicans to be like: evangelical and catholic and charismatic.

We worked in that little parish as faithfully as we knew how for a
number of years, trying to be a Bible-believing, people-loving, com-
munity-serving church of Jesus, and God blessed that. And then he sent
me back to the United States. I did not want to come. I had fallen into the
trap of believing that England is the holy land, even though it is in desperate need of renewal.

It was a hard awakening, to come back to the Diocese of Southern
Ohio where I felt marginalized. Much to my shame, I tried to figure out
how to live a normal life in the Episcopal Church. I found that being an
evangelical-catholic-charismatic Episcopal priest in Southern Ohio didn't
cut it. After a year or so of being labeled a fundamentalist by men and
women that I loved in the home diocese of my childhood, I went underground. I'm not proud of it, but I have nineteen years of parish experience, including seven of them in Knoxville, trying to be a secret evangelical-catholic-charismatic. And I can tell you, it's not worth it. If you
are playing with that idea, or living in it, give it up! Heaven isn't worth
risking for business as usual in the Episcopal Church.

By the grace of God, I have never served in a church that didn't
grow, but after those nineteen years the Lord said to me, "Most of what
you are doing is like vomit, because it's not making disciples, it's making church people." So I asked the Lord to forgive me, and I began a
journey now in its fifth year of trying to come out into the open and find
a new way. I am convinced that God is doing a mighty thing on the earth
in our day. Having been called into this church, raised up in this church,
finding the Lord in this church, and knowing the heritage, goodness and
life that God has in this church, I have a desire to see this family to
which I belong share in the global revival that God has already inaugurated.

In addition to that, through some mystery, twenty-five years ago God put it into my heart to form a group of folks who were willing to covenant together to plant churches where there weren't any, in the Episcopal tradition. In 1977-1978, as I went underground as a parish priest, I survived by getting in a prayer group. We prayed for two years about whether God wanted us to start a missionary community of people who would be willing to go anywhere to plant new churches, but God would not open that door. Our lives went on.

After hearing me speak in Baltimore, Alden came up to me after it and said, "I have a dream that I think God has given me to start a North American Missionary Society that would be a Great Commission society. I think your passionate sense that God is calling you to work for the Great Commission in the Episcopal Church is related to this. Will you come and talk about it?" In my Day-Timer, I still kept the papers on which my prayer group had blocked out a beginning covenant in 1978 to go where there wasn't a work, and how we would plant self-sustaining, self-replicating, disciple-making churches. I had saved those plans all these years, and now Alden told me why.

So I replied that I had just made a kind of crazy commitment to a new venture, with a board of people from around America, and I have agreed to work with them on a short term basis to try to lift up a vision of the Great Commission as the mission of the Episcopal Church, calling the church to a season of reform in the light of that mission. I said, "I don't know if Shaping Our Future and the North American Missionary Society are the same thing; I don't know if they are converging, but I know this, it's the call of God that it should happen and I want to help."

HATHAWAY: In the summer of 1992, Tom Prichard took a group of us from SAMS down to Lima, Peru, to look at a church-planting project sponsored by the Christian and Missionary Alliance Church. During the course of twenty years, from one small congregation, they have planted over thirty churches in Lima, Peru, with a membership of more than 11,000, and probably two or three times that number attending worship services. We were so impressed with that work of planting churches in urban settings that I wrote some articles about it for my diocesan paper. Over and over the Lord said, "Why can't you do this in Pittsburgh or elsewhere in the United States?"

The North American Missionary Society would be an agency within this denomination of planning a strategy for building a church for the twenty-first century, organizing the resources and people to go do it, and—to put it delicately—to protect it from the political processes that so compromise most of the rest of the church. That's not to do it in a rebellious way, but simply to offer a workable project that can stand on its own, present a challenge and be in dialogue with the church, obedient to its ecclesiastical authority and its pastoral relationships. I think of the example of Trinity Episcopal School for Ministry, which was established fifteen years ago at a time when churches were shutting down seminaries and saying we didn't need any new ones. But Trinity went forward by an independent board and resources, simply putting together an agency that has challenged the whole Episcopal Church. The Episcopal Church is different for that, and the established seminaries are, too; they have gotten better. That's the way in which I see this happening.

SHULER: Conceptually, we have talked about going only where invited. If the bishop of a diocese is not willing to have us, then we won't go. This would be a North American Missionary Society congregation, not a diocesan parish, for a set number of years. That means that the authority and oversight of the congregation is vested in the society, not in the diocesan bishop. Therefore, the link to the entire Episcopal Church is through the society, much as would be true of a religious order. Consequently, if the bishop or the neighboring parishes are upset, they have to deal with the Society and not intervene in the congregation.

HATHAWAY: We can learn something from or English brothers and sisters about how the English patronages worked. I know that there are societies that support congregations and works in England that have a life of their own, but are in complete fellowship with the bishop and with the diocese.

SHULER: During this predetermined length of time, the financial responsibility for the congregation is the society's, and the giving of the congregation is not diocesan giving unless they are moved to do so. We have played with the idea of a maximum of six years of society planting, after which in the seventh year—the Jubilee Year—the congregation becomes diocesan. We believe that in six years God can grant growth in a cell-based, Great Commission style of church life, such that congregations become strong enough to change the diocese and not get devoured by it. We would operate on the basis of a team going in, not an individual. What God showed me in a big, flourishing congregation in Knoxville was that cells make disciples. Therefore, I would like to see every congregation structured to be cell-based: self-replicating cells make self-replicating cells; disciples make disciples; congregations make congregations. So that is the DNA of the concept.

HATHAWAY: In terms of demography, we are not going after Episcopalians. We are going after new, unreached people, so these congregations would not necessarily be in competition with classical Episcopal parishes. That is going to be a tough idea to sell. In Pittsburgh we started two congregations at the same time: Orchard Hill, a contemporary church, and St. Brendan's, a classic Episcopal parish. They were started within a mile of each other, and there was tremendous strife about that; however, both of them are doing well, because they both created an entirely different kind of church. Dioceses and bishops will have to be very farsighted to be able to understand that where these churches would grow, they would not only generate interest and vitality in the Christian faith, but all churches would profit from it. But that's an idea that is very foreign to our church.

SHULER: Recruiting and training need to happen in the midst of teams that are already doing the mission. Each congregation planted would become a recruiting and training station. Mentoring is key. I have a dream that God is primarily going to call lots of lay people to this. So, I think of the kind of training and planting we are describing as being non-seminary, even though open seminaries may help us with resources. I don't see us sending people away to teach them how to do this. I envision a leader saying, "Phoebe, you know how to do this. You are in charge until I get back."

I pray that God will lead us to places that can be very strong early on, using a Pauline strategy to the "hot" areas. It is not hard to know where to plant an Episcopal Church that will work. Whether you want to plant an Orchard Hill or a St. Brendan's, you can look at the demographical data and know where to put one if the gifts of God have been given to do so. But I don't want to close the door that the Holy Spirit cares about all people, whether they are in those places or not. In time, as he equips and gives resources, we may be called to send people into all kinds of places and cities. If the Holy Spirit says to plant in Sandy Plains, North Carolina, and somebody hears the call, I hope we will send them.

In large measure, we are describing something the people we want to reach couldn't ask for. The downfall of this will be disgruntled Episcopalians wanting to start new churches. That is not going to cut it. It has to be men and women with a heart to reach people that would never darken the door of ninety-eight percent of the existing Episcopal churches in the United States.

Our heritage is to be an evangelical, catholic and Spirit-filled community, with a connection to those various large movements of God in history, time and place, and that at our best we have a bridge role. I believe, pray for, work for and long to see visible reunion. I think God is displeased with our divisions. Part of our calling is to work for unity in the church as a eucharistic community connected with history, the catholic and evangelical traditions, and alive to what the Spirit is doing today.

HATHAWAY: We have fallen prey to the belief that in this country Episcopal churches can't really do this kind of thing, but that is not true. People are planting Episcopal and Anglican churches in massive ways all over the world. We need to learn from our Anglican brothers in other places how to do it.

PARTICIPANT: We are working towards planting apartment churches. We are able to work because there is an interdenominational organization in Arlington that has five hundred of them ranging in size from thirty to five hundred, but they are non-sacramental. I'm praying about how God is going to let us bring the sacramental aspect into that kind of a network because we can't carry it. I am a solo priest with a five hundred member church.

HATHAWAY: When the African priest came to spend a year with us at St. Christopher's, I introduced him to the church by asking him, "Philemon, tell us how many people are in your congregation." He said 40,000! Perhaps we can learn from people like him how to handle the sacramental thing. Or maybe we can have a different notion of sacramental ministry. There are a lot of things up for grabs here, but it is a new world. I think in order to be true to the Great Commission, we are going to have to be open to the way in which the Spirit is going to lead us in other ways. If we are going to go after the masses and bring them to faith in Jesus Christ, the Lord will show us how to get the sacraments to them.

SHULER: It's difficult to answer questions about an organization that is just in the formative stage. The Pauline model seems to be our guiding example; it rapidly identified indigenous talent and gifts. There are those with an apostolic anointing who are called to go where they are sent, and where the door is open.

This concept really is for global mission but with a particular target of North America that God seems to be laying on our hearts. Very particularly, we are feeling a burden not only for the United States, but also for the people of Mexico and Canada.

PARTICIPANT: If we go to witness with our natural mindset, it is going to be to prosperous suburbanites. The demographical data is going to point right toward the new communities with a lot of yuppies and all the rest. I would encourage you to look in very different contexts than where the Episcopal Church normally goes.

HATHAWAY: That's terribly important. Remember that this is a strategy for mission, not simply a method to build up the Episcopal Church. It is using church planting to effect mission: to carry the gospel to save the lost.

SHULER: God is blessing congregations in every pocket and corner of this society where he is finding faithful men and women; in every demographic area, in every culture, in every city, town and niche. There is a sense in which he calls us to reach everyone, but there is also a sense in which he has gifted us to reach some. If we ignore the gifts we have, we will not be faithful. There is a balance. There is a dynamic thing the Spirit does with different kinds of people and different parts of the world. My desire is that we would stay fluid to what God begins to do. I am desperately afraid of locking God in to what we think he will do or how we think he should do it.

HATHAWAY: Let me close with this thought. Around Pittsburgh, just about on every street corner, there is a new British Petroleum gas station. They are slick, they are beautiful, and they are up-to-date. Obviously they were designed with an eye to the community, because some have a car wash and store, and others don't. But they are all over the place. Now somebody in that organization made the decision that they were going to go for it, and they decided to design outlets to effectively sell their product. That is what I want to do in the Episcopal Church. We have got the best product in the world. Let's get out there and share it!

SHULER: Let us pray. Father, I pray that you would bring to pass in each of us exactly what your Spirit is calling us to do and to be, and that this dream which you have placed in so many hearts will come to pass in our generation. Lord, give us the faith and the boldness to step out of the boat, not heeding the voices that say, Who said you could do this? Lord, if it is you calling us to walk on the water, may we come to you. In Jesus' name, Amen.

PRESIDING BISHOP'S FUND FOR WORLD RELIEF AND UNITED THANK OFFERING

Mrs. Nancy Marvel

Come, you that are blessed by my Father, inherit the kingdom prepared for you from the foundation of the world, for I was hungry and you gave me food, I was thirsty and you gave me something to drink. I was a stranger and you welcomed me. I was naked and you gave me clothing. I was sick and you took care of me. I was in prison and you visited me. (Mt 25:34b-36 GNB)

The Presiding Bishop's Fund for World Relief is a major response by the Episcopal Church to God's call to serve Christ in all persons, to love our neighbors, and to respect the dignity of every human being. The United Thank Offering is a joyful witness to Christ's presence within us by sharing our blessings, a reverent and thoughtful giving of thanks to God, the forming of loving bonds that unite us into one community in Christ. The offering grows out of thanksgiving to God for blessings received, those blessings shared through gifts of money that are given away in grants and multiplied as blessings for others.

The Fund raises, receives and uses monies for the relief of human suffering. The Fund provides emergency relief in times of disaster. There was an emergency grant to the Diocese of Los Angeles within twenty-four hours after the earthquake hit, emergency grants to Alabama and North Carolina immediately following the touchdown of the devastating tornados, an emergency grant to the Diocese of New Jersey to assist those affected by the gas explosion. The Fund helped in Rwanda recently, as you are all familiar with the horrors in that country. The Fund assists in the rehabilitation of lives, property and organizations. The Fund continues to assist those affected by Hurricane Hugo, Hurricane Andrew, the Midwest floods, to name just a few.

United Thank Offering grants support long-range planning to meet mission needs in special areas and to relate to missions and to compelling human need. Compelling human need includes conditions such as poverty and violence which create unjust situations, steps to humanize institutions, programs that maintain and nurture people's development toward just and humane self-sufficiency. For example, think of homeless families given emergency shelter in a motel and think of the joy of common space like a living room where parents may congregate and children can play in central Pennsylvania. Or think of homeless, low-income families, the working poor in Maine, who now have access to a free health clinic offering early intervention, education, and preventive care.

Through development projects, the Fund joins in partnership with those who identify and address the root causes of suffering. The Fund partnered with the Methodist Church with Grassroots, International to develop water resources in Eritrea. These water resources are extensive, providing water for the people, with a separate irrigation system for crops and animals. The Fund received an "End to Hunger" award for this.

Also, United Thank Offering grants support to missions, new or disadvantaged congregations, new or developing dioceses or provinces, new or innovative mission outreach, indigenous ministry, and renovation to meet mission needs. Many of the grants outside the United States relate to church infrastructure, what it takes to strengthen or expand church presence and church operation. For example, the Caribbean region received $27,000 to establish a regional office as dioceses of five different countries, three islands, and two languages work toward becoming an autonomous province. At the same time, the one of the dioceses used grants to build a multipurpose hall and to purchase property for a new church. In Mexico, which is also moving to autonomy, the diocese moves steadily to build churches and rectories in strategic locations. The Diocese of Alaska also has steadily built churches combining growth in middle class areas, where the church can be self-sustaining, with the more remote areas where it will take much longer. Theological education in Brazil reflects the vastness of the country itself and the diversity within the country. UTO also supports culturally-sensitive theological education by extension in South Dakota.

There are guidelines for assessment of the grant applications received for consideration by the board of directors of the Fund. Is the Anglican Church involved and supportive? Each application must have the signature and support of the bishop in whose diocese this project or program is located. Is this endorsement indicative of strong commitment? What local church funds are involved? Will the project extend visibly the church's local mission of compassion and relief of human suffering? What human needs are directly addressed by the project? Is it timely? Effective? Appropriate? Does the project encourage initiative and self-support among intended recipients? Are local people, including the intended recipients, involved in an appropriate way in developing the project? Such thoughtful questions need to be part of the process, because the Fund receives each year in excess of $50 million in grant requests. The Fund is currently receiving approximately $6 million in contributions.

The United Thank Offering committee invites a limited number of applications each year through structures within the Anglican communion. Every diocese of the Episcopal Church USA, and dioceses and provinces generally where the church is not self-supporting as well as related churches, such as the Union churches in India are also included. All applications must show Episcopal connection and support. Each must either seek to complete a project, such as one-year training or renovation for a shelter; seed money to begin start-up, such as for an after-school tutoring program, or show development to attract permanent funding, such as a home health aide program moving toward Medicare reimbursement. As you well know, UTO is associated with building. Why? Because buildings are a vehicle for mission, for meeting human needs with substantiating church presence. UTO does not fund buildings so much as the people who will use them and the transformation in life and society that will come through their use. Why else? Other sources do not loan capital, particularly for church-related work. Yet UTO funds by deep commitment and not by default.

In dioceses of the United States and Province Nine, the committee also seeks to build up screening committees involving UTO diocesan coordinators searching out appropriate programs to apply and screening requests. The tasks of the grant cycle serve as tools, particularly for women who promote and administer the Offering, to deeper knowledge of relationships within the church. This helps make decisions, and also helps tell the story to those who have shared and will share their prayers and gifts of thanksgiving. As with the Presiding Bishop's Fund, the United Thank Offering invites and nurtures deeper and wider relationships within the church family and the world. That would be necessary even if we could fully fund every request that came.

Recently the United Thank Offering has been asked for five to eight million dollars each year and has had close to three million dollars with which to fund grants. You can imagine how difficult it is for the board to make final grant decisions, thus the Annual Appeal to raise more undesignated gifts in order to respond to the needs where they are greatest. How much more could be done if the resources were $10 million, even $20 million. In order to better serve, it is important that we all recognize that undesignated giving better assists response where the need is the greatest. Monies are transmitted as quickly as possible at a low administrative cost.

Offerings come from a response to God, not with focused intent for how it will be spent. The UTO grant policy attempts to remain open to respond to the diocesan and provincial self-defined plans. At the 1991 triennial meeting of the Episcopal Church Women, there was much discussion as to how the United Thank Offering would respond to requests related to women and children. There are no simple answers. The struggle is really profound. In one respect, it is the question, do we make policy around an ideal world, or around the world in the way it exists? In another, it is what are the accompanying consequences, such as do we create a perception of women and children as victims only? It's a question of power and authority. When you look at primarily United States laywomen, working through ecclesiastical structures that are primarily male, it's a question of breadth versus focus. While policy struggles must be complex, the written policy has to be simple, readable, doable, and user-friendly to varied localities around the world. A policy to address these incoming requests and the grants awarded help us all to understand and mold the work of the church that we love so well.

Remember those familiar words from the Gospel According to Matthew, "For I was hungry and you gave me food." The Fund was there on your behalf in the Diocese of New York. Holy Apostle soup kitchen is the largest, private on-site feeding program in New York, feeding almost one thousand people a day. The Food and Hunger Hotline links destitute and homeless people with community-based emergency food programs. The Fund was, and continues to be, in Somalia on your behalf through support of the Church World Service and Lutheran World Relief hunger relief programs. (In 1993, UTO funded only five programs that related directly to hunger, a difference from the late 1970s and the early 1980s when those programs were on the rise.) In Central Florida, basic costs for diocesan participation in SHARE, Self-Help and Resource Exchange, a nationwide, low cost commodity program which is carried out locally, was funded. A warehouse in Vermont was funded also.

"I was thirsty and you gave me something to drink." The Fund was there on your behalf providing water to those affected by the hurricanes, floods and earthquakes which have affected the United States the past few years. The fund was in the Solomon Islands on your behalf providing assistance for the completion of a water system for a village in North Malaita.

United Thank Offering is not so likely to fund water programs, although it has for the guest house in Uganda and a system in Ethete, Wyoming, on the Wind River Reservation. So I look at "thirsty," as people hungering, as they hunger after righteousness. I share this as "thirst" after righteousness. I share this also as the thought of children searching for greater life, as in Michigan, when UTO bought snow shovels and lawn movers for a program that provides role models and teaches entrepreneurial skills for young males, in Long Island, with a multicultural after-school program, and a West Missouri program for abused women.

"I was a stranger and you welcomed me." The Fund, on your behalf, in Westchester County, supported Project Hope. This project is a program of St. Peter's Church in downtown Peekskill which provides immigrants free information and referral services in Spanish and English. The Haitian Project assists Haitian homeless families with the purchase of permanent housing. The Fund was in Costa Rica on your behalf to assist in completing the electrical work needed so that Hogar Escuela Episcopal can continue with skills-teaching courses.

I guess it should be no surprise that a good number of the 1993 United Thank Offering grants were in this category. UTO resources assisted a deaf congregation in Alabama in relocating to a safer area; worked with children of traditional fishermen, those outside the usual caste system in India, and Hmong refugees in Eau Claire, Wisconsin; boats for mission expansion along river settlements in Guatemala; facilities for elderly and those with Alzheimer's disease in Oklahoma and Oregon.

"I was naked and you gave me clothing." The Fund was in Liberia on your behalf during the height of the relief efforts during the last two years, providing not only clothing, but necessary medicines and medical supplies. The Fund also provides clothing after major earthquakes and other natural disasters in this country. Much of the outreach that receives UTO funding is multipurpose in nature and does include clothing supplies, but again, I take license to think about what "naked" might mean in societies today, what it takes to be clothed in dignity. I think of employment and advocacy programs in which adults seek to gain or regain a place in society. Six of the 1993 UTO grants in Africa address such. In

Ghana, workshops for employment; in the Indian Ocean, college facilities; Kenya, agriculture and livestock production; Liberia, a soap factory; South Africa, community development; Uganda, a rural women's credit scheme; here in the United States in Pittsburgh, Pennsylvania, a community loan fund; in Minnesota, an employment readiness program for single parents.

"I was sick and you took care of me." The Fund was and continues to be in Uganda on your behalf as a partner to the Ugandan AIDS Project, providing medical care and education programs. This project's orphans program has also been supported by the Fund. The project is now called African AIDS Project. This successful educational program will be expanding into Kenya, and God willing, into Burundi this year. The Fund provides $100,000 a year on your behalf to supply medical missions overseas with medicines and medical supplies, including books. These are donated medicines and medical supplies obtained through Interchurch Medical Assistance. The money is used to pay a low handling and packing charge as well as the shipping fees. If there is a great need for a specific medicine, it can be purchased through this program, either in the United States or in Europe.

In 1984 UTO funded the Diocese of New York to provide housing for those with AIDS who lost their apartments. Yearly, an increasing number of grants are given for AIDS projects, as you can see compassionate response awaken throughout the United States. The Diocese of Bethlehem received $30,000 last year to renovate a facility. Also, $20,000 went to ecumenical partners wanting to bring a Christian perspective to an international AIDS conference. Help for substance abusers in Western Massachusetts, Connecticut, New Jersey, Central Gulf Coast, Nebraska. Handicapped accessibility. Now I don't believe being handicapped is sickness. This could be put under "stranger," but for these purposes in New Hampshire, ramps; in Washington, East Tennessee and Florida, stands for the physically handicapped.

"I was in prison and you visited me." The Fund was in Alabama on your behalf in providing literacy programs in a prison to assist those who need to acquire job skills. The Fund was in Massachusetts to enable a support program for recently released prisoners. There always is an interest in prison ministries, and a few such requests. We see work with offenders, ex-offenders, families. In 1993, a most unusual grant was given to the Diocese of Taiwan, not to work with Taiwanese prisoners, but to work with expatriates in Taiwanese prisons; a modest sum of $5000.

There is more. The Fund was and continues to be in the Middle East on your behalf before and during Desert Storm, and through the unrest of today by assisting projects and programs of the Episcopal Church in Jerusalem and the Middle East and the Middle East Council of Churches. It must be very difficult for people who are in the path of disaster to believe in the goodness of the Lord. It must be impossible for the people of Bosnia-Herzegovina to think in terms of goodness when everything they hold dear dies slowly before their eyes.

As a program of prayer and giving, as well as of granting, UTO has double duty in relating to parts of the ECUSA. For instance, the Philippines have moved to autonomy and the Caribbean central region of America, Mexico and northern South America are considering such moves. The grant relationship can change much more simply. But how will the diocesan and parish UTO network of giving change? For five years, the UTO committee and women in the Philippines have worked informally with a covenant relationship, and now that covenant is up for renewal. Out of that, an Episcopal Church of the Philippines UTO panel not only promotes the offering, which continues with ECUSA for now, but serves as an advisory committee to the Philippine Executive Council which accepts and prioritizes the five annual requests that the Philippines have been allotted during this transition, an exceptional number because it is a new province. The UTO committee has been a strong advocate to assure that women have a decision-making role in grant requests and are not merely relegated to raising the money. Each of the Latin American and Caribbean regions has a different culture and relationship with women in general and women in the UTO network. For the next triennium, there will be one Province Nine representative on the UTO committee. However, the UTO committee is also recommending that a woman from each of those regions work with her and with the UTO committee members who are part of the covenant committee. It gets complicated easily. However, it is all built around seeing all of UTO as deepening relationship, and this is yet another facet of that belief.

It touches us all to hear those affected refer to God's goodness when they witness how their fellow human beings come to their aid. This is what we all can point to when we speak of the goodness of the Lord: the active love of others toward those who suffer. None of this would be possible without you. You are the ones who make it possible for people who seem forgotten to remember that the goodness of the Lord is for them also now in the land of the living. You make it possible by supporting the Presiding Bishop's Fund for World Relief and by your thanksgiving offerings to the United Thank Offering.

SOMA: SHARING RENEWAL OVERSEAS

Mrs. Edwina Thomas

The international mission organization, Sharing of Ministries Abroad (SOMA) was born at a conference called by people in renewal from all over the world and held prior to the Lambeth Conference in 1978. Bishops, priests and lay people involved in renewal had come to this conference with the determination to hear what God was saying about renewal. What they heard from God was that they were to take the message of the Holy Spirit, the power of the Holy Spirit, to the Anglican Church around the world. The first director was the Rev. Canon Michael Harper. Since that first meeting over fifteen years ago national SOMA organizations have been formed in Australia, the United Kingdom, Canada, the United States, Northern Ireland, and New Zealand.

The work of SOMA is to share renewal all over the world by training and equipping pastors and leaders who are already involved in the church and by modeling ministry in the power of the Holy Spirit for them. God has given us the opportunity to go in and nurture them spiritually and share with them the good news that the spiritual gifts of the Lord are for his church today. This is truly exciting because they know the language, they know the people, they have a constituency, they live in the community and they have a church to pastor. Our primary responsibility is to teach and model ministry with the goal of reproducing what we do.

Does the Episcopal Church today need renewal? From my own experience I can relate that I was an Episcopalian for many years, went to church every Sunday, was very faithful and even observed a sacrificial Lent. Yet, in the crises of my life, I could not find hope or the assurance that God walked with me. Even though I knew Jesus as my Savior, I felt as if there was no life to my faith. It was through the empowerment of the Holy Spirit that God brought that life to me. He brought the reality of a personal relationship with him and the joy of walking out a life lived in him. There were some difficult times because he disciplined me; there were frustrating times because he took me through a desert. There were hard times because he does not always answer prayers immediately. It has been a walk of twenty-one years of discipleship with him. There are times when I am disobedient, but my heart's desire is to be obedient to him and to walk in forgiveness.

Does the Anglican Communion around the world need renewal? I believe it does. The world-wide church needs the empowerment of God's

Holy Spirit, and those within the church need a personal relationship with Jesus Christ. Once the church all over the world understands and embraces this, it will be able to proclaim Jesus Christ in a more powerful way.

Ministry Principles

In Acts 2, Peter cites the prophet Joel, "In the last days, God says, I will pour out my Spirit on all people. Your sons and your daughters will prophesy, your young men will see visions, your old men will dream dreams. Even on my servants, both men and women, I will pour out my Spirit in those days, and they will prophesy." I am bold to say that it is an apostolic ministry to carry renewal to our community, to other churches and to people abroad. It is a ministry of bringing life to the church.

That is the commitment of SOMA. The principles involved are applicable not just to our organization, but to anyone doing ministry wherever God gives the opportunity. First of all, we believe that it is important to work under ecclesiastical authority. That means that insofar as there is an Anglican Church where we are working, we work with the blessing and under the authority of the bishop. If it is work for another denomination, we work under that authority. If we do not encourage the vision of that church, we are inviting destruction by undermining the vision of those in authority and allowing the enemy a foothold.

A second principle is to bring the overseas church into partnership with us. We have accomplished this by asking the overseas diocese to participate in what we do by supporting some of our ministry while we are in the country. Team members are responsible to raise their own funding to travel overseas and to provide for the incidental expenses of food, lodging and miscellaneous items. The host bishop and diocese are asked to provide room, board and transportation once the team has arrived. In some areas, this is not difficult. In other areas, it is almost impossible. Being in partnership means that the diocese has some investment and ownership of what happens. It is the difference between accepting a gift simply because it is offered and desiring something enough to make the effort to sacrifice to get it. This also means that the diocese has a say in the ministry and has the opportunity to evaluate the ministry and to offer suggestions for improvement, for ways for follow-up, and for return visits.

Another principle involves preparation and flexibility. SOMA teams put a great deal of prayer, planning and preparation into each mission effort. The goal is to be sensitive to the Holy Spirit, to discern the needs of the host church, and to be flexible in conducting meetings and conferences. The key to ministering renewal is to move under the power of God's Holy Spirit and that means submission. It is a joyous adventure to go on a trip prepared, lay the plans before God and have the Holy Spirit rework the plans to meet the needs of the people.

The Mission Team

SOMA is very careful about team selection. We talk to pastors and rectors asking for their best people, those people who have been faithful to minister in the gifts of God's Holy Spirit. We are a teaching ministry and we have to be sure that we take teachers with experience in these matters. We do take people with other gifts as well. One of the most valuable is the gift of hospitality. That particular gift somehow crosses the cultural lines, inviting people and making them comfortable. Even without knowing the language, the servant heart, the joy and real love of Jesus Christ draw the people to them.

The gift of healing also transcends the language barrier. When we are willing vessels for the Holy Spirit, God will honor our prayers. We have witnessed this when we have worked through interpreters to determine the needs of the people, we have prayed in English and any tongue the Lord has given and there have been healings. We have learned that the sovereign power of God's Spirit does not depend upon the right words. When we trust his mercy, the Holy Spirit does the work.

We also look for team members who are teachable and flexible. People who are flexible and willing to take risks can live into the mission experience. The Holy Spirit is always at work teaching us, so it is important to be willing to learn. Each trip reveals more about God and more of his character.

Flexible team members are able to work in cross-cultural settings. There are the realities of frustration, confusion, tension and embarrassment in the unexpected and unfamiliar circumstances overseas. In some countries, there is a very strong military presence everywhere, and this is certainly unfamiliar for most Americans. In some cultures, the attitude towards time and punctuality is totally different and calls for some understanding. Being the only white person in a black environment can be different. We work with team members to prepare them for these experiences. It is important to be familiar with the culture and to know how to respond. We encourage team members to be open, to accept the circumstances, and to trust the people who have invited the team to come.

The unexpected is always an event on the mission field. How we handle these events reflects the attitude of the heart. There will always be options in these circumstances and choosing to observe, listen and inquire will build understanding, compassion and a rapport with the people. Teaching team members to use these tools and communicating with them along the way helps to maintain cultural sensitivity.

We have now assembled a training program for all SOMA teams who go into the field and have made that training available to others as well.

The Intercessory Prayer Team

In order to lay a solid foundation for prayer support, every team member is asked to build an intercessory prayer team for themselves. These intercessors receive letters and faxes when the team is in the field encouraging them to pray and keeping them informed of specific needs.

During an exploratory mission to Pakistan in 1992, God impressed upon me in a very real way the need for intercessory prayer. The team consisted of six members, and we experienced oppression, spiritual warfare, fear and sickness. One team member had a fear of travel, and travel by vehicle in Pakistan seems to have no rules; a priest on the trip experienced medical problems causing several trips to emergency rooms; one team member broke her leg and spent ten days in bed. This did allow the team member to be an intercessor from her bed, but the trip taught a valuable lesson.

To prepare for the trip the next year, I prayed and discerned that God wanted a strategic team assembled to pray specifically for the strongholds of the country and the spiritual issues the team would confront. A packet of material about Pakistan was sent to these intercessors with instructions to read it and highlight the issues that they felt needed prayer. They were to discern how to pray over Pakistan and the ministry of the team. While we were on the trip, we faxed to this group what was happening on the trip and our specific prayer needs. In turn, these intercessors communicated our needs to intercessory prayer teams in our churches so they could be more effective in prayer.

We also asked the intercessory prayer teams to do concerted prayer as a corporate group, because there is additional power in that. God's lesson was dramatic because this time we experienced spiritual "elbow room." The powers of darkness were pushed back, and we had room to praise and worship, to hear God, and to discern his voice and move in his power. This allowed us to work offensively rather than to be on the defensive.

The SOMA Vision Lived Out

The vision of the ministry of SOMA is to bring and share renewal in an equipping ministry. Teaching and modeling the spiritual gifts, and giving encouragement and support to others, puts a local team in place that can continue ministry after the missionary team departs. We go to the mission field as givers who function as a pipeline through which the Body of Christ can be reproduced. People are encouraged, trained and equipped to be more powerful in their own ministry.

Nandyal is a diocese in South India where this teaching and equipping ministry has been most effective. SOMA was invited there by a bishop who knew that the priests were not at all interested in renewal. This bishop, however, had a deep concern for the future of the church in India because he looked to the day when the borders of India would be more tightly closed. He knew that the church needed to understand the value of moving in the Holy Spirit and that there would come a day when it would not be able to rely on the Western church for anything. His approach was to have us hold one conference for youth (folks from about fifteen to twenty-eight years of age) and another for diocesan workers. Included in the group were six hand-picked clergy who were to do our translating and be with us as we did the ministering so we could teach them. Over a period of several years and several mission trips, this team of six grew to be a team of fifteen to eighteen lay and clergy.

The youth conference was conducted using a team of eight lay and clergy team members and the bishop had specifically instructed that two of his clergy were to do the translating. They had never translated before, and there were frustrations as they struggled with the language. As a result, there was so much focus on making the conference happen that no one was hearing God's word and message. As a team, we prayed about the situation and I know that God gave the gift of wisdom. His answer was to let the Indian team of eight priests do the teaching. When we presented this idea to them, they were eager to do it. We discerned who would do each task, gave them our prepared material, and within forty-five minutes the first young man had to give his talk. Our team just sat; we could not do a thing except pray and trust. We watched as they were so much more effective that we would have been. They didn't need anyone to translate for them and they were getting all the correct reactions in all the right places. We saw people laugh and people cry. That night we put these ministry people in a circle, laid hands on them and prayed for the power of the Holy Spirit and leadership of this ministry time. Then we turned the whole thing over to them and simply said we were available to be their servants and to help in any way. Then we stepped back and they did it. The joy is that they went on to do more conferences. Now they have the skill, the confidence and the ability to move in ministry.

Last January another diocese in India invited us to come but due to some health issues relating to an American team member, we were unable to honor the request. The invitation was referred to the group in the Diocese of Nandyal. The inviting bishop was initially disappointed there were no Americans coming, but he later wrote me the most incredible letter saying that this team was more effective and more powerful than the white man. I personally wrote the check to get the Nandyal team to this diocese and it was for $70 to send four people. How much would it have taken to get an American team over there? Now this team can go back to the diocese and train a team to continue the ministry.

SOMA Missionaries Learn as Well as Teach

It is possible for mission teams to learn something from every church they visit. For example, I visited with Bishop Dinis Sengulane in Mozambique in 1991. At that time, Mozambique had just been declared the poorest nation on the earth, even poorer than Bangladesh. Civil war had raged since 1979 and the churches had all been nationalized, locked and nailed closed or turned over to secular uses (except in the major cities where foreigners would see). The war had torn the country apart with internal refugees everywhere. When we asked Bishop Sengulane about the state of the church, he told us about the glory of God. He told us of a church that was multiplying in spite of the fact that the people did not have enough food and medical care. He pointed to victory in the face of suffering and pain. He told us stories of how the Christians under persecution had gone back to using the symbol of the fish as the early persecuted Christians had done. They were flourishing and growing. The church that is under persecution has much to teach us.

Our Western culture so influences us that we often cannot separate the culture from the truth and the nuggets of the gospel. Outside our borders we get new eyes. A priest in Uganda once asked me some very uncomfortable questions. We were discussing the people who live in the northeast of Uganda, near the Sudanese border and Kenya, who do not wear clothes. They are nomads who wear a drape over one shoulder, carry a staff and something like a stool that is used as a seat. As we talked about this, the priest asked me about the people in our country who are nude on the beaches and about the abortion in our country. I immediately thought about the string bikinis on the beach in my home town. This gentleman was not being cruel, but by being away from my culture and separated by thousands of miles, I got a different perspective on my own culture and I grieved. I saw what is normal at home viewed more from God's perspective. I saw this and I wept and ultimately found myself in confession to this priest. Going to the mission field does put in perspective who we are when we see ourselves through the eyes of other people. It is not always pretty, it can be painful and change lives, but we need this if we are to be healthy ourselves.

When you go to the mission field, I would challenge you to journal, meet people and maintain relationships through writing because it is through these relationships that we can be involved. It is through these relationships that we learn of such unique needs as someone who feels called to seminary but who lacks the money. I have heard it said that if you go to the mission field and it does not change the way you spend your money, it did not touch your heart. I once was on a trip to India with a lady who had a very difficult cross-cultural experience. However, she came back from that trip and began to work with the homeless. She has moved on to another ministry now, but her church is still involved with the homeless in her community. It has to matter. It is a challenge to take the experiences of mission and infuse them into a congregation or community of faith. My answer is to become a storyteller, telling about real people and situations, making them and the principles of mission real.

Mission is people; mission is relationships. Mission is bringing people into relationship with Jesus Christ, into living a victorious Christian life, overcoming and persevering with the power of the Holy Spirit. Be persistent in sending people on mission. Send the young people with such organizations as YWAM, partner with other parishes, or develop your own missions. We want to be enablers, not only for ourselves, but for our church, our diocese, and other churches who do not have a vision for mission. It is not possible to go to the mission field and come back without being changed and transformed and knowing more about God the Father, God the Holy Spirit and Jesus Christ.

SOUTH AMERICAN MISSIONARY SOCIETY

The Rev. Canon Tom Prichard

> But how are men to call upon him in whom they have not believed? And how are they to believe in him of whom they have never heard? And how are they to hear without a preacher? And how can men preach unless they are sent? As it is written, "How beautiful are the feet of those who preach good news!" (Rom 10:14-15, RSV).

One of our missionaries, a nurse, was driving alone at night through San Pedro Sula, Honduras. Her car began coughing and wheezing and she soon realized that the auto was not going to make it to her destination. She began to pray, "Lord, lead me to the right place to get my car worked on. Show me where I should get help." She saw a garage ahead but didn't feel it was the right one, so she kept going. She passed another, then yet another, and still didn't feel that any of them were quite right. Finally she saw one that didn't really look any different from the others, but she obeyed a nudge from the Lord that this was the place. She stopped the car and the mechanic walked up. He first said, "Are you an Episcopalian?"

She thought that was strange, since she didn't have a sticker or seal to identify herself as such, and the Episcopal Church in Honduras is tiny. She replied, "Yes, I am."

Then he said, "Will you tell me about Jesus?" Well, she did. She shared how during a moment of crisis in dealing with the tragedy of her mother's suicide, she found the Lord Jesus Christ and he changed her life. Soon the mechanic waved over a friend who came to listen, and during the evening he accepted the Lord. They then fixed her car.

I'd like to begin with that thought. Are you an Episcopalian? Will you tell me about Jesus?

The Lord is doing a wonderful and marvelous work around the world. The piece of the church's mission that the South American Missionary Society (SAMS) is involved with is in Latin America. SAMS is the largest voluntary missionary society in the Episcopal Church. Right now we have a total of forty-five missionary personnel, including thirty missionaries on the field, and there is a wonderful revival going on.

I served for five years on the cathedral staff in Little Rock, Arkansas, then as a missionary for three years in Bogotá, Colombia. I found my ministry was transformed by those three years in Colombia. There were more people coming to the Lord and being touched by him in a week in Bogotá than I saw during five years in Little Rock. It was a tremendously renewing and life-changing experience. God's hand was at work in powerful ways, answering prayers, changing lives, doing exciting and vibrant work.

It is tragic that so many churches are disconnected from that work. This is an exciting time to be involved in helping to bring in the harvest. It is something that is renewing for churches.

The first concept I want to communicate is that SAMS exists as a ministry to help your congregation be faithful to the Great Commission in sending missionaries. The Great Commission was not given to a parachurch missionary society; it was given to you. The mission of the church is not our responsibility as a missionary society, it is your responsibility and we exist to help the local church succeed at that.

One misconception we are constantly combating is that local churches tend to think that they can pass someone along to us, and then SAMS is responsible. Two weeks ago we visited a church in Jamestown, New York, which said they had two members who are going to be serving in Latin America with SAMS. I tried to make it very clear: They are not going to be our missionaries, they are going to be St. Luke's missionaries serving *through* SAMS.

We want to be an agency that provides a framework so that Episcopal parishes can be missionary-sending churches. It's incredibly renewing to make a commitment to send out missionaries as the Lord mandated—to be engaged in missions to the end of the earth. St. Luke's in Jamestown told me how these two missionary candidates asked the vestry for $25,000 a year to send them out. Imagine the reaction of the vestry, which had never given anything to send missionaries. They were probably thinking, "Well, maybe $500 or $1000—but $25,000?!?" I think it took the vestry three months of wrestling with the idea before they finally were able to say two months ago, "The Lord is in this. He has commanded us to make this outrageous pledge of $25,000 a year for three years. We're going to be a missionary-sending church!" The next morning the rector got a letter from a lawyer saying that the estate of a parishioner who had died three months earlier was going to leave the church $75,000. So the morning after the vestry made a decision to give away $75,000, exactly that amount to the penny was given to them in a special bequest. And that church is now saying, "God is at work. He is doing something, and we are part of it!"

Over and over again we see that when churches get involved in mission, the Lord starts to work in a new and exciting way.

So, SAMS exists to help your church send out missionaries.

The second concept has to do with awakening your church to mission. We exist to help you bring about revival to mission in your church, to go forward step by step in obedience to the Great Commission. We can provide a missionary or two to speak at your church. They will share some true stories about what God is doing in other countries and how he is using them. They will demonstrate that the life and vitality of the early church is going on today. Then they will invite your congregation to participate, asking, "Wouldn't you like to be part of such a ministry?"

We can also offer you the opportunity to have a long-term relationship that could eventually lead to a short-term mission. Your church could be involved with a particular missionary who is doing church planting, and you may want to send out a team of six people to help build on the effort there. With the connection to a long-term missionary and through the door of short-term mission, your parish's awareness will be much more focused, instead of having the scatter-shot approach of sending a check here or there. You will be able to say that the ministry of this church, in addition to being right here locally, is also to be planting a church in Uruguay or supporting a children's home in the Dominican Republic. You can then send a short-term mission team to this targeted ministry, which opens up the whole world of mission to your congregation on a very personal level. So, these are ways in which we help open the door of the local congregation to world mission.

The third concept to remember about SAMS is that we are engaged in a very special kind of urban ministry not being done anywhere else in the Anglican Communion. It is a strategy that comes from the Christian and Missionary Alliance Church in Lima, Peru, focusing resources to start from scratch and build up a church with more than one thousand members. That church then sends out teams of two hundred people, usually once a year, to begin a daughter church. That strategy in Lima caused a church of 180 people to grow into thirty churches with a combined Sunday attendance of 30,000 in less than twenty years.

The goal of this strategy is to win cities in the name of the Lord Jesus Christ. In 1950, forty-five percent of Latin America's population was located in cities; by 2000, that number will be around seventy-eight percent. Also by the year 2000, about half of the world's largest cities will be in Latin America. One of the focuses of SAMS ministry has been to cities, so we are trying a brand-new strategy. A year-and-a-half ago our ministry in Tegucigalpa, Honduras, started from scratch with a team of fourteen missionaries. They are in the early stages of that church's growth, having a series of evangelistic campaigns, with their Sunday attendance now around seventy. Our goal in the next eight years or so is to build up a church that will have more than one thousand people which will begin planting daughter churches. (This strategy is detailed in Chapter 3: "Church Planting in Latin America.")

We have a need for ten times as many churches to be involved with SAMS. Right now out of six thousand Episcopal churches in the U.S., three hundred are involved; out of a 2.4 million-member denomination, we have about 2,500 individual supporters. The Episcopal Church does not have a tradition of supporting missionaries on deputation, so it is difficult.

At the same time, we are receiving more and more requests for missionaries from the field. The Bishop of Uruguay called me once and said, "I am on my knees begging for help." He is trying to develop a new diocese with only three clergy, including himself. Over and over again, we hear the same plea from Latin American bishops: they want youth workers, teachers, church planters, medical personnel, social workers and others. People with almost any background are needed for long-term mission service.

Seventy-five percent of the requests we get for missionaries go unmet, and yet the greatest obstacle to our growth is not the lack of missionaries, but the lack of parishes willing to support them! It costs between $22,000 and $58,000 per year to send a missionary, depending on the number of people in the family and the cost of living in a particular country. What about the role of the national church? Twenty-five years ago there were 480 people in our national Appointed Missionary Program. Now that program sponsors only twenty-two. Where does the responsibility lie for missionary sending? With all of us—with our congregations. If we're not going to do it, who is? And if we're not going to do it now, when will we do it? The needs are there for missionaries; the fields are white for the harvest.

The local church is the first level of screening for new missionaries. We really depend upon parishes to raise up people and say, these folks would make fine missionaries. You may have people in your own church who would be good candidates. Perhaps they have never even thought about it because no one has ever challenged them by saying, "You really ought to look into missionary service." Perhaps they are retired and looking for something new. Perhaps they are young people, or perhaps a family looking for a door into ministry. I would encourage you to challenge them. In Scripture, it is very clear that no one was called to missionary service who wasn't set apart by the church. It wasn't something that an individual just felt, but it was the church confirming the call, setting them apart and sending them out.

Several team members will now share some of their thoughts about the role of parish support and deputation.

DOROTHY McGUINNESS (a member of the SAMS team to Tegucigalpa): My home parish was extremely supportive of me. The biggest blessing was to know that I had that body of people with me; come rain or shine, hard days or good days, they were with me in prayer and in financial support. They had a vision for missions and made a commitment to tithe to the mission field. I was one of the first that was actually sent, and I felt enveloped by that body. The broad vision of missions was being promoted and uplifted from the pulpit, by the leadership and in the small groups. I was part of a small group fellowship, and they were very faithful in their day-to-day sending of letters, cards, sermon tapes, and those little things that really helped me know in the field that a body of people was part of my ministry.

MALCOLM ALEXANDER (another member of the Tegucigalpa team): The hardest part about deputation—raising 100 percent of your own support—is having to go out and try to persuade people to do something. Sometimes you feel as if you are selling yourself; that you have to get up in front of all these people and convince everyone what a great person you are, and then sit back down and wait for the returns to come in. As I began to see the Lord working in people's hearts while I was talking to them, I soon realized that I was not a salesman exhibiting myself, but rather I was sharing the Lord's work with these people. They were getting excited about being partners, rather than just buying something that I was trying to sell them. It gets easier as you see the Lord working through you, and it's actually a lot of fun now.

DAN KLOOSTER (who finished studies at Trinity Episcopal School for ministry, and with his wife, Kathy, is now completing deputation work for service in Uruguay): The hardest part of deputation for me is the ride home after my wife, two kids and I have traveled hundreds of miles to give a presentation. Sometimes you are asked go all that way to share your testimony, and then they give you a check for maybe twenty-five or fifty dollars. It's obvious from the way it's done that this is their "thank you" for your trip to their parish. How you feel about yourself then, on that long drive home, is one of the hardest things. It's a real attitude check to look at yourself in the rearview mirror and say, "Okay, was this just a transaction? Or am I serving Jesus Christ, and have I performed something valuable for him that can never be put into monetary terms?" Deputation is definitely about relationships, not money. If you don't fund your budget then you don't go to the field, but developing relationships is even more important. Our motto has become, "You can't go without money, but nothing happens without prayer."

PRICHARD: Missionaries Russ and Heidi Smith were on their deputation six years ago when a congregation said, "We're sorry, we're not large enough to give you any gift at all, but if you can come, we will promise to pray for you every time we gather for worship." Russ and Heidi replied, "If you're serious about that promise we would be happy to come, even if you can't give a penny." They visited that church, and it is now their strongest supporting parish. Besides faithfully remembering the Smiths in prayer, the members have done all sorts of creative things to be partners with their ministry. For example, ten families organized a progressive Mexican dinner and raised about eight hundred dollars above their normal parish giving to support the Smiths.

We are seeing extraordinary things happen in the field: lives changing and ministries blossoming. Part of the excitement comes from our brand-new short-term missions program.

BILL CONNER (SAMS Director of Short-Term Missions): My wife and I were short-term missionaries for a period of ten months on an island in Honduras, during which time we did administration to run a hyperbaric chamber to treat mostly Miskito Indians for diving sickness. Honduras exports a large amount of both rock lobster and conch that was being hand-caught by divers violating every safety rule you could think of. They were coming to the clinic suffering from decompression sickness ranging from paralyzation from the waist down to complete unconsciousness. The treatment for diving sickness is a pressure chamber.

Through this experience, I found that evangelism does not require someone to go out to the street corner and preach the gospel. We discovered that for nearly three hours we had a captive audience in that tank! We put Bibles in there, and after about an hour or two of boredom the divers would begin reading them, and many wanted to keep their copies.

Generally speaking, a short-term missionary is someone who goes into the field as an individual or on a team for as little as one week or as long as one year. We have a two-and-a-half page list of needs that short-term volunteer missionaries can fill in Honduras, Puerto Rico, the Dominican Republic, Chile, Spain and other countries. Short-term mission helps build awareness in your church. No parish should ever let a person or team go out without backing them with involvement and prayer. If the parish is spiritually supporting a short-term volunteer team, it will begin to grow from it.

While Eleanor and I were in Honduras, a short-term missionary team came to construct a small church. Their home parish in Indiana was building their own church, and had decided from the beginning to tithe their building fund. With that tithe, they wanted to provide a church building for a congregation somewhere that otherwise could not afford it. During their year of planning, a group of about twenty people met weekly to pray and learn some Spanish. They also learned to sing some Spanish songs, and what a Spanish worship service was like. They practiced how to build something in a short period of time using available tools and equipment. They came and with the Honduran people built a church in four-and-a-half days on a foundation that was provided for them. The Indiana team was able to witness the church's consecration when the bishop visited that Sunday. Through that joint venture, there is a long-term relationship between these Americans and Hondurans. They correspond regularly, and people that were on that building team are financially supporting two barrio children to attend a bilingual school in Honduras.

Once most churches begin short-term missions, it becomes an important part of that parish's life and outreach program. It's a life-changing experience.

There is an enormous need for teachers in the bilingual schools of Honduras. These schools are primarily taught in English and attended by middle-class Hondurans who are the potential leaders of this country. The Bishop of Honduras once said that the people from the United States have the greatest opportunity to influence the long-term outcome of Honduras through teaching in these bilingual schools.

SAMS has missionaries on the field in six countries who know which strategies will be effective and which will be a waste of time. They can help short-term volunteers reap the most results from their efforts.

For example, last summer we organized a group from St. Stephen's Church in Sewickley, Pennsylvania, on a short-term mission to Tegucigalpa. They did a crazy thing; they went there to offer a Vacation Bible School in English. What was the purpose of that? Well, there were forty Honduran young people who wanted the opportunity of having an immersion experience in English to improve their skills. At the same time they heard the gospel, and thirty-one of the children prayed to ask the Lord into their lives. From that, our long-term church planting team had the chance to follow up with eighteen families. If that short-term mission had happened apart from the efforts of the long-term missionaries, it might have been just a little flash in the pan. We want to couple short-term volunteers with long-term missionaries to reap the maximum benefits for the good of the kingdom.

We are also working on how to reach the professional, upper-class people. Often in the Anglican Church in Latin America, we have established the church among the more blue-collar part of the population. We become stuck in a sense, because if the church is only made up of people from this background it is unable to reach up to professionals (who have the financial and human resources to extend the mission of the church). But what we're doing in Tegucigalpa, the first generation of our new church-planting effort, is to reach out to professionals. For example, two months ago we had an evangelistic conference at which the former president of ALCOA, an Episcopalian, gave his testimony to a Honduran businessmen's luncheon. They were very interested to hear how Jesus touched the life of a man of his stature. One man on our board, whose family owns an international oil company, shared how the Lord Jesus Christ had changed his life and healed his marriage. At a nice tea with nearly forty-five Honduran ladies, his wife shared how the Lord had changed her life and their marriage. There are different strategies needed to reach that element of society, but when they're touched by the gospel, they can do profound things.

PRICHARD: We seek to have a positive impact on the community. It is tragic that in many places some groups try to develop a congregation by preaching against another denomination and sometimes pulling members away from it, which is really sheep stealing. I don't believe SAMS has ever engaged in that. When we share the gospel with people, we simply encourage them to find a church where they can grow.

As Anglicans, we have a very special role as a bridge church in Latin America. Unfortunately, Christendom is divided there. Generally the relationships are very poor between evangelicals and Pentecostals on one side, and the Roman Catholic Church on the other side. The Anglican Church is in a unique position to be an instrument of healing and evangelism. Many people who have been alienated from other denominations are open to the Anglican Church. Many times people have told me, "I feel like I am coming home." We have a very distinct niche in evangelism, as well as a special role in reconciliation. Together, let us make the most of these opportunities.

10

Bearing Fruit That Remains: Jesus' Call, Our Response

CALL TO COMMITMENT

The Rev. David Harley

So, after receiving all this information about missions, what are we going to do? I wonder what the Apostle Paul's reaction would be? I think Paul's first reaction would be to weep.

In Romans 9:1, Paul said, "I have great sorrow in my heart, continual grief." Paul thinks about the people who are dearest to him and is convinced that they are not "okay." And so in Romans 10:1, "My heart's desires and prayer to God for Israel is that they might be saved." Paul respects and highly regards the Jewish people and he speaks of their sincerity and devotion. He is not criticizing their zeal. Rather, he would say to us, as Gentiles, "I wish you had the kind of zeal which some of these Pharisees have!" They were exemplary, as many orthodox Jews are today, and we can learn much from them. He says that they have gone so far, but the burden of his heart was that they had not gone far enough. No human can go far enough, and Paul knew that because he had tried as much as any of them. The only person who can take us all the way is Jesus.

421

Rosemary and I worked amongst Jewish people for eight years. It is an incredibly sensitive and difficult ministry. If you have seen *Schindler's List,* you will be aware of something of the suffering of Jewish people. Christians, in humility, need to go on their knees to Jewish people. But we cannot be silent about Jesus. The greatest comfort, I believe, for Jewish people who have lost loved ones in the Holocaust is the comfort of God that comes to them through Jesus by the Holy Spirit. If we do not believe that, we do not believe the gospel.

So, as we reflect on the information here, let us react as Paul would react and let us weep. Let our tears lead us to the same prayers that Paul had. We can start a new chapter of intercession in our prayer lives. We can use *Operation World*, calendars of prayer, and every means at our disposal to intercede regularly and with discipline for all the peoples of our world.

A second reaction to all this information is to preach. We read these wonderful words in verse 14, "How shall they call on Him whom they have not believed? How shall they believe in Him of whom they have not heard? How shall they hear without a preacher?" Four out of every ten people on our planet have not yet heard about Jesus in a way in which they can understand and respond. How shall they hear without a preacher? We must also remember those, too, who live among us and seem somehow sadly hardened to the gospel. A concrete result of this information needs to be a commitment by all to be involved in reaching the world for Jesus.

I am English, and we English are shy and introverted. I don't find it easy to talk about Jesus. Yet we cannot be silent, any of us; we are all called to witness. We are all called to have an answer for the hope that is in us. God help us to overcome our shyness. Let us be committed to preach and to proclaim Jesus in whatever way the Lord particularly has laid on our individual hearts. We can show hospitality, show love by opening our homes, by breaking down those divisions within our community that are often reflected, sadly, in our churches. We can become involved in social action and combating racism and anti-Semitism. We can also tell our own story of what Jesus has done for us.

We can preach through our giving. Most of us will not go to another country, but we can support those who do through our generous and sacrificial giving. By saying "no" to things that we would like but do not need, we can invest more in the proclamation of the gospel to the world. I believe that God is calling us, in Britain and perhaps you, too, here in the States, to invest in the proclamation of the gospel through giving in a way we have never done before. A concrete result of this information must be a greater involvement in sharing Jesus with the world in proclaiming the love of God in deed and word.

A third concrete result of this information can be found in Romans 10:15: "How shall they preach unless they are sent?" We are all commissioned to preach, and all, in one sense, are sent. But let us think particularly of the sending of people in cross-cultural mission, both here within the United States and in other parts of the world. The Lord has been speaking to some of you, calling you, as he called Abraham, to leave your father and your mother, your country and your security, to go to another land which he will show you. I hope that the messages and the statistics contained here have convinced you that there is still a key role for missionaries from the United States to play in the world. We are all going to be involved, either in being sent, or in doing the sending.

There are three things in the area of sending that are of vital importance. They are these: the importance of partnership, the importance of training, and the importance of the right attitude.

First, the importance of partnership. "How shall they preach unless they are sent?" God is not just sending you, he is sending others. Traditionally in Britain we have thought of missionaries as being from the West, from Europe and North America. In these days, God is sending out an increasing number of missionaries from Korea, Nigeria, Singapore, Brazil, and so on. They are hearing the same call from God that we hear. They are responding to him, and they also are being sent. From all over the global family, and from the Anglican Communion worldwide, our heavenly Father is calling out men and women to work in mission. I think it's important that we take them on board, that we work with them now. We are no longer carrying the burden and responsibility of world evangelization by ourselves. It's great to hear Africans and Brazilians and Indians saying, "God is giving us now the torch or the baton to carry on the task." So we are working in partnership. That needs to be reflected in the way we operate.

We are not always going to be calling the shots, dictating the strategy. I must confess that I sometimes become embarrassed when I hear Westerners telling Africans how to evangelize Africa. Shouldn't it be the other way around? I know it is difficult to work out the practicalities, but we must learn to share resources. There are gifted, mature Christians in Africa whom God is calling to serve not just in that continent, but all over the world. Often their going is prohibited by a lack of resources.

Secondly, the importance of training. Have you noticed in Acts what pains Paul takes to communicate the gospel sensitively and in a way that is culturally appropriate to the group to whom he speaks? So to

Jews, he preaches from the Old Testament, the Hebrew Bible; to Greeks, he quotes from their poets and prophets; to polytheists in Asia Minor, he speaks of the great, high God that they recognize. Paul was familiar with the three cultures of his contemporary world: he was a citizen of Rome and he knew Latin; he had a Greek education; he was a Jew with a Ph.D. in Jewish Law. God took great pains to prepare Paul academically, spiritually, ministerially, and cross-culturally. I would urge those of us who have heart for mission not to shortchange those we send out in mission, but to provide them with comprehensive training for their missionary work.

Currently, the rate of attrition among Western missionaries is cause for concern. The statistics on mission failure are a tragic testimony to the inadequacy of the present system of training. A purely academic course is totally inadequate preparation for the spiritual and emotional demands of missionary work. A Western theological degree is a totally inadequate preparation for the presentation of biblical truth in another culture. The training of men without making provision for their wives and children leaves the latter totally ill-equipped for cross-cultural life and service. To send out people with inadequate preparation is to court disaster for the missionaries, for their partners and for their children. Please do not let our enthusiasm to get the job done deprive our missionary candidates of proper training.

Lastly, the importance of the right attitude. Our model is to go as servants, as our Lord Jesus did. He came to identify, to live among us, to wash the disciples' feet, to be misunderstood, to die on the cross. Sisters and brothers, it is very difficult for those of us in the West who are white to go as servants. An African pastor came to our training school at All Nations and said, "If you come as white missionaries to Africa, do not come as if you were the fourth member of the Trinity."

I would like to say to those who feel God is calling them to full-time missionary service overseas to be realistic about the cost. It is hard to kiss your mother and father good-bye at the airport; it is hard to leave the security of a good job; it is hard to live in another culture where you are misunderstood. Jesus calls us to be servants. If you answer that call, will you be a servant?

May the Lord Jesus enable us to make a response to him that is real and concrete. May we learn to weep and pray, may we learn to commit ourselves to preach, and may we be willing to go as servants.

Contributors

Mr. **George Anglin** is a young Jamaican who is an international studies major at Mary Washington College and graduate of Rock the World's Josiah Project.

Captain **Steve Brightwell** is the National Director of the Church Army which focuses on reaching those outside the church through evangelism and practical response to human need, particularly in the inner city.

Kerk and Gwen Burbank were Appointed Missionaries of the Episcopal Church, working for seven years in Kenya starting a diocesan-wide community development organization for Bishop Gitari. From 1986–1988 Kerk worked with CORAT-Africa as a management consultant working with Christian churches and organizations in Africa on community development. He has a Master's degree in International Agriculture and Rural Development and teaches at Eastern College in their graduate Economic Development program where he holds the Templeton Chair for Christian Service through Entrepreneurship.

The Rev. **Antoine (Tony) Campbell** has worked nationally in congregational development, outreach ministry, stewardship, raising capital funds, and youth ministry. He has led Black congregational development conferences, youth conferences, and renewal conferences. He is Rector of St. James Episcopal Church, Houston, Texas.

The Very Rev. **Ronald A. Campbell** is a Dakota Indian born and raised on the Sisseton-Wahpeton Reservation in South Dakota. He is a Korean War veteran. He and his wife have been married forty-three years, have nine children and twenty-nine grandchildren. He graduated from the Church Divinity School of the Pacific and was ordained in 1968. He served on the Pine Ridge Reservation and at the University of South Dakota at Vermillion. He has spent the last sixteen years on his home reservation serving five mission churches. Young people and teenagers are a main focus of his ministry.

The Rev. **José D. Carlo** was born in Puerto Rico and studied in New York City where he graduated as a civil engineer. He worked in the space industry before graduating from the Church Divinity School of the

425

Pacific in 1961. He served for nineteen years as an Appointed Missionary of the Episcopal Church in Costa Rica where he established a parish, a national youth work, family centers, and training for future priests. He is the Rector of St. Simon's, a thriving bilingual parish in San Fernando, CA. He is a former President of the Board of ECMC.

Mr. **Leiton Chinn** has been a resource and catalyst for ministry to internationals since 1977. He founded the Truro International Program and Services and has helped six churches develop ministries to international students.

The Rev. **Brian Cox** is Rector of Christ the King Episcopal Church in Santa Barbara, California, and the Executive Director of the European Reconciliation Fellowship. He was U.S. Director of SOMA (Sharing of Ministries Abroad) from 1985-1990.

The Rev. **Tad deBordenave** left his position of seventeen years as Rector of St. Matthew's Episcopal Church, Richmond, Virginia, to found and become Director of Anglican Frontier Missions in 1993. Anglican Frontier Missions concentrates exclusively on people groups who have not heard the gospel. He has served as Chairman of the Board of SAMS and is now on the ECMC's Board of Directors.

The Rev. **Ian T. Douglas**, Ph.D., a priest of the Diocese of Western Massachusetts, has served as a Volunteer for Mission in Haiti as well as Associate for Overseas Leadership Development at the Episcopal Church Center. He is Associate Professor of World Mission and Global Christianity and Director of Anglican, Global, and Ecumenical Studies at the Episcopal Divinity School and Chair of the Standing Commission on World Mission for the General Convention.

The Rev. **Bill Francis** served twenty years with Youth With a Mission, a short- and long-term missionary organization. He has led many short-term mission outreaches and directed long-term mission work. He is currently ministering at St. Clement's Procathedral in El Paso, Texas.

The Rev. **Paul Frey** is Assistant Rector at Truro Church in Fairfax, Virginia. Along with David Case, he oversees Truro's ministries with internationals in the Washington, D.C. metropolitan area. Prior to his studies at Trinity Episcopal School for Ministry, he helped start a Hispanic church in Houston, Texas and worked for six years as Assistant Director of St. Francis Center in Denver, Colorado, a ministry to homeless people which serves over 500 people a day.

Mrs. **Dorothy Gist** joined the staff at the Episcopal Church Center in 1988 as the Associate for the Volunteers for Mission; in 1991 she became the Director of Mission Personnel for the overall administration of the Appointed Missionary and Volunteer for Mission patterns of service, including recruitment, screening, placement, maintenance of mission personnel worldwide. Currently she is the Mission Personnel Officer in the Office of Anglican and Global Relations.

The Rt. Rev. Dr. **David Gitari** is Bishop of the Diocese of Kirinyaga, Kenya, (formerly of the Diocese of Mount Kenya East which is growing so fast it had to be divided). The diocese is reaching out to twenty-six unreached tribes in northern Kenya. Bishop Gitari has built up theological education, community development, and schools throughout the diocese, and was awarded an honorary doctorate for his contributions to the community.

The Rev. **Anne Halapua** is now the Project Home Again coordinator in the Diocese of Los Angeles.

The Rev. **Walter and Louise Hannum** founded the Episcopal Church Missionary Community in 1974. They have given missionary orientation to more than 300 Episcopalians preparing for overseas service, taught numerous one-week Introductory Courses on World Missions, and presented seminars in dioceses and churches throughout the USA. They are adjunct professors of World Mission and Evangelism at Trinity Episcopal School for Ministry. Both served in Alaska, where as Archdeacon of Northern Alaska, Walter prepared Indians and Eskimos for the ordained ministry and for leadership in the church and community. Louise assisted in the leadership training programs and taught pre-school. They both have graduate degrees from the School of World Mission of Fuller Theological Seminary in Pasadena, CA.

The Rev. **David and Mrs. Rosemary Harley** are coordinators for the Evangelical Mission Resources Network, facilitating cross-cultural mission between dioceses of the Southern Hemisphere. They are missionaries of CrossLinks. They had previously worked in a parish in North London, then went to Ethiopia to work as missionaries with the Ethiopian Jews. Following the communist revolution and death of Haile Selassie, they returned to London to work among Jews there. David and Rosemary were members of the staff of All Nations Christian College, an interdenominational, vocational, missionary training school in the U.K. for 15 years, and David was President of the college for eight years.

The Rt. Rev. **Alden Hathaway,** Bishop of the Diocese of Pittsburgh, is a member of the Joint Commission on Evangelism and Renewal.

The Rev. **Whis Hays** is the Executive Director of Rock the World: Youth Mission Alliance and an Assistant Director of the Stanway Institute for World Mission and Evangelism at Trinity Episcopal School for Ministry.

The Rev. **J. Eugene Horn** is the President of Episcopal World Missions, Inc.

The Rev. **Richard Jones**, formerly a missionary in Ecuador, is Associate Professor of Mission and World Religions at Virginia Theological Seminary.

The Rev. **Richard Kew** is the Director of the Russian Ministry Network and the former Executive Director of the SPCK/USA (Society for Promoting Christian Knowledge). He and Roger White have co-authored two books: *New Millennium, New Church* and *Venturing into the New Millennium.*

The Rev. **Geoffrey Little**, formerly a missionary in Peru and Recruitment Officer for the South American Missionary Society, is on the staff of the Overseas Ministries Study Center in New Haven, Connecticut. He is the rector of St. James, a bilingual congregation in New Haven.

The Rev. **Charles Long** was a missionary in China and Hong Kong in the 1940s and 1950s, Missions Professor at Philadelphia Divinity School in the 1960s and 1970s, and Director of Forward Movement Publications from 1978 through 1994.

The Rev. **Kevin Martin** served for five years as the Director of Leadership Training for Episcopal Renewal Ministries. He has also served as rector of three congregations, has led leadership, evangelism, and healing training events, and has taught at the College of Preachers in Washington, D.C. He presently serves as Canon to the Ordinary for Mission and Congregational Development for the Episcopal Diocese of Texas.

Mrs. **Nancy Marvel** is the Assistant with the Presiding Bishop's Fund for World Relief.

The Rev. Canon **Patrick Mauney** serves on the Presiding Bishop's staff as Director of Anglican and Global Relations at the Episcopal Church Center.

Mr. **Keith McCaffety** is Director of the Episcopal Medical Missions Foundation.

The Rev. Dr. **Don McCurry** served eighteen years as a missionary in Pakistan, where he pioneered new concepts of contextualized approaches in cross-cultural evangelism and church-planting. Founder of the Zwemer Institute of Muslim Studies, he trained 800 missionaries now serving in fifty-three countries. As President of Ministries to Muslims, he has traveled to sixty-three countries to assist and equip nationals in Muslim evangelization and church-planting.

The Rev. **Duc Nguyen** is the Director of World Vision's Indochinese Church Development Project. He was the first Vietnamese Episcopal priest in the United States.

The Rev. **Marty O'Rourke** is Rector of Church of the Messiah in Chesapeake, Virginia, and is now the President of the Board ECMC. While at his former parish, Church of the Resurrection in Sharon Center, Ohio, he led short-term mission trips to Jamaica involving about seventy people from various parishes. Resurrection has sent one family into full-time missionary work on YWAM's medical mercy ship, the *Anastasis*.

The Rev. **Titus Presler,** Th.D., teaches Mission Studies and World Christianity at the Episcopal Divinity School. His mission experience includes eighteen years in India and three in Zimbabwe. He is the rector of St. Peter's, Cambridge, Massachusetts. He co-chairs the Volunteers for Mission Committee of the Diocese of Massachusetts and recently led the American Pilgrimage to the Centenary Festival of Bernard Mizeki in Zimbabwe.

The Rev. Canon **Tom Prichard** has been Executive Director of the

South American Missionary Society since 1987. Since then, the number of SAMS missionaries has tripled. He and his wife served as SAMS missionaries in Bogotá, Colombia.

The Very Rev. Dr. **John Rodgers** is the former Dean and President of Trinity Episcopal School for Ministry, founder and former Director of the Stanway Institute for World Mission and Evangelism, and a member of the Board of ECMC. He is now retired and is a past President of the Board of ECMC.

The Rev. **Alfred Sawyer** is the National Director of Shoresh, a Christian Ministry Among Jewish People (CMJ/USA). Previously he pastored Christ Church in Jerusalem for eight years and helped start the first Messianic Jewish congregation in London, England.

The Rev. Dr. **Jon Shuler** is President of Shaping Our Future, Inc., working to see the Great Commission adopted as the mission of the Episcopal Church and working to reform all structures to accomplish that mission. He is the founder of the North American Missionary Society.

The Rev. **Alfredo Smith** has pastored churches in Quito, Ecuador, and Buenos Aires, Argentina, and helped to found the Encounter With God church planting strategy in Lima, Peru. He is currently serving in Miami, Florida.

Ms. **Sharon Stockdale** taught in China from 1981-1985. Since 1985 she has given orientation to more than two hundred Western Christian teachers who have gone to China. She is Director of the Episcopal Church Missionary Community.

The Rev. **Toni Stuart** was the Project Home Again coordinator for ten Episcopal Churches in the Diocese of Los Angeles. She is Vicar of the Chapel of St. Francis in Los Angeles.

In 1965, the Rev. **Ed Stube**, his wife, and five of their seven children went to Indonesia to start a center in Indonesia to train young nationals to reach unevangelized tribes. The ministry flourished and the whole project was indigenized by the time the Stubes returned to the US in 1977. Fr. Stube has served in a small town parish and in the inner city. He is Executive Director of the Holy Way, a prayer and support group for the mission in Indonesia.

The Rev. Dr. **Andrew W. Swamidoss** is a priest in the Diocese of Tirunelveli, Church of South India. He is Director of the Yavatmal College for Leadership Training and Professor of New Testament. YCLT trains Indian nationals to be missionaries and in its first ten years has had about three hundred graduates, now working in many places in India as missionaries.

Mr. **Tom Telford** is the Northeast Regional Consultant for Advancing Churches in Missions Commitment (formerly Association of Church Mission Committees).

Mrs. **Edwina Thomas** has served since 1991 as the National Director of Sharing of Ministries Abroad (SOMA-USA), a Christian mission agency in the Anglican Communion dedicated to fostering renewal in the Holy Spirit throughout the world. Edwina has participated in almost thirty short-term missions. She has served on the Episcopal Church Missionary Community Board of Directors.

Mr. **Reachsa Uch** is a resident of Canada and a Cambodian citizen who is in training to take the gospel back to his people.

The Rev. **Valarie Whitcomb,** a former ECMC board member, is Associate Rector at All Saints Episcopal Church in Woodbridge, Virginia. She has been involved in world missions in one aspect or another since 1974 and has ministered in Uruguay with SOMA on two different occasions.

The Rt. Rev. **Roger White** is the Bishop of Milwaukee, a diocese deeply involved with the Diocese of Haiti. He is also the Presiding Bishop's appointee to chair the coordinating committee for developing a new relationship between the Episcopal Church and the Russian Orthodox Church.

Mr. **Stewart Wicker** and his wife, Laura, taught and ministered with students and families for three years in Tela, Honduras, at the Holy Spirit School, a bilingual outreach of the Episcopal Church. He is Director of Missionary Personnel for South American Missionary Society (SAMS), providing pastoral and logistical support for missionaries.

The Rev. Dr. **Sam Wilson** is the Director of the Stanway Institute for World Mission and Evangelism and Professor of Mission and Evangelism at Trinity Episcopal School for Ministry. He has been a missionary in Peru, the Director of the Missions Advanced Research Center of World Vision and the Director of Research for the Zwemer Institute of Muslim Studies.

Dr. **Ralph Winter** is a former missionary among Mayan Indians in western Guatemala and Professor of Missions at the School of World Mission at Fuller Theological Seminary. He is founder of the American Society of Missiology and the U.S. Center for World Mission.

The Rev. **James Wong** is Vicar of the Chapel of the Resurrection in the Diocese of Singapore and Dean of Indonesia. Active in church planting in Singapore, he also travels widely in Asia in a Bible teaching ministry. He is the international vice-chairman of the Evangelical Fellowship of the Anglican Communion and he serves on the executive committee of the Asian Lausanne Committee for World Evangelization.

Mr. **Mike Wurschmidt** is one of two regional coordinators for World Vision's Project Home Again, a ministry he helped found in 1988. He served three years as an associate pastor in an inner-city church with Vineyard Christian Fellowship in Denver, Colorado. For nine years he has been active in ministry to the urban homeless. He is now studying for the priesthood at Trinity Episcopal School for Ministry.

The Rev. **Don C. Youse, Jr.,** M.D. is a Board Certified Family Physician who is currently Priest-in-charge of Emmanuel Episcopal Church, an inner city parish in Pittsburgh.

Mr. **Tyler Zabriskie** currently works as a consultant with Consensus Planning Group, a community relations firm in Los Angeles, and attends the Executive MBA program at UCLA. At the time he led this workshop, he was serving as the Director of Outreach Ministries at All Saints Episcopal Church in Beverly Hills, California. He is a former Volunteer for Mission in Zaire, has participated in several SOMA short-term missions, and is a former member of ECMC's Board of Directors.

RESOURCES

Recommended Mission Books

Austin, Clyde N. *Cross-Cultural Reentry, A Book of Readings.* Abilene, TX: Abilene Christian University, 1986.
People returning to their own country of origin after a period of living and working in another culture often find it more difficult to adjust to than to the foreign country. This book addresses reverse culture shock through a variety of readings on personal experience and has practical suggestions to avoid or alleviate many psychological and social problems. Helpful to mission committees as well as to returning missionaries, business people, and internationals.

Bradshaw, Bruce. *Bridging the Gap: Evangelism, Development and Shalom.* Monrovia, CA: MARC Books, 1993.
Bruce Bradshaw urges a holistic approach to Christian ministry, using the biblical concept of shalom to bring together evangelism and development. Using case studies, he looks at the worldviews of indigenous people and cross-cultural workers and calls readers to examine their cultural biases in the light of biblical truth.

433

Garrison, V. David. *The Nonresidential Missionary: A New Strategy and the People It Serves.** MARC/New Hope, 1990.
The nonresidential missionary strategy is an innovative approach in which a missionary uses the latest technology and inter-agency cooperation to spread the gospel while living outside the area because of restrictions and barriers to traditional missions. Includes a list of the world's unevangelized peoples.

Gibson, Tim, Steve Hawthorne, Richard Krekel, Ken Moy, eds. *Stepping Out: A Guide to Short Term Missions.* Seattle, WA: YWAM Publishg, 1992.
Stepping Out will help you examine how God wants to use you, how to get prepared and trained, search for a mission agency, care for yourself on the field, and integrate this whole process into your life.

Gordon, Alma Dougherty. *Don't Pig Out on Junk Food: The MK's Guide to Survival in the U.S.* Wheaton, IL: EMIS, 1993.
Don't pig out on junk food is one piece of great advice for young people returning to the U.S. from places all around the world. And it is just one of the many valuable insights from experienced missionary kids you'll find in this book that will help equip MKs to make their cross-cultural entry to the U.S. successful. Beginning with family preparations the book includes practical advice about education, money, work, social adjustment, and personal issues. Each chapter includes special assignments for family discussions.

Hale, Thomas. *Living Stones of the Himalayas: Adventures of the American Couple in Nepal.* Grand Rapids, MI: Zondervan Publishing Corp., 1993.
A fascinating account of everyday and sometimes incredible experiences of Thomas and Cynthia Hale who have worked as medical doctors in Nepal since 1970. Written with humor, understanding, and love for the Nepalese people, the majority of whom are subsistence farmers who share much in common with the poor of all developing countries.

Hale, Thomas. *On Being a Missionary.** Pasadena, CA: William Carey Library, 1995.

A readable book about what it's like to be a missionary—the problems, challenges, heartaches, and joys. A book for everyone who has an interest in missions from the sender to the missionary on the field or about to be. Helpful insights for avoiding many of the common problems. Being a missionary is a joyous and rewarding career, and this book aims to make it even more so.

Hiebert, Paul. *Anthropological Insights for Missionaries.** Grand Rapids, MI: Baker Book House, 1985.

A mission-oriented text providing basic anthropological insights in lay terms. A great book for anyone in cross-cultural ministry, at home or overseas.

Johnstone, Jill. *You Can Change the World: Learning to Pray for People Around the World.** Grand Rapids, MI: Zondervan Publishing Corp., 1993.

Referred to as the children's version of *Operation World*. A marvelous book that enables families to learn about and pray effectively for the nations and unreached peoples of the world. Lots of full-color illustrations.

Johnstone, Patrick. *Operation World: A Day-by-Day Guide to Praying for the World.** Grand Rapids, MI: Zondervan Publishing Corp., 1993.

This small prayer encyclopedia has a wealth of information and specific items for prayer for every country of the world. An eye-opening look at the world's nations and peoples.

Lewis, Jonathan, ed. *Working Your Way to the Nations: A Guide to Effective Tentmaking.** Pasadena, CA: William Carey Library, 1993.

A book of essays on effective "tentmaking" by experienced, knowledgeable mission specialists from around the world. Emphasizing the importance of accountability structures, the local church, and the preparation needed for effective service, this book is a valuable resource for mission committees to use with those whom God is calling to serve in the mission field in traditional and non-traditional roles.

Murray, Andrew. *The Ministry of Intercessors*. Whitaker House, 1982.
According to Andrew Murray, prayer is the most dynamic opportunity available to God's children. It enables us to intercede for others with tremendous results. This book will be an inspiration and encouragement for those who already pray for missions and for those who wish to begin.

Myers, Bryant L. *The Changing Shape of World Missions*. Monrovia, CA: MARC, 1993.
The Changing Shape of World Missions describes the state of the world from the perspective of evangelism and Christian mission. This book provides a bird's-eye view of the context of mission without oversimplifying the world's complexity: How will missions address the special needs of women, children, youth, the growing cities? What is happening to world population, income, poverty? What resources are available for mission today? What are the dimensions of the unfinished mission task? What new structures for mission are needed now?

Pirolo, Neal. *Serving as Senders: Six Ways to Support Your Missionaries.** Emmaus Road, 1991.
This key book makes the strategic point that mobilizers—the senders—are as crucial to the cause of missions as the frontline missionaries. It is a book crammed with solid, exciting insights on the most hurting link in today's mission movement.

Stearns, Bill and Amy. *Catch the Vision 2000.** Bethany House Publishers, 1991.
An exciting glimpse into what God is doing in the world, such as the stories of Chinese believers sent to live among un-

reached ethnic groups in China, and a revival among Koreans who were resettled among Muslim Uzbeks. Gives a multitude of practical ways individuals and churches can become involved.

Taylor, William, ed. *Internationalizing Missionary Training: A Global Perspective.* Grand Rapids, MI: Baker Book House/ Paternoster Press, 1991.
How is the missionary force for the twenty-first century to be trained? Western and non-Western training models and programs are examined. This book is full of excellent material on effective missionary training.

Winter, Ralph, and Steven C. Hawthorne, eds. *Perspectives on the World Christian Movement: A Reader,* rev. ed. Pasadena, CA: William Carey Library, 1981, 1992.
Used in over 100 schools and many special courses, this text is a compilation of ninety-four excellent articles by seventy-four authors on biblical, historical, cultural, and strategic aspects of missions.

*Available from William Carey Library, P.O. Box 40129, Pasadena, CA 91114; (818) 798-0819.

Recommended Mission Periodicals

(Contact the mission agencies to receive their newsletters.)

Anglican Cycle of Prayer, a yearly publication of Forward Movement Publications, 412 Sycamore St., Cincinnati, OH 45202.

Anglican World, published four or five times yearly by the Anglican Consultative Council, Partnership House, 157 Waterloo Road, London SE1 8UT, England.

Church School Missions Study: A Yearly Lenten Program for Children. Education Office, Episcopalian Church Center, 815 Second Avenue, New York, NY 10017.

Evangelical Missions Quarterly, four issues a year, Box 794, Wheaton, IL 60189.

Global Prayer Digest, a monthly publication of Frontier Fellowship with stories and daily prayer items for unreached people groups, 1605 Elizabeth Street, Pasadena, CA 91104.

The Great Commission Handbook, a yearly publication of Berry Publishing Services, Inc., 701 Main Street, Evanston, IL 60202.

Health and Development, published by the Christian Community Health Fellowship, P.O. Box 12528, Philadelphia, PA 19151.

International Bulletin of Missionary Research, published by the Overseas Ministries Study center, 490 Prospect Street, New Haven, CT 06511.

International Journal of Frontier Missions, published quarterly by International Coalition for Frontier Missions, P.O. Box 27266, El Paso, TX 79926.

Missiology, An International Review, a quarterly publication of the American Society of Missiology, 616 Walnut Avenue, Scottsdale, PA 15683-1999.

Mission Frontiers, published bi-monthly by the U.S. Center for World Mission, 1605 Elizabeth Street, Pasadena, CA 91104.

World Pulse, published semi-monthly (twenty-four issues a year) by Evangelical Missions Information Service, P.O. Box 794, Wheaton, IL 60189.

Episcopal Agencies for Training and Sending Missionaries and Evangelists

Anglican Frontier Missions is a voluntary mission society of the Episcopal Church that concentrates exclusively on unreached peoples. AFM works in close partnership with all Great Commission Christians using non-traditional methods and strategies and relies heavily on research to direct decisions about placement. AFM does not operate by going only at the invitation of Anglican churches because in most instances it goes where there is no Anglican church. Anglican Frontier Missions, P.O. Box 18024, Richmond, VA 23226; (804) 355-8468.

The Church Army is part of a worldwide cadre of evangelists in the Anglican Communion. It has a two-year training program and officers are commissioned evangelists by the Presiding Bishop. The particular focus of the society is on reaching those outside the church through evangelism and practical response to human need, bringing them into saving knowledge of Jesus Christ and into lively and worshipping fellowship in the church. Officers serve in the inner city, rural, Indian, and overseas missions, and as parish and institutional workers. The Church Army, P.O. Box 1425, Pittsburgh, PA 15230; (412) 231-5442.

Episcopal Church Center. Volunteers for Mission and Appointed Missionaries. Appointed Missionaries of the Episcopal Church serve in many countries. Volunteers serve full-time from six months to two years and are sent in response to requests for skilled personnel from provinces and dioceses within the Anglican Communion. Episcopal Church Center, Anglican and Global Relations, 815 Second Ave., New York, NY 10017; (212) 867-8400.

Episcopal Church Missionary Community enables Episcopalians to be more knowledgeable, active, and effective in mission. It raises mission awareness in the Episcopal Church, trains missionaries and missions committee members, equips Episcopalians to witness in cultures with no viable church, and undergirds all outreach with prayer. ECMC has given orientation to more than three hundred Episcopalians who have served overseas with the Volunteers for Mission, SAMS, etc. ECMC runs a clearinghouse to inform Episcopalians about Episcopal and interdenominational mission opportunities and sponsors the New Wineskins for Global Mission conferences. Episcopal Church Missionary Community, P.O. Box 278, Ambridge, PA 15003; (412) 266-2810.

Episcopal World Mission, Inc. sends Episcopalians for long-term service in Africa, Asia, Europe and the Pacific. The vision of EWM is to see Episcopalians effectively serving Christ around the world. Founded in 1982, EWM has missionaries serving in Madagascar, Zaire, Malawi, Pakistan, and the Solomon Islands, and a couple preparing to go to Russia. Episcopal World Mission, Inc., P.O. Box 490, Forest City, NC 28043; (704) 248-1377.

Rock the World: Youth Mission Alliance (formerly Youth Quest) seeks to "call and equip kids to lead the world to Christ." It offers several programs for youth ministry leadership training: at the graduate level, a Diploma and a Masters of Arts in Missions and Evangelism in conjunction with Trinity Episcopal School for Ministry; at the college level, the Josiah Project, a two-summer program which includes cross-cultural mission experience. Rock the World: Youth Mission Alliance also offers various ministry and training events for young people and their leaders, and a consulting and job listing service for people and parishes interested in youth ministry. Rock the World: Youth Mission Alliance, Box 43, Ambridge, PA 15003; (412) 266-8876.

Shoresh Ministries trains Christian leaders in Jewish evangelism and offers seminars to educate the church on its Jewish roots. It also gives educational tours to Israel which center on Christ Church Jerusalem, a congregation of Christian Arabs and Messianic Jews. A few volunteer positions are available for short-term mission work in Israel. Shoresh Ministries, P.O. Box 551593, Jacksonville, FL 32255-1593; (904) 730-9751.

SOMA (Sharing of Ministries Abroad) is committed to worldwide renewal to enable and equip the church to fulfill the Great Commission of proclaiming God's Kingdom and ministering in the Holy Spirit's power. Working within the Anglican Communion by invitation of bishops in overseas countries, short-term mission teams lead seminars for clergy and lay leaders. SOMA, 5290 Saratoga Lane, Woodbridge, VA 22193; (703) 878-7667.

South American Missionary Society, USA, is the largest voluntary mission agency in the Episcopal Church with over fifty missionaries. It carries out church-planting missions and social ministries in seven countries in Latin America, the Caribbean and Spain. SAMS missionaries serve a three-year minimum as teachers, evangelists, clergy, church planters, in medical ministries, and in homes for abandoned children. SAMS short-term missionaries (one month to one year) help in children's homes, teach English in bilingual schools, etc. SAMS assists churches in training and sending teams on short-term mission trips, such as Vacation Bible School, offering medical care in remote areas, and renovating facilities. SAMS is also engaged in an innovative team effort church-planting in partnership with the Diocese of Honduras. SAMS' week-long Crossroads Conferences, held three times a year in Ambridge, Pennsylvania, are designed for inquirers who want to learn more about long-term missionary service. South American Missionary Society, P.O. Box 399, Ambridge, PA 15003; (412) 266-0669.

Trinity Episcopal School for Ministry. The Stanway Institute for World Mission and Evangelism offers a Diploma and a Master of Arts in Missions and Evangelism to train missionaries and cross-cultural workers for effective service in the U.S. and overseas. It is a goal of the seminary that all graduates be eager and able to raise mission vision in their parishes. Trinity Episcopal School for Ministry, 311 Eleventh Street, Ambridge, PA 15003; (412) 266-3838.

Recommended Interdenominational Mission Agencies

Educational Resources and Referrals–China seeks to manifest the servanthood of Christ to the intellectuals of the People's Republic of China. Since 1980, China has invited foreign teachers and experts to teach English, literature, science, technology, business, and many other subjects. Presently more than forty universities and research institutions in the major cities of China send their requests for teachers and consultants directly to ERRC. Over one hundred positions are now available through ERRC. Educational Resources and Referrals–China, 2606 Dwight Way, Berkeley, CA 94704-3000; (510) 548-7519.

Educational Services International answers requests for teachers of English, business, and law for universities in China, Eastern Europe, and the former Soviet Union. More than one hundred year-long and summer positions are available. Educational Services International, 1641 W. Main Street, Suite 401, Alhambra, CA 91801; (818)284-7955.

English Language Institute/China places Christian professionals in university-level teaching positions in Mongolia, Vietnam, and the People's Republic of China. Over four hundred positions are available. ELIC, P.O. Box 265, San Dimas, CA 91773; (800) 366-3542.

Frontiers sends teams of tentmakers to reach Muslims in North Africa, the Middle East, Asia, Eastern Europe, and the former Soviet Union. Frontiers, 325 N. Stapley Dr., Mesa, AZ 85203; (602) 834-1500.

Global Opportunities sends tentmakers throughout the world in a wide variety of careers and professions. Global Opportunities, 1600 Elizabeth St., Pasadena, CA 91104; (818) 398-2393.

Overseas Missionary Fellowship is committed to the evangelization of East Asia through well-taught, witnessing churches. Its nine hundred members, drawn from East and West, are involved in evangelism, church planting, literature, translation, literacy, Bible teaching, discipleship training, medicine, radio/TV and more. OMF has work in Japan, Korea, Hong Kong, Taiwan, Philippines, Indonesia, Singapore, Malaysia, and Thailand. U.S. headquarters: Overseas Missionary Fellowship, 10 West Dry Creek, Littleton, CO 80120; (303) 730-4160.

Wycliffe Bible Translators. WBT and the Summer Institute of Linguistics work together on the task of providing God's Word for all language groups in the world. While SIL does on-site translation, linguistics and literacy work, WBT is responsible to represent the work in sending countries, stimulate prayer and financial support plus recruit and process candidates. Around fifty Episcopalians work as translators or support personnel with WBT/SIL. Wycliffe Bible Translators, P.O. Box 2727, Huntington Beach, CA 92647; (714) 969-4600.

Youth With a Mission is an interdenominational, international mission organization with permanent ministry centers in one hundred countries. It was founded thirty-five years ago and has 7200 full-time staff and missionaries. YWAM focuses on both short- and long-term missions, in three categories: mercy, evangelism, and training. Discipleship training is given before all ministries, with continued training for long-term missions. Youth With a Mission, International, P.O. Box 55309, Seattle, WA 98155; (206) 363-9844.